THE CLASSICS OF **WESTERN SPIRITUALITY**

THE CLASSICS OF WESTERN SPIRITUALITY
A Library of the Great Spiritual Masters

President and Publisher
Lawrence Boadt, C.S.P.

EDITORIAL BOARD

Jewish Mystical Autobiographies
BOOK OF VISIONS AND BOOK OF SECRETS

TRANSLATED AND INTRODUCED BY
MORRIS M. FAIERSTEIN

PREFACE BY
MOSHE IDEL

PAULIST PRESS
NEW YORK • MAHWAH

Cover art: Derekh Ez ha-Hayyim (The Path of the Tree of Life) by Hayyim ben Joseph Vital. Scribe: Elkanah ben Shimshon ha-Levi. Jerusalem (?) 1720 (ms. 2178). Courtesy of the Jewish Theological Seminary of America.

The Publisher gratefully acknowledges use of the excerpts from *The TANAKH: The New JPS Translation According to the Traditional Hebrew Text.* Copyright 1985 by the Jewish Publication Society. Used by permission.

Library of Congress Cataloging-in-Publication Data

Jewish mystical autobiographies : Book of visions and Book of secrets / translated and introduced by Morris M. Faierstein.
    p.   cm. — (The Classics of Western spirituality; 94)
    Includes bibliographical references and index.
    Contents: Book of visions / Hayyim Vital — Book of secrets / Yizhak Isaac Safrin of Komarno.
    ISBN 0-8091-0504-7 (cloth). — ISBN 0-8091-3876-X (paper)
    1. Vital, Hayyim ben Joseph, 1542 or 3-1620. 2. Cabala. 3. Dreams—Religious aspects—Judaism. 4. Rabbis—Israel—Tsefat Biography. 5. Safrin, Isaac Judah Jehiel, 1806-1874. 6. Hasidism. 7. Hasidim—Ukraine—Komarno Biography. 8. Rabbis—Ukraine—Komarno Biography. I. Faierstein, Morris M. II. Vital, Hayyim ben Joseph, 1542 or 3-1620. Sefer ha-hezyonot. English. III. Safrin, Isaac Judah Jehiel, 1806-1874. Megilat setarim. English. IV. Series.
BM755.V48J49   1999
296.8 ′33 ′0922—dc21
[B]   99-31838
                                                                      CIP

Published by Paulist Press
997 Macarthur Boulevard
Mahwah, New Jersey 07430

www.paulistpress.com

Printed and bound in the United States of America

Contents

CONTENTS

Translator of This Volume
MORRIS M. FAIERSTEIN studied at the City College of New York, Hebrew University, Jewish Theological Seminary of America, and received his Ph.D. in Religious Studies from Temple University. He is the author of *All Is in the Hands of Heaven: The Teachings of Rabbi Mordecai Joseph Leiner of Izbica* (Yeshiva University Press/Ktav, 1989); editor and translator of *The Libes Briv of Isaac Wetzlar* (Brown Judaic Studies, 308; Scholars Press, 1996); and editor of Abraham Joshua Heschel, *Prophetic Inspiration After the Prophets: Maimonides and Other Medieval Authorities* (Ktav, 1996) and numerous articles in Jewish mysticism and intellectual history. He is an independent scholar and has served as a chaplain in the U.S. Air Force.

Author of the Preface
MOSHE IDEL, Max Cooper Professor of Jewish Thought at the Hebrew University of Jerusalem, Israel, was born in Rumania in 1947. He is a graduate of the Hebrew University, where he also received his Ph.D., and author of numerous articles on the history of Kabbalah and Jewish Renaissance thought.

To Our Grandmother
CLARA S. TRITT
For Her Ninety-Second Birthday

Foreword

Jewish mystics, unlike mystics of other religious traditions, rarely describe their mystical experiences explicitly in their works. To the extent that they do describe their experiences, they are couched in highly symbolic language or ascribed to rabbinic figures of the Talmudic period. Rabbi Ḥayyim Vital is one of the most notable exceptions to this generalization. His *Book of Visions* is a full-fledged mystical autobiography in which he not only described his mystical experiences in great detail, but also wrestled with two questions central to all autobiographies—who he was and what his purpose in the world was. Vital identified himself with a range of figures from the Messiah of Joseph to the king of Israel and saw himself as the reincarnation of many of the most important figures in Jewish history associated with messianic hopes and expectations. Similarly, the task he envisioned for himself ranged from bringing the redemption to causing the people of Israel to repent, which he saw as the necessary precondition for the advent of the Messiah.

Vital was more than just a mystic with messianic pretensions. He was also the foremost disciple of R. Isaac Luria, one of the most important mystics in sixteenth-century Judaism, who founded a major new school of Jewish mysticism known as Lurianic *Kabbalah*. Vital was the most influential transmitter of these teachings. Other Jewish mystics during the sixteenth century, such as R. Joseph Taitazak, R. Joseph Karo, and R. Eleazar Azikri also wrote mystical diaries, but their writings differ from Vital's work. Their diaries are not primarily autobiographical, but records of the mystical revelations transmitted to them by their Heavenly mentors. The personal references that occur in their writings are incidental to their central concerns, which are the mystical teachings they have received. Vital's work remains the closest work we have to an autobiography written by a Jewish mystic.

The second text in this volume, the *Book of Secrets* (or *Megillat Setarim*) is by Rabbi Yizhak Isaac Safrin of Komarno, an important Hasidic master of the nineteenth century who shared many characteristics with R. Hayyim Vital. He also saw himself as a potential messianic figure who had direct access to the mysteries of Heaven. In his writings, he often claimed direct contact with long-dead figures, like Israel Baal Shem Tov (1700–1760), the founder of Hasidism, and saw himself as a transmigration of Vital's mentor, R. Isaac Luria (1534–1572).

The *Book of Secrets* is divided into two parts. The first part is entitled "Book of Visions" and consists of incidents in his life and visionary experiences. It is clearly modeled on Vital's work of the same name. Unlike Vital's work, it is much more fragmentary and does not aim at completeness. The last entry is more than twenty years before his death. Appended to the "Book of Visions" is a section entitled "The Deeds of the Lord," which consists of stories about the Baal Shem Tov that Komarno heard from his father-in-law and others. Some of these stories are found in the hagiographical biography of the Baal Shem Tov, *Shivhei ha-Besht*, while others are not known from other sources.

I have left a number of Hebrew words and abbreviations untranslated in the text. English translations of these terms and a list of the Hebrew months of the year can be found in the glossary at the back of the book.

This project had its origins in a request by Professor Moshe Idel that I translate the *Book of Secrets*. I would like to thank him for this initial suggestion and for his support and encouragement during the various stages this project went through before achieving its final form. My sincere thanks to Professor Paul B. Fenton and Professor Ze'ev Gries, who graciously read a draft of the translation and offered many helpful comments and suggestions. I am also grateful to Professor Elliot R. Wolfson, who responded to a number of queries and clarified some complexities. An anonymous reader made some helpful suggestions that improved this work and I would like to thank him for his insights. I would also like to thank Professor Bernard McGinn, editor-in-chief of the Classics of Western Spirituality, for including this work in this series. My editor at the Paulist Press, Kathleen Walsh, has been most helpful in turning the manuscript into a finished book. I appreciate her support and encouragement.

Aharon, aharon, haviv. The support and encouragement of my wife, Ruth Anne, for my scholarly endeavors has been invaluable.

7 Tishrei 5759
27 September 1998

Preface

Autobiographies in general and mystical diaries in particular are rare in Jewish literature. Much of this scarcity has to do with major presuppositions that inform this religious literature and prevent a flowering of such literary genres. First and foremost is the basic concept permeating biblical thought, an emphasis on the collective personality, which fosters the assumption that the Israelite individuals form one great unit named the people of Israel. The individual's identity is shaped by his role in the religious group, and the well-being of the group is crucial for the purpose of life. The historical drama and the religious vicissitudes of the Jewish people, described oftentimes as the wife of God, absorbed much of the imagery of Biblical Judaism. The Bible is, to a certain extent, the national and official biography of the ancient Jews.

The second factor that stifled the growth of autobiographical diaries is related to the basic style characteristic of the main strata of Jewish literature, namely, the propensity for an objectivistic type of discourse. As it had been pointed out by Erich Auerbach, the Bible is less concerned with depicting the interior landscape, preferring much more the external action. This proclivity for the external does not mean, automatically, a disdain for the internal states of mind or intimate feelings, but rather a cultural decision that the community is to be shaped by common denominators that are religiously oriented, synchronized performances. This attitude remained critical for the two main modes adopted by rabbinic literature: the Midrashic-interpretive and the Halakhic-legalistic. Both layers expand upon topics crucial for the Bible, and neither indulges in creating an emotionally inclined literary genre. So, for example, the Halakhic discussions and prescriptions are concerned with the minutiae of the ritual dromenon without elaborating upon problems of intentionality. Again, I do not assume that there were not mystical experiences involved in some aspects of the religious life, as would be found in prayer and the study of the Torah, but those elements do not come to the fore. The technical aspects of the Rabbinic approach were intended not to suppress the inner life, but to liberate it from prescriptions involved in deliberations on matters of faith and emotions. With the creation of a solid common denominator by the Halakhic literature, the theological convictions and the feelings of individuals remained their patrimony.

Medieval speculative literature, which emerged in some segments of the Jewish elite, contributed crucially to the emergence of discussions dealing with the intensification of the inner life. Whether in the different forms of Jewish philosophy or in the various schools of Kabbalah, a dramatic expansion of discussions dealing with mental and emotional processes is conspicuous. Mystical techniques and questions related to Kavvanah, or inner intention while performing the commandments, flowered in substantial bodies of literature that developed in several centers of Judaism dating back to the end of the twelfth century. Whether in the Near Eastern literature written by Jewish masters under the impact of Sufic practices and thought, in the Ashkenazi Pietists active in the Rhinelands, or in small groups of Kabbalists that surfaced in Southern France and Northern Spain, the demand for an intensification of inner life looms prominently. However, it is very rarely that those medieval masters confessed the details of the attainments that culminate the adherence to the mystical practices, a point that has been duly pointed out by Gershom Scholem.[1] To a great extent, an overarching concern with the details of the performance of the commandments is reflected in the Halakhic mode mentioned above, but it also prescribes ways to intensify the inner life. Like the Halakhic prescriptions, the paths are offered without delving too much into descriptions of the most intimate spiritual moments as a specific mystic would have experienced them. This general reticence to confess mystical spiritual attainments is quite obvious in the main trend of Kabbalah, the theosophical-theurgical one, which is much more impersonal than the other, secondary school, the ecstatic Kabbalah. It is in the latter that a much greater propensity may be detected. There are two different reasons for this propensity. One is the messianic and redemptive nature of this school. Its founder, Abraham ben Samuel Abulafia (1240–c. 1292) believed himself to be the Messiah, a concept that he understood as involving much more an extreme spiritual experience than an external redemption.[2] It is in his writings that we learn about details of his life, of his study and mystical experiences incomparably more so than in the works of any of his antecedents or contemporary Jewish mystics. There can be little doubt that this surge of the confessional and autobiographical has much to do with his messianic mission, an awareness that emerged in a period relatively free of traumatic events in Jewish history.

In the case of one of his followers, the anonymous Kabbalist who authored *Sefer Sha `arei Tzedeq,* the autobiographical propensity is quite obvious, contributing greatly to our understanding of events and processes involved both in the external history of ecstatic Kabbalah and in the inner development of the anonymous Kabbalist.[3] Unlike Abulafia, the anonymous Kabbalist did not indulge in messianic aspirations, and the details of his external and spiritual life are introduced in order to attract students to this Kabbalah. In his short treatise we may find the second important reason for his adoption of a confessional mode: the propagandistic impulse. A relatively belated mystical phenomenon, ecstatic Kabbalah had to compete with the attraction exercised by Jewish philosophy and apparently also by the theosophical-theurgical Kabbalah, two types of lore endorsed by authoritative figures like Maimonides or Nahmanides. The testimony as to the personal mystical achievements in this book should be attributed to a struggle for recognition and the pragmatic approach involved in the testimony of one's experience as part of the effort to convince others to delve into the new mystical lore. Some other examples of reporting personal experiences, close to that of *Sefer sha `arei Tzedeq*, are found in the early fourteenth-century R. Isaac of Acre's *Sefer `Otzar Hayyim*.[4]

None of those Kabbalists provided a full-fledged Kabbalistic autobiography. It is only in the Safedian Kabbalah, which flowered since the mid–sixteenth century that mystical biographies began to appear. This century, described by Michel de Certeau as the century of the mystics, has a fine parallel in the development of Jewish mysticism, and the concomitant flowering of the two types of mysticism invites comparisons and explanations that will take in consideration commonalities that were marginalized by modern scholars.[5]

The existence of several mystical diaries, like those of R. Eleazar Azikri, *Millei di-Shemaya*'[6] and the two more famous treatises: Rabbi Joseph Karo's *Maggid Mesharim* and Rabbi Hayyim Vital's *Sefer ha-Hezyonot*, is a phenomenon unmatched earlier in the history of Kabbalah. All the three have been composed by persons living, at least for a significant period in their lives, in the same small town, within a relatively limited span of time, and there are very good reasons to assume that they knew each other. Further, it is implausible to assume that it is a matter of accident that they turned to a literary genre of confessional writing independent of one another. In my opinion, their emergence is part of a larger phenomenon that may be described as the turn from an objective form of Kabbalah to a much more subjective one concerned with such topics as the details of one's transmigrations, an intense interest in dreams, and the ascent of the importance of the charismatic figure who is able to guide the individual Kabbalist and even the non-Kabbalist in the religious life, a phenomenon that is quite negligible before the end of the fifteenth century.[7] Another interesting factor related to this subjective turn is the dramatic ascent of the number of reports related to possession, known as *dibbuq*, that may be seen as an inverse phenomenon to Maggidism.[8] In the span of two generations, namely, since the middle of the sixteenth century, the evidence regarding possession by demons multiplies in a geometrical progression.[9] It is quite interesting that Karo, the person who reported to have been visited by the Maggid, was also an exorcist.[10]

While the first two diaries do not contain messianic aspirations, the third one, that of Rabbi Hayyim Vital, which is translated and annotated in this volume, definitely does. This is also the case with the second autobiography translated here, the mid–eighteenth century mystical diary of Rabbi Isaac Aizik Yehudah Yehiel Safrin of Komarno. Both Kabbalists were, in addition to their messianic aspirations, deeply involved in Lurianic Kabbalah and played a leading role in small groups of persons interested in Jewish mysticism. The Rabbi of Komarno was well aware of Vital's diary, and the two books form, in a certain way, one unit. Common to both of them is the belief in metempsychosis, and the authors make great efforts in placing their own lives within much larger historical contexts. This is certainly part of the messianic role they adopted and, to a great extent, is related to their attempt to find themselves within the larger scheme of lines of important scholars and mystics, and to integrate themselves within the collective personality mentioned above. Personal as these two books indeed are, they nevertheless betray an effort to strengthen feelings of national mission and spiritual importance or, in other words, they are documents whose addressees are much more the authors themselves rather than external readers. This remark may explain why their literary structure is so fragmentary, sporadic, and poor. In other words, the two diaries may serve as an interesting example of the different forms of combinations between the communal and the individual, between spiritual attainments and national mission, and between the preaxial and the axial, to resort to Jasper's concepts.

It may be illuminating to remark that the mystical diaries translated here were composed by a Kabbalist of Italian extraction, Hayyim Vital Calabrese, and one by an Ashkenazi Kabbalist, while the other two composed in Safed had been written by two Sefardi figures, Azikri and Karo. It is therefore fascinating to see the distribution of the messianic elements in a certain literary genre, the mystical diary, in a rather neat manner: It is in the non-Sefardi milieux that messianic aspirations are much more pronounced even when compared with the mystical diaries of Sefardi Kabbalists close in time to the expulsion from Spain.[11]

Dr. Morris M. Fairstein's accurate and elegant translation and his rich comments on the two mystical diaries contribute greatly to the widening phenomenon of scholarly presentations of Jewish mysticism to larger intellectual audiences in English, supplementing the more theoretical treatments with two texts that also evince other facets of Jewish mysticism.

Notes to the Preface

1. See *Major Trends in Jewish Mysticism*, (New York: Schocken Publishing House, 1967), pp. 15–16.

2. On this figure and his messianism, see Moshe Idel, *Messianic Mystics*, (New Haven: Yale University Press, 1998), pp. 58–100, 295–307; "Le temps de la fin: l'apocalypse et sa spiritualization d'Abraham Aboulafia," *Pardes*, vol. 24 (1998): pp. 107–37.

3. See Scholem, *Major Trends in Jewish Mysticism*, pp. 146–55.

4. On this Kabbalist and his book, see Efraim Gottlieb, *Studies in the Kabbalah Literature*, ed. J. Hacker (Tel Aviv: Tel Aviv University, 1976), pp. 231–47 (Hebrew).

5. See Idel, *Messianic Mystics*, pp. 154–57.

6. Cf. Mordekhai Pachter, ed. (Tel Aviv: 1991 [Hebrew]) as well as Pachter, *From Safed's Hidden Treasures*, (Jerusalem: Merkaz Zalman Shazar, 1994), pp. 121–86 (Hebrew).

7. More on these issues see M. Idel, "On Mobility, Individuals and Groups: Prolegomenon for a Sociological Approach to Sixteenth-Century Kabbalah," *Kabbalah*, vol. 3 (1998), pp. 162–69.

8. M. Idel, "Jewish Magic from the Renaissance Period to Early Hasidism," in Jacob Neusner et al., eds, *Religion, Science, and Magic*, (New York: Oxford University Press, 1989), pp. 107–8.

9. See the monograph of Gedalyah Nigal, *"Dibbuk" Tales in Jewish Literature*, (Jerusalem: Rubin Mass, 1983 [Hebrew]).

10. Moshe Idel, "Inquiries in the Doctrine of *Sefer Ha-Meshiv*," *Sefunot*, vol. 17, J. Hacker, ed. (Jerusalem 1983), pp. 224–25 (Hebrew).

11. For a recent reassessment of the distribution of messianic elements between different sorts of Jewish communities see Elisheva Carlebach, "Between History and Hope: Jewish Messianism in Ashkenaz and Sepharad," *Third Annual Lecture of the Victor J. Selmanovitz Chair of Jewish History*, (Graduate School of Jewish Studies, Touro College, New York, 1998), pp. 1–30.

Book of Visions

Translator's Introduction
to the Text

The genre of spiritual autobiography has a long and distinguished history in the Christian tradition that can be traced back to the *Confessions* of St. Augustine. Throughout the medieval period and into the early modern period, the autobiographical, confessional life was an important genre of Christian spiritual and mystical literature.[1] Central to this literature was the conversion experience of the author, the most famous example being that of Augustine himself.[2] On the other hand, medieval Jewish writings that contained a biographical element, such as chronicles and ethical wills, had a didactic purpose, but no real autobiographical intent.[3] They lacked the central feature of true autobiographical writing, "a specific retrospective point of view, the place at which the author stands in relation to his cumulative experience when he puts interpretative meaning on his past."[4]

Similarly, the medieval Jewish mystical tradition differed significantly from the Christian and Muslim mystical traditions in that personal mystical and visionary experiences were not normally discussed.[5] The significant exceptions are the writings of R. Abraham Abulafia (1240–after 1291) and some of his disciples, notably R. Isaac of Acre (mid-13th cent.–mid-14th cent.), which contained significant discussions of mystical experiences.[6] There was a flowering of mystical literature that recorded personal mystical visions and experiences beginning in the early sixteenth century, which will be discussed below. However, neither the works of the Abulafian school nor the later ones can be considered autobiographical in that they lacked the "retrospective point of view" that is central to autobiographies. There is only one work written by a Jewish mystic of the sixteenth century that meets the hallmark of autobiographical writing and that is R. Hayyim Vital's *Book of Visions*. The central motif of Vital's life and work was messianism. In order to understand the centrality of messianism in Vital's life, we must first consider the climate of messianic fervor and expectation that forms the background to Vital's activities.

The persecutions of Spanish Jewry beginning with the anti-Jewish riots of 1391 and culminating in the expulsion of the Jews from Spain in 1492 unleashed within Spanish Jewry a wave of apocalyptic messianic speculation and expectation. Prophets and visionaries appeared who predicted the imminent advent of the messianic age and the destruction of Israel's enemies. During the Talmudic period and throughout the Middle Ages certain scholars and mystics had made claims of divine inspiration *(ruah ha-kodesh)*, visits from the prophet Elijah, and other forms of contact with the divine realm.[7] What was new in fifteenth-century Spain was the centrality of acute messianism and the claims of pneumatic experiences by segments of the population not normally associated with these experiences in Jewish society, such as ordinary men, women, and even children.[8]

Messianism also took on a new importance and centrality among Jewish mystics in Spain. New modes of mystical speculation emerged that combined classical kabbalistic theurgic concepts with magic. A new genre of mystical literature emerged that claimed to be revelations from God or responses by Heavenly angels to the queries of kabbalists. The anonymous *Sefer ha-Meshiv (The Book of the Responding Angel)* is illustrative of this new genre.[9] The legend of Rabbi Joseph della Reina, a kabbalist who tried to bring the redemption by capturing Satan with magical incantations and his failure at the last moment, was emblematic of the mood of Spanish Jewry in this period. In the sixteenth century, this story was popularized and widely disseminated in a variety of versions.[10]

After the expulsion of the Jews from Spain, messianic speculation and messianic movements continued through the sixteenth century. The persecutions and ultimate expulsion from Spain were interpreted as the "birthpangs of the Messiah," the period of persecution and travail that would immediately precede the advent of the Messiah, as had been predicted in rabbinic literature.[11] R. Isaac Abrabanel (1437–1508), one of the major rabbinic figures who lived through the expulsion, dealt with its trauma, like many of his contemporaries, through apocalyptic speculation. He found his consolation in calculations that demonstrated that the Messiah would come in the near future.[12] Many other important rabbis and scholars also calculated and predicted the imminent advent of the Messiah. Numerous proofs were offered for a variety of dates throughout the sixteenth century, claimed to be the time of the eagerly awaited messianic age.[13]

Messianic visionaries and pretenders such as Asher Lemlein of Reutlingen (early 16th cent.);[14] Solomon Molcho (c. 1500–1532),[15] who tried to meet the pope and convert him to Judaism; and David Reuveni (d. 1538?),[16] who claimed to be an emissary of the ten lost tribes who were waiting with a large army to come to the aid of the embattled Jews, contributed to the state of messianic expectation. They made a lasting impression on those Jews looking for signs of the imminent redemption.[17] Molcho's death as a martyr made him a folk hero and a role model for many. R. Joseph Karo (1488–1575), one of the major rabbinic figures of this period, saw Molcho as his role model and dreamed of dying a martyr's death as Molcho had done.[18]

One of the important consequences of this intense messianic activity was the radical spiritualization of religious life. As Rachel Elior has suggested, "This spiritualization was motivated by intense messianic expectation and was founded on the vital connection as formulated in *Tikkunei Zohar,* between the revelation of the kabbalistic secrets through the propagation of the *Zohar* and the attempts to hasten the coming of the Messiah."[19]

A result of this spiritualization was the emergence of a new form of religious authority, which was based on pneumatic inspiration, in contrast to the earlier type of authority, which was based on knowledge, tradition, or rabbinic power.[20] Earlier kabbalists had based their authority on direct revelation from Heavenly messengers, angels, or revelations from Elijah. In principle, this was not an innovation. During the Talmudic period and throughout the Middle Ages these had been invoked as sources of authority.[21] What was new was not only the intensity and urgency of these revelations, but their wide dissemination. Previously, these pneumatic experiences had been claimed on behalf of major innovative figures by their disciples and followers.[22] Now, people were claiming these experiences on their own behalf. One of the most interesting examples of the blurring of rabbinic and pneumatic authority is R. Joseph Karo, the leading *halakhic* authority of the period, who had a heavenly messenger that revealed divine secrets to him.[23]

From approximately 1530 until the end of the sixteenth century, the small Galilean town of Safed became the home of a group of kabbalists who created a spiritual revolution in Jewish thought and life. Its favorable economic conditions[24] and its proximity to the graves of many Talmudic sages, including R. Simeon bar Yohai, the purported author of the *Zohar*,[25] attracted many important scholars and mystics. Major figures like R. Moses Cordovero (1522–1570), R. Joseph Karo, R. Solomon Alkabez (c. 1505–1584), R. Moses Alshekh (d. after 1593), and a host of lesser figures all found their way to Safed, where they produced their most important work.[26] One of the most revolutionary and influential of these was R. Isaac Luria. He lived in Safed for only two years, from 1570 until his premature death at the age of thirty-eight in August, 1572. Yet Luria's teachings as they were preserved by his disciples, particularly Rabbi Hayyim Vital, had a profound and long-lasting influence.[27] Other disciples of Luria also preserved his teachings, but it was Vital's version that became the authoritative version of Lurianic *Kabbalah*.

Hayyim Vital Calabrese[28] was born in Safed on the first day of Heshvan 5303 (1542). His father, Joseph Vital Calabrese, was a well-known scribe in Safed. Vital studied in the *yeshivot* of Safed, most notably under R. Moses Alshekh, whom he considered his teacher in exoteric subjects. He was attracted to esoteric and mystical studies and even devoted two and a half years to the study of alchemy (1563–1565), which he later regretted; he felt he had to atone for this negligence of Torah study.[29] He also studied *Kabbalah* with R. Moses Cordovero, the most important kabbalist in Safed at the time. Vital informs us that the elevated nature of his Soul had been predicted even before his birth. In his youth, a variety of diviners and heavenly messengers also predicted that Vital was destined for greatness. In 1570, an oil diviner told him that a teacher who would teach him great wisdom would come from Egypt.[30]

That year, R. Isaac Luria came to Safed from Egypt. After the death of R. Moses Cordovero in the summer of 1570, Luria began to gather a circle of disciples. Vital initially remained aloof and became Luria's disciple only in the spring of 1571, at least nine months after Luria's arrival in Safed.[31] One source suggests that initially Vital "did not value him [Luria] enough to learn from him. On the contrary, he thought himself more learned in the wisdom of the kabbalah."[32] Ronit Meroz suggests that this relationship never was an ordinary hierarchical student-teacher relationship. Vital acknowledged Luria as his teacher, but at the same time, Luria recognized the messianic potential of Vital's soul.[33] After joining the circle of Luria's disciples, Vital quickly asserted himself as Luria's most important disciple. Vital even claimed that Luria had come to Safed only for the purpose of teaching him.[34] After Luria's death in August 1572, Vital hoped to become his spiritual heir and successor as leader of the group of mystics that had gathered around Luria. He also endeavored to have himself accepted as the only authorized interpreter of Luria's teachings. In 1575, the long-awaited year of redemption, Vital gathered around him twelve of Luria's disciples. The formation of this group may have been connected to the messianic significance of this year. When the Messiah failed to appear, the significance of the year was reinterpreted to mean that it was the beginning of the period when the advent of the Messiah could be expected at any time. The members of this group signed a document in which they pledged to study Luria's teachings only with Vital and not to divulge these teachings to outsiders. Only a small mystical elite was worthy of these teachings, which were to remain the domain of this select few and not

be disseminated to others. Even Vital's teacher in exoteric studies, R. Moses Alshekh, was not deemed worthy and Vital refused
to initiate him into these mysteries despite his entreaties (1.16).[35]
Not all of Luria's disciples accepted Vital's hegemony and some
produced their own versions of Luria's teachings. Notable
among these was R. Joseph ibn Tabul Mohgrabi (c.1545–beginning of 17th cent.), who was disparaged by Vital in the *Book of
Visions* (2.41).[36]

This mystical circle of disciples around Vital lasted less than
two years and dissolved in 1577 when Vital left for Jerusalem,
where he served as a rabbi and head of a yeshiva. G. Scholem
suggests that Vital was not a charismatic leader and had trouble
throughout his life attracting and keeping disciples.[37] His departure for Jerusalem was probably related to his perceived messianic mission. He had asked his teacher, R. Isaac Luria, on a
number of occasions if the time had come for his move to
Jerusalem. He also sought confirmation from other sources that
the time had come for this move. Finally, Luria told him in a
dream that the time had arrived. Vital felt that his true destiny
would be found only in Jerusalem, where he would attain the
peak of mystical inspiration and comprehension. He also had a
more visible omen, which told him the time had come for him to
go. He reports that a comet, which was understood as a portent
of great change, was seen over Safed on the first day of *Kislev*,
1577. Vital left for Jerusalem on the fifteenth of *Kislev* (2.29). M.
Beneyahu suggests that more rational reasons for his move to
Jerusalem may have been conflicts with other scholars in Safed
or the invitation of the Jerusalem community to become the
rabbi of the community.[38] Vital saw himself not only as the heir
of R. Isaac Luria in mystical wisdom, but also as the successor of
R. Joseph Karo, the greatest *halakhic* authority in Safed (2.1). In
Jerusalem and later in Damascus, his public teaching was
restricted to exoteric studies. He desisted from teaching mystical
doctrines.[39] In 1586, Vital returned to Safed. Again, the reasons
for this move are unclear. R. Mas'ud Cohen, in the prophecy he
brought to Vital, speaks of a conflict that would erupt between
the people of Jerusalem and those of the Galilee over Vital, and

that he would return to the Galilee (1.9). Perhaps there is a historical kernel in this "prophecy" that helps explain Vital's return to Safed.

Vital remained in Safed from 1586 until 1592. According to the hagiographical account of R. Shlomel Dreznitz, he became seriously ill in 1587 and was in a coma for a period of time.[40] During his period of unconsciousness, a group of scholars bribed his younger brother, Moses, who allowed them to copy 600 pages of Vital's writings, which were then circulated among a select group of scholars. Vital had been so zealous to preserve the secrecy of Luria's teachings as well as his personal control over them that he had even confiscated the personal notebooks of Luria's other disciples who had joined his circle in 1575.[41] The writings purloined during Vital's illness made their way to Italy and formed the basis for the dissemination of Lurianic *Kabbalah* by the end of the century. In 1590, Vital received rabbinic ordination from his teacher, R. Moses Alshekh.[42] His whereabouts between 1592 and 1598 are uncertain.[43] There are traditions that he divided his time during this period between Jerusalem and Safed.[44]

Vital moved to Damascus in 1598 for reasons that are not specified and remained there for the rest of his life. He served as rabbi of the Sicilian community for a time. However, his sojourn in Damascus was a time of depression and despair. It was also apparently a period of poverty.[45] In 1604, he again had a serious illness, which impaired his eyesight and led to periods of blindness (1.19). Vital assembled his autobiographical notes into the *Book of Visions* between 1609 and 1612. Much of the material in the *Book of Visions* is from the Damascus period and reflects many of his trials and travails. A central motif is his complaints that the people of Damascus would not listen to his sermons and would not heed his calls for repentance. They are rebuked by spirits, demons, Elijah, and even R. Isaac Luria in dreams and visions for not listening to him and not giving Vital the respect due him.[46] He even suggests that the sins of the Jews of Damascus hindered the coming of the Messiah (5.19).

His primary opponent in Damascus was R. Jacob Abulafia (1550?–1622?), who is mentioned several times disparagingly in the *Book of Visions*. Abulafia apparently scoffed at Vital's messianic pretensions and is accused of hindering Vital's attempts to cause the people of Damascus to repent.[47] Toward the end of his life, Vital assembled another group of disciples around him in Damascus. He was married at least three times and had a number of children, some of whom died in infancy and childhood. Vital died in Damascus on the first of *Iyyar* 5380 (1620), at the age of seventy-seven. His son Samuel inherited his writings and edited them in their final form.

R. Isaac Luria wrote very little himself.[48] What we know of his mystical teachings comes primarily from the works of his disciples. There are four independent versions of Luria's writings. Vital's version of Luria's teachings was the most comprehensive. It became the "authoritative" version and was the most influential.[49] In addition to his "Lurianic" writings, Vital also wrote many other works. They include a commentary on the *Zohar* written before he met Luria, sermons, a treatise on alchemy, one on astronomy, and a commentary on the Talmud. Some have been published, while others remain in manuscript.[50]

Vital also wrote, as I indicated earlier, the first autobiography by a Jewish mystic, his *Book of Visions*.[51] The sixteenth century saw a dramatic rise in the writing of mystical diaries, which recorded dreams, visions, and visitations from a variety of heavenly messengers. The reason for the flowering of this particular genre of literature is an important question that remains to be answered. The heightened messianic expectations were certainly a significant contributing factor. Among the better-known examples of this genre are the anonymous *Sefer ha-Meshiv,* R. Joseph Taitazak's mystical diary, R. Joseph Karo's *Maggid Mesharim,* R. Eleazar Azikri's *Milei de Shemaya,*[52] R. Moses Cordovero's *Sefer Gerushin,* and Solomon Molcho's *Hayyat Kaneh.*[53] However, these works are not autobiographies. The autobiographical element in all of these works is at best a secondary by-product of the author's primary concern, which is the mystical teachings received from a divine messenger, ancient sage, or other divine source that he has been able to contact through mystical means. Of these works, the one that perhaps comes closest to being autobiographical is Karo's *Maggid Mesharim*. However, as David Tamar has written,

> Even though the book of R. Joseph Karo is a mystical diary and quasi-autobiography, it is not similar to the work of R. Hayyim Vital in the power of his confessions and in the revelation of the secrets and complications of his soul. In this respect there is nothing comparable to [Vital's book] in all of the Hebrew literature which precedes it, at least that which has been published, and little similar to it in all of the Hebrew literature which follows it. In some respects it is somewhat similar to the *Megillat Sefer*[54] of R. Jacob Emden (1697–1776) and the *Megillat Setarim* of R. Isaac Judah Yehiel Safrin of Komarno.[55]

A work of a different genre that might also have influenced Vital is the legendary[56] autobiography of David Reuveni, who claimed that he had been sent on a mission by the king of the ten lost tribes to hasten the advent of the Messiah. Vital was familiar with Reuveni's work.[57] An intriguing point of similarity is that Reuveni's work was written as an apologia for why he ultimately failed in his mission to bring the Messiah. As we shall see, this is strikingly similar to Vital's motivation.

Vital's book is a highly unusual phenomenon in the literature of the Jewish mystical tradition. Why did he write this most intimate work and who was his audience? The *Book of Visions* was written for an audience of one, namely Vital himself. There is no reason to believe that he intended it to be published or read by others. Considering the lengths to which he went in order to preserve the secrecy of R. Isaac Luria's teachings, which were known to others, how much more so would he have wanted to keep such an intimate work hidden from the scrutiny of others.[58] D. Tamar has suggested that an additional factor may have been his own humility in not wanting others to know the elevated status of his soul.[59] It is true that secrecy was important to him, but not humility. On the contrary, one of the sins that R. Isaac Luria told him to repair was that of arrogance (4.6). In addition, this does not make sense when one considers the many efforts Vital made to confirm his self-assessment of his own spiritual status and the many "signs" that others received of his greatness. I would suggest the contrary. Vital was disturbed that others did not give him the recognition he felt he deserved, particularly in Damascus. His desire to understand the dissonance between his inner elevated status and his external reality was one of the factors that led him to write this autobiography.

Though the entries are dated, I believe that Vital redacted or wrote the final version of the *Book of Visions* during the period of 1609–1612 and that it was a response to a specific spiritual crisis.[60] It is probable that he had notes and other written materials that he used in addition to his memory in writing the *Book of Visions*.[61] A related question is how we are to deal with Vital's assertions when he cites the dreams and visions of others that were supposedly told to him, or when he recounts various "omens" that foretold his greatness in his childhood or youth. Similarly, when he ascribes certain thoughts or actions to others, should we assume that he is a reliable reporter or that these are his own invention? Data that cannot be verified from external sources, and this includes most of the contents of the *Book of Visions,* must be treated as Vital's perception or belief. It would not be helpful to use judgmental terms like fantasy or invention or say that Vital "alleges" this or that. It is obvious that we are dealing with a "visionary" document and it should be approached from that perspective.

Why then did he commit these intimate details to writing at such a relatively late date in his life? I believe the answer is related to the two basic questions that Vital wrestled with throughout his life and that form the central motifs in this work: Who is he and what is his spiritual mission? The answer Vital provides to these questions may have served as a source of solace and strength at what must have been a difficult time in his life.[62] He was already advanced in years, though he had been assured that he would live to the age of 100 (3.53); his mission had not yet been accomplished, and it seemed further from completion than ever. At the same time, he was surrounded by scoffers and enemies who sought to disparage him and his activities. In the summer of 1609, he was rebuked by the angel Zadkiel, who said to him:

> Now you have completely withdrawn and isolated yourself in a corner. Some people dream wondrous dreams and tell them to you. All this is from God, in order to strengthen your heart, but your heart is still undecided and you do not believe strongly in those dreams. Know that your place in Paradise is next to your teacher, the Ashkenazi, and two other *zaddiqim* of the great *Tannaim*. You are completely righteous before God, but that which I spoke of was the reason that the *zaddiq* refrained from speaking to you by means of Unifications. Your teacher is also somewhat angry with you because of this and that is why you do not dream of him as you did previously. If you will return to your work, you will undoubtedly attain all your goals. (1.23)

Vital had hoped to bring the final redemption that had been predicted for more than a century. His teacher, R. Isaac Luria, had tried, but ultimately failed. The mantle had fallen on Vital, but he did not seem to be succeeding and had become depressed and withdrawn. The angel Zadkiel chided him for this despair and encouraged him to return to his task. By collecting the dreams, visions, and revelations that he and others had received he would find the strength and reassurance he needed to carry on his messianic mission to its ultimate successful completion.

Vital reports that he had intimations in his youth, long before he met Luria, that he was destined for greatness. The *Book of Visions* begins with a series of predictions of his greatness, which began even before his birth. When he was twelve, a palmist predicted great things in his future. Not long thereafter, a heavenly messenger told his teacher in exoteric studies, R. Moses Alshekh, that he would be the successor of R. Joseph Karo. A whole series of seers and diviners all predicted great things for him. Finally, he met his true teacher, R. Isaac Luria, who confirmed the veracity of all these predictions and told Vital that he had come into the world for the sole purpose of teaching him (1.16). In addition to these general predictions of greatness, there are dreams, visions, and other omens by Vital and others that identify him with a series of royal and messianic figures from Jewish history.

Vital believed the redemption to be imminent and expected it within his lifetime. A key question for him was what his role would be in the messianic drama. He had asked his teacher this question, but Luria responded that he did not have permission from Heaven to answer it (4.45). Thus he had to fall back on his own devices to answer this central concern, which permeated his whole being.

The most important figure that Vital associated himself with was the Messiah of Joseph. He was explicitly called the Messiah of Joseph in a letter from a scholar who claimed to be the Messiah of David. He assured Vital that he would pray for him at the appropriate time and that Vital would not die as the Messiah of Joseph was supposed to, according to the Talmudic tradition.[63] Vital's name, Hayyim, which means "life," was assurance of this (1.9). A resident of Damascus had a dream in which he was assured that Vital was the Messiah, though the dream did not specify whether he was the Messiah of David or of Joseph.[64] There are several dreams that indicate that Vital was not to be identified with the Messiah of David. In one, a resident of Damascus had a dream in which a deceased friend sends regards from Heaven and assures Vital that the Messiah loves him and prays for him before God (3.11). Vital himself had a dream in which he spoke to the Messiah (2.2) and another in which he received a letter from the Messiah in which the Messiah assured him that he would soon come, but Vital must endeavor to return the people in penance as this will help the Messiah come more quickly (2.42). Decisive for Vital's identification with the Messiah of Joseph was the kabbalistic tradition that the Messiah of Joseph was reborn in every generation, waiting for the propitious moment to be revealed. Should the Messiah-in-waiting die, the mantle was passed to another person worthy of it. Though his teacher, R. Isaac Luria, never personally claimed to be the Messiah of Joseph, this claim was made on his behalf by his disciples after his death. It was only natural that Vital would also take over this aspect of his teacher's identity.[65]

At the same time, in a number of dreams, Vital was identified with King David (3.17), the king of Israel (3.10), and as a member of King David's family (3.62). The Talmudic sage Hillel, who was identified as a descendant of David in rabbinic tradition,[66] looks like Vital in another dream (2.56). In an interesting twist, Vital was also identified with King Saul (3.61). In the fourth part of the *Book of Visions,* where Vital analyzes the mystical sources of his Soul, we find that Vital's Soul comes from the same root as many of the most important figures in rabbinic Judaism. Most notable is his close association with the Talmudic sage Rabbi Akiva, who was considered to be a Soul spark of the Messiah.[67] Not only was he assured a number of times in the fourth part of the *Book of Visions* that his Soul had the closest possible connection to Rabbi Akiva, but also like Rabbi Akiva he would marry a wealthy widow who was a transmigration of Rabbi Akiva's wife (1.10). Thus while Vital's primary identification is with the Messiah of Joseph, he also has some claim to connection with the Messiah of David.

Vital also indirectly identifies with two messianic figures closer to his own time. It is not coincidental that Vital has two dreams that reflect the activities of the well-known sixteenth-century messianic pretenders, David Reuveni and Solomon Molcho. In a dream that is related to David Reuveni's adventures, Vital dislodges a stone in a wall, which turns into a genie-like figure who tells him that the stone he has dislodged has magically held Israel under the domination of the gentile nations. He has broken this magical spell by dislodging this stone. The genie-like figure then fights Vital, who defeats him by excommunicating him (2.44). In the other dream, which is reminiscent of Solomon Molcho's attempt to meet with the pope in order to convert him to Judaism, Vital goes to Rome, where he meets with the emperor of Rome and wins him over to the truth of Judaism (2.36).

Perhaps the most audacious dream Vital reports is that of the Muslim judge Sa'ad al-Din (1.29). In this dream, Jesus and Muhammed are disgraced and all of their followers have seen the error of their ways. When the Muslims and Christians come and ask whom they should now follow, they are directed to a distant vision of millions of Jews who are being led by an old man whose name is Akiva. When they protest that he has long since died, they are told that he has left behind a disciple who is living in this generation and who is the leader of the Jews—clearly an allusion to Vital himself.

Vital also asserts his importance in relation to some of the great scholars of Safed, most notably R. Joseph Karo.[68] He reports that in his youth, Karo was told by his *Maggid* that Vital would be his successor (1.3). This prediction is fulfilled for Vital in several dreams, both in his youth and in old age. The first dream he reports is one in which a wealthy man had died and the whole community, including Karo, attended his funeral. When the cantor told someone to put the deceased's *zizit* on his head, the deceased objected. All the assembled, including Karo, were powerless to do anything, until Vital compelled him to obey (2.1). In another early dream, Vital ascends to Heaven, where he has a vision of God, who tells him to sit at His right hand. Vital demurs, saying that this place had been reserved for Karo. God agreed, saying that He too had thought so originally, but had decided that Karo should sit somewhere else and Vital should sit there instead (2.5).

In his later years (1608), Vital again had three dreams that demonstrated his superiority over Karo. In one dream, Adam is lying ill in the street in Safed near Karo's house, but it is Vital who brings him medications for his weak heart (2.25). In another dream, it is Karo himself who is ill and Vital heals him (2.46). In the last dream, Karo tells Vital that the king is sending his viceroy to destroy and pillage the city and he implores Vital to use his kabbalistic knowledge to save the city. The implication is that Vital's wisdom and powers are greater than Karo's, for he can perform deeds that the greatest *halakhic* authority is incapable of accomplishing. Vital's kabbalistic knowledge is more highly valued in Heaven and more efficacious than *halakhic* knowledge.

Vital also mentions other "signs" that point to his elevated status. One of the more unusual ones is the pillar of fire. According to a story in the Lurianic hagiography of R. Shlomel Dresnitz,

shortly before R. Moses Cordovero died, he said that whoever
would see a pillar of fire over his bier would be his successor. The
only one who saw it was R. Isaac Luria.[69] Vital has modified this
tradition and now the pillar of fire is seen by others hovering
over Vital himself as a sign of his greatness. He reports four different sightings by others between 1568 and 1610.[70] It is noteworthy that the first sighting is placed two years before he met R.
Isaac Luria, implying that his greatness was not dependent on his
association with Luria, but was preexistent.

A related concern for Vital is his place in Paradise. Through a
number of his own dreams and those of others, he is reassured
that he will have a most exalted place in Paradise. He will sit at
God's right hand, teach many disciples, and even R. Isaac Luria,
his teacher, will attend his lectures instead of sitting in his own
Heavenly academy. Indicative of Vital's obsession with this issue
is the story he tells of his father-in-law's death. As his father-in-
law was dying, Vital made him swear that the first thing he would
do when he reached Heaven would be to find Vital's place in Paradise and report back to him concerning it, via a dream appearance (2.24). His wife too was granted a vision of his Heavenly
abode and reported on it when she came out of a coma (1.17).

Vital's grandiose self-estimation is only one side of his complex
personality. There is also the other side, which questions his ultimate ability to fulfill the messianic role he had claimed for himself. This complicated tension between success and failure can be
found in his relationship to his mentor, R. Isaac Luria. Y. Liebes
suggests that Luria saw himself as the reincarnation of Moses,
and Vital as the reincarnation of R. Akiva. In Lurianic *Kabbalah*,
R. Akiva, the personification of the Oral Torah, stands higher
than Moses, the personification of the Written Torah.[71] Thus,
Vital's task was to finish what Luria had started. Luria intimated
to Vital that the latter had a messianic mission in a number of
ways. He repeatedly connected Vital's soul-root with R. Akiva, and
alluded to the greatness of Vital's Soul numerous times without
being specific, but assured him that it was from the highest
sources.[72] Luria, who was an expert in metoposcopy,[73] saw interesting things written on Vital's forehead. Once, he saw the verse

"For whom is all Israel yearning, if not for you" (1 Sm 9:20), when Vital asked him about his Soul (4.23). On another occasion he saw, "Prepare a seat for Hezekiah, king of Judah" (4.28).[74]

On the negative side of the ledger, Luria rebuked Vital seven days before his death and told him that he had done great harm to himself and to Luria by revealing Luria's teachings to others. R. Moses Alshekh had heard about Luria's teachings and had ordered Vital to tell him about them. Vital complied and as a result the number of visitors to Luria's house increased greatly, leaving Luria insufficient time to study with Vital. In addition, further harm was caused to Luria because the others were not ready for the revelation of these secrets. Luria pleaded with Vital to keep the teachings secret, but Vital would not listen, fearing that he might hinder the repentance of his colleagues. Luria died seven days after this conversation and Vital considered himself at least partially responsible, since he had not listened to Luria's injunction (4.44). This would also explain Vital's obsessive secrecy with regard to Luria's teachings in his later years.

Closely related is a story that Vital reports about his teacher's death. When Luria was dying, he told R. Isaac ha-Cohen that if he had found only one of his disciples that was completely righteous, he would not have been taken from the world. In the course of the conversation, he called for Vital, but he was not present. Luria exclaimed, "Where did he go? Has he left me in such an hour!" (5.1) This sense of inadequacy is reinforced by two dreams that Vital had which make the same point. Luria appeared to Vital in a dream three days after his death and Vital asked him why he had died so hastily. Luria responded that it was because he had not found even one disciple who was complete, as he had desired (2.16). Three months later, Vital saw R. Moses Cordovero in a dream. Cordovero assured him that Luria's method of kabbalistic analysis was the one taught in Heaven and even Cordovero studied it. When Vital asked him why Luria left the world, he received the same answer. Luria left because there was not even one *zaddiq* who was complete, as Luria had desired. Had he found him, he would not have died. (2.17)

Thus, Luria's premature death was attributed at least in part by Vital to his own inadequacy and lack of spiritual completeness. Vital himself says, "If we had all been completely righteous and completely repented, we would have had the power to extract all the good Souls from the *kelippot* in one instant and the Messiah would have immediately come."[75] Implicit in this is the assumption, never fully explicated, that Vital might have been the Messiah of David in relation to Luria's Messiah of Joseph. Related to this is the idea developed in Safed that "the Messiah ben Joseph is reincarnated in every generation and if there are *zaddiqim* in that generation who can protect him, then he will not die."[76] However, with Luria's death Vital must assume his mentor's mantle as Messiah of Joseph. This may explain the confusing imagery that is found in the *Book of Visions,* where Vital appears to be the associated with the king of Israel at times and the Messiah of Joseph at other times.[77]

The ambiguity and confusion we have seen in our account of Vital's self-perception is absent when we consider his primary task. Vital sets for himself one central objective: to cause the people to repent and in this way bring on the advent of the messianic age. It is noteworthy that almost all of the material relating to the theme of repentance is from his Damascus period, while the bulk of the dreams and visions that identify him with royal or messianic figures other than the Messiah of Joseph are from earlier periods in his life. The premature death of his mentor, R. Isaac Luria, must be considered a central factor in this transformation. As long as Luria was alive, Vital could see himself as the reincarnation of R. Akiva to Luria's Moses. However, after Luria's death, the focus necessarily shifted, since it was clear that Luria had not succeeded in his mission, forcing Vital to shift his own emphasis.

There are three foci in his discussions of repentance: first, that this was his primary mission; second, reminders and rebukes for not fulfilling his mission; and third, reasons that hindered him in the performance of his task. It is significant that the only successes Vital records in his desire to preach repentance occur in his dreams, never in his waking experience. Vital was reminded in a variety of modes and by a diversity of beings that it was his mission in life to cause the people to repent. He was assured by visionaries (1.15) and by the kings of the demons, who had been summoned by magical means, that he came to this world for the purpose of causing the people to repent and that through this the redemption will come (1.21). The same message was conveyed by angels, similarly called by magical incantations, that his mission was to return the people in repentance (1.23, 1.28). During one period when he was preaching repentance, he dreamed that the king of Ephraim[78] had come in anticipation of the imminent redemption, which, it is implied, would come about as a result of Vital's preaching (2.34). In another dream, he received a letter of encouragement from the Messiah assuring him that the Messiah had already been invited to come to the land of Israel and that Vital's preaching would hasten his coming (2.42).

Much more common are incidents, dreams, and visions by Vital and others that couple Vital's need to preach repentance with rebukes to Vital for not fulfilling his task. Perhaps the most dramatic incident is the long story of the spirit that inhabited the daughter of Raphael Anav (1.22). It is significant that the spirit, who was the sage Piso from Jerusalem, had to return to this world to atone for the sin of not preaching repentance. Vital was also told that his daughter had died in a plague because he had not preached repentance (1.23). When he asked if he would be worthy to be visited by Elijah, he was told that Elijah stopped visiting him because he stopped preaching repentance. If he would return to this task, then Elijah would return to him (1.28). He was further reminded that the redemption depended on him and that if he did not preach willingly, he would be forced to do so (3.33).

The variety of human figures who reminded him of his mission and rebuked him for not pursuing it adequately ranged from biblical figures like Joshua (3.7) to recent scholars like R. Samuel de Medina (1506–1589) (3.29). He also received letters from the sages of Jerusalem asking him why he delayed preaching repentance and thereby hindered the redemption (3.23). He was even rebuked by the kings of the demons (3.47). In another dream, he was compared unfavorably to his nemesis, R. Jacob Abulafia. Vital was dressed in a very plain garment while Abulafia was dressed in elegant garments, all because Vital had been lazy and had not preached repentance to the people (3.28). Even his mentor, R. Isaac Luria, returned in a dream to rebuke him for not preaching to the people and for being arrogant about his wisdom (3.8).

Vital responded to these rebukes by complaining that he was hindered in the performance of his mission because the people of Damascus would not listen to his preaching and would not heed his message. They were rebuked by the kings of the demons for their lack of attention to Vital's message. They were even threatened with losing their share in the world to come (1.21). R. Joshua Altif dreamed that the king had decreed the destruction of the Jews of Damascus because they did listen to Vital (3.58). In other dreams they were threatened with financial ruin (3.53, 3.63) and black hail if they did not harken to Vital and his message (3.50). Even a plague that ravaged Damascus was blamed on the people's indifference to Vital (3.45).

Vital's difficulties were not only with the Jews of Damascus as a whole, but extended to the congregants of the Sicilian synagogue, whose rabbi he had been for a time. The wife of the beadle of the synagogue had a dream that tells much about Vital's relationship with his own congregation. She dreamed that people were preparing for Vital's return as rabbi of the synagogue, indicating that he had previously been fired. Vital entered the synagogue accompanied by a large retinue. Tellingly, the section where Vital and his guests were seated was richly appointed, but the rest of the synagogue was crumbling and in disrepair. When the community was summoned, only one or two people came. The sages who had accompanied Vital left when they saw that the community had not come, threatening the community with destruction as they departed. Vital also left, followed by the beadle's wife. In the courtyard, she saw a kettle of boiling pitch. She was informed that this was for scalding the Sicilian community because they would not take Rabbi Hayyim back as their rabbi (3.49).

This dream was probably an accurate reflection of Vital's difficulty in even maintaining his position as the rabbi of a small synagogue. Vital's constant complaints about the people of Damascus and their lack of positive response to his message support this view. It is only in his dreams that Vital was a successful preacher who persuaded his listeners to repent. It would also explain his depression and the need for constant prodding from the Heavenly messengers that he should fulfill his mission of preaching repentance.

Vital's wrath focused on his nemesis in Damascus, Rabbi Jacob Abulafia, even more than on the people of Damascus. Abulafia was the rabbi of the Spanish congregation and he did not believe in Vital's visions, nor did he accept his approach to *Kabbalah.* Abulafia had been in Safed, had known R. Isaac Luria, and had studied with some of the great scholars of the generation. Thus, his scorn and mockery of Vital must have been influential. Vital's numerous references to Abulafia and the many allusions to his excommunication and punishment in dreams and visions bear witness to Vital's negative feelings about Abulafia. Vital held Abulafia responsible, more than anyone else, for his failure to convince the people of Damascus of the need for repentance.

According to the king of the demons, "There are three people here in Damascus who hate him [Vital] and they are the primary cause of the damage as a result of which the people of Damascus do not listen to his call for repentance" (1.21). Abulafia was certainly among these three. The angel Zadkiel, who was conjured up by Joshua Boom, confirmed this and told them that the Messiah was angry with R. Jacob Abulafia because he mocked Vital's efforts to bring the Messiah. As a result of his actions, he has been excommunicated in Heaven (1.24). Not only will Abulafia be personally punished for his actions, but the inhabitants of Damascus will also suffer. Their prayers will not be answered (3.16), plagues will break out in the city (3.43), and the city will even be destroyed (3.58). All this will occur as a result of Abulafia's opposition to Vital.

Abulafia was even compared to the Primordial Serpent of Genesis. Yet, Vital was assured that the end would be positive and Abulafia's machinations would ultimately fail (3.51). There are also dreams that suggest that Vital and Abulafia would be reconciled. R. Benjamin Saruq dreamed that the honor of the

Torah was being diminished by the dissension and was urged to make peace between them. At the end of the dream he was able to reconcile the two antagonists. In another dream, Abulafia was rebuked by the sages of the previous generation and the prophet Haggai wrote a document concerning everything that had transpired between Abulafia and Vital. Abulafia's garment was mysteriously taken from him on the following Sabbath. After three weeks Abulafia agreed to become Vital's disciple and the garment was returned to him. It is not clear whether this was a dream or an actual reconciliation (3.13). If it was real, it was only temporary.

The spirit who inhabited Raphael Anav's daughter attributed Abulafia's hostility to jealousy (1.24). However, a more rational reason may be the diminution of the messianic fervor that had characterized Safed in the sixteenth century. Abulafia may well have reflected a broader caution with regard to acute messianic tension, which followed the exuberance of the previous generation, while Vital did not give up on the dreams of his youth.

The *Book of Visions* is divided into five parts. The first part has to do with events in Vital's life. It is significant that virtually all of the events described are related to magical practices or supernatural events.[79] The events that do not directly bear on the central questions that Vital has posed are not discussed at all. In his efforts to find answers and confirmation of the two central questions that concerned him, Vital had recourse to a wide variety of magicians (1.21), diviners, and seers who foresaw the future.[80] The methods of divination included oil drop divination (1.6), geomancy (1.21), conjuring angels and demons with mirrors, and posing questions upon awakening.[81] Even visions during comas are reported.[82] Though all of these forms of divination were known and utilized in Vital's milieu,[83] what is striking is Vital's almost obsessive attempts to learn about his destiny and to find assurance of his greatness. Vital even goes so far as to consult Muslim diviners personally (1.19) and to send others to consult them on his behalf (1.21). The most famous and most detailed incident is the story of the possession by a spirit of Raphael Anav's daughter (1.24). This story received wide circulation and was quoted in a variety of sources.[84] It is also closely related to the doctrine of *gilgul* (transmigration), which will be discussed below.

The second and third parts of the *Book of Visions* are reports of dreams. Vital's own dreams form the second part, while dreams about Vital by others are reported in the third part. All of the dreams that he describes, both his own and those of others, are related to the central questions of his identity and his mission. Vital does not tell us how he knows the dreams of others, whether they were reported to him by the persons mentioned as having those dreams or whether he learned of them through mystical or magical means.

A diversity of views concerning dreams can be found in rabbinic and Jewish mystical literature. Some authorities dismissed them completely, but others set great store by the revelations found in dreams. One can find in the Talmud statements that dismiss the significance of dreams, such as that of R. Jonathan who said, "A man is shown in a dream only what is suggested by his own thoughts."[85] On the other side of the spectrum one can find statements that see dreams as a form of prophecy.[86] The kabbalists had a generally positive attitude toward the prophetic power of dreams, but realized that they could be colored by false notions inspired by the *Sitra Aḥra* (the Other Side).[87] One medieval authority, R. Jacob of Marvege (late 12th–13th cent.), even based his legal decisions on the answers he received in dreams in response to questions he posed before falling asleep.[88] Vital considered dreams to be important and gave them a prominent place in his book. Dreams were an important form of communication from the Heavenly realm and he valued them highly. Nonetheless, he felt impelled to defend his reliance on the prophetic quality of dreams. He does so by citing a number of rabbinic passages that speak positively about the prophetic power of dreams (2.(51)[52]).

The fourth part of the *Book of Visions* is the most esoteric and for Vital the most self-revelatory section of the whole work. It is the spiritual autobiography of his Soul and deals with the things R. Isaac Luria told him about his transmigrations (*gilgulim*) and the ultimate source of his *nefesh*.[89] The closely related area of Unifications *(yihudim)* is also discussed. The concept of transmigrations is an integral part of the Jewish mystical tradition. It can already be found in the *Sefer Bahir*, the earliest extant medieval Jewish mystical text. It grew in importance over the centuries. It assumed major importance in the sixteenth century and was discussed by a wide variety of authors.[90] It also occupied a significant place in Lurianic *Kabbalah* and Vital devoted two treatises to this subject in his Lurianic corpus.[91] The doctrine of transmigration posits that a particular Soul may be reborn into several people over a period of centuries. Normally, the reason for this transmigration is to repair some sin or lacunae of a previous incarnation. Vital named his previous incarnations and described the reasons for their transmigration on the basis of what he was told by his mentor. R. Isaac Luria was the source of information concerning Vital's soul-root and also those of the other disciples.

Vital's first transmigration was R. Vidal de Tolosa (second half of 14th cent.), author of the *Maggid Mishneh,* an important commentary on Maimonides's *halakhic* code, *Mishneh Torah.* R. Vidal's "sin" was relatively minor, an error of judgment in deciding a case involving menstrual blood (4.7). The next three transmigrations were into ordinary people.[92] Saul Tristi was negligent in circumcising a child and the child died. Joshua Soriano deliberately ate a part of an animal forbidden by Jewish law. The third transmigration was a youth by the name of Abraham who died at the age of thirteen as a divine punishment for Joshua Soriano's sin (4.8). Each of these sins, not repaired, led to a more serious sin in the next transmigration, following the rabbinic concept of "one sin leads to another sin."[93] Vital's task was to repair these sins by punctilious observance of the commandments violated in the previous transmigrations. Vital must also deal with and repair several sins related to his own life. These included arrogance, mockery, and nocturnal emissions (4.6). Luria also explained Vital's strong attraction to the *Zohar* as a response to the neglect of this literature by R. Vidal de Tolosa, who did not believe in the wisdom of the *Zohar.* Thus, Vital must concentrate on mystical literature to compensate for its neglect by his previous transmigration.

The concept of *ibbur* (impregnation) is closely related to the concept of *gilgul*, but differs in some important ways. *Gilgul* occurs at birth and is permanent. *Ibbur*, on the other hand, is temporary and usually takes place only when one is an adult. Its purpose is to allow the *nefesh* of a sage of a previous generation to enter the body of someone who is spiritually prepared to receive this impregnation in order to accomplish some task or fulfill some commandment that was left uncompleted in the previous lifetime. The choice of host is also determined by a connection or affinity in their respective soul ancestry.

In Vital's case, Luria told him that the Talmudic sage R. Eleazar ben Arakh was impregnated into Vital in order to complete what was deficient in R. Eleazar's teacher, R. Johanan ben Zakkai. Similarly, R. Eleazar ben Shammua was impregnated in Vital during his twenties so that he could complete deficiencies of R. Eleazar's teacher, R. Akiva (4.6). Vital was chosen as the host for these Talmudic sages because of his close association with R. Johanan ben Zakkai and R. Akiva. Both were from the same soul-root as Vital. The concept of soul-root is very important for Vital and he devotes a great deal of space to charting the precise root of his Soul in Adam and the many important persons who shared this root. This concept will be discussed in greater detail below.

A related concept that is alluded to a number of times is that of Unification (*yihudim*).[94] Its purpose was to unite the Soul of the adept with that of a long-deceased sage. This Unification is accomplished either by prostration on the grave of the sage one wishes to commune with or at home after midnight. In both cases a series of prayers and meditations accompanies the prostration. A long period of spiritual preparation and prayer precedes the actual Unification. The goal the adept longed for was to enlist the aid of the departed sage in some project or to learn the mysteries of the Torah. Vital sought Unification with the soul of the Talmudic sage R. Akiva because he had a particular affinity to Vital, both of their Souls deriving from the same root (4.14).

The most intimate and important secret that Vital could reveal was the precise source of his *nefesh*. It was so intimate a secret that R. Isaac Luria declined to tell Vital about his own soul-root when Vital asked about it. As Lawrence Fine has observed:

> The Safed kabbalists were intensely concerned with questions of soul ancestry. This concern was motivated in large part by the conviction that their own destinies were intimately bound up with, and in a sense controlled by, the nature of the souls with whom they were connected. Knowledge of one's soul-ancestry was, in effect, a method of analyzing oneself, of delving into one's spiritual origins and learning about the possibilities in store. No less important, it was a means of fixing one's status within the community, a concern that was especially strong for this group of pietists.[95]

The ultimate goal of the kabbalist was to restore his soul to its Supernal root by completing the process of *tiqqun* (repair). Knowing the precise source of one's soul was the first and most important step in this process. For Vital, who saw himself as the Messiah of Joseph, his own *tiqqun* would be the first step in the redemption of the whole people of Israel.

Lurianic *Kabbalah* is built on a theological and mythological model that utilizes central concepts of earlier kabbalistic schools, which it reshaped into a new system of kabbalistic specu-lation and contemplation. It is a highly complex system and a full description is beyond the scope of this introduction. Only the most basic ideas that relate to Vital's discussion of his soul-root can be discussed here.[96] Lurianic *Kabbalah* is built on three cru-cial events in the life of the Godhead, *zimzum* (contraction), *shevi-rat ha-kelim* (the breaking of the vessels), and *tiqqun* (repair). The first act in the process of creation for Lurianic *Kabbalah* was *zimzum,* contraction or self-limitation. Originally, the Godhead was *Eyn-Sof,* limitless or infinite, whose light filled all space. God's being had to be withdrawn from a space in order to allow creation to take place. He withdrew from "Himself into Himself" in a process called *zimzum* (contraction). Prior to the *zimzum* the ten aspects of the Godhead, the *sefirot,* were in perfect harmony and balance. All of the sources of *Din* (stern judgment) were collected by *Eyn-Sof* in the process of *zimzum* and remained in the "vacuum" *(tehiru)* when the Godhead withdrew. Traces of the positive divine light *(reshimu)* also remained in the vacuum. A ray of divine light, which is termed Primordial Adam *(Adam Qadmon)*, entered this vacuum. The lights that emanated from Primordial Adam's "ears," "nose," and "mouth" constituted a unified structure. However, the lights that emanated from his "eyes" separated into ten distinct *sefirot*. Vessels *(kelim)* were required to contain these lights. These vessels were composed of a "thicker" light.

When the light poured into these vessels, the three upper vessels performed their task properly and contained the light. The seven lower vessels were not able to contain the light poured into them and they shattered. The first six vessels shattered completely, while the seventh vessel, that of the *sefirah* of *Malkhut*, cracked but did not shatter. Most of the divine light returned to the Godhead, but some of the divine sparks were trapped in the fragments of the vessels, which fell into the vacuum. The husks or shells *(kelippot)* were produced from the broken shards. These *kelippot* are the forces of the "other side" *(Sitra Ahra)*, which is the source of evil. They are also the basis of the material world. The sparks of divine light trapped in the *kelippot* are the divine force that nourishes and gives life to the *kelippot*. Without the divine sparks, the *kelippot* would be lifeless and ineffectual. This whole process is called "the breaking of the vessels" *(shevirat ha-kelim)*. A variety of reasons are given in Lurianic kabbalistic writings for this cosmic catastrophe.

Tiqqun (repair) is the process by which the damage caused by the breaking of the vessels is repaired. Lurianic *Kabbalah* devotes much energy to explaining the process of *tiqqun*, but it is extremely complicated. The following is a highly simplified version of this process. The main vehicle of repair was the divine light that continued to flow from Primordial Adam after the breaking of the vessels. This divine light was reorganized into five new configurations called *Parzufim* (lit. faces). The first *sefirah, Keter,* was called *Arikh Anpin* (the long or patient face). The second and third *sefirot,* *Ḥokhmah* and *Binah,* became *Abba* (father) and *Imma* (mother). The next six *sefirot*–*Hesed* (lovingkindness), *Din* (stern judgment), *Tiferet* (splendor), *Nezaḥ* (endurance), *Hod* (majesty), and *Yesod* (foundation)–were all incorporated into the *Parzuf* of *Zeir Anpin* (the short or impatient face). The last of the five *Parzufim* is *Nukvah de Zeir* (the feminine of *Zeir*), which represents the last *sefirah, Malkhut* or *Shekhinah,* the feminine aspect of the Godhead.

The Soul of Adam, the first person, contained within it the four worlds of *Azilut, Yezirah, Beriah,* and *Assiyah.* His body was a perfect microcosm of Primordial Adam. As a result, he would have been able to complete the process of *tiqqun* through mystical activities. Unfortunately, Adam's sin interrupted his communion with the upper spheres. As G. Scholem has put it, "The sin of the historical Adam repeats and re-enacts on the anthropological and psychological levels the havoc wrought by the breaking of the vessels on the ontological plane of the Primordial Adam."[97] As a result, the harmonious existence of the four worlds that depended on the union of the *Parzufim* of *Zeir Anpin* and *Nukvah de Zeir* was disrupted and the lowest of the four worlds descended into the *kelippot.* In addition, the sparks of all human Souls also descended into the *kelippot.* The task of humanity from Adam's fall until the coming of the Messiah is to raise the divine sparks and restore them to their appropriate place in the divine realm. This process will come to its final conclusion with the coming of the Messiah. Kabbalists, whose Souls are purified, play a central role in this process. Through their prayers, proper performance of the commandments, and Unifications, they help raise the sparks and assist in bringing about the harmonious relationship between the male and female aspects of the Godhead, which is one of the central goals of *tiqqun.* Vital believed that he was living at the very end of this process and thus at the dawn of the messianic age.

The Lurianic doctrine of the Soul is closely related to this concept. As mentioned, all human Souls were incorporated into the body of Adam, which incorporated the five sources of Souls, the five *Parzufim*. According to rabbinic science, each person contains 248 organs and 365 vessels.[98] Each of these 613 organs and vessels corresponds to a "great" Soul. Each of these great souls can subdivide itself into a maximum of 600,000 Soul sparks.[99] While 600,000 is the maximum number of sparks into which a Soul can divide itself, it can also divide into any intermediate number of sparks. Each of these sparks constitutes one human Soul. One can speak of families of Soul sparks that derive from the same one of the 613 great Souls.

The precise genealogy of one's Soul spark is an extremely important and valuable piece of information. The *tiqqun* of one's Soul spark is prerequisite for helping effect the *tiqqun* of others. It is also easier and a higher priority to effect the *tiqqun* of Soul sparks within one's own Soul family. At the same time, the Soul sparks of others in the same Soul family can help one effect one's own *tiqqun*. Thus, Vital goes into excruciatingly complex detail in mapping out the genealogy of his own Soul spark. In theory, one can do this with each of the three aspects of the Soul, the *nefesh*, *ruah*, and *neshamah*. Vital's primary interest is the first of these, the *nefesh*. A detailed explication of the location of Vital's "Soul map" is beyond the scope of the present discussion.[100]

Vital gives a long list of people who are from his Soul family. It begins with Cain, proceeds through a whole host of biblical, rabbinic, postrabbinic, and medieval figures. Some are obscure, but the majority are major figures in rabbinic Judaism. The most surprising name on this lengthy list is the first, Cain. G. Scholem has observed about this evaluation of Cain as a "great soul":

> This Gnostic element in the reevaluation of Cain's soul, which is now perceived as a "great soul," is one of the most remarkable and one of the strangest parts of Luria's doctrine, within a system that was strictly Jewish. It is also among the most interesting ideas in Lurianic thought, for which there is no precedent in earlier *Kabbalah*. This innovation demonstrates the possibilities for the development of Gnostic ideas within the context of strictly Jewish traditions. Chapter 21 of R. Hayyim Vital's *Sefer ha-Gilgulim* (The Book of Transmigrations) is extremely revealing in this respect:

the image of Cain is whitewashed there to the extent that he is now seen as a prophet.[101]

The other figure who plays a major role in Vital's spiritual genealogy, as indicated earlier, is R. Akiva. Unlike Cain, the centrality of R. Akiva is readily understandable, especially in light of his close association with the figure of the Messiah of Joseph, discussed above. Vital's Soul genealogy is for him the capstone of his efforts to prove to himself that he indeed is worthy to be the Messiah of Joseph, despite the seemingly contradictory evidence of his external life.

The *Book of Visions* probably takes its title from two biblical verses, Joel 3:1 ("Your old men shall dream dreams and your young men shall see visions") and Job 33:15 ("In a dream, a night vision").[102] A much abbreviated and bowdlerized version of the *Book of Visions* was first published in 1826 under the title *In Praise of Rabbi Hayyim Vital.*[103] This edition was reprinted a number of times[104] and translated into German by Chajim Bloch.[105] The first complete edition of the *Book of Visions,* based on Vital's own handwritten manuscript, was edited by A. Z. Aescoli and published posthumously in 1954. The annotation of sources and other notes had not been completed at the time of Aescoli's death. N. Ben Menachem, who oversaw the publication of the work, added some notes, but the annotation was far from complete. This translation is based on the Aescoli edition of the Hebrew text. I have supplemented Aescoli's notes with additional source citations and references to the relevant scholarly literature that has appeared since the publication of the Hebrew edition. The notes in the translation marked with an [A] are those of the Aescoli edition. The other notes are my own.

Notes to the
Translator's Introduction

1. N. Zemon Davis, "Fame and Secrecy: Leon Modena's *Life* as an Early Modern Autobiography," in *The Autobiography of a Seventeenth-Century Rabbi–Leon Modena's Life of Judah,* ed. and trans. M. R. Cohen (Princeton, 1988), p. 51.

2. Ibid., p. 61.

3. I. J. Yuval, "A German Jewish Autobiography from the Fourteenth Century" [Hebrew], *Tarbiz* 55 (1986): 543.

4. K. J. Weintraub, *The Value of the Individual: Self and Circumstance in Autobiography* (Chicago, 1978), p. xviii.

5. On the Muslim autobiographical tradition, see F. Rosenthal, "Die arabische Autobiographie," in *Studia Arabica I* (= Analecta Orientalia) (Rome, 1937), pp. 3–40; reprinted in F. Rosenthal, *Muslim Intellectual and Social History: A Collection of Essays* (Aldershot, 1990).

6. E. R. Wolfson, *Through a Speculum That Shines: Vision and Imagination in Medieval Jewish Mysticism* (Princeton, 1994), pp. 331f.

7. A. J. Heschel, "Prophetic Inspiration in the Middle Ages," in *Prophetic Inspiration after the Prophets: Maimonides and Other Medieval Authorities,* ed. M. M. Faierstein (Hoboken, 1996), pp. 1–67.

8. See I. Tishby, *Messianism in the Time of the Expulsion from Spain and Portugal* [Hebrew] (Jerusalem, 1985); and A. Z. Aescoli, *Messianic Movements in Israel* [Hebrew] (Jerusalem, 1956), pp. 231–417.

9. M. Idel, "Studies in the Doctrine of *Sefer ha-Meshiv*" [Hebrew], *Sefunot* N.S. 2 (17) (1983): 226–232, 244–250.

10. J. Dan, "The Story of Rabbi Joseph Della Reina" [Hebrew], *Sefunot* 6 (1962): 313–326; G. Scholem, "On the Legend of R. Joseph Della Reina," in *Studies in Jewish Religious and Intellectual History,* ed. S. Stein and R. Loewe (University of Alabama, 1979), pp. 101–108 [Hebrew

sect.]; M. Oron, "Waiting for Salvation—History and Literature in the Metamorphosis of the Legend of R. Joseph Della Reina" [Hebrew], in *Between History and Literature* (Tel Aviv, 1983), pp. 79–90.

11. The classic statement about the "birthpangs of the Messiah" is M. *Sotah* 9:15, which begins, "In the footsteps of the Messiah, insolence will increase and honor will disappear, the vine will give its fruit but wine will be expensive, the government will be transformed into heresy and there will be no admonishing." Additional rabbinic texts on this theme are collected in R. Patai, *The Messiah Texts* (Detroit, 1979), pp. 95–103.

12. B. Netanyahu, *Don Isaac Abravanel* (Philadelphia, 1972), pp. 195–257.

13. On the various dates proposed for the messianic advent in the sixteenth century, see A. H. Silver, *A History of Messianic Speculation in Israel* (Boston, 1959), pp. 110–150. On 1575 as the messianic year, see, D. Tamar, "Expectations in Italy for the Year of Redemption, 1575" [Hebrew], in *Studies in the History of the Jewish People in Israel and Italy* (Jerusalem, 1970), pp. 11–38.

14. E. Kupfer, "The Visions of R. Asher ben R. Meir called Lemlein Reutlingen" [Hebrew], *Kobez Al Yad* N.S. 8 (18) (1976): 385–423.

15. Aescoli, *Messianic Movements,* pp. 266–278, 365–412; M. Idel, "Solomon Molcho as Magician" [Hebrew], *Sefunot* N.S. 3 (18) (1985): 193–219.

16. A. Z. Aescoli, *The Story of David ha-Reuveni,* second edition (Jerusalem, 1993) [Hebrew].

17. Vital was himself influenced by Molcho and Reuveni. Cf. *The Book of Visions* (hereafter—B.V.) 2.36, 2.44, 3.14.

18. R. J. Z. Werblowsky, *Joseph Karo, Lawyer and Mystic* (Philadelphia, 1977), pp. 97–99.

19. R. Elior, "Messianic Expectations and Spiritualization of Religious Life in the Sixteenth Century," *Revue des Etudes Juives* 145 (1986): 37.

20. Ibid., p. 43.

21. Heschel, "Prophetic Inspiration," cites numerous examples from the medieval period.

22. Ibid., pp. 32–37.

23. There was a considerable controversy over the authenticity of Karo's account of his Maggidic experiences. Many people refused to believe that such an important *halakhic* figure would make such extravagant claims. Werblowsky, *Joseph Karo,* ch. 2.

24. On the favorable economic conditions in Safed, see S. Avitsur,

"Safed—Center for the Manufacture of Woven Woolens in the Fifteenth Century" [Hebrew], *Sefunot* 6 (1962): 43–69.

25. Authorship of the *Zohar* was traditionally attributed to him, but modern scholarship has shown that the *Zohar* was actually written in late thirteenth century Spain, by R. Moses de Leon.

26. The classic description of Safed in the sixteenth century remains S. Schechter, "Safed in the Sixteenth Century," in *Studies in Judaism*, Second Series (Philadelphia, 1908), pp. 202–306. See also L. Fine, *Safed Spirituality* (Ramsey, 1984), pp. 1–24.

27. The standard view, that of G. Scholem in his various writings, is that Lurianic *Kabbalah* had a profound influence on all Jewish mystical movements that followed it and on Judaism as a whole. More recently, M. Idel has raised important questions about the dissemination and influence of Lurianic *Kabbalah* up to the eighteenth century. See his article "One from a Town, Two from a Clan—The Diffusion of Lurianic *Kabbalah* and Sabbateanism: A Re-Examination," *Jewish History* 7, 2 (1993): 79–104.

28. Calabrese was the family name, but he is referred to as Hayyim Vital in most sources.

29. B.V. 1.2, 4.11. Despite his words of remorse, Vital returned to the study of alchemy and related subjects after Luria's death. On Vital and alchemy see R. Patai, *The Jewish Alchemists* (Princeton, 1994), pp. 340–364, and G. Bos, "Hayyim Vital's 'Practical Kabbalah and Alchemy': A 17th Century Book of Secrets," *Journal of Jewish Thought and Philosophy* 4, 1 (1994): 55–112.

30. B.V. 1.1–1.6.

31. It is not certain when Luria arrived in Safed. The first significant reference to him in Safed is his participation in the funeral of R. Moses Cordovero. Vital mentions in B.V. 4.1 that his first encounter with Luria was on *Rosh Hodesh Adar* of 1571.

32. Ronit Meroz, "Faithful Transmission versus Innovation: Luria and His Disciples," in *Gershom Scholem's Major Trends in Jewish Mysticism 50 Years After*, ed. P. Schaefer and J. Dan (Tübingen, 1993), p. 267. How this change came about is described in M. Beneyahu, *Toldot ha-Ari* (Jerusalem, 1967), pp. 161–163.

33. Meroz, "Faithful Transmission," p. 268.

34. B.V. 1.7, 4.1.

35. These numbers refer to section and paragraph in the text of the *Book of Visions*. In a few places the numbering system has two numbers for a given paragraph, one number in parentheses and the next in

brackets. The Hebrew text does not explain the reason for this dual numbering. I have kept this numbering system to make it easier for the reader to refer back to the Hebrew text.

36. Meroz, "Faithful Transmission," pp. 269–272, discusses the differing versions of Luria's teachings produced after his death.

37. G. Scholem, "Shtar Hitkashrut shel Talmidei ha-Ari," *Zion* 5 (1940): 141.

38. M. Beneyahu, "Rabbi Hayyim Vital in Jerusalem" [Hebrew], *Sinai* 30 (1951): 69.

39. Ibid., "Vital in Jerusalem," p. 68.

40. Scholem, "Shtar Hitkashrut," p. 135.

41. Ibid. Vital's ostensible reason was that there were many mistakes in the notes of the other disciples.

42. The ordination spoken of here is not the ordinary rabbinic ordination, but the special ordination introduced by Rabbi Jacob Berab in 1538. Only a few of the most distinguished scholars in Safed received this ordination before it fell into disuse at the end of the sixteenth century. See M. Beneyahu, "The Revival of Ordination in Safed" [Hebrew], *Yizhak F. Baer Jubilee Volume* (Jerusalem, 1960), pp. 248–269. On the controversy surrounding this ordination, see also H. Z. Dimitrovsky, "New Documents Regarding the Semicha Controversy in Safed" [Hebrew], *Sefunot* 10 (1966): 113–192.

43. Beneyahu, "Vital in Jerusalem," p. 67

44. G. Scholem, *Kabbalah* (New York, 1974), p. 444.

45. D. Tamar, "The Greatness and Wisdom of Rabbi Hayyim Vital" [Hebrew], in *Rabbi Joseph B. Soloveichik Jubilee* Volume (Jerusalem/New York, 1984), vol. 2, p. 1306.

46. B.V. 1.21, 1.24, 3.9.

47. B.V. 1.22, 1.24, 3.13, 3.58, 3.63.

48. Luria's extant writings consist of a commentary on *Sifra de-Zeni'uta* (The Book of Concealment); a section of the *Zohar*, which was written in his youth and reflects the influence of R. Moses Cordovero; and a collection of pious customs and several Sabbath hymns that attained wide popularity. His customs and hymns have been translated in Fine, *Safed Spirituality*, pp. 61–80. The first attempt to catalog Luria's kabbalistic writings was G. Scholem, "The Authentic Kabbalistic Writings of R. Isaac Luria" [Hebrew], *Kiryat Sefer* 19 (1942): 184–199. More recently, Joseph Avivi, *Binyan Ariel* (Jerusalem, 1987), and Ronit Meroz, "Early Lurianic Compositions" [Hebrew], in *Mashu'ot: Studies in Kabbalah and Jewish Thought in Memory of E. Gottlieb,* ed. M. Oron and A. Goldreich

(Jerusalem, 1994), pp. 311–338, have sought to identify other Lurianic writings found in the works of his disciples. See also the reservations of Y. Liebes, "Early Lurianic Compositions?" [Hebrew], pp. 339–342 in the same volume.

49. Scholem, *Kabbalah,* pp. 424–426.

50. A list of Vital's writings can be found in the entry on Vital in the *Encyclopedia Judaica* (Jerusalem, 1970), vol. 16, pp. 173–176.

51. M. Oron, in her article, "Dream, Vision and Reality in Hayyim Vital's *Sefer Hezyonot*" [Hebrew], *Jerusalem Studies in Jewish Thought* 10 (1992): 299–309, has demonstrated that this work should be considered an autobiography. Much of the analysis that follows independently reached substantially the same conclusions as Oron does in her article. I have not documented each specific point of convergence.

52. *Milei De-Shemaya of R. Eleazar Azikri* [Hebrew], ed. with Introduction by M. Pachter (Tel Aviv, 1991).

53. Ed. A. Z. Aescoli (Paris, 1938).

54. The *Megillat Sefer* was published in a bowdlerized version by David Kahana (Warsaw, 1897).

55. "The Messianic Dreams and Visions of R. Ḥayyim Vital" [Hebrew], *Shalem* 4 (1984): 211.

56. It is legendary in that it is a mixture of fact and fiction. Much of what Reuveni describes of his early history and background is based on popular myths and legends. Other parts are a reasonably factual account of his mission.

57. B.V. 2.44 and n. 68 there.

58. R. H. Y. D. Azulai reports an interesting tradition that Vital ordered that the final version of his Lurianic writings be buried with him and certain rabbis contacted him by means of Unifications after his death and procured permission for these writings be retrieved by mystical means. See *Shem ha-Gedolim* (Vilna, 1853), p. 56, s.v., R. Ḥayyim Vital.

59. Tamar, "Greatness and Wisdom," p. 1297.

60. Tamar, "Messianic Dreams and Visions," p. 212, suggests that it was redacted about 1610. However, there are items dated as late as 1612.

61. Ibid. Tamar believes that the incidents in which R. Isaac Luria participated were recorded during Luria's lifetime and the relevant dates are reliable.

62. K. J. Weintraub comments on Peter Abelard's autobiography that "he [Abelard] may have been the prime beneficiary of the catharsis that

can lie in writing" (op. cit., p. 75). The same sentiment may also be applied to Vital.

63. Babylonian Talmud (hereafter referred to as B.), *Sukkah,* 52a.

64. B.V. 3.14. A second version of this dream is also found in 5.17.

65. D. Tamar collected the relevant material and demonstrates the identification of Luria and Vital with the Messiah of Joseph in his article "The Ari (R. Isaac Luria) and R. Hayyim Vital as the Messiah of Joseph" [Hebrew], *Sefunot* 7 (1963): 169–177; reprinted in *Studies,* pp. 115–123.

66. B. *Ketubot,* 62b.

67. Tishby, *Messianism,* pp. 156f.

68. Vital had a deeply ambivalent attitude toward Karo. Cf. Werblowsky, *Joseph Karo,* pp. 142ff; L. Fine, "Recitation of Mishnah as a Vehicle for Mystical Inspiration: A Contemplative Technique Taught by Hayyim Vital," *Revue des Etudes Juives* 141 (1982): 193.

69. Tamar, "Greatness and Wisdom," p. 1300.

70. B.V. 1.12, 1.26, 1.27.

71. Y. Liebes, "*De Natura Dei:* On the Development of the Jewish Myth," in *Studies in Jewish Myth and Jewish Messianism* (Albany, 1993), pp. 26f.

72. This is the leitmotif of the whole fourth part of the *Book of Visions.* Of course, it must be remembered that we know this only because Vital tells us that it is the case.

73. On this aspect of Luria's knowledge and its importance see, L. Fine, "The Art of Metoposcopy: A Study in Isaac Luria's Charismatic Knowledge," *AJS Review* 9,1 (Spring 1986): 79–101.

74. B. *Berakhot,* 28b. Hezekiah was destined to be the Messiah, but he failed to offer praise to God at a crucial point and this honor was taken away from him. *Song of Songs Rabah,* 4.8.

75. Tamar, "Messiah ben Joseph," p. 115.

76. Ibid., p. 116.

77. Vital is associated with the King of Israel or Davidic figures in B.V. 1.4, 1.5, 1.21, 3.7, 3.10, 3.17, 3.20, and 4.28. For his association with the Messiah of Joseph, see Tamar, "Messiah ben Joseph."

78. I.e., the king of the ten lost tribes.

79. Vital's interest in magic and the various forms of divination was not unusual in this period. For another example, see G. Bos, "Moses Mizrachi on Popular Science in 17th Century Syria-Palestine," *Jewish Studies Quarterly* 3, 3 (1996): 250–279.

80. B.V. 1.4, 1.9. 1.14.

81. B.V. 1.10, 1.15, 1.18.

82. B.V. 1.17, 1.19.

83. The classic study of Jewish magic is J. Trachtenberg, *Jewish Magic and Superstition* (New York, 1939). See also S. Daiches, *Babylonian Oil Magic in the Talmud and in Later Jewish Literature* (London, 1913) and J. Dan, "Archons of the Cup and Archons of the Toenail" [Hebrew], in *Studies in Ashkenazi-Hasidic Literature* (Ramat Gan, 1975), pp. 34–43. See also the two articles by G. Bos cited in notes 29 and 79.

84. Beneyahu, *Toldot ha-Ari*, p. 292 n. 1, cites many of these sources.

85. B. *Berakhot*, 55b.

86. E.g., B. *Nedarim*, 8a; *Genesis Rabah*, 17.5.

87. I. Tishby, *The Wisdom of the Zohar* (Oxford, 1991), vol. 2, pp. 809–830.

88. R. Margulies, *Responsa from Heaven* (Jerusalem, n.d.) [Hebrew]. The Introduction traces this idea through rabbinic literature.

89. In Lurianic *Kabbalah*, the Soul has several parts. The three most important are the *nefesh* (Animus), *ruah* (Spirit), and *neshamah* (Soul).

90. R. Elior, "The Doctrine of *Gilgul* in *Galya Raza*" [Hebrew], *Jerusalem Studies in Jewish Thought* 3, 1–2 (1983–1984): 207–239; M. Helner, "The Doctrine of *Gilgul* in the Kabbalistic writings of R. David Ibn Zimra" [Hebrew], *Pa'amim* 43 (1990): 16–50.

91. *Sha'ar ha-Gilgulim* and *Sefer ha-Gilgulim*.

92. I.e., persons who are not famous or known from other sources.

93. M. *Avot* 4.2.

94. This concept is discussed in L. Fine, "The Contemplative Practice of Yihudim in Lurianic Kabbalah," in A. Green ed., *Jewish Spirituality* (New York, 1987), vol. 2, pp. 64–98.

95. Fine, "Recitation of Mishnah," p. 197.

96. More comprehensive discussions of Lurianic *Kabbalah* can be found in G. Scholem, *Major Trends in Jewish Mysticism* (New York, 1961), pp. 244–286; idem, *Sabbatai Sevi* (Princeton, 1973), pp. 23–66; I. Tishby, *The Doctrine of Evil and the "Qelippah" in Lurianic Kabbalah* [Hebrew] (Jerusalem, 1942).

97. Scholem, *Sabbatai Sevi*, p. 38.

98. See Part 4, n. 82, for the rabbinic sources of this idea.

99. 600,000 is the traditional number for the number of Israelites who received the Torah at Sinai.

100. The primary discussion of this is in Part 4, sect. 37–50.

101. G. Scholem, "Gilgul: The Transmigration of Souls," in *On the Mystical Shape of the Godhead* (New York, 1991), p. 236.

102. This is the suggestion of Tamar, "Dreams and Visions," p. 213.

103. Scholem, "Shtar Hitkashrut," p. 135 n. 2, suggests that the printer gave it this title to capitalize on the success of *In Praise of the Baal Shem Tov*, which had been published in 1815. Another possibility is that the printer wanted to connect it to a similar work, *In Praise of R. Isaac Luria*, which had been published in 1795.

104. C. B. Friedberg, *Bet Eked Sefarim* (Tel Aviv, 1954), vol. 3, p. 960.

105. *Lebenserinnerungen des Kabbalisten Vital* (Vienna, 1927).

The Text of
Book of Visions
by Rabbi Ḥayyim Vital

Part One

———————— EVENTS IN MY LIFE ————————

These are the things that occurred to me since the day of my birth, which was the first day of *Heshvan* in the year 5303 after creation [1542 C.E.].

1. When my father and teacher z"l was living outside the land of Israel, before he migrated there, a great scholar, whose name was R. Ḥayyim Ashkenazi, was a guest in his home. He said to him: Know that in the future you will travel to the land of Israel to live there, and a son will be born to you there. Call him Ḥayyim after me. He will be a great scholar, and there will be none like him in his generation.

2. In the year 5314 [1554], when I was twelve years old, a great expert in palmistry looked at the lines in my hand and said to me: Know that when you will be twenty-four years old, many thoughts will enter your heart which will force you to neglect the study of Torah for two and one half years.[1] Afterwards, two paths will present themselves to you, one to Paradise, and the second to *Gehenna.* The choice will be yours. If you choose the path of *Gehenna* there won't be a more evil person in your generation, and if you choose the path of Paradise, you will ascend to a higher level of wisdom and fear of sin than anyone else in your generation, something that is without measure. None of his words remained unfulfilled.

3. In the year 5317 [1557], R. Joseph Karo[2] z"l commanded my teacher, R. Moses Alshekh,[3] in the name of the angelic *Maggid,*[4] who had told him that he should be very careful to teach me to the best of his ability, because in the future, I will be the successor of R. Joseph Karo.

He also cautioned me about my studies, in the name of the above-mentioned *Maggid,* saying that half the world exists through the merit of my father and teacher, through the merit of

43

the magnificent *tefillin*[5] which he had written, and half the world exists through my merit.

4. In the year 5325 [1565], the sage R. Lapidot Ashkenazi z"l,[6] who could foretell the future, was in Safed. His ability was such that when someone was brought before him, whether living or dead, even someone of a previous generation, he would tell them about all their affairs. One day I went to his house on some errand, and he did not give me any respect at all, since he did not know me. The next day I returned to his house. As soon as he saw me, he immediately rose and accorded me great respect. He said to me: Forgive me for not behaving respectfully yesterday, as I did not recognize the significance of your Soul until this past night, when your virtues were made known to me. I would advise you to turn all your thoughts from matters of this world and devote all your thoughts to raising your Soul to its appropriate place, since it is not a Soul of this generation, but from the Souls of the early *Tannaim*. If you desire, you will be able to ascend to awesome heights according to the vast greatness of your Soul, something that is without measure. Therefore, you should not think of yourself as a humble Soul, but as a very exalted Soul, since this is the truth. Through this, you will be strengthened in your work, as we find concerning Hezekiah, "His heart was elevated in the ways of the Lord" [2 Chr 17:6]. Know that you have only one sin which you committed in the past and if you repair this sin, you will ascend to unlimited heights.

Later, when I met my teacher the Ashkenazi[7] z"l, he spoke to me exactly as mentioned above. I then told him what R. Lapidot had said to me, which matched what he said, and he was very happy.

5. The same year. I saw a woman who was an expert in divining by dropping oil into water and she said to me: I was very frightened by what I saw in this oil—you will undoubtedly rule over all of Israel in the future. It seems to me that this will be in a city on the seashore such as Sidon or Tiberias. I never saw anyone, in my practice of oil divination,[8] on such a high level in this whole generation.

6. In the year 5330 [1570] there was a wise woman who fore-

told the future and was also expert in oil-drop divination. She was called Soniadora.[9] I asked her to cast a spell over the oil as was customary, concerning my comprehension of kabbalistic wisdom. She did not know what to answer me until she assumed a "spirit of jealousy" [Nm 5:30], and strengthened her incantations. She stood up on her legs, kissed my feet, and said:

Forgive me that I did not recognize the greatness of your Soul—the importance of your Soul is not that of the sages of this generation, but that of the generation of the early *Tannaim,* according to what I saw in this oil.

In response to your question, I was shown in the oil the following, written in square letters: "Concerning this man who asks, the Talmudic Sages z"l gave an analogy through the parable mentioned in *Midrash Song of Songs* concerning King Solomon a"h: "Very sweet waters bubble forth from a very deep well. Nobody knows how to draw the waters up until an intelligent person comes and ties together several ropes and descends to drink."[10] You have a desire and thirst to know a discipline called *Kabbalah* and you are asking about it; know that you will comprehend, as in the parable about King Solomon mentioned above, that which none of the scholars who preceded you were able to comprehend. A great sage will come this year to Safed from the south, e.g., from Egypt, and he will teach you this wisdom.

So it was, for in that year my teacher z"l came from Egypt.

I again asked through an incantation over the oil about the wondrous dream that I dreamed on Friday night, 8 *Tevet* 5326 [1566]. She said to me: Am I Daniel to explain your dream? Nonetheless, I will explain it to you. And she told me most of the dream.

7. 5331 [1571]. I began to study with my teacher z"l the Ashkenazi and he told me all the things that I had been told concerning my Soul, which are written in another section.[11]

8. The same year. My teacher z"l sent me to the cave of Abbaye and taught me that Unification.[12] I was united with his Soul and he told me those things that I wrote in the above-mentioned section.

9. 5334 [1574]. Rabbi Mas'ud Cohen[13] came to Safed from

Dar'a.[14] He told me that before his departure he went to take his leave of the great sage and clairvoyant, R. Abraham Avshalom. He said to him: To life [le-Hayyim] and to peace [le-Shalom]. He responded: The meaning of his words is: That he will come to me, I am Hayyim, and he will bring me greetings [Shalom] from him. He gave him all the signs that identified me and that I was a young man living in Safed. And he said to him: Tell him in my name that he is the Messiah, the son of Joseph. He will travel to Jerusalem and will be required to live there for two years. In the third year he will be able to choose whether to remain there. After the first year, the spirit of the Lord will begin to beat in him. From then on there will be controversy over him between the people of Jerusalem and the Galilee. The people of Egypt will aid Jerusalem, but the Galilee will be victorious. He will return to live in the Galilee and many thousands and myriads of Israelites will gather around him. He will reign over them and teach them Torah. Afterwards, I will travel there and I will be the Messiah, the son of David, and he will be the Messiah, the son of Joseph, my deputy. He should be cautious when he travels to Jerusalem and not gather people around him, as this will cause him great harm and also because he will be thrown into jail for this reason. Concerning that which the sages said that the Messiah, the son of Joseph will be killed, I will endeavor with all my strength to save him from this evil decree, since concerning him it is written: "He asked You for life; You granted it" [Ps 21:5]. The meaning of this is: Because the Messiah, the son of David, will ask of God that he give life [Hayyim] to the Messiah, the son of Joseph, who is called Hayyim, and God will grant him life.[15]

10. The same year the above-mentioned R. Mas'ud asked a divinatory question about me, in a waking dream.[16] He was told that after the above-mentioned two years a rich widow, who had heard about me, will come from a Christian country to marry me, and I will marry her. She is a transmigration of the wife of "Turnus Rufus"[17] who married Rabbi Akiva and I am the transmigration of Rabbi Akiva. Afterwards, I will have many disciples and I will provide for their sustenance for fifteen years, and then what God will decree for me will occur.[18]

11. 5337 [1577]. I traveled to Egypt and another scholar from Dar'a came and told me everything as it had been related to me by R. Mas'ud in the name of R. Abraham Avshalom, as mentioned in section nine.

12. 5338 [1578]. I was preaching publicly in Jerusalem one Saturday morning. Rachel, the sister of R. Judah Mashan,[19] was there and she told me that the whole time I was preaching she saw a pillar of fire over my head[20] and Elijah z"l to my right supporting me. They both disappeared when I finished preaching.

She also saw a pillar of fire over my head when I led the *Musaf* service on *Yom Kippur* in the synagogue of the Sicilian community in Damascus, in 5362 [1601]. The above-mentioned woman was used to seeing visions, demons, spirits, and angels, and most of what she said was correct from the time of her youth and through adulthood.

13. 5339 [1579]. One morning in Jerusalem a Muslim servant at the Temple who was hostile to Jews came to me.[21] He kissed my hands and feet and begged me to bless him and that I should write any two or three words that I desire, in my handwriting, so that he could hang it around his neck as an amulet. I asked him: What inspired you now? He said to me: Now I know that you are a man of God and holy. I am a servant at the Temple and last night at midnight I went out the door of the Temple to urinate in the courtyard and the moon was as bright as midday; I raised my eyes and saw you hovering in the air over the Temple for an hour. It was you without any doubt.

14. 5340 [1580]. A man from Assyria,[22] whose name was R. Abba, came to Safed and asked for me. He was told: He is in Jerusalem. He told them everything that he later told me which I will record. From there he came to Jerusalem, to my house, kissed my hands and feet, and said to me: When I left Mosul, in Assyria, a great and venerable scholar who lived there commanded me, his name was so and so, but I forgot it—he is an eminent pietist who lives as a solitary hermit in an attic and does not see people. Elijah z"l is found in his company. He commanded me to greet you in his name and tell you that everything your teacher, Rabbi Isaac Ashkenazi, told you concerning the transmigrations of your

Soul and its attributes is all true and certain. Do not despair of them, for everything will be fulfilled. If you would know the greatness of your Soul, you would be astonished. Therefore, do not belittle the words of your master in these matters, because great goodness will come to Israel through you. And if you [consider yourself] unworthy, you are the leader of the tribes of Israel. All of his life he had a great desire to see you, but he does not have the strength to come. He always regrets that he cannot come and talk to you in person, face to face, about these matters. These words that he has sent through me will suffice.

15. 5350 [1590]. A man named R. Shealtiel Alshekh, who saw visions upon waking, came from Persia. He was wise, understanding, pious, and humble all his life.

He told me that he was always shown that the complete redemption of Israel and Israel's repentance depend on me. The attributes of my Soul were made known to him. Until the present year, 5370 [1610], he writes me letters about his visions concerning my soul and the redemption.

16. That year, my teacher R. Moshe Alshekh z"l established his school in the courtyard of Rachel Ashkenazi. One day, she saw him sitting very saddened, and she asked him why he was sad. He said to her: Should I not be sad that my student R. Hayyim Vital does not want to teach me the wisdom of *Kabbalah*. She said to him: Is your student greater than you? He told her how when my teacher the Ashkenazi z"l was still alive, he went to him one day and cried and pleaded with him that he himself should teach him the wisdom of *Kabbalah* and not through me. He responded that he came into the world only to teach me alone and it was impossible to reveal this wisdom, except through me. He said to him: How is it possible for the teacher to learn from his student? He said to him: I wish that you will be worthy to be his disciple, for had not the sages said, "One is jealous of everyone except for his son and his student,"[23] I would also envy him the great attributes that he will attain in the future, something that is without measure.

His son, R. Hayyim Alshekh, also told me all these things about his father, my teacher z"l. My teacher, the Ashkenazi z"l, also told me something similar that occurred between him and

R. Solomon Sagis z"l.[24] He said to him: If you do not want to sub-
mit to R. Ḥayyim to learn this wisdom from him, you will never
know it, for the above-mentioned reason.

17. That year my wife, Hannah, became extremely ill and one
Sabbath she was in a coma and close to death. At night, at the
conclusion of the Sabbath, we approached her to witness the
departure of the Soul. Suddenly, she opened her mouth, her eyes
were closed and she recited the blessing for fragrant trees. We
asked her: What is the reason for this? She answered in a voice
that sounded like a ghost's from the ground,[25] and she said:

Know that my Soul is now being led to *Gehenna* and I saw they
were lighting the fire that had been extinguished on the Sabbath,[26] and I smelled a strong odor of fire and brimstone. Afterwards they led my Soul and the Souls of others to a field before
the gates of Paradise which contained myrtle trees in order to
smell a pleasant odor and remove the sulfuric smell of *Gehenna*
and then I recited the blessing, "Creator of fragrant trees."

Afterwards, I entreated them to lead me to Paradise to see the
place of my husband, R. Ḥayyim. They led me to Paradise and
brought me into a large courtyard, completely planted with fragrant trees and pleasant fruits. In the middle of the courtyard
was a large pool flowing with fresh water, in the midst of which
was a tall pipe through which the water ascended vigorously into
the air and fell back filling the pool. Glass-like bottles of gold and
silver ascended and descended in the water of the pipe. I said to
them: What are these? They said to her: These bottles are the
Souls of your children who died in infancy and they reside permanently in the waters of their father's spring in Paradise. This
whole courtyard and everything in it is a part of their father's
place in Paradise. Afterwards, I saw on one side of the courtyard
a very tall ladder on which one ascends to an attic which was like
a porch consisting of a roof and three walls. The fourth side facing the courtyard was open, without a wall, in order to see and
enjoy the trees of the courtyard from there. Many scholars sit in
this attic and study with my husband. I saw one scholar wearing a
tallit over his head sitting there. I asked about him. They told me:
This is R. Isaac Ashkenazi, your husband's teacher. I said to them:

Why is he not in his own Yeshivah? They told me that there in Paradise he always sits with my husband.

I wanted to ascend the ladder to see the place where my husband sits, but I was not permitted. They said to me: You do not have permission to enter any of the houses in the courtyard and certainly not in this attic, for all of this is your husband's portion in Paradise, and were you not worthy to be his wife, you would not have been allowed to even enter the courtyard. This is enough for you.

R. Gedaliah Levi, my husband's brother-in-law, ascended the ladder. My husband became angry and rebuked him, saying to him: Quickly, descend from here, for you have no permission to ascend here. He descended and left.

When she finished speaking, she was again silent as before, until morning. She then opened her eyes and returned to her senses. She was asked if she remembered what she had said the previous night. She said that she did not remember anything, nothing at all.

In my humble opinion, this occurred to R. Gedaliah because at that time we were angry with each other.

18. 5354 [1594]. I was in Safed and I arranged study times for them and I preached for them on the day of the *mishmarah*.[27] A woman was there, Francisa Sarah,[28] a pious woman, who saw visions in a waking dream and heard a voice speaking to her, and most of her words were true. The daughter of Rabbi Solomon Albakez[29] z"l said to her: Is it possible that such a holy mouth, someone so eloquent, should die? She responded: Do not worry about this, for the Messiah will undoubtedly come in his lifetime.

19. 5364 [1604]. I was gravely ill and in a coma for twenty-one days. The eve of the twenty-second day was the conclusion of the Sabbath and many people gathered around me to observe the departure of the Soul. During the early part of the night, I opened my mouth four times as if my Soul was departing. Afterwards, I opened my eyes and gazed at the eastern wall that was opposite me. I saw there two pillars of fire, one red and one green, like grass. I bowed toward them and gazed at them until midnight. They moved from there, to the north wall

and remained there until morning. I did not take my eyes off them the whole night. I was like someone in a state of shock, without any sense of the world.

When the people sitting near me saw how I bowed toward the wall and how I cast my gaze there, they said: This is what our Sages z"l said: During their lives they do not see, but during their death they see.[30] They said to me: What do you see? I told them that I had been told that the time of my death had not yet come, because the building of my house and place in Paradise had not yet been finished, since it was a large building. I was like an inanimate stone.

In the morning I forgot everything I had told the people, but I remembered everything that had occurred to me with regard to the two pillars.

The fever departed from me completely and all of my senses returned to me, except for my sight. My eyes remained completely dimmed for seven days. Afterwards, I began to see a little, until the end of forty days. From then on my eyes were dimmed, as if clouds and a variety of flames from those pillars ascended and descended before my eyes.

After a year, I went to Zalahia,[31] to a magician and sorcerer,[32] called Sheikh ibn Ayyub, who was an expert in remedies for people injured by demons. I wanted to examine his wisdom and also to ask about my blindness. I arrived outside the door to his courtyard, and he was in his house surrounded by many important men and women. A small boy came out and I said to him: Go, tell the Sheikh that a Jew seeks permission to enter. The boy went in. Suddenly the Sheikh himself came out hurriedly, and said to me: Enter, *Hakham* of the Jews. Why did such an important person as you bother to come here? If you had sent your servant, I would have run to your house. He honored me greatly and seated me in his place while he sat opposite me.

I was amazed by this, because he had never met me in his life. All the gentiles who were there were also amazed. He said to them: Leave, for as long as this distinguished person remains here, I cannot respond to you. They left.

I then asked him for an incantation, as is the custom. He did not know how to answer me. He tried all sorts of expedients and incantations, but did not succeed. I said to him: How did you know something greater than this—to recognize me without any foreknowledge? He told me: The reason for this is that I engage in adjurations to the seven kings of the demons, and through them I utilize this knowledge. They were the ones who informed me of your attributes, and said to me: A superior and holy Jew is coming to you and we do not have the power to remain here with him, and they left. Behold, I see them standing at the summit of the mountain that is opposite us, until you will leave. That is why I cannot answer your questions, because I only know what the seven kings tell me and they have left.

20. 5367 [1607]. At the conclusion of the Sabbath, the nineteenth of *Ellul,* R. Caleb was reciting the *ma'ariv* prayer in my house. Lights had not yet been lit in the house, and when I rose to recite the *amidah* he saw, while awake, with open eyes, the image of an open eye about a hand's breadth across resting on my head, shining brightly. He was very terrified and became confused in his prayers.

21. 5369 [1609]. The intermediate days of Passover. R. Joseph Segura went to the house of a magician who was expert in geomancy and seeing demons. He first cast the sand lots with a spell, as was customary.

He asked: Who is R. Ḥayyim the Kabbalist and for what purpose was he created? They answered him: You are not asking about yourself, but about someone else. He is a very exalted person, and every day he meditates privately and grieves over one matter that he longs for. This matter is not based on the elements of fire and earth, but is from the elements of air and water[33]—the conclusion of this matter will be very good.

Afterwards, he asked by means of a glass mirror. The seven kings of the demons came with their seven servants. Afterwards another seven came, and then another seven, and another seven, until there were a total of twenty-eight kings and nobles, minus the above-mentioned seven servants who always stand before the seven kings. The twenty-eight sat on golden chairs studded with gems and pearls, crowned with golden crowns studded with gems and pearls. He commanded them to bring my image, which is called "Karina."[34] When it arrived, they all stood before me. They gave me one of their chairs and entreated me, but I did not sit on it. Moreover, I distanced myself in order not to be made impure by them. He asked them: For what reason was this one born into this world, and also, will the redemption come in his lifetime? One of the servants of the king who was in charge that day answered. He said: How can you request redemption when there are great sins among you, causeless enmity, perversion of justice, and denial of charity to orphans and widows? From the day that this man was born, great good came into the world and the world began to be illuminated, because he is a very great and exalted person in Heaven. With his prayers he is able to annul evil decrees and to issue decrees according to his will. Should he want to glue these two walls together, he would be able to do so. All of this is because he has no anxieties about this world, not even about food, clothes, or money; all of his desires are for matters of the world to come. He has already struggled greatly to cause you to repent, but you do not listen to his voice. Had you listened, how much good would have come to you. There are three people here in Damascus who hate him and they are the primary cause of the damage as a result of which the people do not listen to his call for repentance. He does not worry about them, for they will all fall like the dust beneath his feet, and they do not recognize his greatness. You have many troubles, and in the future you will have greater troubles, because you do not listen to his admonitions and sermons. After the coming troubles four nations will fall and be uprooted, the first of which is Malta.[35] Afterwards, the redemption will come. Indeed, it is impossible to be redeemed until ten great men will gather around him.[36] They are on a lower [spiritual] level and he is the greatest of them. Seven of the ten men have already been born, the sage [Vital] and six others. Some are in Damascus and some in Safed. The sage always thinks of going to Safed and now he is ultimately forced to go there. One of the seven has already died, but this is not a hindrance because his merit exists in the world and it is as if he himself still exists. Afterwards, another two great men of the above-mentioned six will come, and later the tenth one will come and they will all gather around the sage. Then they will gather Israel to be redeemed.

If one of them will not be completely perfected, he will have to die and transmigrate until his repair will be complete. The redemption is delayed because of this. It would be necessary that they all love each other completely and that they have attained perfect piety, as has been mentioned.

The sage knows all these things since the ways of Heaven are as clear to him as the noonday sun and nothing is hidden from his great wisdom. However, he is a master of esoteric wisdom who conceals things and inwardly he worries and grieves. All of his thoughts are on this matter.

Since the redemption depends on these ten, and the completion of their repair, we have no information to give you about the time of the redemption, because it depends on their deeds and their repair [*tiqqun*]. However, there is no doubt that if all Israel would listen to his voice, the redemption would come in his lifetime. Indeed, with all this, the sage's future will be very good, prosperous, and joyous. He now has a small son who is very clever, but is not yet mature. His future will be very good, but he is not among the ten, mentioned above.[37]

All this happened on Sunday when the Christian king [of demons] ruled. Therefore he alone spoke through his servant, with the agreement of all twenty-eight, and they remained silent. That day, Joseph Romano the seer decided not to look into demonic matters anymore. That night he dreamed that a man said to him: Be careful, if someone will call you tomorrow to look at this matter today, do not avoid going with them, because through you a great *mitzvah* will come into the world.

Afterwards, the next day, the above-mentioned judge came to my house to see me, since he was astonished at hearing of my greatness that day. R. Joseph Segura and Joseph the seer came with him. I asked them myself, but the kings did not want to come and appear in the mirror, except for one servant.

Joseph said to them: Why are you not coming? They said: Because of the greatness of this man who is sitting here. He said to them: On the contrary, it is with his permission, and he is the one asking the question of you. Then all twenty-eight and the seven servants were reconciled and they came. They brought my image with them. I asked them: For what was I created in the world? They raised a flag, yellow like tumeric. He said: For this you were created, to raise this yellow flag.

I said: Why has my teacher z"l not been revealed to me in a dream for a long time, as he had been previously? Then, they also brought the portrait of my teacher z"l there, who was deceased and lying down. Joseph the seer described him completely, even though he had never seen him in his life. My teacher z"l responded: Just as you forgot to think about me previously, so too I forget about you. Also, you have already been informed that you only came into the world to cause the people to repent. Previously, you responded, but now you desist, therefore I also desisted from coming to you. I said: If so, Heaven forbid, then all the things that he promised me during his lifetime have been abrogated! He responded that everything remains as it was previously. However, I was negligent and prevented their fulfillment. I said: When I perform Unifications and the soul of that *zaddiq* speaks with me, is it literally his speech or is he only imaginary and it is only my speech, particularly with regard to that *zaddiq* who is customarily with me?[38] He answered me: He is the one who is speaking and not I. His Soul is encompassed in my heart and from there his voice rises to my mouth and he speaks with my mouth and then I hear. However, the reason that he does not speak with me at length as I would desire is because of the troubled times and the anguish of Israel's exile and also because I neglected to cause the people to repent. It is not appropriate that I should restrain myself because of a few enemies who stopped me, and I will not worry about them. I said: Perhaps the reason is that I am not worthy of this? He answered me: You have no fault that hinders you, for you are beloved and superior above. I said: Perhaps it is because I do not immerse myself? He answered: It would be better if you immersed yourself, and if not—do not worry. Know that through the diligence of the Unifications you perform, you strengthen the bond with and illumine the Souls of the *zaddiqim* within you. I asked: Who is this particular *zaddiq* who is customarily with me? He answered that it is not fitting for the honor of the *zaddiq* to reveal his name before those who are standing here; however, his name has four letters, the first is "*yud*" and the last is "*aleph*."[39] I said: My teacher z"l always warned me during his lifetime not to teach this wisdom to people, and now you tell me the opposite? He answered me: There are already three people here in Damascus who are worthy to hear, but since they are not completely settled in their piety, they are undecided. Similarly, in Safed there are four people who are more worthy than these three. Hence, you now have seven. In other lands there are three others, one of whom has died, but his merit takes his place. If there will be merits in the world, God will also summon those three to you. All your thoughts are to go to Safed, but since this is a period of troubles wait a while. In any event, you will be forced to go there and to take the seven mentioned people with you. Your wife is very bad tempered and she causes you to be angry. This causes great damage to you and to the whole world. The three images of her father, mother, and paternal grandfather are appearing in this mirror to warn her about this, that she should not lose her share in the world to come, because she causes harm to the whole world. Even these three relatives are harmed because they sit on a high level, and when she angers them they descend to a lower level. Joseph, who has been mentioned, saw the three of them and the two levels mentioned. He said to me: There are two angels with you, the good one on your right shoulder and the evil one on your left shoulder. The power of the evil one is very weak and he is completely subservient to the good one. Joseph also saw this with his own eyes. Until here.

Now I will tell you something about the twenty-eight kings as it was explained to me by the above-mentioned judge, the sorcerer.

The demons are divided into three types. The first type are the demons who dwell under this land, in the seven lower lands, as is known. Each land has a king over it. The second type are those who inhabit our land and they too are under the dominion of the seven kings of the demons mentioned above. The third type are the spirits who live in the Ether of the sky below the firmament. The Ether is also divided into seven levels and each level has a king who rules over it.[40] This third type does not tell falsehoods, whereas the two lower types sometimes lie.

Seven holy angels rule over the seven heavens and they rule over the seven kings of the seven levels of air who rule over the seven lower kings of the demons. Each day of the week a different king rules, and in this way also rules over the seven kings of the air and the seven kings of the demons.

Each of these seven Ethers contains the four winds and in the eastern wind of each of these Ethers there are seven ministers appointed over the seven Ethers in that wind. The highest minister of the seventh Ether is the king over the six ministers in the six lower Ethers.

The seven in this wind are appointed for the seven days of the week; each one has his given day. In this way, with the other three winds, there are twenty-eight ministers corresponding to the twenty-eight camps of the moon which rule over the twenty-eight days of the month and the four highest of these are called the four kings who correspond to the four weeks of every month. One king rules over all twenty-eight and he is the minister who rules over that day of the seven days of the week and on that day he rules over all twenty-eight, because it is his day. Below these ministers are seven servants for these seven kings who rule each day. The servant of the king who rules that day is the one who speaks and all the others remain silent.

22. 5369 [1609]. A great thing occurred in Damascus, but I will only write here that which is relevant to me.[41]

On Friday, the twenty-ninth of *Tammuz,* the daughter of Raphael Anav[42] became distressed and fainted. They took her to the sorcerers, but they were of no help.

That evening, it was the night of *Rosh Hodesh Ab,* after the lighting of the Sabbath candles, she was lying in a coma, like a lifeless corpse.

Raphael heard a voice come from her lips which said:

Raphael, come here.

He asked: Who are you?

He said: I am the sage Piso, and why did you light only two candles as is the custom—you should have lit many candles in honor of the angels and Souls of the righteous who have come to accompany me and to guard me. Prepare chairs for them, for there are six Souls. They have prepared a messenger for you.

He said: I am not like other spirits, for I am a sage and right-eous. I have come only because of a small sin that remains for me to repair and also to be a messenger to you to cause you to repent for your many sins. It is twenty-one days since I left Paradise, fol-lowing the rivers of Paradise and traveled underground until the rivers of Damascus, and there entered a fish. I was caught by a fisherman who brought me to be sold in the street of the Jews on Friday afternoon. Il Tawil, the very evil son-in-law of the head of the Jewish community, happened to be there and wanted to pur-chase me, but God sent Raphael Anav there and he purchased me. I was cut into pieces and he gave one piece to R. Jacob Ashkenazi. Friday night I was eaten, and I was in the head of the fish which was eaten by his daughter and I entered into her. I did not harm her at all, because I am not like the other spirits. I did not have permission to reveal myself and speak until now, because it is the Sabbath and *Rosh Hodesh*. I am very saddened that I did not merit to ascend to my place in Paradise on this holy day. May Joshua al-Boom be excommunicated because he did not assist me with the actions which are found in the book which is in his possession, to extricate me on Friday.[43] Perhaps I might have been worthy to ascend. I am delayed only this one day, for on it alone have I been given permission to speak, and I will return to my place in Paradise, first thing Sunday morning. All the angels and Souls mentioned above are waiting for R. Hayyim the Kab-balist to perform his mission. Therefore, call him and he will come.

Raphael did not want to go because it was at night. He said to him:

Do not worry about what will happen to your daughter. I am a holy spirit and I am able to recite the *kiddush*.

He recited the *kiddush* and said to him:

Why are you not careful to pour water into your *kiddush* cup?[44]

58

When R. Jacob went home, he said to him:

Beware of excommunication. Do not tell a thing.

When he came back after the meal, he said:

Do not allow this excommunicant in here, since he has violated my ban.

Raphael also said to him: Do not enter. Perhaps you ate saffron which is bad for such things.

He said: I did not eat saffron.

The spirit said to him:

You are also a liar, since you ate fish [with saffron]. Your wife is better than you, for when she asked you why you were delayed, you said: Because of the evil spirit which entered that young woman. Your wife is more pious than you and she said to you: If you said that he is a sage, how can you call him an evil spirit?

Afterwards [the spirit] said to him:

I knew that you are a naive and foolish person, therefore you may enter. And he entered.

[The spirit] began to tell each member of the household a little about their sins. He also told them about the sins of those who died in the recent plague.

That whole evening he appeared to them as a pillar of fire in the house. R. Jacob dozed off and he felt as if he was being strangled and awoke. At midnight [the spirit] said:

I have already suffered three days from the pain caused by this transmigration. It is not appropriate to also suffer on the Sabbath. Give me water to drink and an apple to eat.

They gave them to him, and he said to them:

Now sleep a little.

They slept until dawn. He woke them and said: It is already morning. Call R. Hayyim.

They did not want to, until he threatened to excommunicate them. He said to them:

If he does not believe you, give him a sign. This night, before dawn, he had a long dream and he does not understand it and is very melancholy. You will find him dressed, with his head on the ground, thinking about that dream. He will come to me and I will tell him.

What I dreamed was: I saw six *zaddiqim* coming from Paradise to my house and they brought me a sage to heal, and I forgot who they were. Then Raphael and R. Jacob came and told me all the above, and I went there. When I crossed the threshold, [the spirit] said to me three times:

Welcome!

When I came near to the girl, there was a veil over her face and she was like a corpse. I said to him:

From where do you know me?

He said: Are you not R. Hayyim the kabbalist?

I said to him: And who are you?

He said: I am the sage Piso.

I pleaded with him to tell me his name, until he finally told me in a whisper:

I am Jacob Piso and was in Jerusalem, married to the daughter of the sage R. Isaac Ashkenazi and my sister-in-law's name is Esther. I died thirty-five years ago and ascended to my place in Paradise, where I sat until now. There remained for me to repair one small thing, and I have now come to repair it. Therefore: Woe to whoever does not guard himself in this world from even a minor sin, so that they should not come to my situation.

It seemed to me, Hayyim, that his sin was that he caused many to sin by preventing them from learning the ways of repentance, and now he has come to repair the issue of repentance.

This is the dream you dreamed: I am the sage that was sent to you from Heaven so that you should heal him and pray for him by means of the six Souls who are sitting here before you. They are: Elijah a"h, R. Joseph Karo, R. Samuel Emron,[45] R. Aaron ibn Tifah,[46] the sage 'Atiya, and the sage Arha. Even though I studied with your teacher, R. Isaac Luria z"l, he did not come with the above-mentioned Souls, but is above in Heaven praying for me. You know that it is not possible to benefit me in Heaven except through the prayers of *zaddiqim* in this world. Therefore, they are all waiting for you and need you. Therefore, pray for me and heal me. Does not his learned excellency see the great fire burning in the world?

I said: Do you want me to gather all the inhabitants of the city before you?

He responded: If only they would come and fast three times on Monday, Thursday, and Monday, just like on *Yom Kippur*, both men and women—perhaps God will relent from his wrath against them because of the many sins among them.

The author, Ḥayyim, said: This indicates what I wrote above, that his sin was the neglect of repentance, and he returned to repair that lacunae; however, it had to be done through me since I was still in this world. This is sufficient for the knowledgeable.

I said to him: The people of Damascus are not interested in my sermons.

He said to me: All this is known before the Almighty.

I said: If so, I will assemble only the scholars.

He said to me: That is good.

I said: I do not know whom to assemble.

He said to me: Do not bring any of the *Mustarab* scholars, only *Sephardi* scholars, except for Israel Najara[47]—he will not see me.

I said: I will go and recite the *shaḥarit* prayers.

He said: This is more important than prayer.

I said: I do not miss the prayers under any circumstances. Afterwards God will have mercy.

He said to me: Does not his learned excellency want to have mercy on my trouble and repair what I have mentioned? What will I do?

I went to pray. I ate breakfast and thought that Raphael would return to call me, but he did not come. I was undecided whether to go there or not. I sent for R. Jacob. He came to me and said: I did not go there. We sat until the afternoon. Then the spirit said to Raphael: The sage is thinking of coming here and sent for that fellow. After the *minḥa* prayers, R. Jacob went there and the spirit told them: The sage does not want to come. He is obligated to come to me and arrogance is appropriate for God alone. A person should not say: "I do not want to drink from these waters"; perhaps he will be required to drink of them. My whole mission is only for his sake, for I have been sent by Heaven to reveal to him Heavenly secrets which he did not learn from his teacher z"l, in order that he should cause the world to repent. Everything depends on him, to repair the world. I came to reveal to him matters concerning the Messiah. He is on the verge of coming. He always preaches that they should repent so that the Messiah will come. R. Jacob Abulafia,[48] because of jealousy, says to the people: He speaks lies, since the Messiah is not coming in this generation and makes fun of him. Woe to him, for his sin is great, since because of his words and because of the great sins in this city, the Messiah has been bound with heavy iron chains and will be delayed another twelve years. During this time, many troubles will befall Damascus and it will be overturned like Sodom and Jerusalem will also be burned. Only Safed will be saved. Afterwards, Gog and Magog[49] will come and then the Messiah will come with "eight princes of men" [Mi 5:4]. The sage preached three sermons last year, before the plague and the people repented somewhat. Because he refrained from preaching further, his beloved daughter died in the plague. She was a great soul. Indeed, his small son will be a great rabbi in Israel. He has lost the opportunity to hear divine secrets, because I was sent from Heaven for this. When he will seek me, he will not find me because I have been given permission to speak only on this day and tomorrow I must return to my place.

At the conclusion of the Sabbath, he spoke no more. In the morning they came and told me everything he had said, and I went there. He did not wish to speak anymore, and he said to me: I am returning to my place. He gave signs, as is the manner of spirits when they leave. He left and did not return again. Indeed, as he said that he was leaving, R. Joshua al-Boom was standing there, performing his adjurations, and afterwards he left. When [the spirit] left I said to him: Write a particular amulet which is found in a certain book and hang it on the girl so that other spirits may not harm her after his departure. He did so.

Now I will write what I did with the help of R. Joshua al-Boom. Afterwards, I will write other things concerning this girl. This is his story.

23. On the sixth day of *Ab* in that year, R. Joshua al-Boom

brought down an angel, one of the servants of Zadkiel,[50] the lord of that day. He was revealed in a glass mirror—as was customary. I asked him about the wisdom of my teacher z"l, the Ashkenazi, and if what he said concerning my soul and my comprehension were all true. He said: All of his statements are true. I said: Are the things that the soul of the *zaddiq* said to me by means of Unifications true or imaginary? He said that he speaks the truth, but sometimes the soul of the *zaddiq* enters my heart and his words enter my mouth and I hear and sometimes he remains without, comes close to me and speaks to me. I said: Why has he remained distant from me for so long? He said to me: You caused it. Previously, you distanced all matters of this world from your heart and you cleaved to your Creator and engaged in Unifications. You engaged in the study of Torah all day and preached reproof against all the people. You left everything and he left you. You know what your teacher said to you as did others, that the whole world depends on you. You came into the world to cause them to repent and the redemption depends on you. You have already experienced this for ten years, when you preached and reproved the people. A number of people repented and they heard your words, but when you left them they turned from the path and many of them died in their sins and you are to blame for their sins.[51] Now you have completely withdrawn and isolated yourself in a corner. Some people dream wondrous dreams and tell them to you.[52] All this is from God, in order to strengthen your heart, but your heart is still undecided and you do not believe strongly in those dreams. Know that your place in Paradise is next to your teacher, the Ashkenazi,[53] and two other *zaddiqim* of the great *Tannaim*.[54] You are completely righteous before God, but that which I spoke of was the reason that the *zaddiq* refrained from speaking to you by means of Unifications. Your teacher is also somewhat angry with you because of this and that is why you do not dream of him as you did previously. If you will return to your work, you will undoubtedly attain all your goals. However, you still have one small sin within you, and we do not have permission to reveal it before those who are standing here, even if you will allow it. Your beloved daughter was a great soul and because of that sin she died in the plague. Also the name of the *zaddiq* who speaks to you, we do not have permission to reveal it to these people, because of his honor. Indeed, his name has four letters. The Unification that is most appropriate for you now is the seventh Unification of Metatron,[55] which is written in your book, and is also the Unification of your teacher z"l.[56] Thus, the *zaddiq* who is most appropriate for you now is Samuel the Prophet, even though he is very great in your eyes. Know that if you do not listen to our words to cause the people to repent, and they should fast Monday, Thursday, and Monday as on *Yom Kippur,* with fasting and tears, and so forth, great trouble will befall you. Great troubles will also be visited on the inhabitants of Damascus. God only sent this spirit into the daughter of Raphael Anav to cause the people of Damascus to repent. The spirit was very pious and in his place in Paradise. Because of a small sin which he still had to repair he was sent to accept his punishment in a river where he was embodied in a fish which Raphael bought. When his daughter ate the head, he entered her and remained there for twelve days. On Sunday, the first day of *Ab,* the time for his ascent came and he ascended of his own will, not by means of any person's actions. On the previous Sabbath, he sent for you in the morning. You went there, but did not return again until Sunday, when the time for his ascent had already come. He had wanted to reveal divine secrets to you. His whole intent was that the world should repent. Several Souls and angels descended with him on the Sabbath eve and they were all waiting to speak to you about this. However, you did not believe their words, and you lost all those secrets. God only sent them so that the people will hear about the awesome deeds of the Lord and through this they would repent. Perhaps God will relent from His anger against them, for great evil will befall them, because of the many sins among them. God also knows that the people of Damascus will not listen to your voice, because they have committed great sins which hinder their repentance.

You do what is required of you and gather the ten most worthy people that you can find. Even if they are not entirely worthy, cause them to repent, and do what you can to cause the people to repent. He who hears will hear, and He who ceases will cease, and you will have saved your Soul.

24. I have written in section twenty-two what occurred concerning the spirit which entered the daughter of Raphael Anav, what I had seen myself and what was told to me by Raphael and R. Jacob Ashkenazi. All this occurred on the Sabbath, *Rosh Hodesh Ab*. On Sunday morning, he undoubtedly left and ascended to his place. Afterwards, other things happened which were not caused by the above-mentioned spirit while still in this guise. He had already left and the girl returned to complete health, but she said that she sometimes has visions, both while awake and dreaming, of Souls and angels and on rare occasions of that spirit. I am uncertain if what she says is true or is a mixture of good and evil, because of the above-mentioned reason. There is also another reason. I have not seen this with my own eyes as I saw it the first time. However, what amazed me was that all her words were only about repentance, fear of God, and words of moral rebuke. Therefore I will not refrain from writing them because they were from truthful people.

She said that after the spirit left her, she always sees an angel who in her dreams leads her to Paradise and *Gehenna* and shows her the places of the righteous. In the majority of these visions they tell her that she should be careful to cause the people of Damascus to repent—perhaps God will relent in his anger against them.

On Saturday, the twenty-eighth of *Ab:* The spirit told her that it was true that he could not return to his place in Paradise until Sunday morning.

Indeed, if R. Joshua al-Boom had helped him leave by means of incantations on Friday, he would have entered a glass bottle and remained there for the duration of the Sabbath. Afterwards, they should wash the interior thoroughly before using it, so that they should not be harmed by it since he had entered it.

The night of the seventh of *Ab:* She was told to tell me that previously the soul of a *Tanna* would always appear to me by means of a Unification through which I would connect with him. It has been a long time, two and a half years to be precise, that he has not revealed himself to me, for two reasons. First, because I ceased the above-mentioned Unifications. Second, because I ceased my sermons to rebuke the people and cause them to repent as previously. Because of these two reasons, my daughter died in the plague. The night of the eighth of *Ab:* Elijah z"l told her in a waking dream, during the Sabbath *kiddush:* Tell R. Hayyim and the other sages of the city that they are neglecting everything they had heard. Great evil will befall the inhabitants of Damascus because of this, and particularly R. Hayyim. They also told her: Why did he sin on the sixth of *Ab,* to bring down an angel in a bottle to question him—does he not believe what we told him through the above-mentioned spirit? His teacher z"l also told him before his death that he only came into the world to cause the people to repent. The angel that he brought down also told him this, yet he still is uncertain and does not believe at all!

I am afraid for him that, Heaven forbid, many troubles will befall him, because of his importuning.

The tenth of *Ab.* I asked her via her father: Why does the *zaddiq* known to me refuse to speak to me? What is his name and is there any hope that he will return? She responded that on the night of the eleventh of *Ab* she saw my teacher z"l and he said to her: Tell him in my name, that he should not ask these questions so many times. I cannot answer him, except for these three words: "Happy are the dead in your house."[57] He will understand the meaning of these words himself.

The night of the twelfth of *Ab:* In a dream, she saw my teacher z"l in a cave and he said to her: What did R. Hayyim reply to you? She said to him: He told me that he did not understand the three words. He said to her: Such an easy thing. Has his intellect been so retarded that he did not understand? Where is the wisdom that I taught him?

Remind him of the evil spirit that I expelled from him. It has been four years that he has not seen me in a dream. Now I planned to return to him, but since he does not understand my response, I do not want to return to him.

In my humble opinion, the meaning of the above-mentioned evil spirit concerns the resurrection of the dead. He revived me on our journey to Kfar Akhbara because the spirit who was in the grave of the gentile injured me,[58] or perhaps is related to what twisted my mouth with the first Unification that I taught myself. On the twenty-fourth of *Ab,* Raphael went to Sinim,[59] and Rachel Abirlina[60] went to visit them. His daughter told her that on Saturday, *Rosh Hodesh Ab,* everything that the spirit intended for me occurred to me and was sent to me. Afterwards, when I did not want to do his bidding and I did not return there, he complained about me concerning three things. First, because when I went there I thought that he was an evil spirit, like the other spirits of evil people, and therefore I did not behave respectfully toward him and spoke disparagingly to him. Second, because I did not believe his words when he told me that there were angels and souls who were all waiting for my prayers and I did not remain there but left. Third, because I did not return there afterwards to speak to him. He had come on a mission from God to tell me awesome things and divine secrets and therefore I lost them and my end is to regret this and when I shall seek it, I will not find it.

Rosh Hodesh Kislev, 5370 [1610]. Raphael came from Sinim and told me that my teacher z"l appeared to his daughter while she was awake and said to her: Tell R. Hayyim that he is depressed because his sermons to the people of Damascus in the month of *Ellul* were not successful. Previously, I was angry with him because he did not want to listen to that spirit and waited until [R. Jacob] Abulafia would return from Safed and because of this the matter became confused. When the spirit spoke to him, it was a time of grace. Afterwards, the time passed and that is why his sermons were not successful. Indeed, despite all this, your sermons have been accepted before God, even though they did not succeed.

Now I will write what happened to R. Jacob Abulafia and the above-named spirit, after it had left her body, as mentioned above.

I delayed [asking] the people to repent because he was out of the country then and I thought that the two of us would be able to repair the matter. The opposite was the case, for when he came everything was ruined. He came on Friday, the fifteenth of

Ab, and caused it all to go up in smoke before the people, in order that I not receive any honor because of the spirit. Then on Monday, the seventeenth of *Ab,* the spirit revealed himself to Raphael's daughter and told her to threaten her father with excommunication in his name, that he should not eat anything on Tuesday morning until he will go to Abulafia after the *shaḥarit* prayers and reprimand him for the above-mentioned.

Tuesday morning after the prayers he called him and he sat until noon with that reprimand. Raphael and his daughter were there along with his whole household, and other women. R. Joshua al-Boom, his brothers Bezalel and Faraj Allah and other people were on the roof, in order to hear. The girl then said to R. Joshua al-Boom: Bring the glass mirror and bring down the angel Zadkiel who rules this day. The angel and the Souls of four sages who were to be witnesses to the matter appeared. These are the four: R. Joseph Sajjah,[61] R. Joseph Karo, R. Samuel Emron, and R. Aaron ibn Tifah. The girl looked into the mirror, saw them, and spoke to them.

The angel told her: I do not want to reprimand him because R. Jacob Abulafia will not believe things seen obliquely in a mirror, only clear things from the mouth of the spirit himself after he has been embodied in the mouth of the girl. Since he originally came by himself with this mission from above, therefore I will ascend above to call him. He then went and remained there awhile and again descended into the mirror with the four witnesses. He said to her: Tell R. Jacob Abulafia, Bezalel, and Faraj Allah to go outside to the courtyard until the spirit will enter the girl. The three of them went out to the courtyard and the spirit was embodied in the girl and she fainted as if she was an epileptic. After the spirit was embodied he began to speak: Tell R. Jacob Abulafia that he should come to the window. He came close and said to him: Why did you not embody yourself until you told me to go outside? He said to him: Because you are not worthy to see me become embodied since you are a sinner. The Messiah is angry with you because you are always mocking the coming of the Messiah, saying: The Messiah will not come in this generation. When R. Ḥayyim the Kabbalist wants to preach repentance to the people concerning the Messiah, you mock him and make fun of his words because of your envy toward him. If you think you are so wise, give me a reason for the commandments of Passover, *Shavuot, Rosh Hashanah, Sukkot,* and so forth.

He gave him the simple reasons which are well known. [The spirit] said to him: These things are obvious even to the ignorant and had you wanted to know the truth, you should have listened to the secrets of the Torah from R. Ḥayyim. He had wanted to preach and reprove the people on the Sabbath and you stopped him and withheld repentance from Israel. Woe to you the wise men of this age that you do not cause the people to repent! I also saw the scandals of the wise men of Egypt, for there is no wisdom among them and they destroy the city with miscarriage of justice. The people of Egypt have slaves who serve them and when they leave the house, the slaves sleep with their wives. They place cooked food in the oven on the Sabbath and many other such things. Whoever goes to Egypt now, even for business, is condemned above and the result will be that he will lose all his money because of the evils there. Also in Venice, in the future, a sword will be drawn for seven consecutive days and many incomparable, righteous sages, whose likes are not found in this city, will be killed.

Finally: Woe to you sages of the generation who are arrogant and contemptuous and do not safeguard the honor of God to cause the people to repent. You cause great harm in the world. Then R. Jacob Abulafia submitted a little and tears fell from his eyes.

[The spirit] said to him: Since you have submitted and been humiliated by having been told to go outside, that is enough. He gave him permission to enter. After he entered, [the spirit] said to him:

You and the inhabitants of Damascus have no share in the world to come, Heaven forbid, for several reasons. You cause people to sin when you ask them to swear how much money each person has, with regard to taxes and assessments.[62] They swear falsely and you know that they are swearing falsely. Your wives also insolently wear disgraceful clothes and jewelry, like the small conical hats on their heads; their breasts are not covered and they fill their bosoms to show their large breasts, and they wear filmy sashes and veils to show their bodies. They put on citrus oils, perfumes, and scents to arouse the evil inclination in men. They conduct themselves in this way in the markets and streets to show everyone their beauty. Also, rebuke your children and keep them away from these sins. Here, forty-eight people are committing sins with gentile women, adultery, homosexuality, not to mention other sins.

He listed them all, but particularly told me about the following: Elijah Hefez, the sons of Gandor, the son of Kuraydi, and Abraham Mosseri are sleeping with gentile women. The daughter of Qumayri, who became an apostate, is having illicit relations with Joshua Quraysh and many other men. R. Jacob Monides is committing sodomy with Nathan Khulayf, and now has given him his daughter, and still has sexual relations with him—woe to Jacob because his face is black as pitch in the world to come because of his many sins and he has no share in the world to come. Jacob Uceda, your brother-in-law, is committing a sin with a certain woman. Nissim Menashe has no share in the world to come and has no heavenly defender, and whoever does any good for him, even to heal him of this disease that he has been afflicted with from Heaven, through an evil spirit, is worthy to be sawn [to bits] with a saw. Raphael Khulayf and Michael, his son, commit sins with Jewish and gentile women. This past Saturday night, a sage who is called "*Hakham*" by the *Sephardi* community slept with a gentile woman in Jawbar.[63]

Afterwards, we investigated who was on the oven[64] which was in the room, and we discovered that Abraham,[65] the son of R. Moses Galante,[66] was sleeping there with his wife and the gentile woman who owned the house.

The wife and daughter of Meir Perez are complete whores, causing many people to sin. R. David Gavison is a great sinner, because he left his chaste wife here and married a promiscuous woman in Egypt, and because of his sins his wife and daughter-in-law, who were chaste, died.

In addition, another person told me about him that he committed many sins with prostitutes in Egypt and lost his share in the world to come. Perhaps the story of the woman seduced in Egypt also refers to him.

Behold, R. Israel Najara.[67] True, the hymns that he has composed are in themselves good, but whoever speaks to him and whatever leaves his mouth is forbidden, because he always used foul language and was a drunkard his whole life. On a particular day that was between the fast days,[68] he prepared a meal at that hour at the house of Jacob Monides, put his hat on the ground, sang songs in a loud voice, ate meat, drank wine, and even became drunk.[69] How can he decree vigils in Jawbar and preach repentance to them!

I, Hayyim, told him about this incident and he admitted that it was true.

Even now, when he is escaping from the plague, he commits homosexual acts in his drunkenness. On Saturday, he committed two sins: First, when he quarreled with his wife and expelled her from his house, and second, afterwards a gentile woman entered his house and lit the oven. Afterwards, he slept with her. Therefore it is forbidden to employ him, and it is forbidden to allow him to write a marriage contract or a bill of divorce. It is almost appropriate to declare them invalid. His younger son, the husband of the gentile woman, is also completely evil, may his bones be ground into powder. However, his older son is not a sinner.

There is much homosexuality and much perversion and delay of justice in this land.

R. Jacob Abulafia [hereafter, J] responded to the spirit [hereafter, TS]: How did I know all this?

TS said to him: Behold your son Moses, he and Menachem Romano brought a gentile woman to a certain house last *Shavuot* and slept with her, before he went to Aleppo.

J said to him: Perhaps my son sinned in this way?

TS said to him: The children inherit the deeds of the fathers! And you never did anything in your youth that was not good?

J said to him: If so, I will go to Safed.

TS said to him: Having destroyed Damascus, you will now also go to destroy Safed? First repair the destruction in Damascus and then go to whatever place you want.

J said to him: I will wait until the month of *Ellul,* which is a time of repentance.

TS said to him: You have spoken well, but your mouth and heart are not aligned, because you do not believe these things. When I spoke with R. Hayyim the Kabbalist, he hesitated at first, until the angel descended, and then he believed and was reconciled to bringing the people back to repentance—but you do not believe anything. Therefore, in any event gather all the sages of the city and let them urge the people to repent and fast seven days. Leave R. Hayyim the Kabbalist alone and do not call him, because he did not believe at first.

J said to him: But the seventh day is Sabbath?[70]

TS said to him: Do you fulfill all the commandments? Because of necessity, since God's anger is upon you, it is necessary that you fast even on the Sabbath. However, do not preach sermons. Instead, spend the whole day reciting penitential prayers and in tears. If you will not do thusly, know that terrible decrees will befall the inhabitants of Damascus, particularly such a terrible famine that a person will eat the flesh of his arm. Be careful that R. Israel Najara does not come among you in any of these fasts. I decree these things upon you with the severest sanctions. If there was a complete *zaddiq* amongst you, a holy angel would have revealed himself to him and told him all these things directly.

In the course of his talk, he mentioned that R. Joshua al-Boom was a knowledgeable expert in matters of abjuring spirits and demons which he learned from his teacher, R. David the Moghrabi, who was God-fearing and a very learned expert.[71] This disciple of his, if he wished, could heal Simeon the epileptic, the brother of Bezalel.

After the spirit departed, R. Jacob Abulafia made all those standing there swear by the formula found in the *Kol Bo,*[72] that they would not reveal a thing, out of respect for his honor and the honor of the others mentioned by the spirit. They did not pay attention to his worthless oaths and [the spirit's] words were revealed and then he also had to admit it. Indeed, [the spirit] had destroyed his sanctity by impugning his honor and defaming him with his statement, "Is the whole Torah true?" On this he built fortresses and bans and publicly excommunicated the above-named spirit because he had defamed righteous people. Afterwards, the daughter of Raphael sent him a message from Sinim, in the name of the spirit, saying that the spirit stands daily in the Heavenly Academy and excommunicates him and everyone who agrees with what he did.

25. 5331 [1571]. When I was in Safed, my teacher z"l taught me how to exorcise evil spirits with the power of a Unification that he had taught me.[73] When I came to him, a woman was lying on the bed. When I sat down by her side and [the evil spirit] turned his face away from me, I told him to turn his face toward me and speak to me, that he should leave, but he refused. I slapped his face with my hand. He said to me: Because I would not turn my face you hit me? I did not do this maliciously, but because your face burns like a great flame and my Soul would be burnt if I looked at you, because of your great holiness.

26. When Hayyim, the son of R. Yedidiah Penzieri, was born, I was his *sandek*. During the circumcision, Sa'adat, the wife of Jacob Nasar, saw a heavenly pillar of fire on my head. It seems to me that this was in the year 5328 [1568].

27. 5370 [1610]. On the seventh day of Passover I left the synagogue after the prayers and a group of women were walking in front of me. One woman turned around to see my face. She saw a pillar of white light to my right glowing much more brightly than the light of the sun and filling the whole width of the street. Its height was twice my height and glowed and glittered, blinding the eyes. She could not see my face at all, and from great anguish entered the doorway of a courtyard to hide there.

The name of that woman was Simha, the sister of Zabda, the wife of Cuencas.

28. Thursday, the twenty-eighth of *Ellul* 5370 [1610]. R. Joshua al-Boom brought down the angel of the day in a glass mirror. I asked with a spell if I had the possibility of seeing Elijah z"l and speaking to him. He told me: Seven Souls are present and are speaking to you, but you ask about someone who is very great.

He is an angel and the Soul of a *zaddiq*. The whole world depends on him and the whole salvation will be through him. The first three letters of the Tetragrammaton and the two letters *aleph"lamed* are in him,[74] and because of his greatness I cannot explicitly mention his name in front of the people who are sitting here with you. Previously, he would be found near you, but since you stopped your earlier practices, he too has stopped coming to you. These are the issues of ritual purity, ritual immersion, and preaching repentance to the people. Even if you want to return, you cannot, for you have grown old and your powers have weakened and you can no longer do what you once did. Despite this, do not despair completely. Though it is impossible for it to be as in the past, yet it will be close. If you will immerse yourself, he will speak to you in clarity and will reveal himself, but in the manner in which you see in these times, in great secrecy and in brevity.

29. Sunday night, the eighteenth of *Tishrei*, 5373 [1612]. The judge Sa'ad al-Din the liar, the impurity of the Islamic nation, had a dream. He was sitting alone in a desolate desert. He saw a man approach him dressed in rags and torn clothes and his face smeared with ink. The judge asked him: Who are you? He responded: I am Muhammed, the prophet of the Muslims. He said to him: If you are that prophet, why are you in this condition? He said to him: Because I misled such a great nation and my time, which was a thousand years,[75] has passed and my religion, which is empty foolishness, has been abolished.

There were six men in front of him. Two of them grabbed Muhammed, one on his right and one on his left. Two others grabbed the judge from the right and left and the last two walked in front of them until they came to a place where there was an outhouse. They extracted a man from it, completely covered in excrement from head to foot, and brought him before the judge. He asked: Who is this? They answered: This is Isa, the son of Miriam.[76] He asked him: Why are you in this condition? He responded: Because I misled the Christian nation with a false religion for such a long time. Its time has passed and this empty and meaningless religion has been abolished.

74

Millions of Muslims came before them and asked: In whom shall we believe and which religion shall we adopt? The men answered them: Raise your eyes to the distance and see the nation of the Jews in their millions. At their head is an old man with a white beard down to his navel. His name is Akiva. Enter his religion, the true religion.

They went there. After a short time, all the above-mentioned Muslims returned to them and complained loudly: Give us a religion, since the man to whom you sent us is dead. The men then said to them: He has left a disciple to replace him. They said: Who is he? They said to them: He "lives" in this world and "lives" doubly so in the world to come.[77] He is now living in this generation in this world. Go to him, since he is now the head of all the Jews that you have seen.

They turned and went to him. These three, the judge, Muhammed, and Isa, remained behind in great anguish, restrained by the six men. The judge tossed in his bed and screamed in anguish. His mother saw him in anguish and woke him from his sleep.

He had this dream three or four times and told it to members of his household and his students. That day he sent for sorcerers expert in the arts of oil and mirror divination. They conjured up spirits and kings of the demons and asked them to tell him what he saw in his dream. They conjured up a Muslim blackened and torn in the above-mentioned manner, and his face was smeared with dirt; similarly, a Christian besmeared with excrement and his face smeared, and so forth. He asked them: Why are they in this anguish? They took off their turbans from their heads and flung them on the ground, to symbolize that their kingdom has been destroyed and fallen to the ground.

Then they conjured up a Jew sitting on a chair in a garden full of wonderful fragrant plants, with two attendants before him to his right and left, fanning him. He asked them if the visions that he had seen in his dream were from the evil side, just a vision caused by demons and evil spirits, or were they from above, from Heaven? They raised their hands Heavenward, indicating that it was all from the Blessed One.[78]

75

Part Two

——————— MY DREAMS ———————

These are the dreams that I dreamed, even though I have forgotten many dreams.

1. The seventeenth of *Heshvan*, 5322 [1561]. On that day I had
an old book in my hands, written in *Ashkenazi* script. The following was written in it: The name of love was the [divine] name
that the High Priest mentioned on the Day of Atonement. That
night I dreamed that a wealthy man died and the whole community came to his funeral, including R. Joseph Karo, R. Solomon
Alkabez, and R. Joseph Ergas[1] the cantor. We accompanied him
to the largest synagogue in Safed to eulogize him. Afterwards,
they started to lift his bier.

The cantor said: First put the *zizit* of the *talit* on his head. The
deceased spoke and said: I do not want it. All those standing
there could not do it until I angrily got up to do it. The deceased
said to me: Why is your power greater than all these others? I
said to him: Because I know the Ineffable Name and I will
excommunicate you with it. He said to me: Who told it to you? I
said to him:

I hereby excommunicate you with the 426[2] pillars of light that
are in *Keter* and with the thirty-two paths of *Hokhmah* and fifty
gates of *Binah* and with the seventy-two bridges over the waters
of *Hesed* and the forty-two torches of fire that are in *Gevurah* and
with the Ineffable Name that is in the *sefirah* of *Tiferet*, which is
the Tetragrammaton with the punctuation *holam, zeire, kamez,
zeire.*

He then fell to the ground and I put the *zizit* on his head. They
carried his coffin down a very steep path to where the cemetery
was and he was buried.

Afterwards, a man appeared on his grave, with an iron chain
in his hand. He opened the grave, placed the chain on his neck,

76

and took him out. The deceased changed into the image of a dog and he was led around as a wanderer in the world.[3] I said about that man: This man was one of the dignitaries of the city. Why are you punishing him in this manner? He responded: You did not recognize his evil in this world.[4] This is the way we punish all evildoers after their death.

2. That year I dreamed: I was standing on the top of the mountain that is to the west of Safed, between its two peaks which are above Kfar Meron. I heard a voice announce: The Messiah is coming! The Messiah was standing before me, blowing the *shofar,* and myriads of Israelites were gathering around him.

He said to us: Come with me and see the revenge for the destruction of the Temple. We went there. He did battle there. He vanquished all the Christians who were there and entered the Temple, and also killed those who were inside. He commanded all the Jews and said to them: My brothers, purify yourselves and our Temple from the impurity of the blood of these uncircumcised corpses and the impurity of the strange gods within it.

We will purify and build the Temple on its foundation and the High Priest will offer the daily sacrifice. He [the High Priest] looked like my neighbor, R. Israel ha-Levi. I asked the Messiah: How can a levite be a priest? He answered me: It is your mistake, because he is not a levite but a priest.[5] Afterwards, he brought out a torah scroll from the sanctuary of the Temple and read from it. And I woke up.

3. 5324 [1563]. On the first night of *Heshvan* I asked a dream question, about a certain woman, whether she was my predestined mate.

I saw in the dream: There was a large house with two entrances, one in the east and one in the west. The woman's father was in the house and I was outside at the western entrance. I had two wings, like the wings of the large eagle.[6] Her father said to me: Come into the house and we will see if I can catch you. I said to him: Don't you know my name—everyone calls me the winged one—how will you be able to catch me? He again said to me: Come in and we will see if I can. Then I lifted my wings and flew in through the western entrance and out the eastern entrance. Afterwards, I flew in the air at will and the woman's father was like an inanimate stone, unable to move from his spot.

4. 5325 [1565]. My wife, Ḥannah, was engaged to me and we had a dispute. I asked a dream question as to whether I should marry her. I was answered with a verse: Go, say to them, "return to your tents" [Dt 5:27].

5. 5326 [1566]. Friday night, the eighth of *Tevet*. I recited the *kiddush* and sat down at the table to eat. I was shedding copious tears and was depressed and melancholy because the previous tenth of *Heshvan* I had married my wife, the above-mentioned Ḥannah, and I had been bound with witchcraft.[7] I said to God, Blessed be He: I went back to her as the result of the above-mentioned dream question. How is it possible for such a great tragedy to befall me—in particular, since it relates to the sin of nocturnal emissions, from which I guard myself?[8] I also cried over the two years that I neglected the study of Torah, which I wrote about in the section concerning my Soul.[9] My anguish was so great that I did not eat anything. I lay on my bed crying, face down, until I dozed off from the many tears and I had a wondrous dream.[10]

I saw myself sitting in the house of Rabbi Shem Tov ha-Levi z"l, reciting the *minha* prayers, which is called a time of grace on the Sabbath. After the prayers, an old man stood before me who looked like my neighbor Rabbi Ḥayyim ha-Levi Ashkenazi z"l. He called me by my name and said to me: Rabbi Ḥayyim, do you want to go out to the fields now with me to accompany the Sabbath Queen as she departs, as you are accustomed to do when she arrives,[11] and I will show you wondrous things there? I said to him: I am here. We went out to the wall of the old tower which is on the western side of Safed, opposite the *khan*, a place where there had previously been a gateway in the wall.

I looked and saw a very tall mountain, the top of which was in the heavens. Come up the mountain with me and I will tell you why I was sent to you. In the blink of an eye I saw him ascend to the top of the mountain and I remained at the bottom, unable to ascend, because it was perpendicular, like a wall, and not sloping as other mountains.[12] I said to him: I am amazed. I am a young man and cannot ascend at all and you are old, yet you ascended it in the blink of an eye. He said to me: Ḥayyim, you do not know that every day I ascend and descend this mountain a thousand times to fulfill the missions of God. How can you be amazed at me? When I saw that he had earlier called me Rabbi Ḥayyim and now called Ḥayyim and not Rabbi Ḥayyim, and also when I heard his terrifying words, I knew that he was certainly Elijah z"l of the tribe of Levi.[13] I broke down and began to cry from great fear. I then tearfully pleaded with him and said to him: "Have regard for my life" [2 Kgs 1:14] and bring me up to you. He said to me: Do not fear, this is why I was sent to you. He grasped my arms and brought me up to the top of the mountain with him, in the blink of an eye. I looked and saw a ladder, the bottom of which was standing on the top of the mountain and its top reached the heavens.[14] The ladder only had three rungs and the distance between each rung was approximately the height of a man. He said to me: I have been given permission to accompany you only until here. From here and further, see what you can do. He disappeared and I cried with great anguish.

A distinguished woman, beautiful as the sun, approached the top of the ladder. I thought in my heart that it was my mother. She said: My son, Ḥayyim, why are you crying? I have heard your tears and have come to help you. She stretched out her right hand and raised me to the top of the ladder. I saw there a large round window and a large flame coming out of it, back and forth, like a bolt of lightning[15] and it burned everything found there. I knew in my soul that it was the flame of the whirling sword that is at the entrance to the Garden of Eden [Gn 3:24]. I called to the woman with great grief and said to her: My mother, my mother, help me that the sword should not burn me. [She said] Nobody can help you with this flame; you are on your own! But I will advise you on what to do: Put your hand on your head and you will find there cotton-wool, white as snow. Take some and put it in the flaming window and it will close.[16] Pass by quickly.

In my humble opinion, the cotton, which had been changed to white, was the black hairs of my head—which are judgment—

through certain merits in the secret of "And the hair of His head was like clean wool" [Dn 7:9]. I did so and passed by quickly. In a moment the flame again shot out as before. Then the woman disappeared.

Elijah z"l again appeared as earlier, grasped my right hand, and said to me: Come with me to the place where I had originally been sent to bring you. He brought me to an immensely large courtyard with large rivers flowing through it to water the garden. On both banks of the rivers were innumerable beautifully full and ripe fruit trees. The majority were apple trees, smelling like myrrh and aloe. The trees were very tall and the branches bent downward almost touching the ground. Their ends looked like a *sukkah*. There were innumerable birds in the garden, which looked like white geese, traversing the length and breadth of the garden, reciting *mishnahs* of tractate *Shabbat*. It was then the night of the Sabbath, at the beginning of the dream. In the course of their wandering they would recite a *mishnah* or a chapter, raise their necks and eat apples from the trees, and afterwards drink from the rivers. This was their constant activity. It had been made known to me that these were the souls of *zaddiqim*, Masters of the *Mishnah*.[17] However, I did not know why they had the form of geese and birds and not the form of people. He led me further into the center of the garden until I saw a large and tall attic, as if it was on top of a great height, but there was no house under it. Its height above the garden was about a man's height. Its door was in the west and there was a ladder of three stone steps from the ground to the door of the attic. Elijah z"l disappeared. I ascended the ladder alone and entered the door of the attic. I saw God, Blessed be He, sitting on a chair in the middle of the southern wall. He looked like the Ancient of Days, with a beard white as snow, in infinite splendor. *Zaddiqim* sat before Him on the ground, on beautiful carpets and couches, learning Torah from Him. I knew in my Soul that they were the *zaddiqim* called *bnei aliyah*.[18] They have human features, continually see the Divine Presence and learn Torah directly from Him. This was not the level of Masters of the *Mishnah*. They had the form of birds and geese, because about them it is said: He who

80

sees a goose in his dreams should hope for wisdom.[19] They stand in the courtyard and in the garden, but do not see the Divine Presence regularly, like the inhabitants of the attic, and do not learn Torah from Him.

When I entered and saw his face, I became confused and was seized with fear. I fell to the ground on my face before his feet and could not summon any strength. He stretched out his hand and grasped my right hand and said to me: Hayyim my son, stand up, why did you fall on your face? Do not be afraid. I said to Him: Lord, I could not summon any strength and my beauty turned into corruption out of my great fear and I have no strength to stand. He said to me: Strengthen and fortify yourself, stand up and sit at my right in this empty place, near me. I said to Him: How can I sit at your right in this place, for it has been prepared for Rabbi Joseph Karo? He said to me: I thought so at first, but afterwards I gave him another place and this has been prepared for you. I said to Him that this was the place of the prophet Samuel z"l. He said to me: True, this is his place, but when the Temple was destroyed, he took upon himself not to sit in this place until the Temple is rebuilt in the future. Since then, he went to Jerusalem, to the destroyed Temple, and stands there constantly to mourn it until the time that it will be rebuilt. Therefore, his place remains empty, and I have given you permission to sit there. Then I sat at His right, literally next to Him, on the couch, like the other zaddiqim who were there.

He said to me: Do you like this place? I said to Him: Who can praise the greatness of this attic? Indeed, explain to me: Why are the Masters of the Mishnah different from these inhabitants of the attic, that there should be such a great difference between them as I have seen with my own eyes? Have you forgotten what the sages said, that in the future God will give them wings and they will roam over the waters?[20] They said this about this sect called Masters of the Mishnah, who have the image of birds with wings and they roam over the waters which are the rivers of the Garden of Eden, as you saw with your own eyes. Then I said to Him: Lord, I remember what is written in the introduction to Tikkunei Zohar concerning the verse, "If you chance, etc., the mother sitting over the fledglings, etc., take only the young" [Dt 22:6]—the fledglings are the Masters of the *Mishnah,* the young are the kabbalists.[21] They are the elite, they have the image of children.

I continued and said to Him: Lord, "If my soul is worthy in your eyes" [2 Kgs 1:13, 14], leave me here and do not return me to the mundane world, "for it is clear to you that my intent is to do your will and I fear lest my passions cause me to sin"[22] and I will forfeit this holy place. He said to me: You are still a young man and you still have time to occupy yourself with my Torah and commandments. You need to return to complete your Soul and at the end of your days you will return to this place. If you fear to return to the mundane world, give me your right hand and swear that you will not put aside the Torah for any other task and I will also swear to you that if you do so, this place will not be given to anyone else under any circumstances. This will be your place, at my right, forever. I extended my hand and swore to fulfill all the above and He too swore to fulfill His words. He said to me: Go in peace and do not forget all these things. I then descended from there alone and found myself in the mundane world, in the midst of the dream, and I did not see any of the things that I had seen when I first ascended.

6. Three months later, the night of the Sabbath before Passover, I had a dream and I saw myself walking in a large field. I passed the entrance to the attic mentioned above and I remembered that I had ascended there and I had sworn to the Lord of all, as mentioned above. I then ascended the ladder and entered the door. Everything that had happened to me the first time happened again, that I fell on my face in fear, everything as mentioned. After I rose, I returned to the original place.

He then said to me: Why did you forget what you swore to me in this place? I said to Him: I have already occupied myself with it, but the truth is that I have not sufficiently occupied myself with the study of Torah. Despite this, tell me if, Heaven forbid, your oath has been abrogated. He said to me: Do not fear, your place is still there and prepared for you and our oaths still stand. Therefore, return and fulfill your promise properly and I will fulfill my covenant with you, to give you this place which I promised you.

He continued to speak to me and said: Ḥayyim, my son, go to the *Ashkenazi* community, for they are now bringing a torah scroll. Sing and play before it, as is your custom, to honor the Torah scroll. Take your father-in-law, R. Moses Saadia, with you and tell him not to neglect this commandment, for this is also his custom and it is a very important commandment.

Then I parted from Him with appropriate salutations and He returned my salutation.

I exited the doorway of the attic and found myself in this world. I met my father-in-law, who had come to seek me. He said to me: I have taken much trouble to find you in order that we should go together to honor a certain torah scroll. I told him: I was also commanded in a certain place to come and find you for this purpose.

We went to the main street of Safed and a great crowd of people were escorting a beautifully ornamented torah scroll, carrying lit candles and torches and singing songs before it until they entered the synagogue of the *Ashkenazim*. The congregation was already reciting the *yozer* prayer for the Sabbath, since it was on the Sabbath that I had this dream. We prayed the *shaharit* service with them. Then we opened the torah scroll and seven men read the portion of the week from it, as was customary on the Sabbath. We then prayed the *musaf* prayers and after the completion of the prayers I wanted to leave the synagogue. My teacher, R. Moses Alshekh, my father, and my father-in-law grabbed me and said: Where are you in such a hurry to go? Wait, since a circumcision is about to be performed here. I sat there and they brought a child to be circumcised. They gave me the child and asked me to be the *sandek*.[23] They circumcised him and they said to me: This is your son. Afterwards, they brought a large and elegant feast to the synagogue and we all ate the circumcision meal. And I awoke. Two years later, my teacher, the Ashkenazi z"l, came to Safed and I studied with him. Shortly before his death he said to me: A son will be born to you. Your wife is already pregnant with him. He is 500 levels higher than you, but there is a doubt if he will live, and so forth. My teacher died and that son also died after a year and a half. I called him Joseph and he was the essence of wisdom. A week before his death he spoke things that were akin to prophecy.

I believe that my teacher z"l was the torah scroll of the *Ashkenazim* and he was transmigrated into that son, Joseph, and he was the son that I circumcised in the dream.

7. 5330 [1570]. The fifteenth of *Tammuz*. I asked a dream question concerning the comprehension of kabbalistic wisdom. I saw in a dream an old man who looked like R. Abraham ha-Levi Moghrabi[24] sitting in the window of my house and we exchanged greetings. He said to me: Do you want me to teach you several reasons and secrets concerning the *tefillin*? I said to him: If you want, I will teach you more than eighty wondrous secrets concerning the *tefillin*, which you have never heard. To him it was as if I had told a joke, and he began to tell me several secrets. I was amazed by them. Then he turned to leave. I said to him: Why did you come at first and why are you now leaving? He said: You called me so I came, but since you do not wish to speak with me I will continue on my way. Then I recognized that it was Elijah z"l. I asked him: Will I be worthy to write a commentary on the *Sefer ha-Zohar*? He said to me: I will not be able to respond until the future. He said goodbye and went on his way.

8. 5330 [1570]. Friday night, the thirteenth of *Ab*. I dreamed that it was either the day of *Shavuot* or *Rosh Hashanah* and I was sitting with my father, mother, and relatives eating at the table. There was a niche in the southern wall and in this niche was a serpent's egg which was about to open. I grabbed it, threw it to the ground, and it broke completely. Two large serpents came out of it, one male and the other female, entwined and clinging to each other as if engaged in sexual intercourse.[25] I took a stone, white as snow, and threw it at the head of one of the serpents and cut off its head. Indeed, the serpents remained entwined and the head that had been cut off jumped up and escaped from the house. I went in search of it. I saw a tent made of a very white material. I went inside to see if the serpent's head had entered, but I did not find it. I said to myself: I am not worried about it,

84

since it undoubtedly will only live until sunset and when the sun sets it will die. Then I looked up and saw the following written at the top of the fabric, the first part written in Aramaic and the latter part in Hebrew. This is what it said: Whoever desists from and destroys the evil inclination and whoever chases away evil sinners and impurity from himself, and throws off the evil inclination, I will put his chair above my servant Metatron.

It seemed to me then that this was literally a verse from the Book of Proverbs. Then I said: If so, if the reward for one who desists from the evil inclination is so great, I will go and also kill the second serpent, since I had already killed the first serpent. And I awoke.[26]

This was shortly before dawn.

9. The same year. I dreamed that it was *Simhat Torah* and I was praying in the synagogue of the Greeks in Safed. R. Moses Cordovero[27] was there with another man who was taller than he. After I awoke I forgot whether it was the *tanna* R. Pinehas ben Yair or R. Eleazar ben Yohai, a contemporary of mine. They pleaded with me that I should lead the *musaf amidah* and that I should recite the reader's repetition out loud. I recited the daily *amidah* until the conclusion of the prayer "who causes the strength of salvation to flourish." I immediately stepped back three steps and said "He who makes peace," and so forth. The whole congregation screamed at me and said: Why did you not complete all eighteen blessings? The two above-mentioned sages answered them: Be silent. He knows what he is doing. It is the need of the hour.[28]

After the prayers, R. Moses Cordovero said to me: Why are you so anxious to thoroughly understand the wisdom of the *Zohar*? Are you not satisfied with the level of knowledge attained by myself and the scholars of previous generations? I said to him: I endeavor with all my strength to attain a greater understanding, and if Heaven does not desire it, what can I do? He said to me: Since you have such a great desire to know it at its source, that which previous generations did not comprehend, I will ascend and pray for you in Heaven with all my ability. Then, the other sage who was with him said: What is this man's character that he will be able to attain this level of comprehension? He said to him: He is very pious and has devoted his whole life to understanding this wisdom and he is worthy of it. The other sage said: If so, I will also pray for him above, until he will comprehend it, as is my will.

Afterwards, I left the synagogue and I saw many people going out to the woods for a walk, bringing with them food and drink, since it was a holiday as mentioned. I went along with them to study Torah there, but not to eat. Robbers descended upon us and stole everything we had and they took my outer garment, which was very beautiful. I ran away, entered the city, and went to the synagogue, where I prayed and said: It is known to you that I did not go out to walk or eat as did the other people, but to occupy myself with Torah—why did this happen to me? A man entered with my garment in his hand, and he said to me: Your prayer has been accepted before God, since you only went there to study Torah, and they have returned your garment to you—take it; it is the very garment.

10. That year. Several of the God-fearing and pious scholars in the city of Safed agreed to gather in the synagogue every Friday afternoon and each one would tell the others what he had done the past week, whether good or bad. Through this the person would be embarrassed and would cease sinning.[29] I told them: I do not agree with you in this matter—for who would dare reveal his evil deeds to others? The gathering occurred on Friday afternoon in the synagogue. That night I had a dream: I was walking and descended from the *khan* of Safed following the stone ladder that descends to the market and at the butcher's shop was an intersection. My father, my teacher, came toward me from one direction and Rabbi Moses Cordovero and Rabbi Moses Sagis[30] both came from the other direction, which leads from the cemetery to the *khan*. Many deceased persons descended from Heaven and were coming toward me. From a distance, before they could reach me, I saw a ledger in their hand in which were written the names of several people, scholars, and they were mentioning them silently. The first was R. Solomon Sagis[31] and

after him myself, Hayyim, and afterwards the other scholars. When they approached me I adjured R. Moses Cordovero to tell me what type of ledger was this, lest, Heaven forbid, written in it are the names of people who will die that year. Better that I should know so that I would be able to examine my deeds and prepare myself for the journey. He said: This is only the list of scholars who are worthy of repenting in order to serve God. You have all already gathered today in the synagogue to scrutinize your deeds and you did not want to agree with them in this meritorious act. I gave him the same reason I had given that afternoon, as mentioned. Afterwards, I said to him: Is R. Solomon greater than me that he is listed ahead of me in the ledger? He said: Heaven forbid, that is not the reason. It is because of the honor of his father who initiated this practice. Therefore his son is listed first.

Then all of us went to the street of the Jews and I saw all of Israel were gathered there and at noon the sun set and there was darkness in the whole world and all of Israel were weeping bitterly. One man who looked like a hermit, with torn clothes and long hair which reached to his legs,[32] came from the west, the road from the synagogue of Aragon,[33] to the mentioned street and was singing an Arabic song in a loud voice. The song was composed of stanzas and the whole song concerned the commandment of levirate marriage, the Messiah, and redemption, in the manner which it was interpreted in the *Zohar*'s commentary on the verse, "If he will act as a redeemer, good! let him redeem, etc." [Ru 3:13].[34] Nobody understood what he was saying and did not listen to him at all, except for myself. He went along singing until he came to me. The sun again shined as before.

11. 5331 [1571]. *Rosh Hodesh Iyyar*. During the afternoon I meditated by means of recitation of the *Mishnah* three times, as is known to me.[35] I prepared my thoughts to ask: Who were my transmigrations prior to me? I fell into a trance and saw my teacher z"l. He grasped my arms and said to me: The handsome young man who is standing near us is my brother-in-law, and you were his teacher. And I awoke.

I returned to reading the *Mishnah* and I fell into a trance. I

87

heard a very loud voice calling: Ḥayyim, Ḥayyim. I became frightened and awoke. I thought to myself that my teacher z"l was *Rabban* Gamaliel and he was the brother-in-law of Rabbi Eliezer, the disciple of *Rabban* Johanan ben Zakkai.[36] I went to my teacher and told him the whole story. He said to me: This is undoubtedly a divine revelation. However, I do not want to reveal to you the meaning of these things, because I do not want you to know who is the transmigration of my Soul.

12. Sabbath, the twenty-fifth of *Iyyar*, when the cantor recited the *kaddish* of the *yozer* prayer with a melody, I dozed off and saw my teacher z"l. He said to me: You know that a man is now going to your house with a valuable headdress which you will place on your head, and that man is called *Aleph"Lamed* and *Yud, Heh"Vav*.[37] And I awoke.

I told this to my teacher and he explained the matter to me. On that Sabbath I had been worthy to receive the additional Sabbath spirit which has been prepared for me after I will repair my Soul.[38]

13. During the afternoon I meditated by means of the *Mishnah*, as mentioned above. I asked in my thoughts: Am I a transmigration of Rabbi Judah the Prince?[39] I saw my teacher and he said to me: Know that there are two Judahs, the son of Jacob, our Father a"h, and Judah the Prince. King David a"h stands between them and the letters of their names are equivalent. It is written, "You, O Judah, your brothers shall praise, etc." [Gn 49:8] and the first letters of these four words are *Yud, Aleph, Yud, Aleph*, which is the same as the first letters of "the Lord our God, the Lord is One" [Dt 6:4].[40] This is the secret of what is written in the *Zohar, parshat Mishpatim* concerning the word *atah* [you].[41] It is the secret of "the Lord is One," because He is He and all is One. *Atah* is also written concerning Judah to hint that he is the first father and the last father. He said to me: Why did you not look at the verse which says "Judah *atah*" [Gn 49:8], since you are Judah the Prince. I awoke from that drowsiness of contemplation, since I was not really sleeping.

14. 27 *Iyyar*. I was meditating as above. I asked in my thoughts if the soul of Rabbi Eleazar ben Arakh[42] which has been impreg-

nated in me was still impregnated in me. My soul cleaved to his soul by means of reading the *Mishnah*, "Rabbi Eleazar ben Arakh says: Be diligent in the study of Torah, etc."[43] When I was completely awake and my eyes closed, I saw a group of scholars studying Torah. They said to me: Know that in this book which is in our hands and which we are now reading, several verses are written. Know that the scholar R. Eleazar ben Yohai,[44] when he was alive, said to us that the verses written in this book point to the name Eleazar which is alluded to in them.

15. 5332 [1572]. Friday night, the twenty-fourth of *Tammuz.* Shortly before dawn, I arose and sat on my bed while I was drowsy. While I was still asleep I spoke in a loud voice which came out of my mouth by itself. My mother and father heard it and were astonished, but remained silent. This is what I said: "In that day, the glory of Jacob shall dwindle, etc." [Is 17:4],[45] "Only gleanings shall be left of him, etc." [Is 17:6]. "The glory of Jacob shall be diminished"—this is my teacher, Rabbi Isaac Luria, who is called the glory of Jacob. This is explained in my work, in the homily on the remnant of Israel and the remnant of Jacob, see there.[46] "And the fatness of his body will become lean" [Is 17:4]—these are the two groups that were his students, who are called the remnant of Jacob. "Only gleanings shall be left of him"—this is difficult.[47] If the explanation is that two times three will remain—that is: six. If it is two and three—that is: five. In the same way one can ask about what is written four and five. If it is four times five—that is: twenty. If it is four and five—that is: nine. However, the meaning is: Of our first group which is called "the topmost branch," some will die, and there is some doubt about how many will remain. Will two or three alone remain or two and three, which is five, or two times three, which is six? Similarly, with the second group who are called "the boughs," there is doubt if four or five will remain.[48] Then I awoke, opened my eyes, and remembered everything I said and forgot nothing. On the following Friday, my teacher was stricken with a plague and died on the fifth of *Ab.*

Now, in the year 5370 [1610], those of the first group who remain are: myself, R. Gedaliah, R. Abraham Gabriel, R. Joseph

ibn Tabul the Moghrabi,[49] and R. Judah Mashan. However, my
teacher z"l excluded the last three from this group, when he was
still alive. Of the second group there remained R. Yom Tov
Zahalon, R. David Cohen, R. Isaac Krispin, R. Jacob Altaras, R.
Judah ben Uri, and R. Israel Levi Ashkenazi.[50]

16. Three days after my teacher's death, I saw him in a dream
and asked him why he had died so hastily. He told me: Because I
had not found even one who was complete, as I desired.[51] I said
to him: If so, Heaven forbid, I despair of everything you promised me and of all the good that you told me will come into the
world through me. He told me: Do not despair; when the time
comes I will come and reveal to you what to do. And I awoke.

From then on, he revealed himself to me most nights to console me, that I should not despair. This continued for twenty
years after his death. For the next ten years he only came to me
once a month. From then on he came once every three months.
All the dreams I had of him were always in one form. He taught
me Torah and consoled me that I should not despair. "For there
is yet a prophecy for a set term, etc." [Hb 2:3], and all will be fulfilled, praise God.

17. 5333 [1572]. *Rosh Hodesh Heshvan.* Three months after my
teacher's z"l death, I saw R. Moses Cordovero in the doorway of
the Torah Study Society in Safed. I adjured him that he should
tell me the truth about how *Kabbalah* is studied in the world of
souls. Was it according to his method or according to the
method of my teacher z"l? He told me: Both methods are true.
Indeed, my method is the method of the plain meaning for the
beginners in this wisdom and the method of your teacher is the
esoteric and primary. Even I, in Heaven, only study according to
your teacher's method.[52] I said to him: If so, why did he leave the
world? He said to me: Because he did not even find a single *zaddiq* in this generation who was complete, as he desired. Had he
found him, he would not have died.

18. 5334 [1573]. The night after *Yom Kippur.* I asked my
teacher z"l in a dream if there is an aspect of the *Parzuf* which
corresponds to the upper half of the *Zeir* as there is of the lower

half, the *Parzufim* of Jacob and Rachel.[53] He told me that there is
an aspect of the *Parzuf* which emerges from the letter *aleph* of
"*Eheyeh*"[54] of *Imma* which is clothed in *Zeir*. From there, this emanation emerges from the back of *Zeir* and becomes a *Parzuf*
which rests on the head of Rachel which is in the back of the
lower half. The Talmudic sages hinted at this upper one when
they said that when Jacob had sexual relations with Leah, Rachel
was under the bed.[55] Corresponding to this in the inner side of
Zeir there is above it an aspect which is the hidden foundation
within it. It is the foundation of the first *Zeir* of six directions
which when it grows ascends and is called *Tiferet* and within it
encapsulates *Yesod* of *Abba*. As the emanation of *Yesod* of *Imma*
emerges in the back side and becomes Leah, similarly the emanation of *Yesod* of *Abba* emerges to the inner side above and unites
with Leah, as mentioned.

19. In *Heshvan* I saw my teacher z"l in a dream and he said to
me: Know that just as there is the divine name of forty-two letters, it similarly exists in musical notes.[56] I forgot the rest and I
only remembered the second name "destroy Satan,"[57] since it is
the musical intonation which is called "*TeLiShA*." Perhaps
because the name that was mentioned is in *Gevurah* and *TeLiShA*
is also *T"L A"Sh* which are five "*Gevurot*"—five times "*Elohim*"
which is 430 in *gematria* and together are *A"Sh Gevurah*. Thus the
two names are *TeLiShA* (731) in *gematria*.[58]

20. 5335 [1574]. On *Rosh Hashanah,* when the verses prior to
the blowing of the *shofar*, "God ascends midst acclamation" [Ps
47:6] were being read, I dozed off a little. I saw myself in Kfar
Tanhum[59] at the grave of R. Tanhum[60] who was buried there. I
and several other people were circumambulating the grave. A
man came and gave me a gemstone, which shined like the sun,
and he said to me: Before we gave you a lit candle, the oil ran out,
and the candle was extinguished. Now we are giving you this
gemstone which does not need oil and will not go out. And I
awoke.

Afterwards, in the month of *Kislev,* a son was born to me and
I called him Nehemiah, for the grave of that *zaddiq* and also for
the name of the village. I understood that the extinguished

candle was my son Joseph, mentioned at the end of section six, who spoke prophecies and died at the age of one and a half the previous *Ellul* and this gemstone was Nehemiah. Because of my sins, he also died at the age of thirteen. He also spoke prophecies and had wondrous visions while awake. When he was four years old he saw Metatron on a roof who said to him: You are a transmigration of the prophet Zechariah the son of Yehoyada the priest.[61] In my humble opinion, my teacher was also transmigrated in him.

21. The second night of *Rosh Hashanah* I had a dream with my teacher z"l, who said to me: Do you know why King David a"h was so anguished over the son who was born to him by Bathsheba and died? I told him: I do not know. He said to me: Know that this son later transmigrated into Nehemiah the Tirshatha,[62] who was a descendant of David and was a great man. Also know that because previously he died before he was circumcised, he was not given a name. Therefore, afterwards his book was subsumed under the book of Ezra and is not called by his name.

22. Friday night, *Rosh Hodesh Adar*. I dreamed that I was in Jerusalem and a Muslim with a white turban on his head came and greeted me with great cordiality. Afterwards, he blessed me silently; only his lips moved. It then occurred to me that I recognized him and it was Elijah z"l. I also heard him say silently: "God will arise, His enemies shall be scattered, etc." [Ps 68:2]. Afterwards, R. Jacob Mas'ud came and conducted me to the house of Rabbi Lapidot Ashkenazi z"l. It was the Sabbath and he rose to greet me, accorded me great respect, and seated me next to him. A copy of the *Zohar* was in his hands and we studied it together. In the course of discussion, he was uncertain about one matter and I explained it to him and brought proof from the *Zohar* on Exodus, from the story of a certain person whose name was Yoezer ben Jacob, who walked before R. Eleazar and told him how he entered the Garden of Eden, and so forth.[63] And I awoke.

23. That year. My brother R. Moses became ill and my teacher z"l told me in a dream that I should concentrate on him when I recite the prayer "Heal us,"[64] [and concentrate] on the words "Who heals the sick of His people Israel" because "Heals the

people" in *gematria* adds up to 288 sparks, from which emanate diseases. I should concentrate that these 288 should be repaired and sweetened and through this, healing will come to the sick. I told him that "heals [*rofeh*]" is only 287 in *gematria*, and perhaps it would be better to concentrate on the first letters of "heals the sick of Israel," which is 288. He told me that this is true, and he did not want to say so until I said it, to [give] me the credit.

24. 5336 [1576]. Friday night, the twenty-eighth of *Ellul,* my father-in-law, R. Moses Saadia z"l, died at nine in the evening. Shortly before his death, I grasped his arm at the pulse point[65] and adjured him that after his death he should come to me in a dream and tell me my attributes and place in Paradise. I went home to sleep and did not know if he died that night. At midnight I saw him in a dream and I asked him: What happened to you in the other world? He said to me: It is good, but since I have just died and it is the Sabbath, I have not yet been led into the Heavenly Tribunal in order to know what will happen to me. Concerning your place in Paradise, I have already gone and looked but I was not given permission to enter and see your place, because they said that I am not worthy to see it. Indeed, I heard that it is a very high place.

25. 5337 [1577]. I dreamed that I was in the market, at the door of R. Judah Anconina, and I saw a man more than three cubits tall, lying on a bed along the road, from that doorway until almost before the doorway of R. Joseph Karo z"l. I said to him: Who are you? He said to me: I am Adam your father and I am lying here very ill.[66] Therefore, I ask of you, Hayyim my son, bring me medications from the pharmacy to strengthen my heart which is weak because of my great illness. I went and brought them to him. He ate and drank. And I awoke.

26. Friday night, the twenty-seventh of *Nisan*. I saw that I had a seminal emission in a dream. I woke up and was very anguished over the emission. I returned to sleep and saw my teacher z"l. He said to me: The time has not yet come about which I commanded you when I was alive, that you should go and live in Jerusalem. Now, come with me to a cave of *zaddiqim*, in order to know what

will be. He led me into a particular cave of *zaddiqim* from the
period of the early *Tannaim*. It was a very beautiful and ancient
building, made of large stones over the grave markers, like the
cave of Hillel and Shammai. I saw carved into one large stone
over a grave the name Kastiel and under it carved the name
Samael.[67] There were other names also carved there, but I forgot
them. There, my teacher z"l told me: The time has come and you
have been given permission to go and live in Jerusalem.

27. The following Saturday night. I dreamed that there was a
book open before me and written in it was that the *zaddiqim* are
on a higher level than the "holy animals," since their souls are
hewn out of the divine throne.[68] After their deaths, they return
there and are made the Chariot for the *Shekhinah*.[69] The holy animals are the lower Chariot, below them. It was further written
there that Elijah z"l is also made a Chariot for God.[70] On each of
Elijah's arms which are divided into three joints are written three
names and three angels. They are specific, but I forgot the
details. However, what I do remember is that on the first joint
was written "copper," on the second joint "serpent," and on the
third joint was a word unrelated to the first two, but I forgot what
it was.[71] There was something also written there, that these three
joints together with the three names of angels on them are the
three legs of the Chariot.

28. *Rosh Hodesh Tevet*. We were in a Talmudic academy in the
village of Ein Zeitan[72] and we completed the study of the tractate
Hagigah. We decided to make a festive meal for two reasons: first,
because we had completed the tractate, and second, because of
Rosh Hodesh and *Hanukkah*. That night I saw in my dream the
Soul of Rabbi Isaac Amigo, the singer, who had died three years
earlier of liver and intestinal disease. During his illness, he had
vomited up pieces of his liver. In the dream I saw him in the large
synagogue, as was his custom during his lifetime. Members of
the community and Rabbi Isaac Karo, the cantor, were gathered.
R. Isaac Karo and R. Abraham Lando, the official, came to me
and begged me to repair the Soul of the deceased. The deceased
himself said to me: I have come to you to repair me. And I awoke.
The next morning I told the dream to the scholars. In that vil-

lage, some gentiles were bringing a calf to be slaughtered. It broke away from them and entered my study hall. It jumped up on the ledge where I and the company were sitting. There was a table there on which we placed our books. The calf presented itself before me with two legs on the ledge and two legs on the table. It looked at me and its eyes were filled with tears. The scholars saw this and were amazed. I said to them: This is the dream about which I told you. We then went outside and purchased the calf from its owner and slaughtered it with the intent to repair the Soul of the deceased which had transmigrated into the calf. The calf stretched out its neck willingly, without any trouble. We examined it and found it to be kosher, without any blemishes. I said to the companions: Cut the liver and you will find that it is putrid, as the sick one who had transmigrated into it. They cut it and found all the veins full of blood and long worms without number. I then commanded them not to throw any of it away. They purged all the worms and all the forbidden fats of the rest of the calf and did not lose any of the calf that was permissible to eat. I did not allow any stranger to eat any of it. We alone [ate] with the intention to repair that Soul through a meal at a religious ceremony.[73] The following night, I saw the Soul of the deceased in my dream and he said to me: May you be satisfied as you have satisfied me.[74]

29. 5338 [1577]. *Rosh Hodesh Kislev,* after sunrise, a large star with a long tail, pointing upward, was seen in the southwestern part of the sky. Part of the tail was also pointing eastward. It lingered there for three hours. Then it sank in the west behind the hills of Safed. This continued for more than fifty nights.

On the fifteenth of *Kislev,* I went to live in Jerusalem.

30. Friday night, the second of *Kislev,* I dreamed that I looked up to the skies and I saw a drawing of a square divided into twelve compartments like the High Priest's breastplate. The compartments were beautifully colored and gilded in many colors.

[There were three rows down and four columns across.]

In the first row and first column was written: The flag of Judah. In the second column was written: Lion. I also saw, on each side of the sky, a beautifully gilded drawing. Inside that drawing was written the letters of *Keter,* in large bright letters which flashed like lightning. The letters protruded as if they were embroidered with pearls, gold, and many colors.

I was shown in a dream that this was in my house. I told my mother the dream and explained its meaning to her. It is a sign: The exile will be rescinded after his right, and the right is the face of the lion of the right.

Judah is called the young lion, who is in exile. Now the light of the Messiah, who is from the tribe of Judah, who is called Lion, will shine, and he is on the right. And I awoke.

31. On a Thursday night in 5339 [1579], there was a plague in Egypt and people fled and came to Jerusalem. I arose at midnight and went over to the window of my attic, close to the Temple, to pray to God with weeping concerning the plague, that it should not come to Jerusalem. Afterwards, I sat in my special seat in that room to study Torah. The candle was extinguished and I dozed off in my seat.

I saw in a dream that a gentile general and a large army were marching on Jerusalem, to sack it. I stood up and said to him in a loud voice: Beware, do not attack this city. He said to me: Who are you, that I should listen to your words? People who were there said to him: Know that he is an important person and close to the government. He raised his hand and struck me on the nape of the neck and from the strength of that blow my neck was bent down as far as possible. I awoke and my neck was still bent, as if this really happened while I was awake. While I was astonished at the vision, a large, cold serpent began to wrap itself around my legs. I arose quickly and lit the candle. I saw the serpent enter a crack in the wall near me. I studied Torah until morning, went to the synagogue to pray the morning prayers, and returned home. I entered that room and I was completely dumbfounded until sunset. Then people came to my house for the Friday evening prayers. When they began to recite the verse "A psalm. A song for the Sabbath" [Ps 92:1], my mouth opened by itself and I recited the evening prayers as was my custom.

32. 5340 [1580]. Saturday night, the sixteenth of *Adar,* my teacher z"l said to me in a dream: Know that the source of your

soul in the twelve tribes of Israel is from one of the three tribes which carried Jacob's coffin on the eastern side and it is from the tribe that was closest to the south side.

33. 5346 [1586]. The night of the fifteenth of *Shevat,* after I returned to Safed, I asked in a dream this question: What was the name of the good inclination which entered me in the beginning of my fourteenth year? I saw the sage R. Ḥayyim Moghrabi in my dream and he said to me: I have come to answer your question—know that his name is Saglid, from the phrase "The consort [*sei-gal*] stands at your right hand" [Ps 45:10].

34. 5354 [1594]. During that period I was preaching repentance to the people at night. In that year I had the same dream two or three consecutive nights. I do not remember the details, but I do remember in a general way, that I saw in the dream that I was walking along a great river, and I saw a large and mighty multitude of Israelites who were resting there in tents. I entered one tent and I saw their king reclining on his side. He was a tall person, with a black beard and about fifty years of age. When he saw me, he seated me at his side with great joy and said to me: Know that I am the king of Israel, of the tribe of Ephraim, and we have come now because the time has come for the ingathering of the exiles and I only came here with great anticipation to see you.

35. I saw in a dream a wealthy man who had died here in Damascus, a year before I came. His name was Judah Gano and I had never seen him. He begged me, for God's sake, that I should repair his Soul, because there is nobody else in this generation who is worthy to repair [Souls]. Tomorrow, I will come to your house so you can repair me. And I awoke.

The next day, a girl came to my house who was the daughter of Daniel Romano. She was possessed of an evil spirit and I healed her.

36. 5367 [1606]. The twelfth of *Kislev,* the third night whose star is Mars and whose angel is Samael. It was in the Torah portion *Va-Yishlaḥ,* in which is found the struggle of Jacob and Samael[75] and the matter of the chiefs of Esau, as the sages say:

The chief of Magdiel[76] is Rome,[77] also the *haftarah*, "The Vision of Obadiah."[78]

I saw in my dream a very large and high mountain, made of flint, which was carved and straight on all four sides, like the four sides of a square wall. I ascended the eastern side along the southeastern corner and I asked: What is this city? They told me: This is Nineveh. Afterwards, they said to me: This is the evil Rome.

The writer, Hayyim, says: Remember that this is found in *Sefer Zerubbabel*, which is in manuscript.[79] I saw inserted on the eastern face of the wall, halfway up the wall, a very long peg protruding toward the houses of the city. An inverted sword, with its point downward, was stuck in the peg. Its handle was at the top of the wall: The length of the sword was half the height of the wall. They said to me: This sword has been resting in this peg since the day the world was created until today, and no person has ever touched it. I looked at it and saw that it was a type of brass unlike any other and cuts all sorts of iron as if they were dry straw. It had four edges on all four sides. At the point of the sword, there was something which appeared to be like the mouth of a snake, and they said that whoever is struck by this sword will not recover.

I thought to myself: Perhaps during this lengthy period of time, from the creation of the world until now, the sword has become rusty. I looked at it, and it was literally like new. I took it in my hand. The Roman emperor was told: That sword which no person has ever touched is now in the hands of a certain Jew. The emperor commanded that I be found and killed. While I was still on top of the wall I threw the sword from my hand into the middle of the city and it stuck in the ground, point down, in one of the courtyards of the city. I escaped and hid in a cave in Rome where poor people lived.[80] I remained in hiding there until Saturday afternoon. I then went out and the emperor's men encountered me and they led me before him. He commanded: Let everyone leave![81] He and I were left alone. I said to him: Why did you want to kill me? You are all being led astray by your religion like blind people, for there are no true teachings except for the

98

teachings of Moses alone, and no others are true. He said to me: I knew all this. Therefore, I sent to seek you, because I knew that there is nobody wiser and more understanding of the true wisdom[82] and I want you to tell me secrets of the Torah and some of the names of the Lord, your God, since I already recognize the truth. Therefore do not be afraid that I sought you, for I truly love you.

I then imparted some of this wisdom to him. And I awoke.[83]

37. I dreamed that one of the great ancient sages warned me that every time I recite the prayer "Hear our voice,"[84] I should use the following language:[85] May it be your will Lord, my God and God of my fathers, that you should join me, connect me and unite me, gird and strengthen me with your divine strength, as you said to Moses a"h, "And you will see my back" [Ex 33:23]. And I awoke. I forgot who the above-mentioned sage was. I am uncertain which one of the following two it was: Either *Rav* Hamnuna Saba or *Rav* Yeivi Saba.[86]

38. 5368 [1608]. I saw in my dream that I was traveling on the road near the house of Ḥayyim Monidas and the garden called Bustan il Kat. I looked and a very distinguished-looking man with a black beard was standing in the entrance to the above-mentioned garden. Opposite it was an entrance to a courtyard which had one tomb within it and people said that it was that of an ancient Jewish sage. I crossed over and asked him: What is your name? He said to me: I am your ancestor, Jacob. I was very happy when I heard his words and kissed his hands. And I awoke.

39. In the month of *Ab*. When Murad Pasha, the governor, wanted to return to Constantinople, I dreamed that this governor came here to Damascus, saw me, embraced and kissed me, and said: Ask what you want and I will fulfill your desire. He also had brought before him large sacks full of gold and silver vessels and a set of scales. The scales were hung in front of him and they began to weigh the silver in the scales in order to conceal them in the king's treasury. I saw one silver vessel in the shape of a wine bottle, about a cubit tall. I desired it and surreptitiously took it in my hand. The viceroy said to me: If you want, take it. I took it. They took out another bottle of precious stone, like pure white

glass, and it was divided into many sections, like a series of rings connected together to form a bottle, and covered in silver. I took them and concealed them under the hem of my garment. The viceroy looked at me and said: If you want, take this one also, since it is yours. This is one of the vessels from the Temple and it is yours. During the destruction of the Temple, the enemies plundered it. Therefore do not be embarrassed to take it, since you are taking what is yours. Join the separate parts. I did so and took it. And I awoke.

40. *Ab.* I saw in a dream that I was in the synagogue of the *Sephardim,* on *Rosh Hashanah* when the *shofar* was being blown. A handsome young man, about seventeen years old, stood up with the *shofar* in his hand. He recited the appropriate blessings, but did not blow the *shofar.* Instead, he began to speak words of rebuke. He said: The essence of the blowing of the *shofar* is none other than the awakening of the great repentance. He rebuked them at length, and at the end of his talk he said to them: If you will not do accordingly, it is written, "Your wives will become widows and your children orphans" [Ex 22:23]. Look and see that *shofar* equals "orphans" in *gematria.* I said to him: Their numbers do not equate! He then explained to me how they are equal. I do not remember his explanation.

I saw, sitting next to me, a tall, handsome sage whose name was Moses R"B.[87] I said to him: Is not his excellency concerned with this congregation's lack of dignity, that the only person they have to blow the *shofar* on this day is this youth?[88] Not only that, but he recites the blessings and then interrupts with a sermon, and after the sermon does not blow the *shofar* at all. He answered me: I have also just descended from Heaven and I see their lack of dignity, because they do not have an appropriate shepherd. The "children will shame their elders."[89] I am silent—you also remain silent like me and suffer it. Afterwards, he begged me to give him some of my wine to drink. I took a goblet and turned it upside down and put some brandy, which is distilled from the wine in a still, in the base of the goblet. Since I had not yet recited the blessing over the wine, since it was still morning, therefore I did not give him wine and also not in the goblet itself.

41. 5369 [1608]. Saturday night, during the intermediate days of *Sukkot*. Before dawn, I dreamed that I was in Safed in the synagogue with my teacher, Rabbi Moses Alshekh z"l. He said to me: Why is the city so noisy, has it been verified that the redemption of Israel will come through you? I said to him: The last two days I have begun to attain divine inspiration, and people see that I seclude myself and I attain and see visions, and so forth. Therefore they say this. He said to me: You know what happened to R. Joseph ibn Tabul the Moghrabi. He married the daughter of R. Yom Tov Zahalon and was not able to have normal sexual relations with her and everyone gossips about him. I said to him: If he is as wise as he says he is and attains divine inspiration, why does he not heal himself of this great affliction? And I awoke.

In the morning, a certain captive who had come from Salonika came to my house to collect money to ransom captives. He told me that the previous night he had dreamed that it was *Rosh Hashanah* and he was in the synagogue. The cantor took the *shofar* in his hand and blew it. The sound that emanated from it was not the normal sound of the *shofar*, but the *kaddish*: "Praised and Magnified, etc., And may the Messiah come speedily" and the whole congregation responded appropriately: "Amen, may His name, etc."

42. The twenty-sixth of *Heshvan*. I had a long dream, but I only remember this little bit in a general way:

I saw a dear friend who brought me a letter, the size of a half sheet of paper, written in Hebrew letters like those in which the torah scroll is written. He gave it to me and said: You always desired to see something in the handwriting of the Messiah, the king of Israel. I have brought it to you from a distant land, more than two thousand days' journey, from a place where the [ten lost] tribes dwell. However, I have brought it to you quickly, in a brief time. It is written by the Messiah himself and sent to you.

I made him swear three times that it was true, that it was the handwriting of the Messiah and he had personally sent it to me. He swore to me that it was true and certain. I opened it and it began with lengthy salutations as is customary and afterwards he wrote at length, in general terms, to notify me that he had already been invited to come to the land of Israel soon. Therefore, I need to endeavor to return Israel in penance, for through this I will help him to come more quickly.

43. The eighteenth of *Kislev*. I dreamed that I was very agitated to know a certain matter and I begged R. Moses the Suaz[90] to show me his book. Perhaps I will find written there the reason why I had previously been called the winged one, and now I had lost this ability.[91] It was shown to me in a dream that this book contained teachings of my teacher z"l. Then I saw that I was floating in the air as I had previously.

44. The sixteenth of *Tevet*. I had a long dream and forgot it. I will write what I remember of it:

My son Samuel[92] and I were sitting at the shore of the ocean and I touched the water with my hand to see if it was cold or lukewarm. I saw that it was lukewarm. We ascended from there to a very high mountain that was at the edge of the shore. On the side of the mountain that faced the water there was a stone wall. The mountain was not inclined at that point and there was a clear path between the wall and the water. I pulled out a stone from the top of the wall and threw it along the path. I looked at the stone after I threw it, and it changed into an object about the size of a human head and neck. One end was cut, as if it had been cut from the neck. It continued to change and slowly assumed the form and features of a human head. Afterwards, his eyes opened and they gazed at me with great displeasure. I was astonished by the sight of all this. The head opened its mouth and said to me: As if I do not know that you are the one who tore me from this wall and threw me down. I am Talfas,[93] one who was made by sorcery, and I was placed at the top of the wall so that Israel would be under the domination of the nations as long as I was in place there. Now that you have torn me from my place and thrown me down, my strength, based on that magic, has already dissipated and Israel is no longer under that domination. You caused all this, and therefore I am very angry with you.

I saw how he was completed and how he grew into a tall, strong, fat, redheaded man. He ascended toward me on the top of the mountain to do battle with me; I saw two knives near me;

one was large and the blade was broken. The second was smaller, and the blade was whole, but its handle was made of wood and its upper half, near the blade, was missing completely. I took them and battled with him vigorously. I inflicted great blows to his neck and both sides of his body. The blood poured out copiously.

His friend came to his aid and I did not know from where he came. He was a short black man, weaker and a worse fighter. He came to his aid: I smote him too, like the first one.

I was afraid that the lord of the city would punish me—why have I shed blood—I left them and turned back. Then the first one came and took the knife from my hand. I was afraid that he would overpower me. I began to excommunicate him, and said to him: May you be excommunicated and banned in both worlds by God if you hurt me. Then we began to debate to justify ourselves. Then I knew and recognized who he was. And I awoke.

I had a second dream in which I was writing many wondrous things, but I forgot the subject. In a general way I remember that I was writing all the repairs for my Soul which I had already repaired. I had already repaired all of them or a majority. I was writing other things on another page. Afterwards, I wrote: These are the clarifications[94] that have not yet been clarified among the *kelippot* that need repair: When God will finish clarifying them, the whole world will be repaired.

45. The fourteenth of *Adar* I. I dreamed that I was wearing a *talit katan* and drawn on it were five rows, and each row had three circles like the *segol*,[95] the way that later kabbalists draw in their books to represent the ten *sefirot*—three groups of three, in a vertical pattern. I was surprised because the *sefirot* are three groups of three, and why were there five groups of three on my garment? I woke up and again dreamed all this four or five times. The garment itself was one piece of cloth as is normal, but the ten *sefirot* were woven into it, like the rings of the Tabernacle. It seemed to me that in the dream I said that the five rows corresponded to the five *Parzufim* that exist in the four worlds of *Azilut, Beriah, Yezirah, Assiyah*.[96] Each *Parzuf* has only three *sefirot*, corresponding to the three paths which include all nine *sefirot* of

the *Parzuf*. In my humble opinion, the explanation is that I had completed the repair of my Soul garment[97] of *Assiyah*, which includes the five *Parzufim*.

46. On the fifth of *Nisan* I had a long dream and I will write what I remember. I was together with many righteous *Tannaim*. There was one sage who was our master. Each one of the assembled sang a *kaddish* before him with a pleasant melody, in order to choose which *kaddish* was more worthy and superior to the other *kaddishim*. It seemed to me that this was at the end of days, when Zerubbabel would recite the *kaddish* and Korah and his community would rise from Sheol, during the resurrection of the dead.[98] They were experimenting to see who would be worthy to recite this *kaddish*. I am almost certain that the sage was my teacher z"l. I am also uncertain if it was a Sabbath or a festival. It seems more probable to me that it was a festival. After many of the *Tannaim* recited their *kaddish*, I arose and recited my *kaddish* with a melody. It seemed to me then that the melody was like the *kaddish* of the trumpets, which currently was customary among the *Sephardi* cantors. I raised my voice so much with the melody of the *kaddish* and the responses, "Amen, may His great name," and so forth, with all my strength, that I parched my throat slightly. It seemed to me that my teacher z"l was not pleased with my raising my voice so much that it was parched slightly. I finished the whole *kaddish* with raised voice and melody. I am uncertain if I awoke immediately or if I finished the whole evening prayers, since it was a Sabbath or festival eve, as mentioned. Afterwards, I awoke.

Afterwards, I fell asleep again and I saw Rabbi Joseph Karo z"l come to my house to greet me on a festival. He sat down. R. Shabbatai and his partner brought me as a present, four or five baskets of food, containing cooked fattened hens, melons, and cheese and milk. I put them before Rabbi Joseph Karo and he was pleased to dine with me. He alone ate of these foods. I only eat what I have cooked, which is my custom even when awake. And I awoke. I often dream of Rabbi Joseph Karo, that he is deathly ill and I go visit him and I am sorry for him and prepare medications for him. I do not understand the meaning of this.

47. The twenty-second of *Nisan*. My teacher z"l said to me: I came into this world another time and there were 600 householders in Safed. Now you will return to dwell in Safed and there will be 1,600 householders and I will again return.

48. 5370 [1609]. The eighteenth of *Kislev*. I dreamed that I arranged a marriage for my son Samuel with the daughter of Solomon Ragwan, and I told Solomon: You do not recognize the importance of my level, since all the aspects of *Hanukkah* are alluded to in my name. I explained it to him. And I awoke. I had a second dream that I returned and explained what I had forgotten, and this is it: The *het* of Hayyim is the *het* of *Hanukkah*. Similarly, the *het* of Hayyim alludes to the eight lights of *Hanukkah*.[99] However, the oil of the lights alludes to the two *yuds* of Hayyim, since they are the secret of what is written concerning the candelabra of Zechariah, "And by it are two olive trees" [Zec 4:3], which are the two *yuds* as is found in the *Zohar Raya Mehemna, Pinehas* [III:244b], that each *yud* is the size of an olive tree. They are also the secret of "These are the two sons of Yizhar, etc." [Zec 4:14], since the oil which comes out of the olives is also called "Yizhar," as is written, "Your new grain and wine and oil [Yizhar]" [Dt 7:13]. Yizhar was also the father of Korah.[100] The *mem* of Hayyim is the *mem* of *menorah* which are the lights themselves. Thus, the candle, the oil, and the light are alluded to in my name. The name of the redeemer who was the author of the miracle of Hanukkah, Mattathias the Hasmonean, is also alluded to in my name. The *mem* of Hayyim is a reference to the *mem* of Mattathias. I explained more great things concerning this matter. I only remember that which I have written.

49. The twenty-ninth of *Kislev*. I dreamed that it was Saturday morning, after the prayers, and I was at my teacher's z"l house. He said to me: I am worried about my relative R. David Amarilio, who has come from Egypt with his family to live here in Safed. He is very poor and how will he make a living? Our master taught me: "A man's feet are responsible for him, etc."[101] Perhaps he has some merit that has brought him here to be buried here. He said to me: If so, why is he still living? I said to him: Perhaps it

has been decreed that he should live here for a while and then be buried here.

After this I felt that I was fainting, that a great pain had seized me and afterwards the fainting left me. Four women heard that I fainted and were coming to bring me some medicine. They found me sitting since the fainting had left me. There were many people there and they said: This fainting was the result of his many worries over the people not listening to him to return in repentance. I then said to my teacher z"l: Do not be angry with me and I will tell you something: All this evil—that the people do not repent and do not listen to my voice—you caused all this because you did not teach me everything I needed to know in this art. I do not want to bother you now since it is time for the Sabbath midday meal. I will go home and return after the meal and sit with you the whole day until you will inform me what you will do with me. My teacher laughed good-naturedly. And I awoke.

50. The seventeenth of *Tevet*. During the week of *parshat Shemot*,[102] in which is mentioned the birth of Moses Our Teacher a"h, I had a long dream which I forgot. This is what I remember of it:

Aaron the Priest, the brother of Moses, was living in this world, in this generation, and was a government official. I do not remember if he was in charge of taxes or in charge of minting coins.[103] I also do not remember if I saw him myself or not. On the eighteenth of *Tevet*, during this week, I also had a long dream which I forgot. I do not remember if I saw Issachar the son of Jacob with my own eyes or if I only explained wondrous secrets concerning him.

On the Friday of this Torah portion, the twentieth of *Tevet*, I had a terrifying dream. I forgot its beginning and also several things in the middle of the dream. This is what I remembered: It was either *Hoshana Rabba* or *Simhat Torah* and I was in the synagogue in Safed and the sage R. Jacob Abulafia was the head of it. The members of the community wanted to enhance the synagogue with lovely couches as is the custom of Israel in honor of *Simhat Torah*. We were also shown in the dream that it was the ancient custom of Israel to bring the corpse of Moses a"h into the synagogue.[104] I am uncertain if it was the custom to bring it in every year on this day or only every seventh year on *Simḥat Torah*. On this day, seven years had already passed, and therefore they were bringing him. The reason for this is that this is the day of the rejoicing with the Torah that had been given through Moses. Therefore, they brought him, so that "Moses will rejoice with the portion assigned him."[105] Furthermore, on this day they read the Torah portion at end of Deuteronomy in which the death of Moses is mentioned. Therefore, they bring his corpse to remember the particulars of his death.

I saw them bring Moses' corpse into the synagogue and his length was almost ten cubits.[106] They prepared a long bench on which there were books and they laid Moses' corpse on them. I saw that his corpse was dressed in his garments. As they laid it on the table it was literally transformed into a torah scroll. It was not rolled up, but was spread out the whole length, like a long letter lying the length of the table, and the whole Torah was written on it from beginning to end. It was not like our torah scrolls which are composed of many parchment sheets which are divided into many columns. It was all one page, divided into lines, line after line until the end. They placed his head at the south which was Genesis and his feet at the north which was the end of Deuteronomy. The rabbi of the community sat at the head and I sat at the feet. I said to myself: He did this out of arrogance to place the head [the beginning] of the Torah at his place and the feet [end] at my place. I again said to myself: Even though his intention was to lord it over me, yet it is appropriate that I rejoice with this, since my place is close to the Blessing [*Ve-zot ha-Berakhah*],[107] in which is written the death of Moses. This indicates that there is a cleaving and connection between my Soul and that of Moses Our Teacher a"h. Then the above-mentioned sage said: Bring garments to clothe the corpse of Moses Our Teacher a"h. However, the place where they girded his loins they only brought a thin cord and they girded him with it. This seemed a great novelty to the sage which he did not know at all. I laughed at him inwardly, because this matter of the thread is explicitly discussed in tractate *Soferim*.[108] Afterwards, I saw the Torah return to its original form, the corpse of Moses. They clothed him and girded him with above-mentioned cord, and with two white shawls. I was surprised that he added the two shawls. Earlier he had ordered only to gird him with the thread. Afterwards, they moved the position of the bench and his head was in the west and his feet in the east. I am unsure, perhaps it was the opposite. This occurred at midday and I forget what else happened....Afterwards, I saw myself outside the walls of Safed, on the eastern side. There was a high wide place like a plateau near the wall. I and all the people were sitting on the southern side of the plateau and on the northern side, near the wall, was Moses' place. I do not remember if it was literally his grave site or only his corpse, as earlier. Indeed, we did not actually see him, but were only cognizant of him. It was also time for the afternoon prayers, and I was sad and very worried and said to myself: If only that I would now be worthy to see the resplendent light of the Divine Presence which hovers over Moses a"h, who is here with us. If only my eyes would be opened and I would see. As I was reflecting, I raised my eyes to the large mountain near the cemetery of Safed which was composed of several hills close together, and in the middle of this mountain, near the village of Masuiah, there were three peaks close together. I saw the sun set unseasonably behind the tops of the hills as was customary. I thought to myself that the sun had not yet set much behind the hills and if I stood up—perhaps I would see it. I decided that the sun itself was in a village behind the middle peak. I saw its light shining skyward—the movement...of the sun, but I did not see the sun. And I awoke.

I dozed off again and I saw myself in the synagogue of the *Sephardim* in Damascus, on *Rosh Hashanah,* during the blowing of the *shofar.* R. Judah Apumado[109] z"l stood up and blew the first series of blasts which is *TaShRaT,*[110] but he did not complete them. He blew the *Tekiah* and *Shevarim.* He then blew the *Teruah* and extended it greatly—until he no longer had the strength to blow. He then blew three very short tremolos extremely faintly....We were all surprised at all the changes he had made. The whole dream was at the end of the night. And I awoke.

(51). The fifteenth of *Shevat.* I dreamed that it was during the day on *Yom Kippur* and my teacher z"l the Ashkenazi and I were at the Ark and Rabbi Israel Curiel[111] was leading the service. He began the *Kol Nidre* with a melodiousness that was uncustomary for him. I said: The old man still has some of his original strength. Afterwards he recited "God is King" melodiously; He then took the torah scroll out of the Ark. He was blind. When he approached the Ark he asked my teacher z"l about me, if I was still engaged in the process of comtemplation. He answered him: All of his thoughts are still on this matter. I then cried before my teacher that he show me the path which I should follow. And I awoke.

(51)[52]. Do not be surprised that I am writing down dreams, since in *Midrash Kohelet* R. Johanan asked that common weaver who saw in a dream about *Rav* Asi that the sky was falling and *Rav* Asi held it up. From then on, he was anxious about this dream and treated him with respect.[112] Also in tractate *Berakhot*, Abbaye and Rava, the greatest scholars of the generation, rewarded a common man who interpreted his dreams to them.[113] There are many similar examples. They said there that to a good person, even like David, only bad dreams are shown and if he sees a good dream, he forgets it, but others show him—a good dream. They said there: Three dreams are fulfilled—a dream that a friend has about him, a morning dream, and a dream that is interpreted within a dream. If so, it is better that a friend have a good dream about him than that which he himself dreams.[114]

(53). The sixth of *Nisan*. I dreamed that I was walking along a road and there were large hills and among them villages close to Safed. I came to one village and there were Jews there. I saw a synagogue there and opposite it a school for the children of the village. Their teacher was sitting there and his name was R. Yiashih, who is mentioned in the Jerusalem Talmud and who commanded, "Bury me in the shrouds of children because I am not ashamed of my deeds, etc."[115] He was very pious, retiring, and a hermit. I decided in my heart to ask him about the path of asceticism and seclusion. I asked him. I saw that he dressed me in a silk garment and he was weaving it on my body. It was like a very long silk belt, three fingers wide. At first he arranged it from the top to the bottom of my body lengthwise [the warp] and afterwards he wove it across [the woof], until he completed weaving the garment. He said to me: I am clothing you in a belt. This seemed to me like what Scripture says, "And He made belts[116] for them" [Gn 3:7]. I wanted to say: A garment is made by weaving belts and the belt was already woven from the combination of threads. He then told me many pleasant things about the wholeness of my Soul and its reward in the pleasures of the world to come. I awoke and remembered them. I returned to sleep and I forgot them. I awoke and I was well acquainted with the following verse: "With oil of gladness over all your peers. All your robes [are fragrant] with myrrh and aloes and cassia" [Ps 45:8–9], and also the verse, "Then you can seek the favor of the Lord, etc." [Is 58:14]. I forgot the rest of the dream. This occurred before dawn.

(54). Friday night, the twenty-fourth of *Nisan.* After the birth of my son Abraham, may God protect him, on Saturday, the twenty-fifth of *Adar,* I dreamed that a son was born to me and it was Saturday, the day of the circumcision.[117] I was angry with the *Sephardi* community in Damascus and I prayed at home with a few friends. They said to me: Why do you not send for your teacher Rabbi Moses Alshekh, his soul is in Paradise?[118] I said to them: Because I do not want him to circumcise my son. I prefer R. Solomon Senior and if my teacher will come I will have to allow him to circumcise [my son]. Then I saw a room in my house open on the right wall and there were two windows and Rabbi Joseph Karo z"l was sitting there and praying with us. He came over to respectfully greet me. We exchanged greetings and he came over to where I was sitting and led me to the eastern wall of the house. We were alone. He said to me: You are occupied with circumcising your son. At the same time, the king is sending his viceroy to destroy and pillage the city. At this time the viceroy or his *Qadi* is entering [the city]. Therefore, see if you can annul this evil decree with the power of the kabbalistic wisdom which you possess. I then prayed with uplifted hands and said: May it be your will, Lord God and God of my fathers, that you will see before you the sacrificial blood of my son, whom I will circumcise today, as the blood of the sacrifices on the altar, and so forth, and you will have mercy on your people Israel and on this city, and so forth. And I awoke.

(55). The twenty-second of *Tevet* 5371 [1611]. I saw in a dream that I opened the phylactery for the head and I saw the verse "To the end that you and your children may endure etc., over the earth" [Dt 11:21]. The final *zadi*[119] had changed into the letter *qaf* and a drop of ink covered it. I scraped it away and revealed the letter *qaf* and was astonished. How had this escaped my teacher z"l who had seen it and not told me of this defect? I took a knife and scraped the top of the letter *qaf* and was left with a final *zadi*. And I awoke.

I fell asleep and had a second dream that this final *zadi* was the *yud nun* of Cain,[120] which is the good which is in Cain, the union of *Abba* and *Imma*. Because of Cain's sin, who sinned with them, as is known, they were back to back, as is known, in the final *zadi* and then the *kelippot* held sway over them, which is the *qaf*,[121] and they were changed to a *qaf*, which is the first letter of Cain. Not only that, but the darkness held sway there and this was the drop of ink. I began to repair the fault of Cain in *Abba* and *Imma*. All that was left for me to repair was in the *Zeir Anpin*. I forgot this matter after I awoke. It seems to me that they also told me that the soul and *haya"h*[122] of [the world of] *Asiyyah* had already come to me and I was repairing them of Cain's fault mentioned above.

(56). Monday night, the fourth of *Adar* 5373 [1613]. R. Moses Mizrahi the scribe[123] dreamed that he was in a study hall and an old man was sitting on a mat and 300 students were standing around him. The old man looked just like me and he was teaching with his eyes closed, just as I do. He asked about him and they told him: This is Hillel the Elder. He was surprised that he was sitting on a mat. They answered him that he was similarly a poor man in this world. He was speaking in a whisper far from the old man with three of the people standing near him and said to them: This old man looks exactly like the sage, Rabbi Hayyim Vital. Then the old man answered him from the distance and said to him: Why are you surprised at this? Know that his soul is nobler than mine. They then led him to the study hall of Rabbi

Judah the Prince z"l and showed him his limitless wealth and greatness; but he did not see him [Rabbi Judah].

Almost a year before this, he also had a dream where he saw me and he asked me about it. I also saw the same thing in a dream and I told him that on two Friday nights I had dreams with Elijah z"l.

Part Three

───── THE DREAMS OF OTHERS ─────

These are the dreams of others.

1. 5339 [1579]. In Jerusalem, a gentile builder came to me and said to me: I dreamed last night that a spring of fresh water came out from the wall of the house in which you are now living and provided water for the whole world, even for gentiles.

2. An important judge who had rented his house to me also came to see me early in the morning, riding on his horse. He said to me: This whole night I did not sleep because of the marvelous dream I had this night. I have come to see if there is any change to my house:

I saw in my dream that I entered [the house] and saw in it many couches of silk, silver, and gold. All the walls were built of precious stones and pearls, sparkling like the sun and out of the southern wall there flowed a spring of fresh water which provided water for the whole world, even for gentiles.

3. A Jewish woman who fasted all her life also told me: In a dream last night I saw Sheikh Abd al-Nabih, the greatest judge in Jerusalem, who had died this year after he had taken [the grave of] the prophet Samuel for the Muslims from the Jews.[1] He said to me: Take these keys from my hands. They are the keys of the Temple. Until now we have had dominion over it, but now that you have come, dominion over the Temple has been given to you. Therefore, here are the keys. Take them, for they are yours henceforth. I took them and went with many Jews and we built the Temple, purified it, and offered the obligatory sacrifices.

4. One day I was debating with an important judge through an interpreter and he entreated me that I should endeavor to learn Arabic so that he should not have to hear my words through an interpreter. I agreed to do so. The next morning, Rabbi Isaac Hadidah z"l, a disciple of my teacher z"l, came to see me. He said

to me: I was very amazed that I saw our teacher z"l talking to me in a dream. When he was ready to leave, I said to him: Why do you not give me some message to tell your beloved disciple R. Hayyim? He said to me: You reminded me: Go and tell him that he should be very careful for his Soul and not learn Arabic, because Heaven does not want him to learn this language. Heaven forbid, that he should come to some danger through direct disputation with them, without an interpreter.

5. 5346 [1586]. In Safed, R. S. ben Kai'm asked a dream question about my comprehension. They responded to him: "If you showed yourself slack in time of trouble, wanting in power" [Prv 24:10]. It was shown to me that the meaning of these words was that I should regularly teach others.

6. R. Jacob Mas'ud the blind also asked a dream question about the above and they responded to him with the following two verses: "And as My Presence passes by, etc., and you will see My back, etc." [Ex 33:22–23]. He again asked a dream question on a different night and they answered him: The answer to what you asked about R. Hayyim is hinted at in the letter *Tav*[2] and the letter *Vav*[3] in the alphabetical list of "Happy are those whose way is blameless" [Ps 119:1]. He told me that this response was a dream within a dream and when he awoke his lips were speaking the above response.

7. 5358 [1598]. In Damascus. Sa'adat dreamed that she saw a woman who walked with her to the synagogue for the *minha* prayer. There were many people there. She said to them with great anger: Why do you not wait until all the people of the land will gather and you will pray together? Sa'adat said to her: Who are you that you are not afraid to insult all these people in a loud voice? She said to her: I am the woman who married Rabbi Hayyim the Kabbalist in Egypt. She walked on, to the gate of the city. Sa'adat told her: There is an agreement that no woman should go outside the city gate except to accompany someone who has died. She said: Look up and see. She looked and saw a large coffin, the length of two men, floating along in the air. A voice emanated from the coffin and said to her: Sa'adat, go to

Rabbi Ḥayyim the Kabbalist and say to him: The wisdom that God has given to him was not given to him alone, but in order that he should disseminate it to other people and return them in repentance. Why does he desist from preaching to the people to return them [to repentance]? I, the one who speaks, am Joshua ben Nun, the disciple of Moses Our Teacher a"h. Tell him all these things in my name.

8. 5359 [1599]. The above-mentioned Sa'adat dreamed that she was in a field and she saw seven sages pass by and each was carrying a torah scroll in his arm. Following them she saw my wife Ḥannah walking close to the last of the seven sages, and she was carrying in her arms three large books of the modern type, and they were not torah scrolls. She asked her: Where are you all going? She responded: We are going to Mount Carmel to pray there. [Sa'adat] said to her: Who are these? She said: The first one is the sage the Ashkenazi, the teacher of my husband Rabbi Ḥayyim and he is the greatest of them. The others are Rabbi Joseph Karo, Rabbi Joseph Sagis, Rabbi Jacob Berab[4] the great, Rabbi Joseph Sajjah,[5] and she did not remember the name of the sixth one. The seventh and last one is Rabbi Moses Sa'adiah, my father, and therefore I walk close to him. These three books which I am carrying are books of wisdom which my husband, Rabbi Ḥayyim, wrote in this world. I was his helper and caretaker; therefore I have been given my reward in the world to come.

Afterwards, my teacher z"l turned to her and told her: Sa'adat, go and ask your neighbor Rabbi Ḥayyim the Kabbalist, in my name: Why are his lips sealed from preaching his wisdom to the masses to return them in repentance and why is he so arrogant about his wisdom, since his youngest son who will come from his loins will be a greater scholar than he?[6]

9. 5367 [1607]. On Thursday night, R. Benjamin the cantor dreamed that he saw an extremely old man who said to him: Why do you sin every day, when Rabbi Ḥayyim the Kabbalist enters the synagogue and you do not stand up? He is a great man in Israel and you do not recognize his attributes. This sage is my relative and know that if henceforth you will not repair this sin, you will be punished. Therefore, early in the morning awake and go

115

to his house, kiss his hands and feet, and beg his forgiveness for what you did in the past. He said to him: Who are you? He responded: I am Elijah the Prophet. And he awoke.

10. The daughter of Joseph Sajjah[7] dreamed that she saw me dressed in a garment, green like parsley, with a similar green turban on my head, and I was sitting on a chair. She was being told: This is the king of Israel and when three years have elapsed from today, he will be king over all Israel.

11. *Rosh Ḥodesh Kislev.* R. Caleb Pinto dreamed that he saw Rabbi Jacob Aliyah and he begged him to send regards to me in his name and he should tell me that I am very important in Heaven and the Messiah loves me very much and always prays for me before God.

12. [The twelfth of] *Iyyar.* Rachel the Ashkenazi dreamed that she was sitting in Safed on her balcony, where I had lived. She saw me flying and descending from Heaven and I landed there. I told her about the greatness of the status which I had there and the great visions which I had seen there. While I was there I was given a key and told: Go to a certain treasure which is here, which has not been opened since the creation of the world, and open it with this key, since only you have permission to open it. I went there with a great angel who had been sent to show me the place where the treasure was. I saw a great sage there who had died 500 years previously and he said to me: I would advise you not to open it now, because they will detain you here with it and you will not be given permission to descend to the mundane world. I advise you this out of my great love for you. If you are afraid of not fulfilling your mission, give me the key. I will stand here as if I am occupied in opening it and I will tarry here for a while. Then you will come to open it since no other person in the world has permission to open it.

I listened to his advice and descended to this world.

13. 5368 [1608]. Saturday night, the twenty-ninth of *Tammuz,* R. Elijah Amiel dreamed that we were in Safed. I said to him: Come with me, since I want to gather all the *zaddiqim* and we will go to the Temple. First we went to the cave of R. Judah bar Ilai and he was handsome, fat, and stout. He said to me: Go over to my

master. I went there and I saw ten sages studying with him. From
there to R. Yose of Yokrat. From there to Hillel and Shammai and
R. Simeon bar Yohai and his son R. Eleazar, R. Yose ben Kisma
and R. Pinehas ben Yair. From there to R. Yose the Galilean and I
found him writing a torah scroll. He said: Wait for me while I
write these three words, and they are: "The Lord will battle for
you" [Ex 14:14]. From there to R. Jonathan ben Uzziel and from
there I returned to Safed to Hosea ben Be'eiri. And Rabbi Joseph
Karo, Rabbi Solomon Alkabez, Rabbi Moses Cordovero, Rabbi
Jacob Goivizo, Rabbi Eleazar Azikri,[8] my father z"l, and with them
was Rabbi Moses Galante,[9] who was still alive. From there to
Rabbi Johanan ben Zakkai, Rabbi Akiva, and Rabbi Meir. From
there to Jonah ben Amitai. From there to Rabbi Judah the Prince
who looked like my teacher, Rabbi Moses Alshekh z"l. From there
to Joseph the Righteous, Joshua ben Nun, Eleazar and Ithamar,
the seventy elders [of the Torah], and Caleb ben Yefuneh. From
there to Gad the seer. From there to Adam, Abraham, Isaac, and
Jacob. These four were not buried in the earth, but were sleeping
in a cave and [there was] a very large torch before Adam alone.
Innumerable lights and flames were incorporated in the large
flame of the torch, from top to bottom. R. Elijah asked me: What
are these flames? These are the Souls of all the *zaddiqim* which are
incorporated in the Soul of Adam, which is a torch itself and they
appear like lights before the torch.[10]

From there we went with all the above-mentioned righteous to
the Temple. There was a cave under the Temple and a very old
man was there. I did not tell R. Elijah his name. My teacher z"l,
the Ashkenazi, sat with him. My teacher z"l said: Bring Jacob
Abulafia before us. Rabbi Eleazar Azikri and Rabbi Moses
Galante went and brought him there. All the righteous were
dressed in white and I was also dressed in a white wool garment.
The above-mentioned Jacob came dressed in black garments and
had a black veil over his head, face, and beard. My teacher commanded the two sages who had brought him to remove his black
garment and dress him in a small white garment which reached
only to his thighs. They did so. However, he told them to leave
the veil since the time to remove it had not yet come. Afterwards,

my teacher z"l commanded me to go to Haggai the prophet and he should write me a document in his hand concerning everything that had occurred. We went and found him in a cave, sitting on a bench with a candle burning before him. He wrote it in his own hand and put it into my hand. Haggai remained in the cave and did not come with me to the Temple as had the other above-mentioned *zaddiqim*. While I was still speaking with him, R. Elijah went and told my teacher z"l how the document was written and signed. Then the old man who was sitting there opened his mouth and said to R. Elijah: Go and tell R. Hayyim that he should be sure to remember and not forget the things we spoke about two days ago on Friday night in a certain synagogue and he promised me to fulfill. They are things he is required to do. I was still with Haggai and from there I heard everything the old man said, since the cave of Haggai was close to the Temple. I said: I will do so. I placed my hands on my head like one who promises to fulfill the matter.

"He awoke: It was a dream!"[11]

On the following Sabbath, before dawn, R. Jacob Abulafia was walking around the synagogue and studying *Mishnah*. All of a sudden, someone removed his black garment from him. Since he had not put his hands through the sleeves, he did not feel who took it. He turned around and did not see him. There were also three other people there, but they saw nothing. On the third Friday, he made peace with me. He accepted upon himself to come with his disciple for a half hour every day, so that I would explain to him a little bit of the *Zohar*, in its plain meaning alone, and [the garment] was returned to him.

14. On the twenty-seventh of *Ab*, R. Isaac ben Nun, the cantor, had a dream on Friday night that he was going to Jawbar to pray in the synagogue for a service for the eve of *Rosh Hodesh* and he met a very elegant man, about forty years old, red-headed, tall and handsome. He said to him: What did the Sicilian congregation do to Rabbi Hayyim that he did not want to be their rabbi? He responded: We are already working on this matter to make peace. He said to him: If you knew the virtues of this sage, you would be at his door morning and night, to kiss his hands and

feet and to accept his authority. He said: As if we do not know that he is a great sage? He responded: The whole world knows that he is a great sage, but they do not know who he is. He said: Who is he? He pleaded with him until he responded. He said: He is the Messiah. I will bring you proof from the Torah, from the Prophets, from the Writings, and from the Talmud. From the Torah—from the verse which says, "And Lamech lived, etc." [Gn 5:28]. The letters of Lamech can be rearranged to spell *Melech* [king]. The verse continues, "and he begot a son" and it does not say "and he bore so and so" as it does in other places. The reason is that Noah is the Messiah.[12] If you turn the letter *het* on its side it will look like a *bet*. Therefore you find that "and he begot a son" is the same as if it said "and he begot Noah." Since he was not circumcised by a human,[13] he was called "son" *[ben]*. When the drop of blood was drawn at his circumcision by a person,[14] the *bet* had the strength to stand on its side and was changed to a *het,* corresponding to the circumcision which is performed on the eighth day.[15] Then he was called Noah. Not only that but the *nun* which is the last letter of *ben* moved to the front and became Noah, since the *nun* is the *nun* of *nahash* [serpent], which is the foreskin which was removed from him.[16] Since he is the Messiah of the generation of the Flood and the final generation, therefore it is written, "This one will provide consolation from our work" [Gn 5:29]—in the generation of the Flood "and from the toil of our hands" [ibid.]—in the final generation. In order to also hint at this there are two musical notes[17] for the word *zeh* [this one], to allude that this [*zeh*] Noah will console us with two redemptions. For the same reason, his name is doubled, Noah Noah [in Gn 6:9]. The doubling of his name also alludes to the above-mentioned, since Noah is Hayyim in the following way: The *m* of Hayyim, when spelled out, is *m"m*, which equals 80 in *gematria*; the two *yuds* added make 100, and the letter *het* is doubled, *het"het*, when pronounced in the Supernal world as you pronounce *heh, vav, mem, nun,* in the mundane world—thus it equals 116 in *gematria,* just like Noah Noah. At the time of the redemption of the final generation, the Messiah will be called Hayyim, and the *nun* of Noah

will no longer be mentioned, because it is the *nun* of serpent
[nahash] and of defeat *[nefilah]*. For this reason *nun* is not mentioned in the alphabetical Psalm 145,[18] as is known.

From the Prophets—as it is written, "For he shall produce that
excellent stone; it shall be greeted with shouts of Beautiful! *[hen]*
Beautiful! *[hen]*" [Zec 4:7] and they are the letters Noah. In the
generation of the Flood, the power of the *nun*, which is the serpent and the foreskin, was dominant over the letter *het*, which is
the circumcision. In the future, the power of the *het*, which is the
circumcision, will overcome the foreskin, which is the *nun* of
nahash [serpent]. This will be in the days of the Second Temple,
in the lifetime of Zechariah; however in the final redemption,
the *nun* of *nahash* will be completely neutralized and his name
will be Hayyim, as mentioned above.

From the Writings—as it is written, "while the sun lasts, may
his name endure *[yanon]*" [Ps 72:17]. *Yanon* in *gematria* equals
Noah and *hen hen*, and also Hayyim with the above-mentioned
methodology.

From the Talmud—it is written there, "with the footsteps
[ikvei] of the Messiah, arrogance will increase."[19] The meaning is:
The name of the Messiah is Hayyim, as mentioned above. The
letters of footsteps *[ikvei]* are the same letters rearranged as
Jacob Abulafia, my contemporary, whose arrogance increases
against Hayyim. Another hint is that this Jacob will be hindered
by the above-mentioned Hayyim, since the letter *qaf* of hindered
[yeaqev] when spelled out equals 100 in *gematria:* Therefore
Yaaqov [Jacob] is equivalent to *yeaqev* [hindered].[20] He gave that
man two myrtle branches to smell in order that he not forget this
dream.[21] And he awoke.

15. 5355 [1595]. Before I married my wife Jamilla, she lived in
Sinim. She saw in a dream that she ascended a long ladder from
her courtyard to the roof of her house with the son of her uncle,
Rabbi J. Cohen, at her bosom. When she was close to the roof a
very old man with a red and white beard appeared to her. He said
to her: Woman, if you do not now accept upon yourself to marry
Rabbi Hayyim the Kabbalist, I will throw you and the child to the
ground. She was crying, but the old man was not satisfied until

she vowed to do so. Later she came to live here in Damascus. One night, at the close of the Sabbath, she drank some of the wine from the goblet of wine for the *havdalah*, before anyone else could taste it, and stuck her head out the window, to hear the first voice she could hear.[22] She heard someone read the verse "It is a tree of life *[ḥayyim]* to those who grasp it, etc." [Prv 3:18]. Later, a gentile sorcerer entered her house one day and seeing her said to her unbidden: How lucky you are. For in the future you will marry a great sage, an old man whose name is Hayyim.

16. 5366 [1606]. R. Solomon Walensy dreamed that he was in Damascus, in the *Sephardi* synagogue on a public fast day, and his father z"l was sitting at the reader's desk. In the middle of the penitential prayers, the whole congregation was silent for more than an hour and they were all crying. R. Solomon asked them: What is this silence? There was no response. He asked his father and said to him: You descended from the Supernal world; tell me the reason. He responded: How can we pray to God, if the rabbi of this congregation, R. Jacob Abulafia, has been excommunicated in Heaven by Rabbi Hayyim the Kabbalist. How will the prayers of his congregation be heard? At this, they all cried.

17. 5367 [1606]. The night of *Rosh Hashanah*. Something happened at the fortress of Jumblatt[23] and all the inhabitants of the city concealed their valuables in a cave. R. Samuel Birvani had no place to conceal [his belongings] and he was very upset all night. Tomorrow, *Rosh Hashanah,* the enemy would enter the city. He dreamed that he was upset about this. In the dream, a man standing near him said to him: Do not be upset about this— "I will protect this city for My sake and for the sake of My servant David" [2 Kgs 20:6]. And who will bring David to Damascus to protect her? He said to him: Hayyim is David. He said: How is this? He said: David and Hayyim are of equal importance and in the *gematria* of minor numbers *[mispar katan]* they are equal.[24] He said to him: Who is this? He responded: This is Rabbi Hayyim the Kabbalist. And he awoke.

He had this dream a second time. And again four and five times.

In the morning the army sacked Damascus, but they did not

touch any of the houses of the Jews. Afterwards, on the second day of *Rosh Hashanah* they left. This R. Samuel had never spoken to me or visited my house. He was an understanding and God-fearing person, occupied himself with torah study, was reclusive, and discussed things faithfully.

18. 5368 [1608], the eighteenth of *Ellul.* Nehamah the daughter of Sayyad dreamed that she saw me seclude myself and I was dressed in fiery flames and great lights. This was because I was uttering holy names and reflecting on them.

19. On the twenty-fifth of *Ellul,* Friday night, the older wife of R. Benjamin Saruk dreamed that she heard many people saying: We will go and see the great level that Rabbi Hayyim the Kabbalist has attained. She went with them and saw me in a large house with beautiful couches and carpets, and there was a bed with gilded panels which is called *"Takhat"* in Arabic. Surrounding it were large burning wax torches and surrounding each torch were smaller candles which were attached to the larger torches and also burning. I was sitting on the bed, dressed in white garments, and the garments were very bright, white, and smooth as fingernails, just as the Talmudic sages said about Adam's garments.[25] I knew that the world was created on the twenty-fifth of *Ellul.*[26]

20. On the same night, my wife's aunt had the very same dream: That I was in a large field, sitting on the chair, and I was dressed in white garments, smooth as fingernails and bright as the sun, like the garments of Adam. All of Israel were coming there and bringing me letters and documents from all lands. The content of the letters was that they were all accepting me as their judge and leader. Among them were many disputants and I judged each of them as appropriate—this one with cautions, this one with lashes, and this one with death, and all in a small, still voice.[27] I sat silently and two dignitaries, dressed in green,[28] stood at my side, one to the right and the other to the left. These assistants issued the decrees and I sat silently, like a king. A tall person with a green turban brought me a letter from Sidon and gave it to me.[29] It contained matters similar to those mentioned above. They said to my wife's aunt: All the greatness this sage attained

came to him from Sidon and he was worthy of all this because he was satisfied with little and did not chase after luxuries.

21. On the twenty-ninth of *Ellul,* my son Samuel dreamed that I had a book of teachings by my teacher z"l and I did not allow him to read it. He said to me: Why do you not give it to me? I said to him: Look at the opposite wall. He looked and saw an old man whose face shone like the sun. He appeared and disappeared. He asked me if I also saw him. I told him: Such is the custom. I cannot see him, but you see him, like someone who consults a necromancer. I did not want to tell him who the old man was that appeared whenever I studied the teachings of this book. My son thought that he was the Ancient of Days [God]. Afterwards we went to a garden where there was a house and I entered, but he was not allowed to enter. He cried until he was allowed to enter. He entered and again saw the same sight as before when I read from the book and the old man stood opposite me.

22. 5369 [1609]. The fifth of *Tishrei.* My son Yose dreamed that he saw me with a large group of people and he was with another group of people nearby. One of the people who was with him said: Go, tell your father the following verse: "Harvest is past, Summer is gone, But we have not been saved" [Jer 8:20]. He came and told me. He returned and was asked: Did you tell him the verse? He said: I already told him. He again asked him: How did you tell him the verse—with amazement or quietly? He said: I told him quietly. He responded: If so, return and tell him the verse with amazement.

23. Friday night, the intermediate days of *Sukkot,* R. Caleb dreamed that he was in my house and a messenger came to me from Jerusalem with a letter in his hand. Written in it was: We have sent you several letters that you should come to Jerusalem. Why have you delayed? Hurry up and come. Indeed, you will not come until you leave behind the blind and lame and then gather the children of Israel and bring them with you to Jerusalem. I said to the messenger: I recognize that you were a dear friend. He said to me: Certainly, were I not your dearest friend in the world, I would not have been sent on this mission. R. Caleb asked me to explain the contents of the letter to him. I told him that

123

they were writing me that before I went to Jerusalem I should cause the people of Damascus to repent and to leave behind the remainder of Israelites who are blind and do not see the proper path or who are too lame to walk the paths of God.

24. On the seventh of *Heshvan,* my son Samuel dreamed that we were going to bring wheat to bake *matzot* for Passover. We were walking through a valley that was full of ups and downs, but had no vegetation. Then the whole path was full of thorns. He said to me: How will we be able to walk on the thorns? I said to him: I will mention a [divine] name and we will be able to walk. My daughter Azmi was walking in front of me with a green fig in her hand. I said to them that all the greatness of my wisdom was in that fig which was in her hand. There was a large river which paralleled the whole road on one side until we reached the source of the river. I sat there and took pieces of egg shell and nut shell and on each piece of shell I wrote a letter. The letters on the shells were the following: *ADHYKHTN*. There was a stone ladder there which reached to the sky and was perpendicular and not inclined. We were not able to ascend it. I mentioned a [divine] name and we ascended to the top where there was a large roof and a house in which were fragrances hidden from man. I always milled my own flour and I took one shell and milled it there. I took the flour and scattered it on the rest of the shells and they became long reeds. I returned to the ground. I planted the reeds in the ground at the source of the river. The reeds had many knots, as is customary with reeds; however, these knots were red. I said to my son: Leave here and hide so these people will not see you. He entered a garden and mentioned a [divine] name and a tree split open by itself and he hid in it. The people went to seek him. He left the tree and took some grapes from a good vine which he found there, took out the seeds from the grapes, sowed them, and wheat sprouted. I became very angry with him. Why did you teach this wisdom to these people? He took bad grapes from another bad vine which was there, took out their seeds, and threw them at the sprouting wheat. And they dried up. We returned to the source and I took some of the milled nut shells and threw them on the reeds and wheat for

Passover sprouted. They said to me: With what power do you cause this wheat to sprout? I said to them: Rabbi Eliezer was also adept in planting cucumbers. They said to me: Rabbi Eliezer did it only temporarily through illusion and not in reality as you did.[30] I said to them: I do as Rabbi Akiva did. He created real cakes and delicacies and ate them. Everything else he ate was also created in this manner. Rabbi Akiva always cleaves to me and all my wisdom is from him and it is his power which causes this wheat to sprout. Then the earth at the source split and Gehazi, Elisha's servant, emerged. My son asked him: You are a leper, since these reeds are your bones and the knots are the leprosy which is in them—how were you able to rise? He told him: I already know that what your father is doing is to raise the dead. Then I said to him: But you are one of the four ordinary people who have no share in the World to Come.[31] He said to me: Your son Samuel will give an answer on my behalf. My son said to me: Father, you have already told me that there are several types of World to Come. With regard to what the Talmudic sages said about four ordinary people, who are Gehazi and his children, that they have no share [in the World to Come]? I would say: They will not arise [from the dead] by themselves, like the other dead; however, if you plant these reeds which are his bones and organs again in order to raise him from the dead and the appropriate time has arrived, perhaps he will rise.

Then Gehazi entered the garden and sat there. Afterwards, the earth again was split and Og the king of Bashan emerged. My son said to him: You are a completely evil person and you tried to kill all of Israel with the stone you threw on top of them—how were you worthy of being resurrected?[32] He said to him: Even so, look at the covenant which was inscribed in my flesh by Abraham, the leader of the circumcised, who was more righteous than all the *mohelim* in Israel.[33] Therefore I was worthy to be resurrected. Your father knows me. He said to him: My father was born in this generation; how does he know you? He responded: Your father was one of the three who overlapped [the history of] the world; they are Ahijah the Shilonite, King David a"h, and Elijah z"l.[34] My son thought that I was Ahijah. Og said to him: Why did your father sow so little wheat and not more? I can swallow all this wheat in one gulp. I said to him: You cannot eat even one kernel of the wheat which I planted! I took a kernel the size of an almond, wrote a [divine] name on it, and gave it to him. He put it in his mouth and he started to bleed and he could not eat it. Then Og pleaded with me that I should also give him a place where he can remain and I gave him a small plot in the garden, as I had given Gehazi. He entered and sat there.

25. On the twenty-third of *Heshvan,* my son Samuel dreamed that I, he, my son Yose, R. Caleb, and Musa Najjar were walking in a meadow until we reached a very large garden, surrounded by a marble wall. There was one entrance with an old rotted door. I wanted to enter. R. Caleb said to me: There is another entrance which is better. We went there and there was a new door of elm which emitted a terrible odor. I opened it and entered. The whole garden was full of all the varieties of fruit trees found in the world. They were so tall they reached the heaven's and even their leaves had a wonderful fragrance. All the barks of the trees were white. We went further in the garden and came to an incredibly tall ladder, built of stones, with a banister on both sides. At the top of the ladder was the closed door to an attic. Near the door was a window without a shutter, but it had a wood lattice over it. R. Caleb said to me: An old man whose name is Ephraim dwells in this attic, but it is not appropriate to enter until he awakens from his sleep. My son Samuel ascended the ladder to the top. From there he grasped some of the branches of the high trees and entered through the spaces in the lattice, until he was halfway in. The old man grasped him and helped him enter completely. He saw the old man standing on beautiful couches and on his head was a turban of a greenish color. Samuel opened the door from within and R. Caleb ascended. He returned and told me: The old man is sick and is sleeping. Then Samuel begged the old man that he should also open the window and the door completely and show himself to us, so that we will believe that he is not sleeping. He did as he was asked. We then all ascended and sat there with him.

The old man said to Samuel: Give them something to eat.

Samuel descended and gathered leaves and fruits from the trees of the garden. He put them before us. He put three leaves before me and put a fig on the first leaf, an apple on the second, and a pear on the third. Before R. Caleb, he put only one leaf with grapes on it. I do not remember what he gave the others. I ate from the fig and the pear which were on the right and left, but I did not eat from the apple, which was in the middle. Afterwards, I said: Let everyone leave and I will remain alone with my son Samuel and the old man. I alone spoke to the old man in a whisper. Those who had left were hanging on to the branches of the trees opposite, hoping to hear what we were saying. My son said to them: While my father and the old man are talking, come with me and I will show you a nice garden. He did this so that they should not hear our conversation. He took them out the first door, the old one, and took them into another garden in which there were lovely trees like those in the first garden. He left them there and he returned to the first garden and ascended to the top of the wall. From there he saw them going deeper into the garden where there were only grasses. They said to him: Why did you deceive us and bring us to this garden, whose entrance seemed as nice as the first garden, but now only has grasses? He said to them: I did this in order that you should not hear what my father was discussing with the old man. Afterwards, the old man revealed to Samuel some of the secrets that we had discussed together. I was upset because I did not want him to reveal them to him. Samuel woke up and it was a dream.

[26] (25). The twenty-fifth of *Heshvan*. R. Nissim Cohen dreamed that a group of people came from Constantinople to Damascus and they stayed in a certain place. They asked him: Do you know R. Hayyim the Kabbalist? He said to them: Yes. They said to him: You do not know how great he is. Among the group was a great scholar, handsome, red-haired, with blue eyes. He said to R. Nissim and two other people: Recite the prayer after a bad dream for me.[35] He began in a loud voice: May He who blessed Abraham, Isaac, and so forth, also bless so and so. Before he could mention his name he became agitated and was unable to mention it. They said to him: Perhaps his name is Abraham?

He said: No. They continued to mention other names, and he said: No, until he gathered his strength and said: May He bless Rabbi Hayyim the Kabbalist, and so forth. Afterwards, the son of the above-mentioned sage stood up and said: I want to bless him a second time with more force and more clearly. He said in a loud voice: "May He who blessed Abraham, etc., may He bless Rabbi Hayyim the Kabbalist." Afterwards, the sage and his son said to the people who were standing there: Know that we only came here from a distant land on account of the sage, Rabbi Hayyim the Kabbalist.

[27] (26). On the fifth of *Kislev* R. Nissim dreamed that he was being sent to tell me [something] and he was too lazy to tell me the dream.

Afterwards, the night of the fifth of *Kislev* he dreamed that he was being rebuked for not telling me. They were also flogging him and saying to him: Tell him that he should go and live in Jerusalem, in any event. He said to them: How can he go when he is afraid of the *Sanjak*,[36] the ruler of the city? They said to him: He should not fear any harm. If he is afraid, take this golden plate which is in the shape of a T, with three corners, and each corner has a [divine] name written on it. He should put it on his forehead, like a diadem, and the middle corner will hang between his eyes. Give it to him and he will fear no harm. He then came to me in a dream and conveyed the above-mentioned message. I said to him: This is my whole desire, but what can I do when my wife hinders me? If she would not hinder me, I would go and take twenty-eight householders along with me to live in Jerusalem. And he awoke.

He did not remember what the three names were, only that the first was written with a *Shin*, the second with a *Dalet*, and the rest he forgot.

[28] (27). On the twentieth of *Teveth*, my wife's aunt dreamed that she saw me dressed in short white garments which were not nice and new and R. Jacob Abulafia was dressed in elegant garments. She was upset by this. There was a very important woman present, who was dressed in beautiful white garments, who said

to her: Do not be upset by this, for R. Hayyim has many elegant
and valuable garments, the likes of which are not found in the
world. Those are his primary garments and are truly beautiful.
These garments of R. Jacob appear elegant to the eye, but not
according to the truth. Indeed, since Rabbi Hayyim is too lazy to
preach in order to return the people to repentance, as a result he
is now not dressed in the important garments which he has.

[29] (28). On the eleventh of *Shevat,* R. Mordechai Cohen
dreamed that he saw Rabbi Samuel de Medina, the rabbi of
Salonika,[37] who told him: Take this message to Rabbi Hayyim the
Kabbalist and say to him: Why does he refrain from preaching
and returning the people to repentance and sit in a corner—is he
so important that he should leave the world in such a state? The
time has already come for the repair of the world and everything
depends on him, since he is the greatest one of this generation.
He already knows all this, and I should not have needed to
inform him.

He said to him: Will he listen to me? He will not believe and
pay attention to my words. He responded: Go and give him this
message and if he does not believe, tell him that if he wants I will
come and speak to him, if he desires in a dream or if he desires
while awake.

He said: If his excellency has been dead for this length of time,
how will you speak to him while awake? He said: What do you
care? Tell him these things and he already knows in what manner
I can speak to him while awake, if he so desires. Also, take this
book and give it to him and he will see how, at the beginning of
this book, this message is found there and how the repair of the
whole world depends on him. He brought it before me and it was
a very old book, of parchment like that on which phylacteries are
written, and the square script was very beautiful. He gave it to
me and conveyed the whole message. I said to him: Why do I
need this book? Do I not already know all this very well? He then
opened the book, but did not see this matter written there. I said
to him: The whole message is written at the beginning of this
book in an allusive and hidden manner and you are the one who
does not understand it. He said to me: I already know that all of

129

this is in a dream since the above-mentioned sage has been dead for a long time, but how does he speak to me while I am awake? Nevertheless, he gave me a response that I should give to him, since he is waiting for me to bring back the answer, and he also ordered me to tell his excellency that he should endeavor with all his strength to repair the world, without any laziness, for the time has already come and there is nobody else who can repair it. Do not worry if people do not listen to you, and do not fear or be afraid of any person in the world. Then I said to him: What can I do, if they do not want to listen to me? I am occupied with this thought all the time and I do not know what to do. And he awoke.

[30] (29). On the fifteenth of *Shevat*, Suleiman Raqaq dreamed that it was *Simhat Torah*, and he saw a sage riding on a white horse among the gentiles and he was amazed at this.[38] They said to him: This sage fasted sixteen fasts, and if he had fasted a seventeenth day, the Messiah would have come. The name of the sage was R. Moses Riki.[39] Afterwards, he saw me in the synagogue. They took out a torah scroll and read from it. Afterwards, I stood up and preached wondrous sermons which terrified the people. Later, I invited them to a large banquet and we ate together.

[31] (30). On the same night, R. Zadok the scribe dreamed that it was *Simhat Torah* as above and I was dressed in a white woolen garment in my house. I had a torah scroll which had a large crown on it and a wondrous covering. They were saying: We have never in our lives seen such a beautiful crown. I preached wondrous sermons to them. Afterwards, I escorted them to a lovely garden and I prepared a large banquet of stuffed chickens and loaves of bread for them there. They were saying: We have never eaten such a meal in our whole lives.

[32] (31). On that night, R. Caleb dreamed that we were studying in the Yeshiva and my teacher z"l, the Ashkenazi, came there and said to us: I wanted to teach you the meaning of "a *halakhah* from Moses on Sinai," ordinary *halakhah*, deduction, and tradition. He explained wondrous things. And he awoke.

He returned to sleep and saw how we were in a synagogue

studying Torah and there were more than 200 oil lamps burning, but their light was very dark. My teacher z"l returned and entered in great haste. R. Caleb said: I do not know why these lamps are so dark. My teacher said: I will repair their light. He stood up and repaired one large candelabra that was there, close to me. Then it was very bright. My teacher said: I do not need to repair all the lights that are here; since I repaired this large candelabra the other lights will be illumined by themselves.[40] So it was, as he had spoken.

[33] (32). On the twenty-fourth of *Shevat,* my son Samuel dreamed that two Turks came to my house and I closed the door. Then one of the boards fell off the door by itself, and they entered the house. They sat next to me and said: Fear not, for we are righteous Jews and we have come disguised as Turks in order that you will accept our words with joy and fulfill them. One was wearing a white turban and the other one had a green turban. I recognized that they had come to hear words of Torah from me, and I preached to them. In the course of the sermon I preached to them about the attributes of the firstborn and his importance before God. My son said to me: What is this attribute? I said to him: The Messiah is the firstborn and from his father's side he is of the tribe of Judah, though his mother's family is from the tribe of Reuben, the firstborn, even though a part of the birthright was given to Joseph. All of this is from the aspect of his body, but the aspect of his soul is from Joseph, who took the primary aspect of Reuben's birthright. He is also the firstborn to his mother Rachel. Then my son turned to the visitor with the green turban and said to him jokingly: I am my mother's firstborn. Perhaps the Messiah will come from me? He said to me: Perhaps it will be you or one of your descendants. Afterwards, he spoke to me and said: Know that we have come to you with a message from the old sage who lives in Jerusalem permanently and he loves you completely. Take this letter that has been sent to you. I said: I am acquainted with him and he is a dear friend. Is it possible that he is still alive? He said to me: Why are you surprised at this, and why is he not alive? I took the letter and read it. Many things in it were discussed at length. However, what he remembered was brief:

You, Rabbi Hayyim, already know what is thought about you in Heaven and how wonderful it is. You also know that the redemption will not come except through you. Therefore, it would be good if you would hasten to bring the redemption and receive a great reward. If you hesitate, the result will be that you will be forced by Heaven to do it, and then you will be forced to do it and will not receive a great reward. Indeed, it is impossible for the redemption to come except through you, whether of your own will or by coercion.

These were the words of the letter.

After I read the letter, the [visitor] in the green turban repeated the message orally, exactly as it had been written in the letter. His colleague said to him: Why do you have to tell all this? Does he not already know this very well? Afterwards, I gave them to eat and drink. And he awoke.

[34] (33). On the sixth of *Adar* I, R. Caleb saw me in a dream dressed in a red silk robe with a drawn sword in my hands and I was saying: "To impose retribution upon the nations, etc." [Ps 149:7].

[35] (34). On the fourteenth of *Adar* I, R. Caleb saw a certain deceased person in a dream and asked him: What do they say in Heaven about the redemption? I do not have permission to tell you. However, go to Rabbi Hayyim the Kabbalist and tell him the verse, "You have the thousand, O Solomon" [Sg 8:12], and he will tell you what he knows. In this verse, the time of redemption is hinted at, and just as Solomon built the first Temple, similarly, with the name of Solomon the Temple will be built in the future.

[36] (35). On the fourteenth of *Adar* II, R. Caleb saw my son Samuel in a dream and he had a long red beard, and he was amazed. I said to him: This son is a transmigration of my teacher z"l, the Ashkenazi, and he has now been transmigrated into him in order that I should teach him this wisdom, to repay him for what he taught me.

[37] (36). On the twentieth of *Adar* II, my son Samuel dreamed that it was the great Day of Judgment and Adam and Rabbi Akiva were judging all of humanity. They were sitting in the middle

room of my house near the windows and Baruch ben Neriah was their bailiff.[41]

Baruch was sitting in the outer room of my house and he was flogging R. Eliezer, R. Joshua, and R. Simeon bar Yoḥai, since no person is exempt from the Day of Judgment, as is known from the verse, "Why have you disturbed me and brought me up?" [1 Sm 28:15]. Afterwards, he flogged Haman the Agagite. My son was astonished: What merit did Haman have, to be judged next to the three great people mentioned? They responded: Because from one side of him, the one closest to them, Rabbi Samuel bar Shilat was descended and he was judged with them and not Haman himself as you think. Afterwards, they brought into the room a sage to be judged whom they called Ḥakhamim. He asked about him: Who is this? They said to him: "Who are the Sages [Ḥakhamim]?—R. Meir."[42] They judged him and he was acquitted. Then my son said something. R. Meir rebuked him. My son became angry. R. Meir said to him: I am amused with you, since we are all close in our Souls and we are all from one root. He spoke words of consolation to him. Then they judged Baruch ben Neriah and said to him: Previously, you were worthy to be called cursed, because of one thing, and afterwards you entered the category of blessed [baruch]—you need to accept punishment for the earlier time. Baruch said: Since I have already entered the category of blessed through my relative the prophet Jeremiah, everything that went previously has already been uprooted. Then they acquitted him from punishment.[43]

He asked them: Why is my father not sitting here with you, since he is the owner of this house? They said to him: Do you not know that he is Rabbi Akiva? Thus, it is as if he is sitting here himself. Furthermore, your father is also Adam who is standing here. He said to them: All the Souls are incorporated in Adam![44] They said to him: It is not the same—the other Souls are incorporated in a general way, but your father is Adam himself, from the most select and important aspect of him.

[38] (37). On the twenty-eighth of Adar II, Rachel Ashkenazi· saw in a dream that I was in a house and before me was a table laid out with books to study and I was eating a salad of radishes

and lettuce. She said to me: Why are you eating this? I told her: Radish and lettuce are never absent from my table and I always eat only vegetables.[45] She saw a large pile of straw and hay which was afire in my house, but it was not consumed. A light emanated from the fire which illuminated me and the house with a great light. She was astonished at the sight and asked me: What is the meaning of this? I said to her: This is what Scripture says, "The house of Jacob shall be fire, etc. and the house of Esau shall be straw, etc." [Ob 1:18]. She said to me: You quote me a verse as it is written, but I see that it is a literal reality.

[39] (38). On the third of *Nisan,* R. Caleb dreamed that I was sitting in my house and teaching wondrous secrets to the people who were there, concerning the verse "The glory of this latter house shall be greater than that of the former one, etc." [Hg 2:9]. During the lecture I said: "Let everyone leave me!" [Gn 45:1]. They all left and he was left alone with me. He said to me: Why did you order this? I said to him: Did you not see these who entered? He looked up and saw two women dressed in white, of equal height. He asked me: Who are they? I said to him: The one on the right is Leah and the one on the left is Rachel. He looked up to gaze at their faces and his eyes were dimmed, since splendorous rays of light, like the rays of the sun, emanated from their faces. I stood up before them. Leah spoke to me and said: We have come to plead with you to empathize with the pain of Rachel who has now been betrothed to the evil Esau and she is in great pain. Therefore, increase your prayers for her to God that she should be freed from his dominion and the redemption should come soon.

R. Caleb wept greatly at this and said: Originally, when Esau came to greet Jacob, Joseph stood in front of her, in order that he should not look at her at all[46]—and now, how has she been literally given over to him?

I seated myself on the ground and prayed and wept before God, with great tears and several varieties of bowing, prostration, and kneeling. I offered one prayer asking God, may He be blessed, that He should hasten the redemption of Israel and that He should rescue Rachel from the dominion of the evil Esau, and so forth. Then we saw someone, but do not remember who it was. He said to us: Do not cry too much, since this is the month of *Nisan*. Then I ended my prayer. The two women went on their way. When they first came before me it was from the west and their faces were toward the east, and I was sitting in the south of my house.

This dream occurred literally at dawn. He awoke in the midst of crying and his eyes were full of tears. From there he came to my house for the morning prayers.

40. The intermediate days of Passover. R. S. Hayyati dreamed that people were coming to me to repent. I would say to them: Know that I was only born into this world to cause people to repent and all the Souls which have been repaired will be left with me and the Souls that have not yet been purified will return to Heaven to be refined and distilled until they will be repaired.

41. On the twentieth of *Nisan*, R. Joseph Segura dreamed that he saw all the gentiles in Damascus gathering in groups and saying: The king of Israel has already been revealed and has undoubtedly come into the world. On that day, R. David Gavison left Egypt to come here. They were asking each other: Where did this idea originate? They said that ten of their sages gathered in one place and performed certain magic rituals and they comprehended intellectually that it was undoubtedly true. And he awoke.

He fell asleep again and awoke a second time, speaking the following verses: "His command runs swiftly. He lays down snow like fleece, etc. He tosses down, etc., He issues, etc., He issued his commands to Jacob, etc." [Ps 147:15–19]. And he awoke.

He fell asleep a third time and dreamed that he came to my house to tell me the first two dreams. I, R. Jacob Monides, and other people were in the synagogue. R. Jacob was saying to me: Give us a sign and wonder concerning the things that you are telling us. I became angry at them and said: As much as I am struggling on your behalf, for your benefit, and you do not believe me! Look and see what I wrote during the lifetime of my teacher z"l. Also, look at the names of the ten colleagues whom I will assemble in the future for this purpose. They looked and found their names. One of them was called Jacob Mishneh and he forgot the other names. R. Joseph Segura was amazed that Jacob Mishneh was worthy to be one of the ten. He said: This is only because he is very charitable and always invites visitors. Then I showed them in the same document, on another page, the name "Jacob Abulafia" and a line of blood was drawn around his name. I said to them: Know that as long as this one is drunk, he has no repair. Later, he told me the two dreams that he had dreamed, as mentioned above. And he awoke.

[42] (41). The same night, R. Nissim dreamed that he was traveling to Jerusalem with R. S. Ḥayyati. When they departed from Damascus, there was a large river and they entered a small boat to cross the river. A large wave rose up to sink the boat. They came across a small island in the middle of the river. The whole island was surrounded by a wooden wall similar to a nice porch and it had many windows open on all four sides, facing the river. They grabbed on to the wood of the wall and entered the island and were saved. They saw that the island was beautifully green with plants. They asked: Whose island is this? They were told: This is called the island of Hayyim the venerable. They saw a large palm tree growing in the middle of the island. I was there with R. Isaac Al-Latif and other people. I was saying: There are already nine people here, and if there were one more, we would be ten and able to recite the *kaddish*.[47]

[43] (42). On the twenty-second of *Nisan*, R. Nissim dreamed that he was asking a man about me, and the man said to him: If he will purify the chariot of Hezekiah, he will not fear anyone.

[44] (43). During *Iyyar*, R. Isaac Al-Latif dreamed that one day I fainted for about an hour. Innumerable old men and many women came to see me. The house was completely filled. They were all worried about me. Afterwards, I woke up and opened my eyes and I said to them: Know that my Soul has now ascended to the Throne of Glory and my Soul was sent back to this world in order that I should preach to you and lead you to repentance and acts of charity.

They all kissed my hand. Afterwards, my wife Jamilla came and removed my garment and dressed me in a fine white garment.

[45] (44). In the month of *Iyyar,* Mira, the sister of R. S. Hayyati, dreamed that she was in a village and she saw a long synagogue, of immeasurable length and splendor, which was filled
with an endless number of people wearing *zizit* and *tefillin,* who
were praying with seriousness and awe. At the end of the synagogue was a window and there was a very tall man there, attired
in *zizit* and *tefillin.* In the midst of the prayers, a Heavenly voice
was heard, which said: Charity, charity, charity and "Charity
saves from death" [Prv 10:2; 11:4]. Afterwards, she saw two
guards grab R. Jacob Abulafia, from the right and left, to bring
him to judgment. His father, R. Solomon, and his uncle, R. Abraham, cried out and said: He is not guilty, since the people of
Damascus are evil and he was not able to reprove them. Then the
above-mentioned sage turned to them with great anger and
rebuke and said: You are telling falsehoods, since the whole sin is
his responsibility. The above-mentioned Jacob broke away from
them. Another ten guards came to seek him, but they did not
find him. One of the guards raised his hand and took hold of his
beard[48] and said: Even if he will hide in the most hidden place, I
will bring him from there, for he has caused an evil decree to
befall this city for a reason that cannot be cleansed and the
decree stands before you.

They lifted their eyes Heavenward and a great darkness, thunder, noises, and catapult stones descended and shook the world.
Then Rabbi Moses Cordovero, Rabbi Elisha Gallico,[49] and his
brother, Rabbi Mordechai, all tried to plead for him. Then the
above-mentioned sage screamed at them, and said to them: There
is no flattery or partiality in this world, and the truth is that the
whole sin is his responsibility, since he did not rebuke them. And
she awoke. That week the plague raged terribly in the city.

[46] (45). On the ninth of *Tammuz,* Merhavah, the wife of R. S.
Hayyati, dreamed that she was walking in a field. She saw a doorway and she entered a very large garden and the trees there
smelled of myrrh and aloe wood. There were also many beautiful
houses there. A wondrous thing. Pools of water flowed in the
garden and ornamental fountains emerged from them, flowing
with water. Around the pools were many benches for people to

sit upon. She did not see anyone in the whole garden and she entered all the houses to see what was inside of them. She looked up and saw an important woman, lovely and fat, sitting in a high attic. She said to her: How did you enter this garden, which no person has permission to enter? Then she thought to herself: Who is the owner of this splendid garden? She heard a voice say: This garden is the place of Rabbi Hayyim the Kabbalist, but she did not see from where the voice emanated. In a short time, she saw me standing next to her, and I was saying to her: Here, this is the true place.

[47] (46). On Friday night, the eighth of *Ab*, Mira, the sister of the above-mentioned R. S. Hayyati,[50] reported that she saw in a dream, R. Mordechai who had died, Rabbi Moses Cordovero, Rabbi David ibn Zimra,[51] and Rabbi Moses Baruch, her husband, standing at the end of the small street on which she and I lived. Her husband was very angry with her and said to her: Why were you lazy with regard to the message that I sent you in the month of *Iyyar*? She said to him: R. Jacob Abulafia has gone to Safed. He said to her with great anger: What is it to us, if he is here or in Safed? Go and tell your neighbor Rabbi Hayyim the Kabbalist that until now we have endeavored to find merit for the inhabitants of this city. Look at the sweat that is pouring from us, which testifies to our exertions. Yet, our prayers are not able to defend them from the abundance of sins that are in its midst.

[48] (47). On the eleventh of *Ab*, my son Samuel dreamed that I sent my daughter to buy cucumbers. She returned immediately and said: Red, yellow, green. I said to her: Are the three kings of the demons coming to my house? I saw the three kings of the demons enter the door of my house, the red, the white, and the green. They did not enter erect, but were seated and dragging along on their shanks. First their feet entered, then their bodies, and they sat inside near the door. Then I bowed to them three times. The red one liked Samuel very much. Samuel said to him: This week we asked the demons called rulers of the mirror and they told us such and such, as is mentioned in the treatise on matters concerning my Soul, in section 23.[52] Afterwards, Samuel again turned to him and said: It was not so, but with an angel

called Zadkiel. He said to him: It is so, since each of the seven kings of the demons has an angel appointed over him. Then I asked him: Why have you come to me now? He said to me: When you brought down the above-mentioned angel you did not sin, since you desired to know the things you asked of him. However, you did sin in that you did not believe him when he told you that you are required to return the people in penance and you did not fulfill his words. Know that all the words of the angel are truthful and it is he who sent us to speak of these things to you, in his name. Then the white king also opened his mouth and said: Until now I have been silent, but know that everything which that king told you is true and certain. If you do not want to believe him, you should know what will happen to you! However, the green king did not speak at all. The red king was dressed in a handsome red wool garment. The white king was dressed in a fine garment of white wool and the green king was dressed in a green silk garment. Indeed, the white king was very short. Afterwards, the red king went with Samuel to the bakery in our neighborhood and said to the owner: Give Rabbi Ḥayyim a loaf of bread and he did not want to do so. He came close to hurt him and then he kissed his feet and gave him the bread which they brought to me. Then the white and green ones disappeared leaving only the red one. He said to us: If you wish, I will give you a sign that all of the above is true. Then we descended into the pit which was in the courtyard and at the bottom of the pit was a hole. We exited from there and we entered a lovely house with fine couches and many windows. Each window opened to a different direction and they exited to the place that one wished to go. We went out one window and we went to the Mediterranean Sea and in one corner of the sea there was a great darkness. In the midst of the darkness was a small hole, the size of a pomegranate, and in it was a light, like a burning candle. There was a very large and deep pit there, without walls around the pit so that the waters of the sea should not enter. Despite this, the waters of the sea did not enter it. He said to him: You see this wonder? Know that through this path we ascend from beneath the earth, for there is our habitation. We ascended through this path when we came now to you to give you the message of the above-mentioned angel.

[49] (48). On the twelfth of *Ab*, the wife of Uziel, the beadle of the Sicilian synagogue who lived in the women's section of the synagogue, dreamed that she saw people cleaning and sweeping the streets that led to the Sicilian synagogue. She asked them and they told her: We are doing this in honor of Rabbi Hayyim the Kabbalist who is returning to be the leader and rabbi of the Sicilian community, as previously. She saw me enter the synagogue and about 200 people followed after me, dressed in white; after them, about 100 people dressed in *murado*,⁵³ and behind them about 80 people dressed in black. I and my son Samuel seated ourselves in our places near the Ark. The 200 dressed in white sat in front of us and those dressed in *murado* behind them and those dressed in black in the back, in the place of the mourners, near the door. Samuel said to me: Look and see how our places alone are elegantly decorated with golden weavings and all the walls of the synagogue are peeling. Ten deceased sages were sitting in front of me—seven from Safed and Rabbi Isaac Karo, Samuel Emron, and Rabbi Joseph Piso from Damascus. This woman said to her husband the beadle: Hurry and gather the whole Sicilian community, that they should come before these sages who have come. The sages said to him: We do not need you, since we have messengers to gather them. They sent a messenger to gather them. He returned and said to them: Isaac Ureibi is in the houses of the Christians collecting taxes, R. Hayyim Barur went to Aleppo, and the third, Joshua Shanina, is coming. The above-mentioned Joshua came with Israel D'ali alone. Joshua said: This synagogue is falling down and a ruin. I wish that it would be completely destroyed, since what can we do when the rest of the community does not come. Israel said: We do not have the ability to repair this destruction. Then the above-mentioned sages said: Since this community does not fear us, we will leave and other sages, stronger than us, will come and punish them.

The women's synagogue was also full of women and Rachel the Ashkenazi was there. The wife of Uziel said to her: How is it that Rabbi Isaac Karo was completely blind in this world and

R. Samuel Emron was blind in one eye and R. Joseph Piso was corpulent and now they are the complete opposite? She said to her: In the World to Come, all afflicted people are healed and similarly, whoever was fat in this world is skinny in the World to Come, by means of the Torah which weakens the person's corporeality.

Then I also left. The above-mentioned woman followed me. We saw a large kettle of boiling pitch over a fire in the courtyard and her husband Uziel was near the kettle. His wife asked him: What is this? He told her: This is for the scalding of the Sicilian community, because they did not want to return Rabbi Hayyim as their rabbi. Then her hand touched the kettle and a drop of pitch fell on her hand.

I went out of the courtyard and a completely white cow, without a hair of another color, was brought to me. A white spread, woven with silver, was on her. On top of it was a white pillow woven of silver. A plaited silken cord bound the pillow and cover to the cow.

An endless number of people were before me. She saw three people approach the cow and they had very wide sleeves, like the sleeves of the Arabs. These three people had no hands. The people were amazed at how the three people without hands would help me mount the cow. Then each one of them took out two large wings, like the wings of eagles, from their sleeves and they took me with their wings and mounted me on the cow. And I went.

The woman asked the women standing there: Where are they taking the rabbi? They told her: To Mount Carmel. We are all going to our houses now to get our nicest garments and will go with him.

She said to them: How is it that the wife of the rabbi is not going with him? They told her: She will ride on the animal and is standing at the door of her house, ready to go with him.

I went and there was a man in front of me whose name was Elijah Amiel and he had a long spear in his hand, at the top of which was a large flag woven of silver, like the flags of kings. He carried it and walked before me on the road mentioned above.

The sun rose and the cantor entered the synagogue and began

to recite the *Selihot* prayers, in a loud voice. She woke up from her sleep in great fear and heard the cantor say: God has heard, God has forgiven. She said: Amen, so may God say. She looked at her hand and saw a black drop, like pitch, and she remembered the drop of pitch she saw in her dream, as mentioned above. She washed her hand well and it came off.

[50] (49). On Friday night, the fifteenth of *Ab,* Merhava, the wife of R. S. Hayyati, dreamed that she saw herself in a certain place and she said to herself: This place is Tiberias. They said to her: Yes, it is. She saw that she was at the doorway to a synagogue, and it was crowded with a large congregation of Jews and a certain sage was standing and preaching to them. That sage and two other sages who were with him said: We are preaching to the masses in this Supernal world, and why does not Rabbi Hayyim the Kabbalist want to preach to the masses in the mundane world, to return people to penance? By not preaching to them, he is bringing great evil upon them. Someone got up and said: How can he preach to them if they do not wish to listen to him and fulfill his teachings? The above-mentioned sage said: It is true that they do not want to listen, but there are many other people who will listen to him.

Rain descended from the sky and it rained small black stones, like black hail instead of rain. They said to her: This is the black rain which descends because they are not listening to Rabbi Hayyim the Kabbalist.

[51] (50). That night, R. Jacob Abulafia came from Safed and confounded the penance. R. Joshua the teacher was then in the synagogue of the *Sephardim,* just before dawn. He was sitting there studying Torah half asleep, but almost awake.

He saw a very large spring pouring forth fresh water which flowed out of the synagogue through the door. He said by himself: This is what Scripture says: "A spring shall issue from the House of the Lord and shall water, and so forth" [Jl 4:18].

At the source of the spring, he saw a copper pot which was blocking the flow of the water. He said to those standing there: That which stops up the mouth of the abyss, that it should not ascend is a clay pot, as the [sages] z"l said concerning King David a"h, when he began to dig the pits.[54] Why has this clay pot been transformed into copper, which is called *"Nahash"* in Arabic? They told him: It is all the same. He again asked. They said to him: Go and ask Rabbi Hayyim the Kabbalist and he will tell you. He implored them very much and they told him: Clay pot *[heres]* and *Nahash* have the same numerical value in *mispar katan*. He said to me: Who is it that left the clay pot here? They said to him: Jacob Abulafia. However, know that the end will nonetheless be good and this spring will not be cut off. It will be good, since *Nahash* in *mispar katan* with the *kollel*[55] equals "good *[tov]*" in *gematria*. Afterwards:

[52] (51). On Friday night, the twenty-seventh of *Ellul,* when he was again half asleep, before dawn, in the above-mentioned synagogue, he again asked about the above-mentioned clay pot. They said to him: The name of Jacob Abulafia is also alluded to in all the above. Jacob, in *mispar katan* is *"Nahash"* in *gematria*. He said to them: How is it? They said to him: Already in Scripture, Jacob is written with a *vav*[56] and in *mispar katan* it equals *Nahash*.

[53] (52). *Rosh Hodesh Ellul*. The sister of R. S. Hayyati was expert in incantations with drops of oil in a goblet of water.

I asked: Will I succeed in causing the people of Damascus to repent? She responded: It is from God to implant penance in their hearts. Many people will repent, but not all of them, since their source is bitter and the evil inclination has been implanted in their hearts. Nonetheless, it is appropriate to cause them to repent, since it is not my obligation to finish the work.[57] There will be great disputes between the *Mustarabs* and the *Sephardim* and they will lose much money. The controversy has already started, but God has silenced it. Afterwards, the controversy will be very great, as mentioned above. An old and wealthy sage, who had seen children and grandchildren, will die. He will be a *Mustarab* of medium height. He will be sick for four or five days and die prior to the next *Rosh Hashanah* or earlier. After his death, the controversy will again be renewed, and afterwards the land will become quiet and they will be united.

I asked further: Where is my fortune? She said to me: All the days that I will be outside the land of Israel or here in Damascus,

I will not find any satisfaction, not for my Soul, not for my body, and not for my money. If I would go to Safed, I would have many times the satisfaction that I have in Damascus. Indeed, my fortune, in all of its details, exists only in Jerusalem, in my life, in this world and in the World to Come. God, all the Souls, and all the angels are angry with me that I am living here. Previously, I lived there, but I left because of the controversies and slander that occurred there. If I had not left, perhaps the redemption would already have come in my days. Indeed, all the people who sought to kill me have already died and if I went there now I would have an important position, great honor, wealth, and spiritual perfection. Not only that, but my tomb would be there. When I go there, my son Yose and three friends will go with me to visit the land and then will return to bring their households there. Eight householders will go to live there because of me and in a short time the number of householders will increase greatly to almost 500, from all places. As soon as I go there a certain very rich person from another land will send me overland a large gift by means of a messenger. Afterwards, he will come with three other wealthy persons and they will stand there with me and bestow great presents upon me. They will also bestow [gifts] upon the inhabitants of Jerusalem, for my sake. When they come, they will find a great commotion between Jews and gentiles concerning money, and they will quiet the above-mentioned commotion. This journey will take place sometime between today and seven months from now. In the eighth month the thought will suddenly enter my mind to go there, and there I will marry off my sons and daughters to people from other lands and not with the inhabitants of this land. From there I will write letters to all the lands. My words will not be wasted and they will send much money to rebuild the land upon its ruins. I will see signs and wonders there on the path to redemption, but concerning the redemption itself, these ministers do not have the power to know when it will occur. When I will be there, I will constantly give praises to God that he has taken me out of Damascus and the many troubles that will befall her in the future. Among them is that fire has broken out three times between the doorposts in my house in Damascus. We do not know from where the fire descended, but it could only be from Heaven. When I will be in Jerusalem, I will hear many times terrifying rumors that the nations are gathering to attack her, but it will all be empty talk, since peace and truth will be in my days.

[54] (53). The ninth of *Ellul.* Mazzal Tov, who divines over drops of oil, also heard a voice speaking to her. She told me that all the greatness of my zodiac sign is only in Jerusalem, in all respects—with regard to my complete comprehension of the wisdom, with regard to my livelihood, with regard to power and honor. The completion of my wisdom will be in the seventy-fifth year of my birth, and the days of my life will be 100 years. And there in Jerusalem will I be buried at the age of 100. I will have three male children from my wife Jamilla and Samuel will greatly increase in wisdom from the age of fifteen. The son who will be born this year will greatly exceed me in wisdom.

[55] (54). 5370 [1610]. On the first night of *Rosh Hashanah,* R. Jacob Romano who lived in Jerusalem saw in a dream a bridge built in the shape of a bow extending from the southeastern corner of the Temple Mount to the Mount of Olives, going over the Valley of Kidron and the Valley of Jehosaphat, and on this bow was a chair. He asked: For whom is this chair? They told him: God will sit in it to judge all the nations in this valley.[58]

He saw the valley was full of people wrapped in *zizit* and wearing *tefillin.* He saw me, Hayyim, coming from a distant place to this valley, and following me were innumerable numbers of people, like the sand of the sea, who were wearing *zizit* and *tefillin.* When I got there, I stood up like the prayer leader and prayed with the whole assembly and I said: "And He passed, etc."[59] and recited the thirteen attributes [Ex 34:6–7]. And he awoke.

[56] (55). The sixth of *Tishrei.* R. Baruch Fuleistro dreamed that he saw R. Isaiah Sini a"h entering my house [dressed] in white shrouds and a golden necklace. He sat opposite me and said: I have now come from Heaven with a message. Since they previously sent the spirit in the daughter of Raphael Anav to cause the people of Damascus to repent and they did not believe

him,[60] now I have come with that message, in a manner that they will not be able to deny. This is your sign: This book which is in my hands was written in Heaven. I looked at it, and it was written in a script we call "Rashi script" and the letters were gilded. He showed me that all the details of his mission, that they should return in penance, exactly as had been the mission of the spirit, were written in the book.

[57] (56). On Friday night, the second of *Heshvan,* my son Samuel dreamed that the Sea of Reeds was before him. It was very long, but not very wide. The waters split along the width and there was dry land between the two parts. On one side of the waters were two tribes of Jacob's children, Dan and Naphtali, with their whole armies in the water, next to the dry land that had split. Their two flags were in the hands of their ancestors, Dan and Naphtali. On the other side, next to the dry land, were two other tribes, Gad and Asher, with their armies. The two flags were in the hands of their ancestors, Gad and Asher, and they were also near the dry land. I was standing in the middle of the dry land and the flag of Judah was in my hand. I and the four tribes were traveling to leave there and we turned to one side of the water. R. Jacob Abulafia was standing opposite me on the dry land and his face was turned away from us, to go in the opposite direction, and in his hand was the flag of Joseph. My son asked me: Is he worthy to carry the flag of Joseph? They said to him: Even though he is not worthy, nonetheless, since he is a scholar he is carrying it. Indeed, he is walking in the opposite direction of all the tribes. And he awoke. Perhaps the solution of the dream is in the secret, "I, you, and the son of Jesse [the Messiah] will walk in Paradise."[61] He said, and who will lead, and so forth. He did not want to go and remained behind. Understand this.

[58] (57). Thursday night, the twentieth of *Tevet,* R. Joshua Al-Latif dreamed that the king decreed destruction on the *Sephardim* in Damascus, Heaven forbid. I got up before the Ark and said to them: All this has happened to you because you did not listen to my calls for repentance. Therefore, if you will come to hear my sermons and return in penance, it will be my respon-

sibility to remove this evil decree from you. They answered: We will not do and we will not listen.[62] Then the armies of the king entered the Jewish quarter and killed everyone they found. R. Jacob Abulafia and all the *Sephardim* with him hid in burrows under the earth. R. Joshua Al-Latif saw R. Benjamin Saruk hiding from house to house and "he came to entreat my favor"[63] that I should allow him to enter my house. I said to them: Since the decree has been decreed, I wish I could do so for the members of my family. R. Benjamin went to hide and R. Joshua Al-Latif went out to the fields. He saw R. Jacob Monidas there and said to him: Will you not admit that this whole decree came about because of R. Jacob Abulafia, when he prevented R. Hayyim the Kabbalist from causing them to repent? He said to him: Undoubtedly, it is so.

Rabbi Joshua Al-Latif fled to Safed. He saw the sages who were there secure and quiet and he said to them: How is it that the troubles of Damascus did not also befall you? They said to him: They sinned in that they listened to their rabbi, R. Jacob Abulafia, who prevented the sermons and rebukes of Rabbi Hayyim the Kabbalist, but not so us.

[59] (58). On Wednesday night, the nineteenth of *Tevet,* R. Joshua Al-Latif dreamed that a decree was issued by the king to destroy and uproot a third of the houses of the Jews who were in Damascus. This is the place called Tel[64]—"strip her, strip her to her very foundations" [Ps 137:7], and it should never be rebuilt, as a result of their many sins, "because their evil has become so great before the Lord."[65] He saw that they were destroyed in a moment to the foundations, and no memory remained of them.

[60] (59). On the twenty-fifth of *Tevet,* R. Caleb dreamed that we were in the street and an old sage came from Safed and said to me: What are you doing here? I said to him: Do you not know that I remain in this world to be the gatherer of all the communities? He said to me: If so, you are from the tribe of Dan.[66] I said to him: I am from another, more important, tribe, but I have come to gather all the communities.

[61] (60). On *Rosh Hodesh Shevat,* R. Caleb dreamed that I was in the street and I was much taller than the other people. They

were all amazed, since previously I had been short. R. Caleb said to them: Whoever wishes to see King Saul look at him, for this is he, since Saul was also taller than all the people.[67]

[62] (61). On Friday night, the twentieth of *Shevat,* my son Yose dreamed that he was in his house and heard a heraldic voice announcing: The king of Israel is passing and whoever is a Jew should come and accompany him. All who heard were coming and many thousands and tens of thousands of Jews were gathering. He also went out into the street and he saw many platoons, one following the other. One platoon carried swords, the next platoon carried spears, another platoon with bows, and a platoon carrying poles, that is, thick poles and clubs, and many platoons with all the varieties of weapons in the world. When he went out, he took with him a club made of gold. One man whose name was Isaac said to him: Why are you standing with this platoon? Go with the platoon in front of us who are carrying clubs. Then he went with them. He saw at the head of the whole procession a group of three people and the king of Israel was in the middle. He was about sixty years old and his beard was a mixture of black and white. I was on one side of him and another person on his other side, but he did not remember who he was. Behind the three of us came the whole throng mentioned above, platoon after platoon. He was told in this dream that the first group following the king and me were all members of King David's family. He saw that many of this army were prophets and righteous people of previous generations. There were also many people of this present generation. He recognized them all. Afterwards, when he awoke, he forgot them. He also said that he thought that the first city mentioned above was possibly Jerusalem, may it be rebuilt speedily in our days. He also said that Joshua the son of Nun was fat and a valiant warrior, his beard was black and his face was reddish, like an orange.

We were all on foot and did not ride on horses. There were many Muslims before us who were asking: What is the meaning of this great army? My son and others told them: This is the king of Israel. The gentiles said: The kingdom of Ishmael [Islam] has undoubtedly already fallen and Israel reigns, and they were silent. We passed before them and they did not say anything. The Jews were amazed that the gentiles were silent. I said to them: "But not a dog shall snarl at any of the Israelites" [Ex 11:7]. We walked until we came to a gate and entered a large courtyard belonging to the king of Israel. There was a porch there and it had an immeasurably tall ladder. We all ascended the ladder, and from there to other ladders, one above the other until we entered a large attic.

The dream then was transformed in the mind of my son Yose and he saw me sick on my bed on one side of the above-mentioned house and my wife Hannah a"h, sick on another bed in another side of the house. I said to him and to my son Judah, his brother: Go to Joshua ben Nun and ask him what is the reason that I became sick now and how will I be healed. They said to me: Where is he? I said to them: He is living in this city, in a certain house. They went there and gave him my message. Then Joshua quoted many verses from the Torah, the Prophets, and the Writings, and explained wondrous things and secrets and divine names which emanate from these verses through abbreviations of both first and final letters of the words *notarikon* and *gematria*. They said to him: We only came here so you could tell us how to heal our father from this illness. He said to them: These verses and divine names which I told you allude to his illness and his cure—how could you understand this? Go and tell him these things which I told you and he will understand these things on his own. They came and told me his response. They also told all this to my wife Hannah and she was very happy with this response. Go back and ask him: How is it possible in this age and also when he is living with us in this city that there should be among us a Jew, a certain person, who is a great magician and necromancer? They went. He said to them: This is surely no question, since in the period of the first king of Israel, King Saul, who himself eradicated all the necromancers from the land, later himself went to consult a spirit.[68] They returned and told me the answer. Then all of us, along with the king of Israel, descended via the above-mentioned ladders. At the bottom was a plain full of wondrous plants and lovely grasses. Horses, light as eagles,

149

were prepared for all of us and for the whole large crowd mentioned above, and we all rode on them. My sons were surprised at how the horses happened to be there now when they had not been there previously. We traveled on the road outside the city in order to travel to another city. In the middle of the road was a large river which was very wide. The whole army stopped at the edge of the river since they did not know how they would cross. I was at the side of the king, in front of the army, and I said to them: Was it not so with the Jordan, which split before the Israelites and they crossed on dry land? We will do the same—follow us. Then, the three of us, the king, I, and the other man mentioned above, who were in the first row, entered the waters of the river riding our horses. The waters split and the whole army followed us. We crossed the river on completely dry land to the other side. Then my son awoke from his sleep and he only remembered what I have written. Indeed, the dream was very long.

On the same night, R. Nissim Cohen dreamed that he saw a red-haired gentile soldier. He had a book in his hand, written in Arabic characters and in another place Hebrew characters. He said to him: Who are you? He responded: I am the son of the daughter of Muhammed, the prophet of the Muslims. I am a Jew and with me are five other colleagues, disciples of Rabbi Jacob Abulafia. We think that he is a greater sage than Rabbi Hayyim the Kabbalist. He said to them: Come with me to him and listen to his wisdom. They came to my house and heard explanations from me. They said: Now we know that there is a God in Israel and Torah in Israel. Therefore, we will remain all of our days with this sage. What was written in his book was: God is king, and so forth, and we were also praying God is king, and so forth. That night R. A. Hayyati dreamed that it was *Rosh Hashanah* and nobody knew how to blow the *shofar* and I got up and blew the *shofar*. The sound exploded throughout the whole city and they were amazed that a weak old man like me could blow with such great force.

R. Habib also dreamed that it was *Simhat Torah* and they were all praying in my house with great joy. They took out a torah scroll and many people read from it, and there were lovely couches throughout my house.

[63] (62). On the nineteenth of *Adar,* R. Benjamin Saruk dreamed that the viceroy sent four of his servants to take me to him. He was concerned with a question concerning the six signs that will occur in the future prior to the coming of the Messiah. Four of them had already arrived and he wanted to ask about the two signs that had not yet come. I was the only scholar in the generation who could know anything about them. He then said: I fear that I may bring great harm to R. Jacob Abulafia because of this, lest the viceroy ask about his evil actions toward me and I will tell him. Then he saw a very elegant old man approach him and say to him: Know that it has been decreed that three important people in this city will die this year and it is because they have thrown the honor of the Torah to the ground through two sages, Rabbi Ḥayyim and Rabbi Jacob Abulafia, because there is dissension between them. Each speaks evil about the other and my Torah is diminished among the ordinary people. R. Benjamin entreated him and said: "Refrain! How will Jacob survive? He is so small" [Am 7:5]. He said to him: If so, the decree will be that the inhabitants of Damascus will forfeit 3,000 piastres this year. The old man disappeared and he saw another man whose name was R. Moses, and he asked him: What happened to you that you were delayed? He responded: Because I had a dream with such and such an old man. He said: Is this something insignificant in your eyes? Then the above-mentioned old man returned and revealed himself to them. The two of them adjured him with a variety of oaths that he should tell me and R. Jacob Abulafia the above-mentioned dream. Afterwards, he again saw the other sage, whose name was R. Moses, and the old man was also with him. R. Benjamin told them the dream and they returned and adjured him many times that he should tell us the above-mentioned dream. He said to them: They will not believe me. They said to him: Take an oath on a torah scroll that you dreamed this. He said: I have never taken an oath on a torah scroll in my life. They said to him: If so, take an oath on God's name. He woke up and had the same dream six times. Finally, they told him: See, this dream is true. It is a dream that has been interpreted in a dream six times and also because it is an

early-morning dream.[69] There was also a third reason, but he forgot it. Then he brought the two of us together and made peace between us. And he awoke.

[64] (63). On the twenty-fourth of *Adar,* my son Samuel had a dream and he forgot it all. This is what he remembered: The Messiah had already come to Israel and we were all walking together, until we reached a large wide river. Its shores and the whole valley were green and fertile. They were all afraid to cross. We were riding on horses. Moses and Joshua were there. Moses was a very strong and handsome man. I said that I will begin to cross the river. Joshua said: I will begin. I said: No, I will begin since you are a descendant of Joseph and I am a priest and similarly, the priests crossed the Jordan before all Israel. My son said to me: Not so, since they stood in the Jordan until all of Israel had passed [Jos 3:17]. I said to him: Nonetheless, they crossed and entered before all of Israel. My son said to me: Will you cross before Joshua who split the Jordan? Joshua said to him: Be silent, since your father is also the greatest of his generation. Then I said: He crossed in his day and I will cross now in my day. Then Joshua became sad and tarried in the back. Then I begged him to come and when we reached the river, I went first into the waters of the Jordan and then the waters split and became dry land and we all crossed. Moses tarried and remained sitting in one spot. My son said to him: Why did you not cross earlier? He responded: Since my father died in this year and I am mourning him, I left it to your father to cross first, since it is his time. Then my son remained behind with him and the two of them crossed after all the people.

[65]. On the twenty-fifth of *Adar,* my son Abraham, may God protect and preserve him, was born. He became unconscious and we called him several times with the name Abraham until he awakened.

On the night of the twenty-seventh of *Adar,* R. Joseph Sajjah dreamed that he heard a disembodied voice say: How much has Rabbi Hayyim the Kabbalist exerted himself to return the people of Damascus in repentance and he was not able to do so. Now the venerable Rabbi Abraham ha-Levi has come and he will return them in repentance against their will and the redemption will come in his day. He said: It is written, "Behold I will send you Elijah the prophet" [Mal 3:23], who is of the tribe of Levi. They said to him: Elijah will change his name and will be called Abraham.

On the third of *Nisan* I circumcised my son and called him Abraham and I did not know about that dream at all. He also did not know that when he was born he became unconscious and he was called Abraham, as mentioned.

[66] (65). On the nineteenth of *Nisan*, Simḥah, the wife of Cuencas, saw her brother who had been dead for several years in a dream. In his hands was the front half of a slaughtered lamb without its forelegs. Behind him came a certain man. She asked her brother: Who is this man? He did not answer. Then the man said to her: I have come now to notify you that this decree is coming upon you because you did not listen to the voice of the spirit which God sent you in the daughter of Raphael Anav, to cause you to return to repentance,[70] nor to the voice of Rabbi Ḥayyim the Kabbalist. She said to him: If they repent now, will the decree be annulled? He said to her like a madman: Until they repent.

On that day, Rabbi Yom Tov Ariful, may his soul be in Paradise, the cantor of the community, died. Perhaps he was the slaughtered lamb.

67. On Monday night, the twenty-fourth of *Sivan*, 5370 [1610], R. Samuel Penzieri dreamed that it was *Yom Kippur* during the hour of *Neilah* and they began to recite the liturgical hymn "Awesome God of Deeds." I prepared a table for the whole congregation for the meal after the prayers. I said to them: After the meal I will show you the two tablets of the Ten Commandments. They lay at the end of the table and were covered with a shawl. R. Samuel, mentioned above, approached and lifted a corner of the shawl and he saw white stone tablets which looked like pure crystal and radiated a great light. He repented for what he had done so that what befell the people of Bet Shemesh when they looked into the Ark of the Lord should not befall him.[71] He saw them and their length was only that of a little finger. He asked me: The Talmudic sages said that the length of the Tablets was six handbreadths.[72] I said to him: Since we are

now in exile, their length has been diminished to only the length of a little finger.

68. On the day before *Rosh Hodesh Ab,* 5370 [1610], Rabbi Samuel Adajis, may God protect and preserve him, was in the synagogue of Jubair engaged in a vigil, fasting, wearing *talit* and *tefillin,* and a certain sage was preaching. He dozed off while he still sitting near the Ark. He saw a dignified man call to him: Samuel Adajis! He said: I am here. He said to him: You are a friend of the sage Rabbi Hayyim the Kabbalist? He responded: It is so. He said to him: If so, listen to what I will command you with an oath, that you will go this day, before you eat, to the house of the above-mentioned sage and say to him, why has he not overseen the repair of this land. He is to blame for the sin of not returning them to repentance. He caused all this because he does not pretend [to like] a few people who do not like him. For this reason they retard the repair of the land, because they think that with this they make him angry. He said to him: And if he humbles himself before them? He said to him: We find that the greatest sages of the generation humbled themselves before unworthy people in order to return them in penance, when they will see that he shows them a bright face. He is the greatest one of this generation and the greatness of his sin is related to his greatness. He does not endeavor to repair the whole world, for it all depends on him.

69. On the first night of *Rosh Hashanah,* 5371 [1610], my son Samuel dreamed that he was standing at the end of our street and he saw a very handsome, red-headed Muslim. On his forehead was a crown with a projection in the center, surrounded by a golden ring which looked like an open eye which shone as brightly as the sun. My son ran away to the entrance of our courtyard as I was going out. The Muslim said to me: What do you plan to do about that matter? You know that if you do not do it, you will suffer great harm. Do not be afraid of those leaders of the *Sephardi* community who advise you to do the opposite, like Gavison and others—do not listen to them and do not fear them at all, and so forth.

70. On the second night of *Rosh Hashanah* 5371 [1610], Rabbi

A. Najjar dreamed that he saw a sage but he did not recognize him. He gave him an open letter which was signed by many sages of previous generations. The signatures were at the top of the letter and the contents below the signatures. He said to him: Look and see who are the signatories. At the top he saw three signatures, one below the other. The first seemed to be that of *Rabban* Johanan ben Zakkai, or similar to it, [written] in a mystical alphabet. The second was that of *Rav* Yeivi Saba and the third Raba bar bar Hana. Below them were the signatures of a great many other scholars, whom he did not remember. He said to him: Take this letter and bring it to Rabbi Hayyim the Kabbalist and tell him to guard it well along with the other letter that he has, since he is obligated by it.

He woke up and told me this dream and I said to him: I do not want to accept the significance of dreams. He again had the same dream. The sage told him: In any event, go to him and tell everything mentioned above. This happened to him five or six times. He dreamed and awoke and it was all one dream. When he awoke he forgot the contents of the letter written below the signatures.

Part Four

—— THINGS MY TEACHER TOLD ——

ME ABOUT MY SOUL

These are the things that my teacher z"l told me which relate to me and the source of my Soul.

1. On *Rosh Hodesh Adar* in the year 5331 [1571], he told me that he began to attain his comprehension when he was in Egypt. There, he was told to come to the city of Safed because I, Hayyim, was living there, in order to teach me. He told me that he came to live in Safed, may it be rebuilt and reestablished speedily, only for me and for no other. Not only that, but the primary reason for his transmigration this time was only for my sake, to complete me. He did not come for his own needs, because he had no need to come.

He also told me that he was not required to teach any person other than myself and when I will have learned there will be no reason for him to remain in this world.

He also told me that the essence of my Soul was on a higher plane than numerous very exalted angels and I would be able to ascend with my Soul, by means of my deeds, higher than the firmament of *Aravot*.[1]

2. I asked him to inform me about my Soul, but he did not want to reveal all the details. Indeed, he told me the following in general terms:

Previously I was R. Vidal of Tolosa, author of *Sefer Maggid Mishneh,* and his name was the same as mine is now.[2] Afterwards, I transmigrated into a man named R. Joshua Soriano. He was wealthy, long-lived, charitable, and frequented the synagogue morning and evening. Afterwards, I transmigrated into a boy whose name was Abraham, a thirteen-year-old who died in his fourteenth year. Finally, I have come to this transmigration at this time and my name is Hayyim as was the name of the first Don Vidal, the author of the *Maggid Mishneh*. He told me that should I need to transmigrate again, the reason for this would be that in one of my earlier transmigrations I did not believe very much in the wisdom of the *Zohar*. From his words I understood that this was during the transmigration when I was the [author of the] *Maggid Mishneh*, but he did not want to reveal the matter.

He told me that the primary thing that I needed to repair in this transmigration was to occupy myself with the wisdom of the *Zohar*.

He also told me that when I was in the transmigration of the [author of the] *Maggid Mishneh*, I was a profound student of philosophy. Therefore, I have no desire to engage in the study of philosophy at present. He also told me that all these transmigrations are only from the aspect of my Animus *[Nefesh]*, but the aspects of Spirit *[Ruah]* and Soul *[Neshamah]* have different concerns from other transmigrations.[3]

3. He also told me that when I was thirteen years old, the Animus of R. Eleazar ben Arakh, the disciple of *Rabban* Johanan ben Zakkai z"l, was impregnated in me through the secret of impregnation.[4] Later, when I was twenty, the Animus of R. Eleazar ben Shammua, the disciple of R. Akiva z"l, was impregnated in me. Since he was one of the ten martyrs,[5] his merits were greater than those of R. Eleazar ben Arakh. Now, in the year 5331 [1571], when I am twenty-nine years old, the Spirit of Rabbi Akiva is hovering over me and surrounding me in order to be impregnated within me. From this it seems that his Animus is transmigrated in me, with my Animus.

4. Afterwards, on the first intermediate day of Passover, I went with him to a village called Akhbara and there, in the orchard, we entered the cave of R. Yannai. A stream flowed out of the entrance of the cave and the entrance was very narrow.

He told me that R. Yannai was not the only one buried there. However, R. Dostai and R. Nahorai are not buried there—as is stated in *Sefer Yihus Zaddiqim*.[6]

There, his Animus cleaved to the Animus of R. Yannai and in the course of his conversation, R. Yannai said to him: I am

R. Yannai, whose tomb this is. Know that thus has God, Blessed be He, said: Go and tell this man, Hayyim, who came with you that he should guard himself from gossip, tale bearing, and idle chatter. He should be very humble and I will be with him everywhere.

5. My teacher, the sage z"l, also told me on that day that my Animus also had a connection to and basis in the Animus of Moses our teacher a"h, since the whole collectivity of Souls was included in his, particularly the Souls of the *zaddiqim*. A part of my Animus was definitely from him, but he has not yet told me about the aspects of Spirit and Soul. This Animus then transmigrated several times until it transmigrated into *Rabban* Johanan ben Zakkai z"l and then into Rabbi Akiva z"l. It then transmigrated several more times until it transmigrated into Abbaye, called Nahmani, the colleague of Rava. He told me that this is the esoteric meaning of the Talmudic statement that three people lived for 120 years: Moses, *Rabban* Johanan ben Zakkai, and Rabbi Akiva.[7] Moses spent forty years in the house of Pharaoh, forty in Midian, and forty he sustained Israel. Similarly, *Rabban* Johanan ben Zakkai spent forty years in business, forty years he studied, and forty years he taught. Similarly, Rabbi Akiva: Forty years he was an ignoramus, forty he studied, and forty he taught. The transmigration afterwards into Abbaye was also hinted at in the Talmudic statement that *Rabban* Johanan ben Zakkai did not desist from [the study of] Scripture, *Mishnah*,...and the discussions of Abbaye and Ravah.[8] Understand this matter.

Afterwards, this Animus was embodied in one of the *Saboraim* called *Rav* Ahai, about whom the Talmud says "*Rav* Ahai objected."[9] He told me that it seemed to him that this *Rav* Ahai is the same *Rav* Ahai of Shabha who was the author of the *Sheiltot*. Afterwards, this Animus transmigrated into *Rav* Dostai Gaon. Several transmigrations then passed until it transmigrated into R. Aaron ha-Levi, the grandson of R. Zerahiah *ha-Levi*, the author of *ha-Maor*.[10] Afterwards, it transmigrated into the rabbi, the author of *Sefer Maggid Mishneh*. Afterwards, into R. Joshua Soriano. Afterwards, into a boy called Abraham, as mentioned. Afterwards, it transmigrated into me; I am now the young man Hayyim.

6. He told me that there was a close relationship to Maimonides z"l and therefore he wrote the commentary, *Maggid Mishneh*, on Maimonides' *Sefer Yad ha-Hazakah*, as is known.[11]

He told me the reason was that since R. Eleazar ben Arakh was a disciple of *Rabban* Johanan ben Zakkai, who is the source of my Animus as mentioned, he has therefore now come in the present to be impregnated in me when I was thirteen years old in order to complete what was deficient in his teacher *Rabban* Johanan ben Zakkai. He is now leading and helping me, because the disciple is obligated to preserve the honor of his teacher. R. Eleazar ben Shammua was also impregnated in me in my twenties, in order to complete the portion of R. Akiva his teacher, for the reason mentioned, because he was his disciple.

He told me that this is a sign that I am a transmigration of Rabbi Akiva. Whenever I see a group of people preparing to execute someone I run away, because my Animus remembers the anguish that it suffered when Rabbi Akiva z"l was killed. It is truly so. He also gave me another sign. When I was young, I had a great desire to study the *Pirke de R. Eliezer*.[12] The reason is that the author was the teacher of Rabbi Akiva.

He told me the reason was also that both *Rabban* Johanan ben Zakkai and Rabbi Akiva were both ignoramuses in their youths, in their first forty years—particularly Rabbi Akiva, who said, "If someone would give me a scholar, I will bite him like a donkey."[13] From this you can understand other things, that he was an ignoramus for forty years and certainly had youthful sins. He told me that the reason for this was because their Animus was an aspect of a drop of semen of the ten drops that Joseph exuded from between his ten fingers, as the Talmudic sages said.[14] Therefore, they were ignoramuses their first forty years and the evil forces were able to influence them somewhat, in those days. For this reason they had to transmigrate into all the transmigrations mentioned. For the reasons mentioned, such a great and holy Animus entered into R. Akiva, who was the descendant of a proselyte and was not of Israelite seed.[15] The reason is that it was a drop of semen that exuded from between his nails during the time he was tempted by his master's wife, as is known.[16] What the *Zohar* wrote in *Vayikra* [III], at the top of page 14b, is known—that it is difficult for proselytes to remove the filth from themselves even to the third generation. Afterwards, since R. Akiva was the son of a proselyte, it is certain that some of the evil still clung to him. He told me that since I am a transmigration of them, therefore that sin occurred to me, since they were connected to me on the day of my wedding and I remained connected to them for nine consecutive months and it was necessary that I have a nocturnal emission at that time. This occurred to me because I was from the drop of Joseph's semen, as mentioned, and because R. Akiva was the descendant of a proselyte, as mentioned, from whom it was difficult to remove the filth. There was also another reason: because of my great arrogance when I was a youth. Even though it was not apparent to other people, but only within my own thoughts, this caused the above-mentioned sin. As is known, "one sin leads to another sin."[17] He told me that these two above-mentioned things, the seminal emissions I had when I was joined, as mentioned, and also the matter of the great arrogance which I had when I was young, are the two sins that I have in this transmigration. They are the greatest sins I have during my whole lifetime and therefore I now need to repair them. To counter the arrogance I have to behave with humility to the utmost degree. I have to be careful not to have sexual relations until after midnight, because of the nocturnal emissions. I should remain on my stomach until the drops of semen have ceased completely and to talk little with my wife during intercourse. I should fast for eighty-four consecutive days, as mentioned by me concerning the repair of sins, see there. They are related to the eighty-four years that Jacob refrained from seminal emission, until he married Leah, who gave birth to Reuben.[18]

He also told me that because one of my previous transmigrations was someone who did not believe in the wisdom of the *Zohar*, I now needed to constantly occupy myself with the wisdom of the *Zohar*, to the extent of my ability. This is the primary thing that I need to do in this transmigration. He also told me that I

should not ask many questions about the *Zohar* until I had studied a certain period of time with him, for the above-mentioned
reason. Afterwards, I will have permission to question and ask
about anything I wish to investigate in the *Zohar.*

He also told me that I also have the sin of mockery in this
transmigration.

7. Later, he told me one day that the three above-mentioned
transmigrations which preceded me were required to transmigrate because of the sins which I will mention:

The primary reason that the rabbi, the [author of the] *Maggid
Mishneh,* transmigrated was because of his inadvertent transgression with regard to the sin of menstrual impurity. Therefore, he
was transmigrated into me to repair this sin. As a result, this sin
befell me. The first night of my marriage I did not immediately
separate from my wife when she saw the virginal blood after our
first intercourse. If this sin had not occurred to me, I would have
completed the years of the rabbi, the [author of the] *Maggid,*
who did not complete his years and died before his time. Forty-
four years were missing from his allotted lifespan, and I would
have added additional years. The above-mentioned sin occurred
to me, even though it was only virginal blood and is not such a
great sin, especially since it was accidental. Nonetheless, since
the whole purpose of my life was for this and I did not repair it,
therefore I only have these forty-four years alone, and this is the
secret of "Substance is swept away for lack of moderation, etc."
[Prv 13:23]. Heaven forbid that this is sufficient to balance the
previous sin concerning menstruation, since it was the primary
reason for my coming into the world, even though this current
sin is not entirely a sin.

He told me that it might be possible in the future that I will
repair this through repentance. Afterwards, I fasted for three
consecutive days, as I will write below, and then he told me that
this decree has already been abrogated, thank God.

8. Another thing occurred to the rabbi, the [author of the]
Maggid, for which he transmigrated, even though the primary
reason for his transmigration concerned the sin of menstrual
blood, as mentioned. Once, he had to decide a case concerning a

married woman and he allowed her to marry, making a mistake in judgment. He told me that I also erred in a similar manner. When I was a youth, a case came before my teacher, Rabbi Moses Alshekh, may God preserve him, concerning a married woman. We discussed the case and I told him that I was inclined to allow her to marry. He said that he was similarly disposed and permitted it. I made a mistake, since I did not consider the law sufficiently. He told me that this situation came before me in order to repair that sin. Had I considered it, I would not have made this mistake and would have repaired the past. In any event, another similar legal question will come before me in the future. A sage will ask my opinion and I will answer correctly. With this, the above-mentioned matter will have been repaired. The sin was not in the deed, but only in speech. Here too the matter depended on speech, in order to repair the previous defect.

The reason that R. Joshua Soriano transmigrated is that he once ate forbidden fat deliberately and with knowledge, and he did not guard himself [from this sin].[19] He told me that for this reason I am now repairing this sin. He pointed out to me that I sit for two hours with the porging of the meat and that I throw away almost twice as much meat as is necessary with the fat: Henceforth, I will also be careful for the rest of my life to only eat meat porged by a pious expert.

He also told me that the transmigration of R. Joshua Soriano was preceded by another transmigration of a man whose name was R. Saul Tristi. He committed one sin, which was: He was a *mohel* and early in his career he was not expert and a child died because of the circumcision. This was unintentional, but almost negligent. The sin with menstruation of the rabbi, the [author of the] *Maggid,* which preceded him, led to the shedding of blood, which was the sin of R. Saul Tristi. These two sins caused the deliberate sin of R. Joshua, into whom R. Saul transmigrated immediately after his death. We may conclude: The [sin of the] rabbi, the [author of the] *Maggid,* was unintentional; that of R. Saul after him was unintentional with some intent and that of R. Joshua after him, completely intentional—since "one sin leads to another sin."[20] He also gave me a sign that in this transmigration

I am very careful to distance myself from being a *mohel* or a slaughterer. On the contrary, I cannot even look when someone is being circumcised or an animal is being slaughtered. Occasionally, I am even careful not to kill fleas.[21] After R. Joshua, I was transmigrated into a youth whose name was Abraham, who died at the age of thirteen years, by divine punishment, because of the deliberate eating of the fat by the transmigration of R. Joshua.[22]

9. Afterwards, on the second Passover,[23] the fifteenth of *Iyyar,* he explained these matters to me more clearly. He said to me: Know that even though it says in the *Zohar* that Cain was the filth of the Serpent and Abel was from the side of Adam,[24] the meaning of this matter is as follows. As a result of Adam's sin, good became intermixed with evil and Cain and Abel emerged. Both were composed of good and evil, but the majority of Cain was evil from the filth of the Serpent, while the majority of Abel was from the side of Adam and the evil minority was from the side of the Serpent. However, the good part of Cain is a very great thing. The reason for this is that he was the firstborn and took the birthright of the good, as is mentioned in *Zohar, Bereshit,* [I] page 36b and throughout *[Tikkunei Zohar], Tikkun* 69. Afterwards, Cain began to be repaired through Kenan and Mehalalel, as is mentioned in *Zohar, Terumah* [II:168a]. Afterwards, when Jacob and Esau emerged, they were in the secret of Cain and Abel, and when they were born, Jacob was born "holding on to the heel of Esau" [Gn 25:26], which was the good of the birthright which Esau took, which was the good of Cain that was intermingled with the evil, as mentioned above, in the secret of "you shall strike at their heel" [Gn 3:15]. He was called Jacob on account of the heel which he took from [Esau].

Afterwards, when Issachar was born, he bequeathed to him the part of the good that he took from Esau, which was from Cain's good. Concerning that which is written, "And he lay with her that night" [Gn 30:16], it was Jacob himself who is called Jacob on account of the heel as mentioned,[25] and was given to Leah in the secret of union. Issachar was born from this union. This explains what is said in *Midrash Ruth,*[26] that Rabbi Akiva is a descendant of Issachar, who is the above-mentioned "heel."

Afterwards, he transmigrated into Nadav and Avihu, since they are two halves of one body, as is mentioned in *Zohar, Ahre Mot* [III:57b].

Afterwards, they were impregnated, through the secret of impregnation, in Pinehas, who is the prophet Elijah z"l,[27] until the time that he went to the cave. He lost them as a result of Jepthah's slander and prophecy disappeared from him. Afterwards, they returned to him in the cave of Mount Horeb, as is mentioned in the *Zohar*. During the time that they disappeared from Elijah z"l, they were transmigrated through the secret of transmigration into the prophet Samuel a"h. My teacher z"l told me that this is the reason that he was shown in a dream that my place in Paradise was the place of the prophet Samuel a"h.

Afterwards, they returned and were again impregnated in Elijah z"l. Then they were impregnated in the prophet Elisha z"l. Then they were transmigrated into Hezekiah, the king of Judah z"l. Later they were transmigrated into Mattathias, the High Priest, the Hasmonean. Later they were transmigrated into Akaviah ben Mehalalel, then into *Rabban* Johanan ben Zakkai, then into Akiva ben Joseph, then into *Rav* Yeivi Saba of *[Zohar] parshat Mishpatim,*[28] then into Abbaye. Then they were impregnated into *Rav* Ahai, who is mentioned in the Talmud, "*Rav* Ahai objected."[29] After this, in *Rav* Aha of Shabha *Gaon*, the author of the *Sheiltot*. Afterwards, it was transmigrated into *Rav* Dostai *Gaon*; then into R. Aaron ha-Levi, the grandson of R. Zerahiah ha-Levi, author of *ha-Maor*; then into Don Vidal of Tolosa, author of *Sefer Maggid Mishneh*; then into R. Saul Tristi; then into R. Joshua Soriano; then into a youth whose name was Abraham; then into me, the young Hayyim.

10. Afterwards, he told me at length about many people who are from the source of my Soul and all of them are from the aspect of my Animus. Furthermore, there are other people who are also from the aspect of my Animus. These are the ones mentioned in the Bible: Cain; Kenan; Mehalalel; Issachar; Shelah ben Judah; Nadav and Avihu; Yuval; Lamech his father; Nahshon ben Aminadav; Netanel ben Zoar; Korah; Dathan and Abiram;

Jethro; Pinehas; Othniel ben Kenaz; Carmi, the father of Akhan;
Shamgar ben Anat; Samson; Elkanah; the prophet Samuel;
Aviha ben Samuel; Hever the Kenite; Yael, the wife of Hever the
Kenite; Rahab the prostitute; Eli the priest; Aflal; Sismi; Hever,
the father of Sokho; Yishbah, the father of Ashtimoah; Yishuvei
Lehem; Jesse, the father of David; Avishai ben Zuriah; Shima, the
brother of David; Doeg and Ahitophel; Aviha ben Rehaboam;
Elijah the prophet z"l; Elisha the prophet; Jonah ben Amitai;
Hiel, of the house of Eli; Nabot the Jezreelite; Micah the Mur-
shatite; Nahum the Elkoshite; Hezekiah the king; Menashe, the
son of Hezekiah; Uriah the priest; Zechariayhu ben Yevarhiyahu;
Ezekiel; Elihu ben Berakhel, the Buzite; Hananiah, the friend of
Daniel; Nedaviah ben Yekhonia the king; Annani ben Elionai.
These are those who belonged to the *Tannaim*: Mattathias the
high priest the Hasmonean; Yose ben Johanan of Jerusalem; Nitai
the Arbelite; Akavia ben Mehalalel; *Rabban* Johanan ben Zakkai;
R. Akiva ben Joseph; R. Yose the Galilean; R. Nehorai Saba, [men-
tioned] in the *Zohar*, at the end of *Tezzave* [II:187a]; *Rav* Yeivi
Saba, [mentioned] in the [*Zohar*], *Mishpatim*; Jonathan ben Hyrcanus; Hananiah ben Hezekiah ben Garon; Aba Saul; R. Ishmael
ben Elisha, the High Priest; R. Huzpit the translator; R. Yose ben
Meshullam of the holy congregation [of Jerusalem]; R. Judah
ben R. Ilai; R. Ahi bar Yishai; *Rabban* Gamliel. My teacher z"l told
me that one of Rabbi Simeon bar Yohai's colleagues who is
found in the *Idra Rabba*[30] was from the source of my Animus. He
did not want to reveal him at that time nor did he want to explain
the reason.

There are also a few other *Tannaim* to whom I have some connection, but I do not know the explanation of the matter. They
are: *Rav* Shimai Hasidah, the teacher of the child prodigy of
[Zohar] parshat Balak;[31] R. Zadok the priest; R. Kisma, the father
of R. Yose ben Kisma; R. Krospodai *Hamud Libah,* in *Zohar,*
Shelah Leha [III:164b].

These are the *amoraim: Rav* Huna who was the Exilarch in
Babylonia during the time of Rabbi Judah the Prince, whose coffin was brought to Israel during the time of R. Hiyya; Judah and

Hezekiah, the sons of R. Hiyya; Levi bar Sisi; R. Simeon ben Yehozodok; *Rav* Yeivi Saba, *amora*, disciple of *Rav*, father of *Rav* Hana and also the father-in-law of Asian ben Nidvakh; Pinehas, the brother of Samuel; R. Miasha, during the time of R. Johanan;[32] R. Shila, of tractate *Berakhot* [58a], for whom the miracle occurred; *Rav* Yisa *amora*, and he is *Rav* Asi the priest; R. Zadok, the disciple of Rabbi Judah the Prince; R. Jeremiah bar Abba, during the period of Rav;[33] R. Helkiah bar Abba; *Rav* Shemen bar Abba; Mar Ukba; R. Zerikah; *Rav* Sahurah; R. Akiva the *amora*; Ula bar Koshav, during the time of R. Joshua ben Levi; Abbaye, who is called Nahmani; Rami bar Hama; *Rav* Bibi bar Aboi; *Rav* Dimi of Neharda'a; *Rav* Nihumi; *Rav* Mishrashia; Rami bar Ezekiel; *Rav* Yeimar; R. Samuel bar Shilat; R. Abin Nagra;[34] Nathan of Zuzita, the Exilarch;[35] R. Tanchum of Noi; *Rav* Yeiva, the father of *Rav* Sama and *Rav* Safra, during the days of Ravina; Rami bar Tamri;[36] Rapram bar Papa; R. Zeira bar Hillel; R. Zeiri of Dehabat;[37] Ravin and *Rav* Dimi, who left Babylonia for Israel; *Rav* Hana Begaditah; Shabhat, the son of Ravina;[38] *Rav* Hama bar Buzi; *Rav* Shisha, the son of *Rav* Idi; R. Hiyya of Dafti; Joshua bar Zarnoki, who is called in the Talmud Hiyya bar Zarnoki,[39] but this is a mistake; Io;[40] Avdimi; Bali;[41] *Rav* Judah Handoah;[42] *Rav* Tavyomi; *Rav* Malchio.[43]

These are the *Saboraim: Rav* Ahai; Ravah of Pumbeditha.

These are the *Geonim: Rav* Aha of Shabha; *Rav* Dostai *Gaon*; the first *Rav* Zemach *Gaon*, son of *Rav* Paltoi *Gaon*; the first *Rav* Nehilai *Gaon*.[44]

These are the *Posekim:* Rabbi Solomon ben Adret z"l; *Rabbenu* Aaron, the grandson of Rabbi Zerahiah ha-Levi z"l; Don Vidal of Tolosa, author of *Sefer Maggid Mishneh*; Rabbi Joseph Karo, author of *Sefer Bet Joseph*, [a commentary] on the *Turim*; my brother, R. Moses Vital; and me, the young Hayyim. Know that all of them are from my source in the aspect of the Animus, but many of them have a Spirit which comes from another source. Even Rabbi Akiva's Spirit was from another source. Only Abbaye had a Soul, Spirit, and Animus which were all from the same source as mine. We find that all of these transmigrations which I have mentioned, from Cain until me, Ḥayyim, are all only from the aspect of the Animus. Shabbatai, the hoarder of provisions,[45] is one of the *kelippot* of the source of my Animus.

11. He asked my Soul about my comprehension and it told him that I should fast for forty consecutive days, in sackcloth and ashes, and then I should fast the first Monday, Thursday, and Monday of each month for two and one-half years and then I will attain complete comprehension, without any admixture of the evil inclination, as occurs to others.

Another day he again asked and was told: I should spend a whole month in sackcloth, ashes, and fasting and I should behave humbly and not mock any person. He told me that the essence of my comprehension depends on these two things in particular, humility and refraining from mockery.

On another day he again asked and was told that it would not be possible to attain true comprehension like him, before the completion of the two and one-half years. Indeed, if during the above-mentioned period I would behave in a penitential manner and particularly if I would fast forty consecutive days in sackcloth and I would sleep in sackcloth every night, then divine inspiration will be awakened in me unexpectedly, about every three months. After the two and one-half years, I will truly attain comprehension, as he does. The reason for this period of time is that I spent two and one-half years in my youth without studying Torah and my deeds were not worthy and needed repair. Therefore, I needed another two and one-half years of repentance, equivalent to that period of time.

12. One day he again asked and was told that I should fast for forty consecutive days in sackcloth, ashes, and tears. In particular, I should sleep all forty nights on the ground dressed in sackcloth. I should also put a stone under my head and meditate on the name of God, which consists of the four letters of the Tetragrammaton.[46] Afterwards, I should fast on the first Monday, Thursday, and Monday of each month, with all the above-mentioned practices, until the completion of the two and one-half years. During this whole time I should behave with the utmost

modesty and humility and be extremely careful to abstain from anger and arrogance.

One day, he told me that I should be very careful, since according to what he was told, it is certain that in the course of time my thoughts will become confused and I will not want to suffer the burden of so much penance. Therefore, since the choice is in my hands, I should be very careful and strengthen myself in this matter.

One day he told me that during that week he saw a pure Spirit which encircled me and this showed that I would certainly be required to attain comprehension. Even though I pushed it away, I will be compelled by Heaven until I will attain, praise God, complete and true comprehension like him.

One day he said to me: Everything that I will attain in the future is because of my desire for it and because his Soul is helping me very much and it is almost as if he is impregnated in me. He said to me that there is a great closeness with him, particularly because once in a previous transmigration, I was his student just like now, and if I will cleave to him always with my thoughts, he will help me greatly.

13. One day he said to me that I should be very careful to recite "Hallelujah. I Praise the Lord with all my heart, etc." [Ps 111]. Afterwards, I should meditate on the divine name "MNZP"KH,"[47] and I should do this every night when I arise at midnight. It will greatly help me to attain comprehension.

He also told me that I should be very careful to always don the phylacteries which are according to the opinion of *Rabbenu Tam*.[48] They are the secret of the permutation of the divine name *YHHV*, which is derived from the first letters of "But only in this should one glory: In his earnest devotion to Me" [Jer 9:23]. Therefore, donning these phylacteries will be very helpful in attaining comprehension, understanding, and knowledge.[49]

He also told me that the essence of comprehension depends on the intentions of the person and his punctiliousness in reciting the blessings over foods. Through them he negates the power of those sparks of evil which are found in physical foods and cleave to the person who eats them. These blessings, when recited with proper intention, remove the sparks of evil from them and purify their physical aspect and make them pure and rational; I should be very careful with regard to this.

He also commanded me that I should be very careful to read regular sections of Bible, *Mishnah*, Talmud, and *Kabbalah* every day with the mystical intentions which have been transmitted to me, as is written in my book.[50] He also told me to be very stringent in observing and honoring the Sabbath, more than all other commandments.[51]

14. One day I was with him and I had neglected to perform any of the Unifications which he had arranged for me. He recognized this in my face and said: "If you will leave me for one day, I will leave you for two days."[52] You have caused great harm by this. You caused the Souls who wanted to cleave to you to separate themselves from you. I gave him the excuse that I only wanted to occupy myself with Torah during that time, particularly since those Souls did not come openly, as is appropriate. He responded that despite all this I should not refrain from performing these Unifications every day, because it is greater than studying Torah, since it unites the Supernal worlds and it is Torah study and Unification, all in one. He cautioned me that when I perform Unifications, my intention should not only be to attract the Soul, but to repair it above.

When I went with him to Tiberias, he also told me in Rabbi Akiva's cave that Rabbi Akiva said to him that I should mention Rabbi Akiva ten times consecutively before each of the three daily prayers. Through this he will become impregnated in me and will help me very much. He told me that there is no need to say "Rabbi Akiva," but Akiva alone [is sufficient].

He also told me that until the festival of *Sukkot* of the year 5334 [1573], I will need help and he will assist me during the time of Unification. However, after that time I will not need any assistance, since the two and one-half years that I sinned when I refrained from the study of Torah will have been completed. Previously, even if he had helped me it was haphazard, since it was impossible for it to be regular. However, henceforth it will be regular, praise God.

15. He also commanded me not to cease performing the Unifications which he transmitted to me. If I should go to prostrate myself on the graves of *zaddiqim*, I should do so on the eve of *Rosh Hodesh* or on the fifteenth of the month, because there is greater [spiritual] readiness on those days. I should not go on Sabbaths, festivals, or on *Rosh Hodesh*, because on those days their Souls ascend to Heaven and cannot be communed with on the grave. Once he sent me to the graves of the *zaddiqim* on the intermediate days of a festival to pray there, but I did not prostrate myself.

He told me concerning the Unification of the *Yuds* and *Vavs* of the thirteen "white parts of the head"[53] that I should perform it with greater regularity than the other Unifications. On weekday nights it should be after midnight because this is a time of grace. On Friday nights I would perform the Unification even before midnight, after the evening meal. On *Rosh Hodesh* I performed the Unification which is based on the divine name "*Shaddai*," since this Unification is the secret of *Rosh Hodesh*, because the name *Shaddai* equals *Rosh Hodesh*, when written in the expanded form of *gematria*. This Unification is good even for prostration on the graves of *zaddiqim* on *Rosh Hodesh*. The Unification of the verse "They are renewed every morning" [Lam 3:23] is also good for weekday nights after midnight, or on Friday nights before midnight, since both these times Leah spreads over the whole length of *Zeir Anpin*. Also, on Friday nights before midnight I should perform the Unification of the ten movements which are in *Da'at*. He also commanded me that every Friday night after the meal and the Grace after meals, before midnight, I should read tractate *Erubin*, in the secret of the *eruv* [Sabbath enclosure] and the secret of [the names of] 72 and 216.[54]

Know that the essence of all these Unifications, whether on the graves of *zaddiqim* or every night after midnight, even when not on the graves of *zaddiqim*, will help. After midnight is a time of grace and then it is the chosen time of all the hours.

16. He also told me that *Rav* Yeivi Saba was more connected to R. Joshua Soriano, who ate nonkosher fat, as mentioned.[55] If I will be able to repair this, *Rav* Yeivi Saba will be connected to me

more than the rest. *Rabban* Johanan ben Zakkai is connected with the rabbi, the [author of the] *Maggid*, with regard to the menstruating woman. Rabbi Akiva is more connected to R. Saul Tristi concerning the shedding of blood, as mentioned. The reason for this is because Rabbi Akiva sinned with regard to the deserted corpse which he carried on his shoulders several miles. The sages said to him that for every step he took he was shedding blood.[56] Therefore, he is connected to R. Saul. However, he did not want to reveal why with regard to the others, since the sages did not reveal it, but concerning Rabbi Akiva, the sages already revealed it and therefore he had permission to reveal it.

He also told me that he saw written on my forehead the verse "To think thoughts about making with gold" [Ex 31:4], an allusion to the sin of wasting time, which I wasted with the study of alchemy.

He also commanded me concerning the removal of the knife from the table [before the recitation of Grace after meals], that I should be very careful to remove it completely. Just to cover it is not sufficient, particularly since I come from the source of Cain, which is the secret of weapons.[57]

He also told me that in this transmigration I am repairing Yuval, who is from the source of my Animus and who sharpened iron and copper from the side of judgments and I did not repair him properly. Therefore, I unintentionally cut my hand or fingers when the knife is in my hands or through all iron utensils. He told me that the aspect of Yuval is the aspect of Cain, which is in the *Parzuf* of Jacob, because he too incorporates Cain and Abel and all the sources such as the *Zeir Anpin* which are called Israel and incorporates Cain and Abel, the first people. He is required to repair Yuval before the coming of the Messiah in the secret of "shall bring *[yovilu]* tribute to the Awesome One" [Ps 76:12]. This Yuval was impregnated in Moses a"h to be repaired by him, since Moses a"h also had some sparks of Cain. This is alluded to in the first letters of "The Lord was wrathful with me on your account" [Dt 3:26].[58] This is the secret of "Sending forth its roots by a stream *[Yuval]*" [Jer 17:8] since he has all the sources of Cain as are found in *Zeir Anpin*, as mentioned, since

Cain is the aspect of Cain in *Zeir*. Yuval is the aspect of Cain in the Supernal *Parzuf* which is called Jacob, as is known. We find that this Yuval begins to be repaired by Moses a"h, as is alluded to in the first letters of "The Lord was wrathful with me on your account" [Dt 3:26].

17. Once I went with my teacher z"l to the place where Rabbi Simeon bar Yohai and his colleagues gathered when they composed the *Idra Rabba*.[59] There, on the east side of the road, is a boulder with two large fissures in it. Rabbi Simeon bar Yohai sat in the fissure on the northern side during the Great Assembly. Rabbi Abba sat in the fissure that is on the southern side. Rabbi Eleazar sat next to a tree that is opposite the fissures and to the west of them. My teacher z"l sat in the northern fissure, in Rabbi Simeon bar Yohai's place, and I sat in the southern fissure, in Rabbi Abba's place, without knowing it. Afterwards, my teacher explained this matter to me. I did not know that one of the participants was from the source of my Soul. It was Rabbi Abba and therefore I sat in his place without knowing it. I am uncertain if it was not the reverse of what was mentioned with regard to our sitting in the above-mentioned two fissures.

He told me that when I was a child, I once cursed my mother a"h. He commanded me to fast for three consecutive days and nights and to be certain that it is for seventy-two hours. This is related to the two crowns of *Hasadim* and *Gevurot* of *Abba* and *Imma*, which are hidden in the three fathers, *Hesed, Gevurah*, and *Tiferet*, which are seventy-two, as is known, since the seventy-two letter name of God is incorporated in *Hesed, Gevurah*, and *Tiferet*. Since I damaged and caused these two crowns to be removed from the Supernal son, therefore I must concentrate on returning them to him through these seventy-two hours, which contain these three fasts.

He told me that I should fast these three days on the three days prior to *Shavuot*. I should also concentrate on the secret of "Be ready for the third day" [Ex 19:15],[60] because then the filth was removed from Israel and through this fast the filth of my physical being will be removed from me, in order to receive the knowledge of the secrets of the Torah on the night of *Shavuot*.

On the night of *Shavuot* I studied the secrets of the Torah with him the whole night and did not sleep at all that night.[61] He also told me that these three fasts will help me annul the decree of the forty-four years which were missing from the rabbi, the [author of the] *Maggid*, as mentioned above. See there.[62]

18. On the first day of the sixth week of counting the *Omer*, he told me that this week corresponds to *Yesod*,[63] as is known, and I should meditate on this and concentrate on repairing the defect which I caused during my honeymoon, as mentioned above.[64]

One day, I was fasting and crying greatly and I argued with God, saying: Why was he blocking me from the paths of repentance and had not inspired my teacher z"l to teach me what I desired, and many other such things. I went to his house and he recognized this matter in my face. He told me that the Supernal Tribunal had wanted to punish me for being insolent toward Heaven, had he not been able to defend me by saying that my intentions were positive. He told me that I should be very careful not to utter such things again, because "the cow desires to nurse more than the calf wishes to suckle."[65] However, there is a set time for everything, as is written: "A season is set for everything, a time for every experience, etc." [Eccl 3:1]. How could I possibly say that, Heaven forbid, God is hindering my repentance! On the contrary, who would have caused this awakening of repentance to enter my heart, were not God infinitely merciful to his creatures? He said to me that what prevented him from telling me everything I wanted to know was only for a set time and this time has now passed. From this day forward, he will no longer conceal from me anything about which I will ask him. He did so from then on.

19. He told me that in a previous transmigration I fulfilled the commandment of slaughtering. However, he warned me in the strongest terms that I should not slaughter at all in this transmigration. Not only that, but he also cautioned me not to kill any living being, not even lice or fleas.

He told me that since I am a new spark, I am required to fulfill the commandment of being fruitful and multiplying since I have not existed previously.

He told me that I am deficient in only eleven commandments, even though I am a new [spark]. After I have completed them, I will then need to fulfill the commandment of sending away the mother bird,[66] even though I had already fulfilled this command- ment in a previous transmigration. The commandment is the last of all the repairs [tikkunim] that I need to make. The intent of the matter is to teach that sending away the mother bird has already been repaired through the eleven commandments previously mentioned. Then the Spirit will come by itself and it will also be repaired. After it has been repaired, the Animus, which has already been repaired, will then also come and will be a throne for the repaired Spirit. Understand this very well and remember it, since this is an important source and do not forget it.

He told me that these eleven commandments are among those that are not far from me. He told me that one of them is the com- mandment of the foreleg, the cheeks, and the stomach.[67]

20. On another occasion he thoroughly explained the matter to me and said that there are both masculine positive and nega- tive commandments and feminine positive and negative com- mandments. There was not a single one of Adam's 248 limbs which is not composed of flesh, sinews, and bones. The flesh and bones are the positive commandments and the sinews are the negative commandments. The source of my soul is in Adam's left shoulder in the aspect of Leah which is in the back. The posi- tive commandments which are in this limb are eleven in number, like the value of *Vav Heh*, the last two letters of the Tetragram- maton, which has the numerical value of the word *qatef* [shoul- der], in the following way: *VYV* [22] times *HY* [15] equals 330; *VV* [12] times *HY* [15] equals 180, totalling 510. If you subtract 11, you are left with 500 [sic] which is the numerical value of *qatef*. The negative commandments equal 15 which is the same as *YH*, the first two letters of the Tetragrammaton. As my teacher wrote: *YH* with *shemi* [my name] equals 365, and *VH* with *zikhri* [my remembrance] equals 248.[68] They also equal *qatef* in *gema- tria*, in the following way: *YVD* [20] times *HY* [15] equals 300. *YVD* [20] times *HH* [10] equals 200. The total equals 500 which is equivalent to *qatef*. The ten that are hinted at in the letter *Yud* are

the ten masculine negative commandments and the five hinted at in the letter *Heh* are the five feminine negative commandments. The six hinted at in the letter *Vav* are the six masculine positive commandments and the five hinted at in the final *Heh* are the five feminine positive commandments. All the clarifications which are found in this limb are inscribed on the skin which covers the shoulder. The sage, may God preserve him, told me that with Cain's sin, my Animus descended to the heel. My father and teacher z"l raised me to the level of the navel by giving birth to me. I now need to repair and raise it to its original place. My teacher z"l did not convey to me the ten masculine negative commandments. However, the five feminine negative commandments are: 1. Do not murder [Ex 20:13], including not embarrassing one's friend publicly.[69] 2. Do not steal money [Ex 20:15]. 3. Do not cook a goat in its mother's milk [Ex 23:19, 34:26; Dt 14:21]. 4. Do not eat forbidden fat [Lv 3:17]. 5. Do not eat any blood [Lv 17:14]. The six masculine positive commandments are: 1. Let your brother live by your side [Lv 25:36], which is very close to the commandment of charity, which is to seek a means to enable your brother to live with you, as is known.[70] 2. To eat the second tithe in Jerusalem [Dt:12:17–18]. 3. To make a parapet for your roof [Dt 22:8]. 4. The commandment to be fruitful and multiply [Gn 8:17]. 5. To circumcise one's son and particularly to do it yourself. [Gn 17:10]. 6. "Love your fellow as yourself" [Lv 19:18]. The five feminine positive commandments are: 1. Lend to the poor. The evidence for this is: "If you lend money" [Ex 22:24]. Do not read *Im* [if], but read it as *Eim* [mother].[71] 2. The commandment of *zizit* [Nm 15:38], which includes putting them on the shoulder, since my source is from the shoulder. 3. Sending away the mother bird. The evidence is "Let the mother go" [Dt 22:7]. 4. The Sabbatical year [Lv 25:4]. 5. To remember the exodus from Egypt [Dt 16:3].

21. My teacher z"l cautioned me and all the colleagues in our group to be punctilious to accept upon ourselves the positive commandment of "Love your fellow as yourself" [Lv 19:18] every day before the morning prayers and we should have the intention of loving every member of the community of Israel as our own

Animus.[72] Through this, one's prayers will ascend combined with the prayers of all Israel and will be able to effect a repair above [in the Supernal realm]. In particular, the love of our colleagues should be such that each of us sees himself as if he was one of his friend's limbs. My teacher z"l emphasized this matter greatly. If any colleague should, Heaven forbid, be in a difficult situation or if anyone in his family is sick, we should participate in his troubles and pray for him; he should similarly participate with each of his colleagues in all his affairs.

In addition, my teacher z"l did not kill fleas, lice, or any insects at all. He told me that since the source of my Animus was from Cain who killed Abel and also since R. Saul Tristi was transmigrated in me because of the actual sin of shedding blood when he circumcised the child and it died, therefore I need to be very careful not to kill any living thing in the world and also not to slaughter at all.

I also performed a repair and fasted under my teacher's z"l direction for the transgression that occurred to me during my honeymoon when I had a seminal emission [in an improper context]; for the transgression of not honoring father and mother; for the nonkosher wine which I drank with a Jewish apostate who deceived me and told me that he had come to the city of Safed to return to the faith of Israel—this was only for show and he later returned to his evil ways; for the sin of arrogance; for laziness; for shedding blood, as mentioned; for neglecting the reading of the *Shema* and [wearing of] phylacteries.

My teacher z"l told me that since I am from the source of Cain who is the secret of the stern judgments which are called fire, therefore I become very excited and confused by the sight of water, because fire which enters water becomes extinguished. I am also very afraid of demons, because the demons were created through the birth of Cain, as is known.

22. He also told me that Cain is the secret of drawing and doing, while Abel is the Supernal breath of the mouth, which is speech.[73] Therefore, Abel is the source for preachers and orators. However, since I am from Cain, I am not a speaker or a man of

words. I have little eloquence, but I have more ability in drawing and practical work.

My teacher z"l told me that I am only required to memorize the Order Women *[Nashim]* of the *Mishnah* but I am not obligated in the other Orders.

He also told me that the correct days for me to fast two consecutive days according to the source of my Soul are Tuesday and Wednesday.

He also told me that there is no person who does not have one particular day during the week and the month which is an auspicious day for all things, since his luck depends on that day, according to the source of his Soul. On that day he is not afraid of any negative thing or malady and he will not die on that day. This is the secret of "repent a day before your death."[74] He is not afraid that he will die on that day and therefore can repent on that day, since there is a fear on all other days. He told me that the day of the week which is appropriate for me according to the source of my Soul is Monday and the day that is appropriate to me during the month is the thirteenth day of every month.

He also gave me another mystical intention in the *Kedushah* prayer and told me that even though every person needs to meditate on it, I need to do so more than any other person. There are three *Kedushah* prayers: First is the *Kedushah* of the morning *amidah;* second is the *Kedushah* of the afternoon *amidah*; third is the *Kedushah* of "*u-Vo le-Zion*" which we recite on Saturday night after the *amidah*. It was already known that the intention of the *Kedushah* is the jump by which *Malkhut* ascends from her place to receive knowledge *[Da'at]*, since her knowledge is weak and this is the secret of the small jumps we do when we say three times "Holy, Holy, Holy, etc.," as is mentioned in *Pirke Hekhalot*.[75] It was already known that every ascent is by means of the divine name of forty-two letters. Therefore, it is necessary to meditate on the *Kedushah* of the daily afternoon *amidah* with the first two letters of *ABGYT"Z*.[76] For the *Kedushah* of the daily morning *amidah* he should meditate on the two middle letters, GY. For the *Kedushah* of *u-Vo le-Zion* [To Zion shall come] on Saturday night, he should meditate on the last two letters, *TZ*. This [divine] name is the first one which incorporates the whole divine name of forty-two letters and is the essence of the forty-two-letter name, since it is in the secret of the *Sefirah* of *Hesed* which is spread through all of them, as is known. Therefore, all the intentions are with this divine name alone.

23. On another occasion, I asked my teacher z"l on a Friday about my Soul's comprehension. He quoted the verse "And for whom is all Israel yearning, if not for you" [1 Sm 9:20]. I pleaded with him to explain his words, but he did not want to explain more than this. I asked him if the meaning of his words was that I am from the source of King Saul, about whom this verse was said. He responded that he did not want to explain the intent of his words.

On another occasion, I again asked him about my Soul. He told me that I was able to comprehend more than the angels because of the great status of my Soul and when my Soul came into this world it was for the great need of the world. He could not explain more than this, since he had not been given permission to do so. If he had revealed the matter to me, I would have floated in the air from great joy over the matter, but he was not given permission to tell me then.

Rabbi J[oseph] Arzin z"l told me that late one Friday night he went to my teacher's house out of great jealousy. He had decided to ask why, though he was older than I, yet he was subservient to me and had to hear the teachings from me. He went to cry before my teacher z"l about this matter. He responded that he had come into the world only to teach me and all the other colleagues were not able to learn even one letter from him, but they all had to study with me. I also heard this directly from my teacher z"l. He also asked him that since there were people who were greater than the source of my Animus, how can they be subservient to me? He responded that the matter does not depend on this, but on the particular Animus of the person, which should be from a very high place.

Rabbi Y. Bagiliar, may God preserve him, also told me that my teacher z"l told him about my teacher's z"l closeness to me. The reason was that the three letters *AB"Y* are alluded to in the name Akiva and they are from below to above. He did not want to explain more than this to me. He also told him that concerning me it was written, "Only that shall happen which has happened" [Eccl 1:9], the abbreviation of which is "Moses." The meaning is, just as Rabbi Akiva taught Torah to 24,000 students and to the whole world, so will I now, praise God.

Once I was sitting before my teacher z"l after the third Sabbath meal and I implored him to explain to me the matters concerning my comprehension and the matters concerning the source of my Animus. In the course of conversation he quoted the verse "At scoffers, he scoffs, but to the lowly he shows grace" [Prv 3:34]. I implored him to explain the verse to me. He responded that the abbreviation of this verse is "Elijah lives." This is related to what is written in the *Raya Mehemna*,[77] that Moses was the teacher of all Israel and his interpreter was Aaron the Priest, as is written, "And he shall speak for you" [Ex 4:16], since Moses stuttered and had a speech impediment. In the future, in the generation of the Messiah, Moses a"h will return in a transmigration and will teach Torah to Israel. Then too, he will stutter and his interpreter will be Elijah z"l who lives and exists. He is Pinehas, the son of Aaron, Moses' brother.[78] Therefore, it is written, "At scoffers, he scoffs," because when Moses a"h will need an advocate and interpreter Elijah will be available, since he is alive; he is an advocate and will be his interpreter. He did not want to explain in more detail how this matter is connected to the first discussion we had.

On another day he told me that he was told in the course of his prayers that in the future I will see an angel and talk to him face to face. I implored him to tell me his name and he told me that it was Elijah z"l.

24. One day he told me, at that time a part of my Spirit began to sparkle within me, accidentally, by means of an addition to my Soul[79] every Friday afternoon for the two and one-half years mentioned above. This period lasted from *Rosh Hodesh Iyyar* 5331 [1571] until *Sukkot* of 5334 [1573]. Afterwards, I will acquire that portion of my Spirit completely and then I will attain complete

comprehension, praise God, as mentioned above. The reason is that the Animus only has the ability to fulfill commandments that are deeds. However, to complete the part of my comprehension dealing with knowledge of the Torah and the comprehension of the Divine Spirit requires the aspect of the Spirit and we find that my comprehension depends on my acquisition of this part of my Spirit permanently and completely, praise God. He told me that this spark of my part of the Spirit which will come is also in partnership with the spark of Rabbi Akiva's spirit and is clothed in it. The reason for this is that just as my Animus is also in literal partnership with the Animus of Rabbi Akiva through the process of transmigration, as will be explained below, similarly, the part of my Spirit is in literal partnership with the Spirit of Rabbi Akiva. When I will acquire my Spirit completely, then the Spirit of Rabbi Akiva will be in partnership with me. It appears that I first need to complete my Animus with the two and one-half years mentioned above, and after I complete it, I will be worthy to receive my Spirit and it will come into partnership with the Spirit of Rabbi Akiva. The Spirit cannot enter a person until the repair of the Animus has been completed, unless it comes by accident with the additional [Animus] on the eve of the Sabbath, but even this requires repentance and good deeds.

He told me that there is nobody who will be with me in the secret of transmigration of all those who are from my source, except for Rabbi Akiva, and he is truly with me in the secret of transmigration. However, the others who are from the source of my Soul, if they cleave to me, it is only through the secret of impregnation and not through the secret of transmigration.

25. On another occasion he told me that all those sparks of the people from the beginning of the progression of Rabbi Akiva's Animus until me, the young Ḥayyim, were all completely transmigrated into me and are partners with my Animus in this transmigration. It is possible that if I will be worthy of it, those who preceded Rabbi Akiva, like *Rabban* Johanan ben Zakkai z"l and others, will also be impregnated in me, but only through the secret of impregnation. The reason for this is that not all of the sparks of this source are as close to the spark of my Animus as is

the spark of Rabbi Akiva's Animus. The spark of my Animus is closer and nearer to him than any of the others and therefore, he was transmigrated into me more than all the other sparks. Just as the spark of the Animus of Rabbi Akiva ascended to the level called "Thought,"[80] I am similarly able to ascend, according to my deeds, to much greater heights than many of the sparks which preceded me.

He told me that my Animus and the Animus of Rabbi Akiva are next to each other in the source of the Animi. Indeed, Rabbi Akiva only partakes of the side of Cain in the aspect of Animus alone, since his Spirit from the aspect of Cain which would have been appropriate to his Animus was not taken from him, but another Spirit was taken from the source of Abel or Adam. I also have two aspects of the Spirit prepared for me: One is from the aspect of the Spirit which is appropriate for my Animus, which is from the aspect of Cain. The second is from the aspect of the Spirit from another source, as we have explained, since through the sin of Adam the Souls in the aspect of Spirit from the source of Abel were mixed up with the aspect of the Animus from the source of Cain and vice versa. The aspect of the Spirit from the source of Adam [is mixed] with the Spirit of Cain or that of Abel and vice versa. The aspect of the Spirit which is within me from the side of Cain is very much greater than the Spirit which is within me from the side of the mixture, as mentioned. If I will be worthy, I will take the Spirit that is appropriate to me from the side of Cain and in the same manner with the Soul. He told me that after the spark of Rabbi Akiva there is none closer to me than the spark of Abbaye, since Abbaye was worthy to take [all three aspects of] Animus, Spirit, and Soul from his source, which is from the aspect of Cain which is not the case with the others, as mentioned. He told me that Abbaye is the same person as *Rav Yeivi Saba* who is mentioned in the *Zohar, parshat Mishpatim.* Abbaye is also the abbreviation of the verse "On none but me He brings down his hand" [Lam 3:3]. The word *yehafokh* [in this verse] alludes to the conversion [*hipukh*] of Yeivi to Abbaye.[81] I asked my teacher z"l to explain the reason for this conversion to me but he did not want to explain it to me.

One day he said to me that the source of my Animus is a drop of Joseph's semen, from the ten drops which exuded from between his nails, as is known.[82]

He also told me that the additional Animus which comes to me in the secret of the Sabbath addition is very elevated and distinguished and is almost from the aspect of *Azilut*. He told me that day that until then I had been worthy to attain this additional Animus only once or twice.

26. Concerning my Animus, he told me that when Cain sinned, all the sparks that were part of this source were included in him and this includes all the sparks until the coming of the Messiah. The spark of my Animus was also included in it. As a result of his sin all the sparks were mixed up with the *kelippot* and all the distinguished and important sparks descended lower than all the others into the depths of the *kelippot* because Cain's sin was in the Supernal Thought, as is mentioned in the *Tikkunei Zohar*.[83] The place of Rabbi Akiva was in the arms in the secret of "His hand holding on to the heel of Esau" [Gn 25:26], as has been explained earlier.[84] He is the heel of the left hand of *Zeir Anpin*. Sometimes the person lowers the hand to the heel and sometimes is able to raise it to the head. Therefore, his arms fell to the heel and afterwards through the death of Rabbi Akiva were raised and ascended to the Supernal Thought, as God said to Moses, "Such is My decree,"[85] in order to repair that which has been damaged. He told me that I and all those similar to me are also able to ascend through our deeds, to ascend from the aspect of the arms to the attribute of height and exaltation without limit, more so than many of the people of previous generations. Indeed, the place of my Animus's spark is in the shoulder portion of the arm and he gave me a sign for this. I have long hair and we find that I am composed of *Hesed* and *Gevurah*, which is the secret of the shoulders. The specific spark of my Animus has not transmigrated and had not come into the world until now. In that respect, I am new. However, I need to complete my Animus, Spirit, and Soul, the part of me that was incorporated in the Animus of Cain, as mentioned. This had been damaged previously, when I was there, as a result of Cain's sin and I need to complete

the part of me that was there. The spark of my Animus is closer than all others to the spark of Rabbi Akiva's Animus and therefore he is transmigrated in me more than anyone else.

27. My teacher z"l told me that three people erred concerning the end of days. They were: Jacob, who called his children together and the date of the end was concealed from him.[86] Similarly, Rabbi Akiva, who contains the letters of Jacob in his name to allude to the fact that their mistake was the same. [Rabbi Akiva] thought that Bar Kosiba [Bar Kochba] was the Messiah.[87] Similarly, Samuel erred in the matter of Eliab, when he thought that the Messiah would be one of his descendants, as Scripture says, "Surely the Lord's anointed stands before Him" [1 Sm 16:6]. For this reason, these three were transmigrated to repair this error.

My teacher z"l told me that the Animus of Rabbi Akiva is not like the Animi of other proselytes which are created from the union of the righteous in Paradise, as is mentioned in *Zohar, parshat, Shelah Leha* [III:168a]. However, his Animus is very elevated, but as a result of the sins of Adam and Cain it was sent out to the outer areas and was required to enter the body of a proselyte. It has come clothed within another Animus, called the Animus of the proselyte, as is mentioned in [*Zohar*], *Saba de-Mishpatim* [II:98b]. It was the Animus of the proselyte which caused him to be an ignoramus for forty years, in the secret of "Proselytes are as difficult for Israel as a skin lesion."[88] Understand this. The same is true of *Rabban* Johanan ben Zakkai who was an ignoramus for forty years.[89] The reason for this is that the source of their Animus was from the drop of Joseph's semen as mentioned. Therefore, I too committed the above-mentioned sin when I was imprisoned for nine months, as mentioned.

He also told me that *Rabban* Johanan ben Zakkai and Rabbi Akiva were the right and left arms of Moses our Teacher a"h, intermingled with Cain. Therefore, all three of them had the same lifespan of 120 years, and therefore, Moses our Teacher a"h wanted that the Torah should be given through Rabbi Akiva, as is mentioned in the *Ottiyot de Rabbi Akiva*.[90] Moses also slew Og, the king of Bashan,[91] and in him was intermingled the spark of Rabbi

Simeon ben Netanel, [whose name is] the abbreviation of
"Bashan," and this is Og, the king of Bashan. Therefore, Moses
was afraid to kill Og because of the spark of holiness that was in
him, which was sin fearing. Later, this spark was the disciple of
Rabban Johanan ben Zakkai.

28. One Friday afternoon he saw the following written on my
forehead: We have prepared a seat for Hezekiah, the king of
Judah.[92] This is to teach that his Animus was revealed in me
through the secret of the Sabbath addition. Later, during the day
I became angered in my house and he disappeared from me.
Afterwards, I repented during the week and on the following Friday afternoon my teacher z"l saw that the Spirit of Hezekiah and
the Spirit of Rabbi Akiva were cleaving to me in the secret of the
Sabbath addition. I again became angry in my house on that day
and he told me that they disappeared. Later that day I cried and
repented for that anger and he said to me that the Spirit of Ben
Azzai alone came to me, even though he is not of my source. This
is because he was the son-in-law of Rabbi Akiva.[93] He said to me
that on Friday morning Akiva was written with a *Heh* [instead of
an *Aleph*].[94]

On the Sabbath I studied two verses according to their kabbalistic meaning. My teacher z"l said to me on the Sabbath morning
that he saw him, Ben Azzai gave me two presents. When he asked
me what new interpretation I had found on that Sabbath and I
told him, he said to me that it was because on that Friday night I
suddenly had the idea and I read one *Mishnah* by Ben Azzai three
or four times that he gave me the above-mentioned two presents.
During that week he said to me that he saw that there was within
me an additional Spirit from the side of the Spirit of Abbaye, as
is written in the *Zohar, parshat Zav* [III:29a], that the scholar has
an additional Spirit even during the week, as the ordinary person has [only] on the Sabbath.

On another Sabbath he said to me that he saw the Tetragrammaton written very brightly on my forehead and this is to teach
that the name of God is called over me. He also told me that all
the sparks that are in the source of my Animus from that of
Hezekiah until that of my own Animus have all come into me in

the secret of the addition on that Sabbath. Even the inner essence of Hezekiah's Spirit came to me then.

29. On *Rosh Hodesh Tammuz*, he said to me that he saw the Animus of *Rav* Dimi of Nehardea was prepared to be impregnated in me, since it was from the source of my Animus and because I participated in the funeral of a deserted corpse on that day.[95] The commandment of accompanying guests or participating in funerals was the one most frequently fulfilled by *Rav* Dimi. Therefore, he wanted to be impregnated in me. He told me that King Hezekiah did not live out his allotted span. Even though fifteen years were added to his life, yet he still lacked a few years.[96] *Rav* Dimi completed the rest of the above-mentioned years, since he was a pure transmigration of Hezekiah a"h without any admixture of any other spark. Thus it is written, "I had thought: I must depart in the middle [*demai*[97]] of my days, etc....For the rest of my years" [Is 38:10], for the rest of his years were in *Rav* Dimi. I, Hayyim, saw that Rabah the *Amora* sent me greetings twice: once during my prayers and once in a dream. My teacher z"l said to me that Rabah wanted to make peace with *Rav* Dimi who accompanies me, because he was in a quarrel with him over what his disciple *Rav* Ada bar Ahava did to him over the matter of the dried figs which *Rav* Dimi brought in a ship, as is mentioned in the Talmud.[98]

30. One Sabbath, *Rav* Mushrashia was revealed within me and my teacher z"l said to me that this is the secret of the complete Sabbath addition from the side of my Animus's source. The matter is that this name is from the aspect of *Abba* and *Imma* which is called *Y"H*.[99] We know that the Sabbath addition is derived from this and the rest of the letters are *MShRSh*.[100] The two *shins* are the two names "*MZPZ*," each of which is equal to 300 *[shin]* in *gematria*. They are two names of the Sabbath addition, of the seven names mentioned in the *Raya Mehemna, parshat Yitro*.[101] The two letters *Mem, Resh* remain and they equal the other five names in *gematria*, which are *H, H, Elohim, El, Adonai,* and are mentioned there. They equal 234 in *gematria* and the seven names themselves equal 241. We find that this name which is the Sabbath addition of my Animus's source incorporates the seven

185

names of the Sabbath and their source is *Y"H*. My teacher z"l told me that King Hezekiah is the aspect of the head of this source of Cain and because Cain's judgment was suspended during the Flood,[102] he was repaired and strengthened by Hezekiah and from there the aspect of the head began to be strengthened and this is "Hezekiah"—"*Hazak Y"H*." Concerning the scriptural verse, "I thought, I shall never see *Y"H*" [Is 38:11], this is because he came to strengthen the aspect of the head, the source of which is *Y"H*. As is known, this name is in the head and he thought at first that it had not yet been repaired. He completed the aspect of the head of Cain, to perfect *Rav* Mushrashia with this, since he has the letters "*ShRSh Y"H*" within him. This source is in the head and his name is also the name *Y"H*. We find that both King Hezekiah and *Rav* Mushrashia are in the head of Cain. Indeed, the prophet Ezekiel strengthened Cain in the aspect of the legs. This is the secret of "O mortal, stand up on your feet" [Ez 2:1], because he was an aspect of Cain, the son of Adam. He told me that "he should stand on his feet" so they will be strengthened and repaired, since he is continued from there. Therefore, he is called Ezekiel, which is derived from the word for "strength." Simeon ben Azzai and Simeon ben Zoma are the two *shins* of *Rav* Mushrashia and therefore, Ben Azzai married the daughter of Rabbi Akiva.[103] Even though these two are not from my source, as mentioned above, nonetheless they have a great affinity with my source. The same happened to Elijah z"l, that Nadav and Avihu were impregnated in him, who are from Cain, since he is descended from the daughters of Putiel, who is Jethro, who is descended from Cain, as our Sages wrote.[104] Similarly, Elisha and Jonah have a great closeness to the source of my Animus. He did not want to reveal more about this.

One Sabbath, Rami bar Ezekiel and *Rav* Bibi bar Abbaye were revealed in me. The sage z"l said to me that he was told in a dream that night that the above-mentioned *Rav* Bibi is alluded to in the first letters of the verse "When you gaze upon Zion, our city of assembly...a tent not to be transported" [Is 33:20], and my teacher himself is alluded to in the first letters of "When you gaze upon Zion, the city of our assembly," since when one

186

switches the *Mem* with a *Yud* using the method of *AT"BaSh*,[105] you arrive at "Isaac," my teacher's z"l name. He also told me in that dream, the first letters of "When you gaze upon Zion, the city of our assembly" equal Rachel in *gematria*, which is the secret of the *Nukvah* of *Zeir Anpin*, which is called Rachel. She is also called "Zion, the city of our assembly" which emanates from the gaze of *Zeir Anpin*. Therefore, he said *"Haze"* in Aramaic rather than "Re'eh [see]" in Hebrew to allude to the above-mentioned and also that Abbaye, the father of *Rav* Bibi, is alluded to in the first letters of "a tent not to be transported." He did not want to reveal to me the essential meaning of these words.

31. Concerning my wife he told me that in all the sparks of my Animus there is none that is as close to me as the spark of R. Akiva. He is closer to me than all others and what happened to him, happened to me.

He told me that my wife Hannah is a transmigration of Kalba Savu'a, Rabbi Akiva's father-in-law. He was transmigrated as a woman, because he had committed sodomy as a woman, who was the substitution for Abbaye, since he was also of Rabbi Akiva's source, as is known. Concerning her it says in the Talmud: "Abbaye said, my mother told me."[106] Afterwards, she was transmigrated into my wife, Hannah. Since she was a transmigration of a man, it was impossible for me to have male children from her, only girls. Even though she could not give birth to girls because she was male, this was possible only through the participation of the Soul of another woman which was impregnated in her. He told me that the Animus of Tinneus Rufus' wife, who later married Rabbi Akiva, as is known,[107] was impregnated in her. This is the reason for the closeness of Rabbi Akiva with my wife, who is a transmigration of his father-in-law, as mentioned. Then she was impregnated in my daughter Angela, when she was born and was separated from my wife. After the death of my daughter Angela, it was then necessary for her to return and be impregnated a second time in my wife and then to give birth to another daughter in whom she would be impregnated and who would be the transmigration of the wife of Tinneus Rufus, as mentioned. If that daughter would live, it would be necessary for the Animus of another woman to be impregnated in her and she would give birth to another daughter and the Animus would be transmigrated into that daughter. However, if that Animus would remain with my wife in the aspect of impregnation and would not separate from her, then it would be possible that the child she would give birth to would be male. He told me that this wife would die and afterwards I would marry another woman with immense wealth, exactly like Rabbi Akiva and the wife of Tinneus Rufus. In this way I would acquire wealth because of my wife, just like him. On another occasion he told me, after I will attain perfection of my Animus I will acquire my Spirit. Just as my Animus is in partnership with the Animus of Rabbi Akiva, similarly my Spirit will also come in partnership with the Spirit of Rabbi Akiva. Then I will be worthy to acquire my true mate. Just as my Animus and Spirit are in partnership with the Animus and Spirit of Rabbi Akiva, similarly the Animus of my true mate will be in partnership with the Animus of the true wife of Rabbi Akiva, who is the daughter of Kalba Savu'a. There is an additional virtue to the daughter of Kalba Savu'a, since she allowed her husband to study Torah for twenty-four years.[108] Therefore, my wife who is in partnership with her has a very great virtue and I am not able to be worthy of her until I perfect my Animus and my Spirit enters within me.

32. On the eve of *Rosh Hodesh Ellul* 5331 [1571], my teacher z"l sent me to the cave of Abbaye and Rava, where I prostrated myself on the grave of Abbaye z"l. I first performed the Unification of the mouth and nose of *Attika Kaddisha*. Sleep overcame me and when I awoke I did not see anything. Afterwards, I returned and prostrated myself a second time on Abbaye himself and I performed the Unification which is found in the manuscript of my teacher a"h. While I was uniting and combining the letters of names of God, as is known, my mind became confused and I was not able to unite them. I ceased thinking about that Unification. It seemed as if I heard a voice in my thoughts saying to me: "Retract them, retract them," many times. I thought to myself: This is the phrase used by Akaviah ben Mehalalel to his son, as is known.[109] I then returned to thinking about that combi-

nation and I completed it. Then it seemed as if they were saying to me in my thoughts: "God will see to the sheep for His burnt offering, my son" [Gn 22:8]. It was as if they were explaining to me the meaning of the verse, and it is: That which I was worrying about, that I had not effected the first Unification, was not so. Indeed, I had effected it and succeeded before God, and this is "God will see to the sheep," and so forth. It seemed to me as if they were explaining to me that the whole first Unification which I performed is alluded to in this verse, since the first letters of "God will see to the sheep" equal forty-six in *gematria*, which is the same number as the Unification of the Tetragrammaton and *EHY"H*. The first letter of "The sheep for His burnt offering, my son" is *HeVeL* [breath], which is the secret of the breath of the Supernal mouth, which I concentrated on with that Unification. It seemed as if they were saying to me that the first letter of "The sheep for His burnt offering" is an allusion to Hillel the Elder, but I do not understand this matter. I imagined all of this in my thoughts. Afterwards, a great fear and trembling came over all my limbs and both my hands were shaking. My lips were also trembling in an exaggerated manner and moving back and forth very rapidly as if a voice were saying very rapidly the following phrase, more than a hundred times: What is he saying, what is he saying. I held on to my lips, but I could not silence them completely. I then thought to ask about the wisdom. Then the voice exploded from my tongue and lips, saying: The wisdom, the wisdom, more than twenty times. Then it returned and said: The wisdom and the knowledge, several times. Then it returned and said: The wisdom and the knowledge will be given to you. Then it returned and said: The wisdom and knowledge will be given to you from Heaven like the knowledge of Rabbi Akiva. Then it returned and said: And more than Rabbi Akiva. Then it said: And like *Rav* Yeivi Saba. Then it said: And more than *Rav* Yeivi Saba. Then it said: Peace unto you. Then it said: From Heaven you are sent greetings. All of this was in great rapidity, a wondrous thing, many times, while I was awake. I prostrated myself on the crypt of Abbaye.

Afterwards, I went to my teacher z"l and he said to me that I had been greatly elevated by my performance of the above-mentioned two Unifications, one after the other. It is appropriate to perform them in this order. I had not been answered for the first Unification since they waited for me to finish both Unifications. My teacher z"l said to me that when I returned from there and entered his house, he saw the Animus of Beneyahu ben Yehoyada accompanying me. He said to me that he is not from my source, but the reason is that he is revealed to all who perform a Supernal Unification, since this was always his habit when he was alive, as is mentioned in another place.

My teacher z"l said to me that he was told during the *minha* prayers that if I will be worthy on the next Sabbath for [the appearance of] *Rav* Yeivi Saba, then he will remain with me always and will not leave, like my other transmigrations. Through him I will be worthy [to attain] great illuminations, particularly during several prayers of the *amidah*. The reason for this is that *Rav* Yeivi Saba is also revealed to *zaddiqim* like Beneyahu ben Yehoyada, as is explained elsewhere. In addition to this, he is from my source and therefore if I will be worthy that he will be revealed to me, he will also reveal great wonders to me, praise God.

32a.[110] On that Saturday night, I performed a Unification after midnight, when I arose from my bed and the above occurred to me. *Rav* Yeivi Saba cautioned me that by means of the Unification from my teacher's z"l manuscript, I will comprehend with wisdom everything that I desire. I should perform the Unification three times every day, in the following manner: during the genuflection in the morning prayers, in the genuflection of the *minha amidah*, and in the *Shema* of the *ma'ariv* prayers. With this I will comprehend that which I desire.

On Monday night I again performed a Unification after midnight. *Rav* Yeivi Saba said to me: Why did you not perform that Unification as you were commanded to do three times every day, as above? With this you will attain complete comprehension permanently. Go to your teacher, Rabbi Isaac [Luria] Ashkenazi, and tell him that he should teach you how to do it during the three times mentioned. Tell him that he should speak to me and I will teach him and he will teach you afterwards. You do not know how great you are before God, for you are a great man like Rabbi Akiva and his colleagues and you will attain what no person in this generation has attained, not even your teacher, Rabbi Isaac [Luria] Ashkenazi. In the future, the angel Elijah z"l will speak to you face-to-face, while you are awake. Therefore, when you will perform this Unification, you will elevate it in the secret of Elijah which is the secret of the divine name *Bet"Nun*,[111] which is the secret of the feminine waters, and you will elevate it in the secret of Nadav and Avihu who are the secret of the Animus and you will elevate me along with them. With this comprehension Elijah and the other angels will speak to you. You do not know how much greater your attributes are than all the people of this generation. God will give you children and wealth, so that you will not be dependent on anyone.

That morning I went to my teacher z"l and told him all the above. Afterwards, he taught me how to perform the above-mentioned Unification during the three prayers, during the genuflection in the *shaharit* and *minha* prayers and during the *Shema* of the *ma'ariv* prayers. I have already explained it at the end of the Unification of my teacher's z"l manuscript. See there.

Also, the matter of the Unification of Nadav and Avihu and Elijah z"l is written about after the first Unification of the mouth and nose of *Attika Kadisha*. See there, in the second Unification.

33. On the Sabbath before *Tisha B'Av* I dreamed that my teacher z"l told me about a pair of *Amoraim* and he said about them: "How abundant is the good You have in store for those who fear you" [Ps 31:20]. In the morning I went to him and he explained this matter to me and told me that it is a great secret. He told me that on Friday he saw written on my forehead, Rami bar Hami and the letters *N"R*. He did not understand it until the matter was revealed to him through investigation. The matter was, as has already been explained, that the 613 sparks of the sages are found in the source of each individual Animus. Thus, the daughter of *Rav* Hisda mentioned in the Talmud[112] is the aspect of *Malkhut*, the daughter about whom is written "abundant in kindness"; This is also the secret of "Your abundant good."

Thus, the Supernal union is the secret of *Da'at* of the Tetragrammaton and *EHY"H*, which equal forty-seven in *gematria*. This name is the secret of Rami bar Hama, as is explained, and therefore he took her first. Afterwards, Raba took her, which contains the letters of the word *Be'er* [well], which is the lower union of *Yesod*, since Raba equals in *gematria* the two lower unions, God *Elohim* and God *Adonai*, which equal *Be'er* in *gematria*, which are [the union of] *Malkhut* with her seven palaces and *Tiferet*, as is known. Therefore it says, "Raba said, Let me be the second."[113] Indeed, Rami bar Hami is Supernal, since if you connect the two lower unions, which are the secret of *Be'er* and Raba, with the Supernal union, it adds up to forty-seven, as mentioned. The three of them equal 250 in *gematria*, which is the same as Rami in *gematria*. Rami is the majestic aspect of *Da'at*, as is known, and it is the fiftieth gate, a path the eagles did not know. This is Rami bar Hama, since Hama equals forty-nine in *gematria* and Rami is the fiftieth gate of the source of my Animus, the secret of the Supernal knowledge of the source of my Animus. This is the meaning of "How abundant your goodness" which I dreamed, since *Mah* [how] is [a synonym for] *Malkhut* who is the daughter of *Rav* Tov who is *Rav* Hisda and she is hidden for those who fear You. Rami and Raba are the secret of *Da'at* and *Yesod*. In addition, the first letters of "How great is Your goodness which" equals Rami in *gematria*. Remember this matter, since Rami is the fiftieth gate of the source of my Animus.

34. We have already explained in another place the issue of the Souls of the *Tannaim* and *Amoraim* and where they are.[114] Now I will explain in some detail about the sparks of the source of my Animus. You already know that *Zeir* contains five *Hasadim* which expand and also five *Gevurot*. It seems to me that all this is within the *Parzuf* of the heel, which is in the encompassing *Parzuf* of Cain whose totality is the *Parzuf* of *Gevurot* of the *Moah* of *Da'at* of *Zeir*. The aspect of the *Gevurot* of greatness is as follows: The *Gevurah* of greatness ascends from *Yesod* to *Nezah* which is King Hezekiah. The *Gevurah* which ascends to *Hesed* is the prophet Ezekiel. The *Gevurah* of greatness which ascends from *Yesod* to *Hod* is Rabbi Akiva. That which ascends to *Gevurah* is Akaviah

ben Mehalalel. The *Gevurah* which ascends to the lower two-thirds of *Tiferet* which are revealed is *Rabban* Johanan ben Zakkai. From the remainder, a third of the *Hesed*, after they are divided, is Mar and Menasseh, the son of King Hezekiah. The upper third is Elihu ben Berakhel the Buzite, of the family of Ram. This one is Mar and is Ram. Afterwards, it ascends to *Da'at* and it is the prophet Samuel of Ramah.

The smallness is the name *Elohim*, as is known. He explained its three aspects, namely the aspect of the *Moah*, the aspect of *Hasadim*, and the aspect of *Gevurot*. The *Moah* that ascends in *Nezah* is Rami bar Hama. The *Hesed* which ascends in *Nezah* is Abbaye and the *Gevurah* is *Rav* Bibi, his son. Afterwards, it ascends in *Hesed*, which is the right arm. The *Moah* is *Rav* Sahurah and the *Gevurah*, *Rav* Samuel bar Shilat. The *Hesed* is Pinehas, the brother of Mar Samuel and he is the aspect of the exalted *Gevurah* which defeats the smallness. The *Hod* of the *Moah* is *Rav* Mushrashia, the student of Abbaye; the *Gevurah* is Rami bar Tamri; the *Hesed* is Rapram bar Papa. Afterwards, it ascends to *Gevurah*. The *Moah* is R. Zarika; the *Gevurah* is R. Zeiri of Dahbat; the *Hesed* is R. Ze'eira bar Hillel. In the *Tiferet*—the lower two-thirds which are revealed—the *Moah* is Ula bar Koshav; the *Gevurah* is Rabin, who left Israel and descended to Babylonia; the *Hesed* is *Rav* Hana Bagdatah; the *Tiferet*—the third which is concealed—the *Moah* is R. Miasa, during the time of R. Johanan; the *Gevurah*—R. Shila, for whom the miracle occurred in tractate *Berakhot* [58a]; the *Hesed*—Shabhat, the son of Ravina. My teacher z"l ordered me to always concentrate on all the above-mentioned every week, divided according to the days. Those that I should concentrate on are *Nezah*, *Hod*, and *Yesod* on Sunday, Monday, and Tuesday; *Hesed*, *Gevurah*, and *Tiferet* on Wednesday, Thursday, and Friday; and *Da'at* on Friday afternoon, because a bit of the Sabbath addition has already begun. Know that all of this was written down on a small piece of paper that I had [written] during the lifetime of my teacher z"l, and at the bottom I saw written, *Rav* Hama bar Buzi, without any explanation and I do not know if I needed to concentrate on him on the Sabbath. I forgot the matter.

35. On another occasion he commanded me to concentrate every day of the week, in every prayer, on these *Tannaim, Amoraim,* and *Zaddiqim,* which I will now list. This is their order: On Sunday: *Shaharit—Rav* Yeivi Saba; *Minha—*Abbaye; *Arvit—Rav* Bibi, his son. On Monday: *Shaharit—Rav* Yeivi the *Amora; Minha* and *Arvit—*Avihah ben Rehaboam. On Tuesday: *Shaharit—Rav* Dimi of Nehardea; *Minha—Rav* Dimi who went to Israel; *Arvit— Rav* Yisa the *Amora.* On Wednesday: *Shaharit—Rav* Ahai bar Yishai; *Minha—Rav* Shisha, the son of *Rav* Idi; *Ma'ariv—Rav* Hiyya of Dafti. On Thursday: *Shaharit—*Joshua bar Zarnoki; *Minha—*Iyo; *Arvit—*Avdimi. On Friday: Nahum the Alkoshite— the whole day. On Sabbath: Micah the Murshatite—the whole day.

I also found all the above written on a small piece of paper and at the bottom I found the following names written. I do not remember the reason. They are: *Rav* Bibi, *Rav* Zerika, *Rav* Tavyomi, R. Krespidoi *Hamid Liba,* R. Zadok the Cohen, R. Kisma, *Rav* Shemaya Hasida. In my humble opinion, I had been commanded to concentrate on each of them, according to the order of the days of the week.

36. On another occasion he told me that Elihu ben Berakhel the Buzite of the family of Ram is in the upper third of *Tiferet* which is covered. Concerning that which is written: "From the family of Ram" [Jb 32:2], Elkanah and his son the prophet Samuel were from Ramah, which is *Da'at* itself, which is the highest level *[ramah]* which incorporates both of them.

On another occasion he told me, the young one, that I am the highest *Gevurah* of *Hod* which is in *Da'at* itself. R. Yose the Galilean is from the left earlock of the head, from the aspect of *El Shaddai* which is in the *Parzuf* of the left shoulder, which is in the *Parzuf* of the source of my Animus. Jonathan ben Hyrcanus is from the *Gevurah* of the *Gevurah* which is in the five *Gevurot* which are in *Da'at.* R. Akiva is from the *Gevurah* of *Hod* which is in *Da'at.* I am from the *Gevurah* of *Hod* which is in the external *Da'at* of Leah. The prophet Ezekiel is from a drop of Adam's semen before Cain was born, like that which I have informed you concerning Micah the Murshatite and Nahum the Elkoshite.

R. Huzpit the translator is from the *Gevurah* of *Hod* which is in *Da'at* which is from the side of *Abba* and her light is split and goes over to the *Da'at* of the external Leah. What remains there is the source of my Animus. In my humble opinion, my teacher told me that it is necessary that when it passes by way of the *Da'at* of *Imma* that it pass by way of *Gevurah* of *Hod* of *Da'at* of *Zeir* from the side of *Imma*, since *Abba* is hidden inside of *Imma*. That which remains in *Hod* of *Da'at* of *Zeir* which is from the side of *Imma* has a great affinity with me. Similarly, all the other sources of my teacher, Rabbi Moses Alshekh, may God preserve him, come and pass along the above-mentioned path and I have a connection with them.

Relevant to the above: My teacher z"l told me: Since Jonathan ben Hyrcanus is from the *Gevurah* of the *Gevurah* of *Da'at*, and Rabbi Akiva is from the *Gevurah* of *Hod* of *Da'at*, therefore, Jonathan ben Hyrcanus had a sharper intellect than he, as is mentioned in both Babylonian and Jerusalem Talmuds, tractate *Yevamot*.[115]

37. He explained to me the concept of the sources of the Souls.

Know that all Souls are derived from Adam, since he incorporates all five sources of Souls, which are: *Arikh [Anpin], Abba, Imma, Zeir [Anpin],* and *Nukvah*. The 248 organs and 365 blood vessels which are in a person are the 613 sources.[116] That is, each of the 248 organs and each of the 365 vessels has within it one *Parzuf* in each of the 613 organs and vessels and are called one source. Each organ consists of flesh, vessels, and bones, as the Talmudic sages said, concerning ritual impurity and the limb of a living animal.[117] However, these vessels are not counted in the 365 vessels, which are independent vessels, separate from the 248 organs. The vessels which are with the organs are the small channels which are spread through the flesh of the organ and are not counted in the 365 vessels. We find that the 613 sources are in Adam and each source contains 613 sparks of Souls. Each of the sparks is called a Soul. All of this is part of the externality of the Animus, as will be explained below. This is the essential truth of the matter. Indeed, through the sins and defects of the lower elements [people], the two above-mentioned aspects separate and divide into a number of parts. Explanation: The 613 great sources are able to divide into 600,000 small sources.[118] Similarly, the 613 great sparks are able to divide into 600,000 small sparks. However, know that it is not necessary that they should divide into 613 or 600,000, but the intent is that it is impossible for there to be less than 613 great sources or 613 great sparks. Similarly, it is impossible for there to be more than 600,000 small sources or more than 600,000 small sparks in each of the 613 sources, but an intermediate number is possible, since it divides into thousands. There are thousands, tens of thousands, and so forth. It is all according to the level of the sin. The reason was mentioned in *Tikkunei Zohar, Tikkun* 69.[119] There are not more transmigrations than those of the 600,000. However, it is possible to be between 600,000 and 613, according to the minimum level of the sin. Cain and Abel are the two shoulders of Adam—Abel the right shoulder and Cain the left shoulder, and he is the aspect of the shoulder which joins the shoulder to the body. Because of the sin which both of them committed, as is mentioned in *Tikkunei Zohar, Tikkun* 69, they cause a defect above and each of their sources, which are 613 great Souls, was divided into 600,000 sparks, and each spark is one Soul. Concerning that which is written in *Tikkunei Zohar* that Moses disseminated them to 600,000, and so forth, it is because he is from the source of Abel. The source of *Da'at* which descends through the spine first descends to the two shoulders and afterwards descends to *Yesod*, to produce the drop of semen.[120] When the drop of semen reaches *Yesod* from the shoulder, then the *Yesod* is called a bundle of dates, since the letters of *KPT* [bundle] and *KTP* [shoulder] are the same. Thus when it descends from both shoulders together to *Yesod*, then it is written, "It shall have two shoulder pieces attached; they shall be attached at its two ends" [Ex 28:7]. Then they are united in *Yesod* and it is written, "You may have the thousand, O Solomon" [Sg 8:12], since *Yesod* is called Solomon, as is written, "my pact of friendship" [Nm 25:12]. Then he is the secret of 1,000, since two times "shoulder" equals 1,000 in *gematria*. However, one shoulder alone is 500 in *gematria*, like the value of the letters alone, which disappears from the [divine] name *Shaddai* in *Yesod*, and when they are united they equal 1,000.

38. I will now explain the matter of the sources, mentioned above. As a result of Adam's sin, the sparks from the rest of Adam's organs were mixed up with the *kelippot* of evil from the sources of Cain and Abel and in the course of the transmigrations, they are revealed and each will return to its original source.

Now, I will explain the source of Cain alone, in whom inheres the spark of my Animus, of me, Hayyim. The source of Cain is the joint of the left shoulder where the arm joins the body and it has flesh, sinews, and bones. As is already known, it is not called an organ [*ever*], unless it has flesh, sinews, and bone. I have already explained above[121] that these sinews are the small blood vessels which are not included in the above mentioned 365 sinews. These three components of the organ are divided into 600,000 small sparks and every organ of this shoulder is one complete *Parzuf*. Indeed, the source of the spark of my Animus is in the lower left "heel" which is in this *Parzuf*, which is the left shoulder of Adam from the second aspect. The left "heel" of this *Parzuf* of Cain contains more than 613 small sparks and they are the Animi which are from the source of my Soul, about which I wrote in detail above, from Cain until my Animus, me, Hayyim. There are others aside from those mentioned above, but my teacher z"l did not explain all the sparks in this "heel" to me.

39. I will now explain the matter of the left "heel" which is in the *Parzuf* of Cain, which is the whole organ of the left shoulder of Adam, as mentioned. Know that the drop of semen which flows from this "heel" until the *Yesod* of *Zeir Anpin* sometimes becomes Jacob, sometimes becomes Akavia and sometimes Akiva,[122] and so forth, and I cannot expand on these details. Know that the secret of *eqev* [heel] is the secret of *Malkhut* and therefore all the sparks of this "heel" have the power to ascend to the "Thought," in the secret of "A woman courts a man" [Jer

31:22]. From this aspect, R. Akiva was able to ascend to the "Thought *[Mahshavah]*."[123] Understand this.

My Animus, of me, the young Hayyim, is from the above-mentioned "heel" of the *Parzuf* of the left shoulder of Adam. Therefore, I have long hairs in my left shoulder, as mentioned above, which my teacher z"l gave me as a sign that Adam's left shoulder is the basis of my Animus. Indeed, I also have long hairs in my right shoulder, but they are more numerous in my left shoulder. The reason for this is when the right side has been damaged as in the analogy of Abel's sin, in which the right shoulder was damaged, then there is no visible sign except in the right side alone. However, when the damage was done in the left side, as in the analogy of the sin of Cain, which damaged the left shoulder, then the damage also reaches the right shoulder, and so forth. Therefore, I also have hairs on the right shoulder, but they are more numerous in the left shoulder, since their essence is there. However, since the damage is not only in the right side, then the sign is not visible only on the right side alone. Understand this.

40. Know that a person does not have to repair all the damages that are in his whole source, as in the following analogy: Whoever is from the left shoulder of Adam, which is called the source of Cain, is from a particular organ which is in this *Parzuf*, like the "heel" mentioned above. No single spark is required to complete and repair all the damage which is found in the whole *Parzuf*, but only in the "heel" itself. We find that all the sparks which are from the left "heel" of this *Parzuf* of the left shoulder of Adam are all guarantors for one another to repair them all, each one for all of them and all for one of them. When the repair of this "heel" will be completed there will be no need for this "heel" to transmigrate, even if the rest of the shoulder will not yet be repaired.

Know that if any one spark of the sparks of this "heel" sins and needs to be transmigrated and repaired, then it transmigrates with another spark from this "heel" and both are repaired together. However, if it is one of those severe sins that destroys his body and he has no life, Heaven forbid, then he alone is transmigrated and his first body is destroyed completely. Similarly, if he transmigrates to complete a particular commandment that he is missing and not to repair the damage of a sin, then too he transmigrates alone as many times until he completes the commandment. Each of the bodies contributes a part according to what has been completed by it.

Know that when a particular spark is missing one commandment, it does not return and transmigrate with a second spark, even though he is from the same source, but with a similar spark and not with the other sparks, even though they are from his source.

Know that if a person causes his friend to sin, then even if they are not from the same source, they are required to transmigrate together and the one who caused him to sin will be impregnated in him to help perform the commandment and repair the sin which he caused.

Know that if a person's Animus will be completely repaired and completed, then all the sparks of this "heel" will be revealed in him and will shine in his body. They need to be revealed on his forehead in order that they should be repaired, and will be recognized there by someone whom God has given wisdom to gaze at the face. There the whole essence of the 613 sparks which are in that source of the Animus, the Spirit, or the Soul needs to be revealed on his forehead, since these 613 are the sages which are found in every source. There are many that are not explicitly recognized, but they are included along with the others that are greater than them. There are some great sparks who are the essence of the 613 lesser sparks. When they are revealed then it is certain that the others are also revealed and included with them. However, because of the great brightness of the primary ones the others are not recognized. My teacher z"l did not explain to me how many of the sparks are the primary ones. If his Animus, Spirit, or Soul was not completely repaired, then some of the 613 of the Animus or the 613 of the Spirit or the 613 of the Soul will be revealed, according to the commandments he fulfills. There are some sparks which are very far from him and some that are very close and there are some which encompass him from a distance and some which surround him and hover very close to him. It is all according to the deeds of the person. If he sins, they will again distance themselves from him, Heaven forbid. The number of sparks that distance themselves is in accord with the severity of the sin.

41. Concerning the sources of the Souls, know that all the Souls are incorporated in Adam.[124] The source of all Souls is Adam and is then divided into the three Patriarchs, then into the twelve tribes, and afterwards divided into the seventy Souls.[125] Each of these [seventy] parts is further divided until we find that the total number of sources that is in the Soul of Adam is 600,000 small sources. If you will examine it carefully, you will see that the 613 incorporate the 600,000, since 600,000 equals *T"R* [600] thousand and they are the two letters *T"R* of *TRY"G*.[126] The *G* of *TaRYaG* is the three Patriarchs. The *Y* of *TaRYaG* is the secret of the seventy souls, since the six directions are the secret of the 600,000, as is known, and the *Yud* completes the seventy, as is known. Also, the two letters *Y"G* are the twelve tribes and the additional one is their essence. Thus, they are 613, and include all the above essences.

Cain is one source of the sources which are in the Soul of Adam. He is the left shoulder of Adam and is divided in the above manner, that is, three Patriarchs, twelve tribes, and seventy Souls. He is not divided further than the seventy, that is, to seventy sources and no more. He is not comparable to Adam who has 600,000 sources. However, since Cain is one of the sources of Adam, he therefore also has some of the essence of Adam and is divided like him into three Patriarchs, twelve tribes, and seventy people. They are seventy sources and no more, since he is not completely identical to Adam who is divided into 600,000 sources. Indeed, these seventy sources of Cain are divided into only 600,000 sparks, but the number of sources is only seventy small sources. The same is true of Adam's right shoulder, which is the source of Abel. He also has three Patriarchs which are then divided into twelve tribes and afterwards to seventy people, which are the seventy sources and no more. They total 600,000 Soul sparks and no more.

Know that each of these seventy sources which are in Cain or

Abel contains one complete *Parzuf*. The totality of this *Parzuf* is called one source, since you do not have a single source of all the sources that is not in the category of a complete *Parzuf*.

In my humble opinion, the sources are the great sages and men of deeds who are called Soul sparks, as is written below.[127] This requires study.

42. The source of my Animus, me Hayyim, is one of the seventy sources of Cain. It contains one complete *Parzuf* and more than 613 Soul sparks. R. Akiva, Akavia ben Mehalalel, and me, Hayyim, are all from the "heel" of this *Parzuf*. King Hezekiah is in the head of this *Parzuf*.

Know that the two shoulders of Adam, which are the categories of Cain and Abel—that is to say, *Abba* and *Imma*—are Adam and Eve and the two crowns which are hidden in them are *Hesed* and *Gevurah*. They are: Abel—*Hesed* and Cain—*Gevurah*.

(In my humble opinion, this "heel" is not the "heel" which incorporates the whole *Parzuf* of Cain, but one single "heel" of one of the seventy sources of Cain. Each source has one "heel," but with regard to the whole source of Rabbi Akiva, I do not know if it is the top one or it is the bottom one or one of the other seventy sources. It is not necessary that this whole source is the "heel" alone, since the whole *Parzuf* of Cain contains seventy sources. This requires study.)

My teacher z"l also explained the source of my Animus to me on another occasion. Know that *Nezah* and *Hod* of *Attik Yomin* are clothed in the two arms of *Arikh Anpin*. *Hokhmah* and *Binah* of *Abba* and *Imma* are made from the two hands of the two arms of *Arikh Anpin*. The two shoulders [of Adam] are the secret of the two crowns called *Hesed* and *Gevurah* which cover the outer holiness [called] *Zeir Anpin*. These four *Mohin* which are the two *Mohin* of *Abba* and *Imma* and the two crowns are the secret of the surrounding light of *Zeir Anpin*. Afterwards, three sparks emanate from these four *Mohin*. Two of them are from *Abba* and *Imma* and the third is a combination of the two above-mentioned crowns. These three sparks from the side of the surrounding light are clothed in the *Nezah, Hod,* and *Yesod* of *Binah* which are the internal *Mohin* of *Zeir*. We find that *Nezah, Hod,* and *Yesod* of *Binah* are the three internal *Mohin* of *Zeir Anpin* and the three sparks of the four comprehensive *Mohin* are clothed in them. The first four *Mohin* are the surrounding light. Since there are only three internal *Mohin*, that is, *Nezah, Hod,* and *Yesod* of *Binah*, as mentioned, therefore only three sparks emanated from the four surrounding *Mohin* and the third spark is composed of the two crowns together, to enter the *Yesod* of *Binah* which makes the *Da'at* in *Zeir Anpin*.

With this, it descends one level, from four to three. Afterwards, with *Malkhut,* it descends a second level, since three become two, because *Nezah* and *Hod* of *Zeir Anpin* are made her internal *Mohin* and [they do] not come from *Yesod*.

Thus, the three internal ones of *Zeir, Nezah, Hod,* and *Yesod* of *Binah* are the surrounding light of *Malkhut*. Only two sparks emanate from them. One is the generality of *Nezah* and *Hod,* which are the two *Mohin* of *Abba* and *Imma*. The second is one crown of *Zeir* and it is the crown of *Gevurah* alone. Thus, first there were four surrounding [lights], then three, and then two.

43. Now I will explain the source of my Animus. There is no mention of the essence of *Malkhut* in *Attik Yomin*, since it only contains the essence of nine "palaces," as is mentioned in the beginning of *Idra, Ha'azinu*.[128] Therefore, the source of *Malkhut* which is in it is only hinted at in the secret of *Hod* which is in it, since it is already known that *Malkhut* is always in *Hod*. This *Hod* is clothed with a "crown" called *Gevurah* of *Arikh Anpin* which is the secret of the left shoulder and *Malkhut* is hinted at there. One spark emanates from this left shoulder to become the surrounding light of *Malkhut*. Cain, who is from the side of the essence of *Malkhut*, is alluded to in the left shoulder of Adam, since his first source is there. Indeed, opposite him is *Nezah* of *Attik Yomin* in the right shoulder of *Arikh Anpin* and the secret of *Tiferet* is in it. Therefore, Abel is alluded to here, and here is his source. From this you will understand the importance of these shoulders and particularly the left shoulder, since it is already known that it is possible for *Malkhut* and particularly in the secret of the surrounding light to ascend higher than the male, since *Hod* of *Attik*

[Yomin] is *Malkhut* and is clothed in the crown of *Gevurah* of the shoulder of *Zeir* which is *Malkhut* and the "heel" of the shoulder is the *Malkhut* in it. The source of R. Akiva and Akavia, and so forth, is from this "heel," which is also *Malkhut*.

Concerning the source of my Animus, it is known that *Zeir Anpin* has two *Mohin, Hokhmah* and *Binah*, and between them is a third *Moah, Da'at*, which is composed of *Hesed* and *Gevurah*. When Adam sinned, *Da'at* descended below the two shoulders of *Zeir*, to the upper third of the body, and *Hesed* descended in the right shoulder and *Gevurah* in the left shoulder. Cain and Abel were born after Adam sinned. The source of Cain is from the *Gevurot* which descended in the left shoulder, after their descent there, since they no longer had as much brightness as when they were above, in the *Moah* itself. The source of my Animus is from Cain. Thus, my whole source, such as Rabbi Akiva and others, is from the *Gevurah* of *Hod*, which is the fifth *Gevurah*. There is one mixture here, since when the Soul leaves here it certainly has an internal aspect and an external aspect, since it has an aspect from the *Moah* itself which is the *Gevurah* of *Hod* which is there and also from the left shoulder itself. If the *Da'at* had been above in the head, the external aspect of the Animus would have been from the bone and flesh of the head itself, but now it is from the shoulder and the external and internal are not related to each other. The result is that the internal aspect of my Animus is from the Supernal *Moah* called *Da'at*. It's external aspect and garment is from the left shoulder. The result is that it has one deficit in its internal aspect, because it is not as bright now as if it would have been above, in its place, and a second deficit in its external aspect, in that it is from the shoulder and not from the head. These two aspects are in the body, that is to say, in the vessel and garment of the Animus. In relation to them are the two aspects of the Animus itself, the external and the internal, which are called lights—see below in the discussion of the garments of the Souls, except for the souls themselves. Through the repair of the person by means of his deeds in this world, he is able to repair this, not now but only later in the messianic age. Then, with the power of the good deeds that a person does now in this world, the damage will also be repaired in the messianic age and the *Da'at* will ascend above and the internal aspect of my Animus will shine as originally. The external aspect of my Animus will then also be above the head. However, concerning the external aspect of my Animus which I now have, which is from the left shoulder, I am uncertain if my teacher z"l told me that it will always remain with me, since it is now connected to my Animus, or if it is the opposite.

As has been explained, *Da'at* descended below with Adam's sin; similarly the aspect of Leah descended from the back of *Da'at* of *Zeir* which was her original place. Now, she descended along with *Da'at* behind the shoulders. As is known, Leah emanated from the *Malkhut* of *Binah* and the *Da'at* which is in the *Yesod* of *Binah*. Rabbi Akiva is from the essence of the *Gevurah* of the *Hod* which is in *Da'at* of *Zeir*. The Animus of me, Hayyim, is from the illumination which emanated from the *Gevurah* of *Hod*, which is Rabbi Akiva, to the *Hod* which is in the *Da'at* of Leah. The result is that I am not in the *Hod* of *Da'at* of *Zeir* and not in the *Hod* of *Da'at* of Leah, but from the illumination which flows between the two and goes from the *Hod* of *Da'at* of *Zeir* to illumine the *Hod* of *Da'at* of Leah. It is possible that this is why my teacher z"l sometimes told me that I am from the *Hod* of *Da'at* of *Zeir* and sometimes he told me that I am from the *Hod* of *Da'at* of Leah. Sometimes he told me that I am from the corner of the left shoulder. Rabbi Akiva is the middle supporting shaft and I am the feather which grows from the central shaft, as will be explained below, with God's help.

My teacher z"l also told me that the internal aspect of my Animus is from the *Gevurah* of *Hod* which is the *Moah* above, but it descended, as mentioned, and the external aspect of my Animus is from the *Hesed* which is in the left shoulder.

Know that just as we have explained the division of Adam into 613 great sources and 600,000 small sources, similarly, each of the 613 sources was divided into 600,000 small sparks and all of this in the aspect of the Animus. The same division is true of the aspect of the Spirit. It is similar with the Soul, and so forth. There is no need to elaborate, since this is obvious.

44. I will now write what my teacher z"l told me seven days before he went to his eternal reward.[129] Know that from the very first hour that he spoke to me, he told me to be extremely careful not to reveal his comprehension and knowledge to other people, since he only came to repair me alone. Others would later be repaired through me. He warned me that if I reveal this, great damage will be caused to him, to me, and to the whole world. It turned out that my teacher Rabbi Moses Alshekh knew about these things and he ordered me to tell him about them. The strength of his order forced me to reveal it to him and from then on the number of visitors to my teacher's z"l [Luria] house increased. I thought that I had done a good deed, to benefit all those who returned and repented. My teacher z"l rebuked me over this many times, because there was not enough time for me to study with him as a result of the many visitors. He would say to me: You caused this, that all these people come here. I am a humble person and although this causes me much harm, I am not able to turn them away. In the course of time he wanted to send them all away, but they did not want to go and implored him with exaggerated pleas, until he said to them: You want to cause me harm so that I will return to the category of impregnation for your sake? They were important people and they implored him greatly and he could not deny them. Not more than three months passed until he took me aside privately one day and said to me: You already know how much I warned you about this matter and how much harm has been caused to you by this. If not for this, I would have raised you higher than the sphere of *Aravot*. Now you should know that great harm has been caused me by the revelation of these secrets to them, since they are not ready for this. I am obliged to tell you everything that you will ask of me, as I have told you many times. For your sake they hear and they are not yet worthy to hear and I am caused great harm by this. Therefore, listen to my advice and do not ask me anything in their presence. Leave me alone and they will all leave and we will be left alone and I will raise you higher than the sphere of *Aravot*. I did not want to listen to his words, and said to him that I did not want to be guilty of the sin of hindering the repentance

of those people for my own benefit. He said to me: I do not know if it is a sin or not. In the end, I did not want to obey him in this matter. When he heard my response he began to explain a little about my Animus, as I will now write, praise God. He thought: Perhaps this will lead me to listen to him when I will hear about the attributes of my Animus and I will be satisfied with helping only myself. Nonetheless, I did not want to do so. We tarried together that whole day, until sunset, but he could not convince me. He said to me: Know that there is no more time beyond this day and if you will not listen to me there will be no further repair for the damage which will be caused to me, to you, and to the whole world by the revelation of these secrets to them, since I still do not have permission for this from above. In my sinfulness, I wanted to be foolishly pious and I said to him: Whatever happens to them will also happen to me and if they will not learn, I will also not learn. They will not say in Heaven that for my own benefit I did not care about the benefit of all these righteous people who come to learn. In particular, I could not think about or imagine what happened, because of our great sins. After three days, on the Friday of *parshat Matot–U-Massaei, Rosh Hodesh* of the month of *Ab* in the year 5332 [1572], he was stricken with a plague. On Tuesday, the fifth of *Ab*, he died and went to his eternal reward.

45. Now I will explain what he told me on the day that he warned me about the source of my Animus. He said to me: Know that I do not yet have permission to tell you why you came into the world and who you are. If I would tell you the details of this matter, you would float in the air out of great joy. However, I will tell a little of what I am now allowed to tell you. Know that the whole world depends on your first repairing yourself. Therefore, listen to my advice and first take care of yourself. He told me: Know that the source of your Animus is from the left shoulder of Adam, and it is the aspect of Cain's Animus from the side of the good which is in him. Know that every limb has flesh, veins, and bones. The bones are the most distinguished, for the aspect of the *Moah* which is in their inner core and not for the aspect itself. Next in distinction are the veins, since the life of the person

206

flows through them and is disseminated via the blood which flows through the blood vessels of the person and they connect all the person's organs and give them life. The lowest of the three is the flesh.

The source of my Animus is from the small veins which are disseminated through the flesh of the limb and not from the 365 large veins. The number of scholars that are in the three aspects of the source of the 600,000 small sources is 613. In each of these three aspects there are sources who are the scholars in each and every source (i.e., in every organ). Surrounding them are the branches who are the householders, the practical people and the common people in each and every aspect (of the organ). My Animus is one of the 613 scholars who are in the source of my Animus. There is a great difference between this source of my Animus and the other sources. The analogy is that whoever is from the hand or the leg, there is a great distance between the Animi. However, whoever is from the source of the shoulder, all the scholars who are there, is connected and very close to one another.

This is the sequence of the source of my Animus: the prophet Samuel; After him Hezekiah, the king of Judah; after him, *Rabban* Johanan ben Zakkai; after him, Rabbi Akiva ben Joseph; after him, *Rav* Yeivi Saba of [*Zohar*], *parshat mishpatim*; after him, the *amora* Abbaye, called Naḥmani; after him, me, the young Ḥayyim. This is why *Rabban* Johanan ben Zakkai said as he was dying: "Prepare a chair for Hezekiah, the king of Judah, who is coming."[130] Though there are many Animi in one source, do not think that their true order is the order of their history and existence in the world. Sometimes, the Souls and sources which are greater and more distinguished are in the depths of the *kelippot* and are not able to ascend until a later time and other less distinguished Souls are able to come into the world before the others. Also know that sometimes three or four Souls are transmigrated together in one body, but more than four is impossible. Therefore it is written: "Visiting the guilt of the parents, etc....upon the fourth generation" [Ex 20:5].

46. I will explain the matter of my Animus and from it you will

learn about other sources. Know that the rabbi, the [author of the] *Maggid Mishneh,* sinned accidentally in the matter of a menstruating woman and was required to transmigrate because of this sin. Another person, called R. Saul Tristi, was required to transmigrate for the sin of shedding blood. He wanted to circumcise an infant, but was not an expert and the infant died under his hand. This sin was accidental, but close to being intentional. Right after him was a man called R. Joshua Soriano who was required to transmigrate for the sin of eating forbidden fat intentionally, as mentioned above.[131] The above-mentioned three Animi were branches of my Animus and therefore they were transmigrated together with my Animus. The result is that I am composed of the four Animi, transmigrated together, since we all need to be cleansed of this sin. Even though I did not commit this sin, nonetheless, since I am from the aspect of the vessels I need to clean the decay that was caused by the above-mentioned sins, in order that the life force should again flow to the whole source. We find that the above-mentioned three Animi were old ones which had already transmigrated, but the spark of my Animus was a new one. From the day that Cain sinned and the sparks of his Animus were immersed in the *kelippot,* this spark has not left [the *kelippot*] until this time. Know that it is not literally called new, since it had already come into the world incorporated in Cain's Animus, as will be explained, with God's help, in the discussion of new and old Souls, in another place.[132] Know that it is impossible for there to be more than three transmigrated Animi together with one new one, as the above-mentioned verse [says], "Upon the fourth generation" [Ex 20:5]. This is the secret of "Two or three times to a man" [Jb 33:29], since three Animi are able to transmigrate with one person and no more. However, it is possible for there to be less than this. For example: It is possible for one Soul to transmigrate alone, for one to transmigrate with a new one, for two to transmigrate with a new one, for two to transmigrate alone, for three to transmigrate alone, or for three to transmigrate with a new one. However, it is impossible for more than this [number] to enter the body of one person.

You should also know that the matter of impregnation in a living person is somewhat similar to transmigration, as will be explained in its place, with God's help. As has been explained concerning transmigrations, it is also so with impregnation: It is impossible that more than three Animi, which come to help the Animus of the person, be revealed in the secret of impregnation, so that together with him they are no more than four in total.

There is a difference and distinction between transmigration and impregnation. Transmigration includes those who are transmigrated and come together with the person from the time of birth and do not separate from him at all until the day of his death. They are made into one Animus and suffer the pains and tribulations of that body. However, impregnation is divided into two aspects: The first is where it comes for the needs of the one who is being impregnated, as will be explained in its place, with God's help. The second is one that comes for the needs of the person [who is the recipient of the impregnation]. When he comes for his own needs, then he does not come until the person is thirteen years and a day,[133] since before this time the deeds of a person are not accountable as he is not yet obligated in the commandments and the whole purpose of his coming is to effect a repair for himself. Therefore, he does not come until this person is thirteen years and a day. Then he enters and disseminates throughout the body of this person, in the image of his Animus, and suffers with it the pains and tribulations of this body, like the person's Animus. It resides there in this way for its allotted span of time until it has completed and repaired what it needed. Then it leaves and returns to its Supernal place. However, when it comes for the needs of the person, to assist and aid him, then it also comes after the age of thirteen years, but it comes of its own volition and it is not forced to suffer the anguish of the person and his body and does not feel the body's pains and tribulations. If it finds satisfaction in this person it resides with him and if not, it leaves and says: "Move away from the tents of these wicked men" [Nm 16:26].

I will explain the source of my Animus and from this you will learn about others. My teacher z"l said to me that if I will be worthy, Abbaye will be impregnated in me. If I will be more worthy,

Rav Yeivi Saba will also be impregnated in me. If I will be even more worthy, Rabbi Akiva will also be impregnated in me. Sometimes, one of them, two of them, or all three of them will be impregnated in me, but more than the three of them is impossible. However, if I will be even more worthy, then *Rabban* Johanan ben Zakkai will be impregnated in me with Rabbi Akiva and *Rav* Yeivi Saba. Indeed, Abbaye will relinquish the illumination of impregnation among them. In the same manner, the others will relinquish the illumination of their impregnation, until the three original ones who are in all of them [are reached] and they are, the prophet Samuel, King Hezekiah, and *Rabban* Johanan ben Zakkai.

47. Afterwards, he explained the source of my Animus to me in greater detail. Know that Cain and Abel received Adam's Animus of *Azilut*. It is known that all the worlds are connected to each other and after Adam completed the repair of the part of *Asiyyah*, he was able to ascend to *Yezirah*, and similarly, in this manner until *Azilut*, as mentioned in the beginning of *mishpatim*.[134] However, this only applies to a new Soul, as has been explained elsewhere. It is the case that all the worlds are connected to each other and each is a throne for the next one. There are aspects of Souls that will never attain more than to repair the Animus of *Asiyyah*, some that will be worthy to attain *Yezirah*, some that will be worthy until *Beriah*, and some that will be worthy to repair *Azilut*. Only a small minority of the sources are those that will be worthy to repair all the way to *Azilut*. These are not found as in Cain and Abel, since they are called a new Soul from the aspect of *Hokhmah*, as I have explained. Therefore, they were able to be derived from the Animus of *Azilut*, but no higher than this. However, the rest of the sources, which were old Souls, as I have explained, did not attain *Azilut*—at most to *Beriah*. Know that Cain and Abel contain the two above-mentioned aspects. One is the aspect of the Souls of Cain and Abel alone, which is from *Beriah* and below, like the other sources of old [Souls]. There is a second higher aspect. This is the part of Adam himself which he bequeathed to Cain and Abel when they were born, but which descended to the *kelippot* with Adam's sin.[135] In my humble

opinion, it is the spark from the father's Animus which is given to the son to guide him, as is known. This spark is one of the crowns which are called the bulwark of the world that remained with Adam himself. The spark which he bequeathed to Cain was larger than Abel's since he was the firstborn and the older brother. From this second aspect there is a continuation of all the worlds from the Animus of *Asiyyah* until the Animus of *Azilut*, as they were in Adam himself, as is known. Whoever is from this second aspect has very great attributes, since he has the ability to repair during the first time he comes into the world up to the Animus of *Azilut*, but no further than this, since they are not called completely new Souls. The whole source of my Animus is from this second aspect. I have already explained elsewhere that in this second aspect there are also two aspects which are the inner light and the surrounding light. My whole source is from the inner light. The prophet Elijah z"l is also from the inner light of this aspect. This whole aspect contains the inner light of the Animus of *Azilut* through *Beriah, Yezirah,* and *Asiyyah.* However, Nadav and Avihu were from the surrounding light of the Animus of *Azilut* of this second aspect.

Know that Cain is in the shoulder of the left arm in all the worlds, including *Arikh [Anpin], Abba, Imma, Zeir [Anpin], Nukvah, Asiyyah, Yezirah,* and *Beriah.* Opposite him is Abel in the shoulder of the right arm. In the three worlds mentioned, that is, *Asiyyah, Yezirah,* and *Beriah,* they are called arms. However, in the world of *Azilut,* they are not called arms, but wings. Abel is called the right wing and Cain the left wing. This aspect of arms and wings contains both an inner light and a surrounding light, as mentioned. Thus, Cain and Abel of the second aspect were worthy to receive only up to the wings of *Malkhut* of *Azilut,* which is called the Animus of *Azilut.* All of these sources are able to comprehend and to receive during the first time they come into the world, up to here. However, from there and higher it is impossible for them to comprehend until their second transmigration. Know that whoever is from this second aspect has the ability to reach the Animus of *Azilut* the first time and therefore is called angel. Wherever you will see a *zaddiq* given the name of "angel," it is because he is from this source. Therefore, concerning Pineḥas it says "and she hid him,"[136] in the incident of Raḥab. The sages say that it was not necessary to hide Pineḥas because he was an angel, since he was from this source.[137] Similarly, the prophet Elijah z"l was an angel.[138] Judah and Hezekiah, the sons of R. Hiyya, are also called angels, as the Talmud says: "The dispute is between two *amoraim* in the West[139]...Judah and Hezekiah,"[140] and to accept them as two ministering angels, since they were from the source of this second aspect of Cain. R. Judah bar Ilai was also from this second source of Cain. It says about him in the Talmud that when he washed his face, hands, and feet and welcomed the Sabbath, he was compared to an angel of God Almighty.[141] Understand this.

Indeed, Enoch, who received the Supernal splendor of Adam, which is as high as the Soul of *Azilut,* was also an angel from that part of his source.[142] Therefore, he was a greater angel than Elijah z"l, since whoever is from the aspect of *Azilut* is called an angel and is able to rise to the level of an angel. Remember this.

48. I will explain the concept of the wing. Know that Cain is the left shoulder of Adam, as mentioned above, and it has three aspects, which are: flesh, sinews, and bones, as mentioned above. In *Beriah, Yezirah,* and *Asiyyah,* in all five *Parzufim* and each of their worlds there is a source of Cain, in the left arm of each of them, in the shoulder. Indeed, none of them has the aspect of the wing. However, in the world of *Azilut* there is an aspect of the wing without the flesh, the sinews, and the bones which are in the shoulder. We find that this source of the second aspect of Cain in *Azilut* is the aspect of the shoulder itself, which is the flesh, the vessels, and the bones. It also has an anchorage for the wing which emanates from there, which is the feathers which emanate from the above-mentioned shoulder in *Azilut.* Below there the aspect of the wing is lacking and there is only the shoulder, as mentioned above. I will explain the concept of the wing, since I have previously explained the concept of the shoulder itself. Know that the left wing, which is that of Cain, has 3,000 feathers: 1,000 large ones, 1,000 intermediate ones, and 1,000

small ones. Each feather has 150 Soul sparks. Each feather has an aspect of a follicle from which the feather grows and it has an aspect of the blood which is absorbed by the feather and the feather itself at the top. In the place where it is connected it has a bit of a stalk that does not have barbs coming out of it. A little higher up it has a bit of stalk that is not connected [to the follicle] which does not have any barbs. From there on it has a stalk with two rows of barbs emanating from it. It continues in this way until the end of the feather. The individual strands of feather also have long ones and short ones among them. Know that the short strands are Soul sparks of those who died in their child-hood. Know that the feather is greater in its attributes than the follicle and the blood, and the stalk of the feather is greater than the strands and the long strands are greater than the short ones. Each feather has 150 Soul sparks which is the numerical value of "wing." The computation of the 150 sparks in each feather is derived from the name Cain, which contains the letters *Quf"Nun* [which has the numerical value of 150]. This is only the left wing which belongs to him. However, in the right wing, that of Abel, the feather is divided in a different way, according to the name of Abel. There, each feather is divided into 5 parts and each part is composed of 32 [parts]. This is Abel: five times 32,[143] which also adds up to 150 sparks [sic], as with Cain. However, the 150 sparks of Cain in each feather are separate and called *Qa"N* [150], while those of Abel are divided into 5 parts and each part is divided into 32 sparks. This is the only difference between them.

49. I will now explain the concept of the left wing. The whole shoulder and the whole wing incorporate the source of Cain in its external aspect, as mentioned above. However, my particular true source is in the second aspect of Cain, which is the aspect of the vessels of the left shoulder, as mentioned above, which is found in the four worlds of *Azilut, Beriah, Yezirah,* and *Asiyyah.* Aside from this, my source also has its aspect in the left wing which is in *Malkhut* of *Azilut,* which also contains a wing. It is in feather number 277 [*EZ"R*] of the 1,000 large feathers and con-tains 150 sparks of Souls. These 150 sparks which are in this feather are the true Souls, which are called my source in the

aspect of the wing, aside from its aspect in the vessels of the shoulder itself, as mentioned above. The follicle of this feather is Abbaye. The blood which is in this follicle is Rami bar Ḥama. A bit of the stalk which is stuck in there is divided into two, since the drop of blood which is in the stalk is divided into two aspects, which is not the case after the stalk exits the follicle. The left side is the prophet Samuel and my teacher z"l did not tell me about the right side. The rest of the stalk which is without measure is Hezekiah, the king of Judah. After this, from there onward, the stalk is divided and disseminates among the barbs and all the aspects of the stalk itself support the barbs. We find that every two barbs, right and left, have one base between them. I, the young Ḥayyim, am from the left side of this feather and my base is R. Akiva ben Joseph. Judah and Hezekiah, the sons of R. Ḥiyya, are not from my feather, which is number 277, but they are from another feather which is greater than feather [number] 277. The spark of the Animus of my brother Moses, may God protect him, is from the feather of Judah and Hezekiah. R. Judah bar Ilai is from another feather, lesser than feather 277, and therefore he was the disciple of Rabbi Akiva. The spark of the Animus of Rabbi Solomon ibn Adret z"l and the spark of Rabbi Joseph Karo z"l, the author of *Bet Joseph*, are from the feather of R. Judah bar Ilai.

Know that Cain has a great advantage over Abel and that is as I have already informed you that the *Gevurot* of *Attik Yomin* which are in *Arikh Anpin*, out of which emerges the Supernal *Imma,* were revealed a long time before the *Ḥasadim*. Furthermore, the *Gevurot* are always revealed. Therefore, whoever is from the second aspect of the source of Cain is able to ascend from level of *Gevurot* to [higher] *Gevurot* until the *Gevurot* of *Attik Yomin* and to be suckled from there. This is not true of the aspect of Abel, since he is from the *Ḥasadim* which are always hidden and are not as open. This is the reason the sages said in *Numbers Rabbah, parshat ḥukkat* [19.4]: R. Huna said: "His eyes behold every precious thing" [Jb 28:10]—these are Rabbi Akiva and his comrades, since things which were not revealed to Moses were revealed to Rabbi Akiva. This is also what [the Sages] said in *Ottiyot de-Rabbi*

Akiva,[144] and in tractate *Menaḥot* [29b],[145] that Moses a"h said to God: You have a person like this and you give the Torah through me? This is because Rabbi Akiva was able to comprehend more than he could for the previously mentioned reason. Concerning that which the sages write in tractate *Menaḥot* [29b], that when Moses ascended to Heaven he found God attaching crowns to the letters, he said [to God]: Who stays your hand? He said to him, and so forth, and Akiva ben Joseph is his name, and so forth. The issue is that those who are from the source of Abel are only able to comprehend up to the crowns of the letters which are the ornaments on the letters. However, the source of Cain of the second aspect, mentioned above, has the ability to comprehend up to the musical notes and even further. Indeed, Moses our teacher a"h comprehended it all by means of his mighty deeds.[146]

There is also another reason that those who are from the source of Cain, which is from *Imma*, [are superior] to those who are from the side of *Abba*, from the *Hasadim* and *Gevurot* of *Abba*. The reason is that *Nezah, Hod*, and *Yesod* of *Imma* which are clothed in *Zeir Anpin*, up to the chest of *Zeir*, have only one garment and one covering and the light which emanates from there is great and powerful and the light of the Soul which emanates from there is great and revealed. However, the Soul which is derived from *Abba*, its light is diminished, since *Abba* is covered with two coverings up to the chest of *Zeir*, one of his own and one from *Imma*. From the chest on down *Imma* is completely revealed and *Abba* is covered with one covering. Therefore the Souls which are from the uncovered *Hasadim* or from the uncovered *Gevurot* are superior to the Souls from the covered place, even though the [covered ones] are higher in the aspect of their place. This is the concept of what was said in the Talmud: I saw a topsy-turvy world, the upper [class] underneath and the lower above.[147] There is also a second reason and it is that *Abba* does not have its own illumination, but is only illuminated by the *Hasadim* and *Gevurot* of *Imma* that pass through there, which therefore are greater. There is also another argument, since the *Gevurot* first pass through *Yesod*, as mentioned above, and therefore Cain was

215

the firstborn, in the secret of "A capable wife is a crown for her husband" [Prv 12:4]. Know that in the messianic age, the sources of Cain will be priests and the sources of Abel that were priests until now will then become levites. In the same way, those who were until now in the category of levites, who are from the side of *Gevurah*—for example, Korah who was from the source of Cain—they will all acquire the priesthood, which is a portion of their birthright. This is the secret of "The levitical priests descended from Zadok, etc." [Ez 44:15]. This issue is only found in Ezekiel, because he was from this source of Cain. Therefore, he prophesied these prophecies for the messianic age, that those who were levites until now will then be priests, the descendants of Zadok, and the sources of Abel who were priests will then be levites.[148]

50. Know that if two Souls from one source are found in the same generation, whether in two brothers or two friends, they will be natural enemies and accuse each other, since one will want to grasp and suckle more than the other and they will be naturally and unconsciously jealous of each other. Indeed, if they will comprehend that they are from one source, then they will certainly not accuse each other. Also know that this is only during their lifetime. However, the Souls of the deceased *zaddiqim* very much desire to complete the Souls of those who come from their source who are still alive, since there is no reason for them to be envious and say that they want to comprehend more than the other one, "For there is no action or wisdom in Sheol where you are going" [Eccl 9:10]. On the contrary, they have great benefit from the deeds of the living.[149]

I will now explain the source of my Animus. You need to know that there is no person who does not have an inner light and a surrounding light, in the image [*zelem*],[150] which is above the top of *Zeir Anpin*. When Nadav and Avihu came into the world, it was the beginning of the repair of this source of Cain. All the Souls of this source were incorporated in their image, in their surrounding aspect. However, only the aspect of the sparks of Nadav and Avihu alone had been purified and all the other Souls of this source which were incorporated in the image of their surrounding light were all mixed up in their individual *kelippot*. Afterwards, when another Soul of this source came into the world, then that individual Soul was purified and revealed and all the rest of the Souls in that source came incorporated in the image, in the secret of its surrounding light. However, each one was still encased in its own *kelippah*. Thus the matter continued until the coming into the world of the rabbi, the author of the *Maggid Mishneh*. He studied the philosophy current in the days of Rabbi Jedaiah ha-Penini Bedersi,[151] as is known and is mentioned in the Responsa of Rabbi Solomon ben Adret z"l.[152] The rabbi, the [author of the] *Maggid*, followed [the path of philosophy] and did not believe in the wisdom of the *Kabbalah*. Therefore, the evil forces wanted to mislead him because of this sin. They extracted the spark of my Animus from the depths of the *kelippot* along with several other evil forces in order to mislead him through me. They thought that I had been lost among them for so long that, Heaven forbid, I had already descended to their level. However, since the spark of my Animus was from a high place, and particularly since it was from the source of the rabbi, the [author of the] *Maggid*, himself, the holiness of my Animus overcame the *kelippah* and I bound them. On the contrary, I strengthened him and helped him in the secret of "While men still had authority over men to treat them unjustly" [Eccl 8:9], as is mentioned in the *Saba de-Mishpatim*.[153] Then I remained permanently in the secret of the image over the head of the rabbi, the [author of the] *Maggid*, even though he was not from my level. Then I began to leave the depths of the *kelippot*.

Know that it is impossible for the Soul trapped in the depths of the *kelippot* to leave there and to be immediately transmigrated and enter the world. First, it needs to come three times in the secret of the image of surrounding light of three people who are from its source. Afterwards, it can come alone into the world in the secret of an inner Soul. This is called the first time, since previously it had come incorporated with other sparks—henceforth it is called a transmigration. Thus with me, the spark of my Animus was in the secret of the image above the head of the rabbi, the [author of the] *Maggid*. The second time I was in the

217

image of R. Saul and afterwards, the third time of R. Joshua, as mentioned above. Now, this time I have come in the aspect of the inner Soul and this is the first time I have come into the world. Now, the three people mentioned have transmigrated with me and have come with me and are connected to me for the above-mentioned reason, to repair themselves. Since this is the first time I have left the depths of the *kelippot*, it is very difficult for me to subdue my inclinations. This is the reason for the depression and doubts that I always have. He told me that my sins are not as serious before God as the sins of others, since I am still among the *kelippot* and require great efforts to emerge from them. If not for this, it would have been very easy for me to be very pious, according to the greatness of my Soul, except that this is the first time that I have left the *kelippot*. The same thing happened to King David a"h, as I have explained in another place. There is also another reason for this, and it is that whoever is from the source of Cain, the good in him is very great, but it is mixed up with many filthy and evil *kelippot* and the evil overwhelms the good. The reason is that it is from the source of the *Gevurot*, to which the harsh judgments and *kelippot* are attached.[154]

51. My teacher z"l told me that since I had been in the aspect of the image three times, as mentioned above, now is the first time that I have come in the aspect of the transmigrated inner Soul. The spark which is now beginning to be repaired in me in the secret of the image over my head, in the manner mentioned above, is Yuval, mentioned in Genesis, as is written: "The name of his brother was Yuval, etc." [Gn 4:21], since he too was from the source of Cain. All the cuts and injuries that I always have on my hands from injuries by knives and iron implements are from him, since I did not properly repair him and he still contains *kelippot*. I have already discussed a little about Yuval in the earlier explanations. See there.[155] My teacher z"l also told me that today, on this day, the twenty-eighth of *Tammuz* 5332 [1572], I have already been repaired in the aspect of the Animus of *Asiyyah* up to the aspect of the left arm of *Nukvah* of *Asiyyah* alone.

My teacher z"l also told me that I will have children who will be from my source. He told me that I will have two other wives.

In the next year or year and a half I will marry a wife whose name is Orah Buena and later I will marry another woman and her name is...she is my true match. This previous Passover he told me that my true mate had not yet come into the world. It is possible that she has emerged in the secret of impregnation, but I do not know.

52. I will now explain the connection I have with my colleagues.

My teacher z"l said to me: It has already been explained how all the Souls were all previously incorporated in Adam[156] and afterwards, because of his sin, his limbs shrank and he was reduced in height.[157] We have explained that the meaning of the matter is the descent of the Souls to the depths of the *kelippot*. Only a few of them were left in him, which is the secret of the hundred ells, as the Talmudic sages said concerning, "You lay Your hand upon me" [Ps 139:5]. There were in Adam a few new Souls which did not come into the world and were incorporated in him before the sin and disappeared. These are called the authentic new Souls.[158] Afterwards, there is another level and they are the Souls which remained in Adam. They are still called new Souls, but are not as important as the first ones. When these Souls were transmigrated for the first time after the death of Adam and separated from him, they were then called new. The reason is that the creation of Adam is still not thought of as the first time since his creation was in the aspect of back-to-back, as is known. Therefore, it is not considered the first time until he will come face-to-face. Then it is called the first time. If after Adam's death this Soul will not be worthy to come into the world except through a union of back-to-back, nonetheless it is now also called the first time since it came after Adam's death. After this level is the level of Cain and Abel, since they are from the Souls which remained in Adam and which he bequeathed to Cain and Abel during his lifetime. This level is still not considered the first time, but when these Souls will return to the world after the death of Cain and Abel, even if they will come in the aspect of back-to-back, it will be called the first time and will also be called a new Soul. From then on, if they will return another time, then they will be called transmigrated. Even though they were imparted by Adam to Cain and Abel, since it was during his lifetime and not after his death, they are not considered to have come the first time in their own right. Indeed, despite all this they are lower than those which remained with Adam and are not called as new as those. Afterwards, there is another level, the Souls which fell into the depths of the *kelippot* with Adam's sin, since these are called transmigrated the first time that they come into the world. Afterwards, there is another level which are the Souls which enter proselytes. All of the individual Souls descended to the *kelippot* except for the truly and completely new Souls, which are the first level mentioned above. However, all the others which descended to the *kelippot* are not equal in their level. Those that remained in Adam himself only have one defect, that of Adam, while those he bequeathed to his children, Cain and Abel, have two types of defect, one from Adam and one from Cain and Abel themselves, when they also sinned, as is mentioned in *Tikkunei Zohar*.[159]

Know that when the Souls emerge from the depths of the *kelippot* in order to come into the world, they first need to be impregnated in *Malkhut* in order to be purified and repaired from those *kelippot* and filth that were in them previously. The Soul will have the strength and merit to tarry there, in accord with its limits. The completely new Souls have the ability to tarry in *Malkhut*, in the secret of impregnation, for twelve months and afterwards they come into the world. Therefore, there is impregnation for twelve months, as is mentioned in the Talmudic story of Rabbah Tosfa'ah.[160] In the second category, the Souls which remained in Adam are also new but not like the first ones. Therefore, they only remain in the secret of impregnation in *Malkhut* for nine months and then come into the world. In the third category, the Souls of Cain and Abel are also called new, but not like the first or the second, since they have two types of defect, as mentioned above. Therefore, their period of impregnation is only seven months. In the fourth category are the rest of the Souls which remained from Adam and descended to the *kelippot*. Even though they are still in their first time, or the earlier categories of Souls when they come for the second time, they are all called transmigrated Souls, as mentioned above. All of these are only able to tarry impregnated in *Malkhut* for forty days, corresponding to the creation of the fetus, and afterwards they come into the world. In the fifth category are the Souls of proselytes and they only tarry for three days, for the absorption of the semen, and then they come into the world.

Know that the greatness of their clarification and purification from the *kelippot* is related to the time that they tarry impregnated in *Malkhut*. Also know that there is another process, that all these Souls which emerge from the *kelippot*, [do so] only through the prayers of Israel which ascend in the secret of the feminine waters, as is known, or by means of some Unification that some *zaddiq* performs, or through some commandment that some person performs. There are Souls that descend to the *kelippot* as a result of some defect in the mundane world or because of their own defect which they caused by sinning when they were in this world. If it happens that some Soul escapes and ascends from the *kelippot* to be impregnated in *Malkhut* and to be repaired, as mentioned above, then that Soul which is in *Malkhut* has the possibility of grasping those damaged Souls before they descend to the *kelippot* and to establish them in their place and to return them along with her above, through *Malkhut*, in the secret of impregnation. There, they will all be repaired together and afterwards will come into the world. The concept is that when the Soul is in the bowels of *Malkhut* it always raises the feminine waters, and with the power of the feminine waters which it raises it is also able to raise the other Soul with her. Indeed, this is impossible except that it puts a little of its Spirit into the body, meaning: The first Soul, which is in *Malkhut*, gives of her strength to the damaged Soul and it is clothed with that Spirit and through this is repaired. This Spirit always remains bound with her until the resurrection of the dead and then they are separated.

Know that if the Soul that was already impregnated is on the level of those Souls which remain in the state of impregnation for twelve months, it has the strength and the ability to retain the damaged Soul with her for the twelve months even if it is from the lowest level, which is three days, which are the Souls of prose-lytes. Similarly, if the first one is from the category of nine or seven months and the other one is from a lower level, that is, from the category of forty days or three days, it will remain with her for nine or seven months. However, if it is the opposite situation, that the first one which retains the second is only from the level of nine months and the second one which is retained is from the level of twelve months, then both remain for twelve months, in the manner of always following the course that will raise the thing.

53. My teacher z"l told me that all the colleagues that were with me were all transmigrated from the category of forty days. However, I am new, from the category of Cain and Abel, and it is the first time that I have come into the world. My time is the impregnation of seven months and I retained them so that they should not fall into the *kelippot*. Through me they were able to be retained like me for seven months. Thus, there is a bit of my Spirit mixed in with them and they all are nourished by me. Therefore, I need to exert myself to repair them, since in this way I am repairing myself through their repair, as I will explain below. I am uncertain about what my teacher z"l told me. Did he say that these transmigrated ones were from the category of Adam himself, but they have come two times, since their original source was from nine months? If so, they have now tarried and been repaired through this Soul. If so, if this Soul is from seven months, both will have tarried for nine months. If this is what I heard, then I also have a doubt about myself, since I know that some of these colleagues are from the category of Adam, and if so, both they and I tarried for nine months. I will return to the discussion. I did not repair all the Souls of the above-mentioned colleagues together. First, I tarried with one Soul and later with the assistance of the Soul with which I tarried, the two of us caused another Soul to tarry. That Soul contains two Spirits—one from me and one from the first Soul which I caused to tarry with me. I proceeded with all of them in this manner until the end. We find that the tenth Soul has one Spirit from me and also one Spirit from the nine colleagues which preceded it.

My teacher z"l did not explain their order to me. However, according to the order which my teacher z"l arranged [for the disciples] to repeat his teachings, I understood that the order was as follows: I, the young one, was first; afterwards, Rabbi Jonathan Sagis z"l, then Rabbi Joseph Arzin z"l, and then Rabbi Isaac Cohen z"l. I do not know the rest.

It is not to be wondered that I am the first, as mentioned above, since I contained them. If so, then how are there colleagues who are older than I and preceded me into the world? The concept is that even though I preceded them in the aspect of impregnation, nonetheless, it is possible that they preceded me with regard to the time of the Soul's going into the world. The explanation of the matter is: Know that after the Soul was in the secret of impregnation in *Malkhut*, there are some Souls that descend to this world immediately after their period of impregnation. There are others that descend to the world of *Beriah* and remain there and serve God like the other angels that are there. After a fixed time, or when some prayer or merit or commandment is performed by some person in this world, it then descends and comes into this world. This is the secret of "As the Lord lives, whom I serve" [2 Kgs 5:16], as was stated concerning Elijah. Since, Elijah z"l, after his Animus left the secret of impregnation of *Malkhut* of *Azilut*, descended to *Beriah* and he tarried there and served God like the other servant angels who were there. This is hinted at in the *Zohar, parshat Ahre Mot* [III:68a], concerning the verse "As the Lord lives, whom I serve." See there. There is also a Soul that descends to the world of *Yezirah* and remains there in the manner mentioned and there are some that remain in *Asiyyah*, in this world. However, they all emanate from *Malkhut* of *Azilut*, just that some remain in *Beriah* in the above-mentioned manner, and some in *Yezirah* and some in *Asiyyah*.

All of this depends on the deeds of those below in this world, since there are prayers which do not have the strength to elevate the Soul in the impregnation of *Malkhut* and there are other prayers that are more intentional and acceptable before God which have the strength to bring down the Soul into this world. There are some prayers that are only able to bring the Soul down to the world of *Beriah*, and so forth. This does not depend on the parameters of the Soul itself, but on the actions of those below who are related to those Souls. Similarly, it is according to the person himself who performs the actions, how he will comprehend and have the strength to attract a Soul into his son, one that is closer to him, according to the aspect of the source of his Soul. The other Soul will remain until it will have a redeemer who is closer to it. This matter does not depend on the attributes of the Soul or its lack of importance, to tarry longer than its comrades. The Soul that immediately after it is born from *Malkhut* of *Azilut* descends to this world without any interval certainly has an advantage, since it is not clothed in any world, but just passes through them. However, the one that tarries above is clothed in that world and afterwards comes already clothed. The one who tarries in *Beriah* is not comparable to the one who tarries in *Yezirah* or *Asiyyah*, since the garment of *Beriah* is much finer than that of *Yezirah* and that of *Yezirah* is finer than that of *Asiyyah*. Sometimes the Soul that tarries and is clothed in a certain world is greater in attribute than a Soul which descends immediately to this world without any interruption or garment, since its attribute is greater than the other one. Indeed, in each Soul there is a difference. If the Soul descended immediately it would be brighter than if it tarried in a particular world and then descended.

My teacher z"l told me that the spark of my Animus did not immediately descend to this world after it left the impregnation. Indeed, it tarried above, but he did not tell me in which world it tarried. We will return to our original discussion. My teacher z"l told me that I am required to strive that these colleagues of mine should repair their deeds since my Spirit is in them and I will benefit if they will be *zaddiqim*. However, their Spirit is not within me and they derive no benefit from my deeds—in the manner that I have a share in all the commandments they perform by means of my Spirit which is within them. The explanation of the matter is as follows. Know that there is not a single *zaddiq* who does not have two Souls, as mentioned in the *Zohar*, in the beginning of *parshat Noah*, in the *Tosefta* [I:59b–60a]. This is its meaning. There is the aspect of the inner Soul which comes with the person and there is the surrounding Soul which rests on the person's head in the Supernal world above. This is the aspect of the conduit that a person has to ascend above by means of that Soul. When, Heaven forbid, the inner Soul of the person sins, it slowly descends below to the *kelippot*, until it descends completely—it is all according to the type of sin. When it descends, decayed, to the *kelippot*, then the surrounding Soul descends into the inner part of the person. We find that both have descended from their level. We also find that the person now only has one Soul, since the other one has descended to the *kelippot*. This is the secret of "That person shall be cut off" [Gn17:14, et al.], since it is cut off and enters into the *kelippot*. However, the *zaddiq* has two enduring Souls—one from the surrounding aspect and one from the inner aspect, as is written there in *parshat Noah*[161] concerning "Noah Noah" that every *zaddiq* has two Souls. This is the path of the surrounding Soul that I have. From there all the light and divine effulgence flows down to those colleagues from that side of my Spirit which is in them and everything follows that path. Then, some of their light which flows to them in this manner also flows to my inner Soul from that part of them [which is part of my Soul]. Therefore it necessary for me to endeavor that they be repaired by me and should learn from me. However, my inner Soul is not in partnership with them and therefore they do not benefit from my performance of commandments.

54. Now I will explain the aspect of the connection of the colleagues, including me, to our teacher z"l and also the connection of them to each other. (See in Part II, p. 118b,[162] how there are seven extremities of *Hasadim* in *Da'at* which disseminate into the body and opposite them, seven *Gevurot* which are the sources for the *Hasadim* and *Gevurot* which disseminate below in the body. These are the fourteen sources in *Da'at* which are the Souls of twelve tribes and Ephraim and Menasseh.)

55. Know that there is no (light of a) Soul which does not have a (vessel and) garment in which it is clothed in this world. This garment is mentioned in *Zohar, parshat mishpatim,* in *Rav* Yeivi Saba [II:98b], on the verse "Her food, her clothing, her conjugal rights" [Ex 21:10] and the verse "Since he broke faith with her"

[Ex 21:8]. Concerning the garment (of these colleagues), know that what happened to Joseph the zaddiq with his master's wife in Egypt, that ten drops of semen exuded from between the sparks of his feet,[163] as is written, "And his arms were made firm" [Gn 49:24]. The same happened in the Supernal world, since Joseph is the archetype of *Yesod*. During the same time, Soul sparks (garments of light) exuded from the Supernal *Yesod* of the male without purpose and were not received by the female, consequently they were trapped by the *kelippot*. Sparks of Souls emanated from all the aspects of *Yesod* that are found in the Supernal world and were wasted in the *kelippot*, since all the *Yesods* are hinted at in Joseph.

There are five types of union in the Supernal world and in each of their *Yesods* sparks were exuded, as mentioned above. These are [the five] in their order of importance:

The first union is Israel, who is *Zeir Anpin*, with Rachel. This union is on the Sabbath during the *Musaf* prayer, since Rachel is then enlarged to the whole length of *Zeir Anpin*, just like him. Then they unite by means of the true *Yesod* of *Zeir*.

The second is the union of Jacob with Rachel during the weekday *shaharit* prayers and he unites with her with his true *Yesod*.

The third is the union of Jacob with Leah after midnight and then both of them spread over the whole length of *Zeir* and then it is the other essence of his *Zeir*.

The fourth is the union of Israel with Leah during the weekday *minha* prayers and it only spreads to his upper half, which is up to his chest. Then he unites with her in the first *Yesod* which he had in *Zeir*, while he is in the secret of the six directions, as we have explained in our discussion of the prayers.

The fifth is the union of Jacob with Leah during the weekday *ma'ariv* prayers, which is the upper half of Israel, and then he is another essence of *Yesod*.

These are the five types of union and the five *Yesods*. Drops of semen exuded from all of these *Yesods*. These drops are the secret of [some] of the Soul garments. (These garments always remain with the Souls and do not separate from them, even after the rebirth. It is the same with all the varieties of garments which

226

are acquired by the other Souls. This is the secret of "She kept his garment beside her" [Gn 39:16].)

56. I will now explain these five categories.

The first category, which is the most superior union of all, is the union of Israel with Rachel. It has two aspects, as do the other unions, and they are: When the true *Yesod* of Israel unites with Rachel, there are *Hasadim* and *Gevurot* which flow there from the *Mohin* of *Imma* and also from the *Mohin* of *Abba*. The *Yesod* of *Abba* which is within *Zeir* reaches and spreads to the *Yesod* of *Zeir* itself. The ten *Gevurot*, which are the five of *Abba* and the five of *Imma*, are the aspect of the ten martyrs,[164] whose Souls were clothed in these drops. The five *Gevurot* of *Abba* are: Rabbi Akiva, *Rabban* Simeon ben Gamaliel, Rabbi Yeshovav, Rabbi Ishmael ben Elisha, and Rabbi Judah ben Baba. It seems to me that this is literally their order. Rabbi Akiva is *Hesed* which is in *Gevurah*, *Rabban* Simeon ben Gamaliel is *Gevurah* which is in *Gevurah*, and so forth. Do not be surprised that Rabbi Akiva, who is from the source of Cain, as mentioned above, is from *Imma* and his garment is from *Abba*. It is the same with all the others, each as he is, and there is no objection to this (as will be explained below). In addition, all of them are mixed together in *Yesod* and Joseph has a closeness with all the tribes, being the aspect of *Yesod*. The other martyrs are from the five *Gevurot* of *Imma*. Since these ten mentioned above are from the aspect of *Gevurot*, they needed to be killed, since the *kelippot* cling to *Gevurot* strongly and particularly to the drops of semen such as these which are the very profound and great ones.

The ten *Hasadim* of *Abba* and *Imma* are the [garments of the Souls] of the ten disciples of Rabbi Simeon bar Yohai a"h. They are: R. Eleazar, R. Abba, R. Judah, R. Isaac, and so forth. Since they are from the aspect of *Hasadim*, it was not necessary that they be killed, since the *kelippot* did not cling to them. The three who died in the *Idra Rabba*,[165] R. Yose bar Jacob, R. Hezekiah, and R. Yisa, were aspects of the three *Hasadim* of *Imma* who are uncovered in *Tiferet*, *Nezah*, and *Hod* of *Zeir*, since these are the ones who ascend above and disappear to illuminate above. Therefore, these three colleagues also died and ascended above.

Rabbi Simeon bar Yohai a"h is himself the *Yesod*, from whom the ten drops exuded, and therefore he came to repair them and teach them. Indeed, in the *Gevurot*, that is, the ten martyrs, we do not find that they had a specific teacher. We have already explained the reason with regard to the verse "He who trusts in the Lord shall be surrounded with favor" [Ps 32:10], concerning the phylacteries of *Rabbenu* Tam.[166] The *Hasadim* of *Abba* are not inside the *Yesod* of *Abba*, since it is very narrow; therefore they are emanated outside and surround *Yesod* from the outside. We find that the *Hasadim* of *Abba* and *Imma* are all inside one *Yesod* of *Imma*. However, the *Gevurot* are separated. Some are in the *Yesod* of *Abba* and some in the *Yesod* of *Imma*. Therefore, it is impossible to designate one teacher and a unique *Yesod* for them. I saw from the words of my teacher z"l, which he did not tell me, but through his evasion and not responding completely, after I asked him about the above, that if this is the case, then they should have two teachers for the two *Yesods*. He evaded [my question] and did not want to answer. I do not know the reason. Know that since these ten colleagues [are] from the aspect of the *Hasadim* of the Supernal union which is in all of them, which is Israel and Rachel, as mentioned above, therefore all the secrets of the Torah were explained and revealed to them without any anguish, something that will not happen until the generation of the Messiah, as is mentioned several places in the *Zohar*.[167]

The second is the union of Jacob and Rachel. Know that, unlike Leah, Rachel does not contain stern judgments *[Dinim]*. In addition, Jacob is from the illumination of the *Mohin* of *Abba* alone, and therefore, they are only the *Hasadim* and *Gevurot* of *Abba* here. Thus, Rabbi Judah the Prince, who arranged the *Mishnah*, is the *Yesod* and his disciples are the drops which exuded from him and they are: R. Hiyya, R. Oshaiah, Bar Kappara, R. Levi bar Sisi, R. Hanina bar Hama, and many others.

Third. The third one in order of importance of the unions is that of Jacob and Leah after midnight—even though it is Leah and she contains stern judgments, but it is the aspect of after midnight, where they are sweetened. They are disseminated over the whole length of *Zeir*, which is also true of the previous union, that of Jacob and Rachel. These are the ten that have five *Hasadim* and five *Gevurot* from *Abba*. Therefore, in these two unions, which are the second one of Jacob and Rachel and the third one of Jacob and Leah after midnight, there is no killing, since they are from the aspect of Jacob, which is from the side of *Abba*. Know that in the darkness before dawn there is more mercy, since it is almost called day. There is a second union of Jacob and Leah, as mentioned, to which they return a second time, as is mentioned in *parshat shemot*.[168] Only two drops are exuded; the first contains five *Hasadim* and the second contains five *Gevurot*. These two drops are on a higher level than the ten mentioned above, which exuded from the union after midnight. These twelve drops are my colleagues who study with my teacher z"l, and he himself is the *Yesod* from which these twelve drops exude.

Know that before midnight Jacob and Leah were up to the chest of Israel, as was explained with the fifth union. After midnight they expand to the end. Therefore, the first impression of the first *Yesod* prior to midnight does not disappear, since Jacob and Leah did not return after midnight in the secret of back-to-back, but were face-to-face when they spread to the bottom. Therefore, what occurred to them previously did not disappear. We find that there are ten other drops which were exuded by the aspect of that *Yesod* which is prior to midnight, but they do not exit until after midnight. There are two others from the darkness before dawn, as mentioned above, and they are superior to these ten. Indeed, these second twelve are on a lower level than the first twelve. It is possible that the two from the darkness before dawn of the second aspect should be included with the first ten, since they are superior to the second ten. Therefore, these second twelve began to study with our teacher z"l, in his school, before we, who are the first twelve, entered. The reason is that they are from the aspect prior to midnight. In addition, they have no independent foundation or teacher, since the aspect of the two foundations *[Yesodot]* prior to midnight and after midnight is included in each other and it is all one *Yesod*. Know and see how four unions are incorporated in this union. The third union and the four of them are called one union, for the above-mentioned reasons. Afterwards, at the end of the discussion, I will explain who are all of these colleagues.

The fourth, according to the order of unions, is the union of Israel and Leah during the *minḥa* prayers. Since it is from the chest and upwards, there is no place for dissemination to the *Hasadim* and *Gevurot*. Therefore, the *Hasadim* gather in the right arm and the *Gevurot* in the left arm and they are called only two drops. Since his union during *minḥa* with Leah contains the stern judgments, they are therefore connected with the martyrs of Lydda, the two brothers Pappus and Julianus.[169] Their attributes increased and they achieved the aspect of Israel. There is no recognizable *Yesod* there and therefore they do not have a particular *Yesod* or teacher.

The fifth, which is the last of all, is Jacob and Leah before midnight and these are completely stern judgments. These are the martyrs of Bethar,[170] and their *Yesod* was Rabbi Eleazar of Modi'in who was killed at Bethar, as is known.[171] (Know that all the lights of the Souls of Israel have internal and external garments which are from the *Moḥin* and the organs which descend are turned into drops of semen from the various types of *Yesod*, mentioned above, but not by means of nocturnal emission.) There are differences and distinctions between these fifty or more drops, as mentioned, of the five unions mentioned, in comparison to all other Souls. They have greater and mightier attributes than the other Souls. All the other Souls come, not by means of nocturnal emission, but by means of union which results from the awakening of the Feminine [aspect of divinity] who is aroused to union and yearns for him and afterwards, he is also aroused. Therefore, when the Male [aspect of divinity] is not awakened on his own, but is aroused by her, those drops of the *Hasadim* and *Gevurot* which flow from this union do not flow from his *Da'at* itself, but only from the *Hasadim* and *Gevurot* which are disseminated by him below, in the three extremities, after they have been clothed and tarried below. However, since the flow of these drops mentioned above was without the arousal of the Feminine, they are the drops of nocturnal emission, mentioned above. It is certain that they emanated from the arousal of the Masculine alone, and the male of that Animus wanted to unite with his Feminine, but did not find her, since she was below in *Beriah* or elsewhere, and then they were emitted needlessly. Since they came from the arousal of the Masculine, it is certain that they are very great and only emanate from the *Moah* of *Da'at* itself of the *Hasadim* and *Gevurot* which are above (since there is the place where desire is awakened). When they leave *Yesod* they do not (first) descend and are clothed in the six extremities (of the male), but pass through from there via the conduit alone (and exit from the *Yesod*). Therefore, the attributes of these Souls are immeasurably greater than all other Souls. Everything we have said concerns the garments (and vessels) of the Souls (themselves, called lights), out of which are made 248 organs in which the Soul is clothed. Since the aspects of the (lights of) these Souls of the above-mentioned ones are all, in the above path, from the aspect of *Da'at* itself and not from the dissemination below, they have also been given garments which are from these drops, mentioned above, which are also from *Da'at*. Even though we have explained that there is a strong connection between all the above-mentioned drops, this is all in the aspects of the drops and the garments. However, concerning the (lights of the) Souls themselves, each is from its own source, but all are aspects of *Da'at* itself, but they are not connected and are not from one source.

Also know that these drops, which are in the category of the garments, also have an internal and external aspect. There are drops which emanate from the external side which is the garment of *Nezah, Hod,* and *Yesod* of *Abba* or *Imma* which is in *Zeir* or in Jacob. There are also drops which emanate from their internal aspect, which are from the *Mohin* themselves which are in *Nezah, Hod,* and *Yesod* of *Abba* or *Imma,* and so forth. All of the above (the drops of the garments) of the internal aspect are the *Mohin* themselves. There are other drops which look exactly like the above, but they are from the external aspect of the garments, mentioned above. However, they also emanate from *Da'at* itself above, but they are from the external aspect which are the garments of *Nezah, Hod,* and *Yesod* of *Abba,* and so forth, as mentioned above. My teacher z"l did not explain to me who they are, except for those of the third union, as I have explained, with God's help.

All the aspects of these drops are called the remnant in the words of the Prophets and those that are in the category of Israel are called the remnant of Israel, as Scripture says, "The remnant of Israel shall do no wrong, etc." [Zep 3:13]. Those who are in the category of Jacob are called the remnant of Jacob, as Scripture says, "The remnant of Jacob shall be among the nations, etc." [Mi 5:6]. There are five aspects in the five unions mentioned above. Therefore, the remnant of Israel and the remnant of Jacob are mentioned many times by the Prophets in connection with them.

57. I will explain the concept of my teacher's z"l associations. Know that even though the order of the attributes of the above-mentioned drops has already been explained above, indeed you should know that these drops of the third union of Jacob and Leah after midnight are the last ones to come into the world, even though this is not their order of attributes, as mentioned above. Since they have come into this last exile, they are alluded to in the prophecy of Isaiah a"h in the verses "The Dumah Pronouncement. A call comes to me from Seir: Watchman, what of the night?, etc." [Is 21:11]. This prophecy concerns this last exile, as is mentioned in the *Zohar* [II:130b]. It is already known that *Leyl* is before midnight and *Laylah* is after midnight as is mentioned in the *Zohar parshat Bo* [II:38a].[172] This is the matter of the two groups of disciples in my teacher's z"l school. All of them are from the union after midnight, but a few of them are from the first half of the night, as mentioned above. Concerning them it says that the *Shekhinah* cries out sitting in her exile in Seir, which is the exile of Edom, and says to God "Watchman, what of the night *[Laylah],*" who are the first group, which is from the union after midnight, which is called *Laylah.* And thus, "Watchman, what of the *Leyl*"—what will you do with those of the second group, who are derived from the first half of the night, which are called *Leyl,* except that they emerged during the second half of

the night, as mentioned above? God answers her: "The watch-man replied, morning came" [Is 21:12], who are the four who are born of the union of the darkness before dawn. "And so did *Lay-lah*"—they are the twenty who are born of the union after midnight, which is called *Laylah*. He said further: "If you would inquire, inquire, etc." [Is 21:12]. Since these groups are in the last generation before the Messiah, they need to increase penance and to increase prayers and supplications. Also in the verse "Only a remnant shall return, only a remnant of Jacob, to mighty God" [Is 10:21], remnant is repeated twice, in relation to these two groups.

My teacher z"l told me that since I and these colleagues are all from the aspect of the union after midnight, therefore we should be very careful to literally rise at midnight and this will help us very much. He cautioned us very much about this matter.

58. My teacher z"l told me that not all of our colleagues will be permanently established and a few of them still need to be clari-fied and changed and others will be put in their place, as I will explain, with God's help. I will now write about the colleagues who study with us, though I do not know which ones will have others exchanged in their places.

The second group who are after midnight includes: myself, the young Hayyim, Rabbi Jonathan Sagis z"l, Rabbi Joseph Arzin z"l, Rabbi Isaac Cohen z"l, Rabbi Gedaliah ha-Levi, Rabbi Samuel Uceda, Rabbi Judah Mashan, Rabbi Abraham Gabriel, Rabbi Shabbetai Menasseh, Rabbi Joseph ibn Tabul, and Rabbi Elia Falco z"l.

This group is from the interior of the *Mohin* of *Da'at*, as men-tioned above. There is another group related to them and they are from the garments of *Nezah, Hod,* and *Yesod,* and they are called the externality of the garments, as mentioned above, and they are my teacher Rabbi Moses Alshekh, may God protect him, Rabbi Moses Najara, Rabbi Isaac Arha z"l, Rabbi Solomon Saba'an, Rabbi Mordecai Gallico z"l, Rabbi Jacob Mas'ud z"l, Rabbi Joseph Alton, Rabbi Moses Mintz z"l, Rabbi Moses Jonah, and Rabbi Abraham Guacil.

The second group, which are from the interior of the *Moḥin*, are also from *Da'at*, from the union after midnight, but they are from the aspect before midnight, as mentioned above. They are Rabbi Yom Tov Zaḥalon, Rabbi Joseph Cohen, Rabbi Jacob Altaras, Rabbi David Cohen, Rabbi Isaac Krispi, Rabbi Simeon Uri and his brother Rabbi Israel Uri, Rabbi Abraham Arovas, Rabbi Moses Alshekh z"l, the Honorable Rabbi Israel Levi, the Honorable Rabbi Joseph Kanfilias, the Honorable Rabbi Judah Ashkenazi, the Honorable Rabbi Naphtali z"l, who were relatives of my teacher z"l.

I have already said that I do not know explicitly if all the above-mentioned are included, but I heard in a general way from my teacher z"l about these three groups.

There is a fourth group, which are the external garments and they are related to the second group of internal ones mentioned. They are the Honorable Rabbi Abraham ha-Levi, the Honorable Rabbi Moses Meshammash z"l, the Honorable Rabbi Judah Romano, and so forth. However, I only heard from my teacher z"l in detail about the colleagues in my group, the first one. In my humble opinion, the matter of the second interior group is more accurate. They are Rabbi Yom Tov Zaḥalon, Rabbi Jacob Altaras, Rabbi Jacob Krispi, the Honorable Rabbi Israel Levi, the Honorable Rabbi Moses Alshekh z"l,[173] Rabbi David Cohen, Rabbi Joseph Cohen, the Honorable Rabbi Abraham Arovas, and the Honorable Rabbi Joseph Kanfilias. Also, Rabbi Elia Almiridi, even though he did not study with them, it seems to me that he was included in their group. It seems to me more explicit that Rabbi Simeon Uri was not included in their group.

It seems to me, with regard to the group of older scholars which is related to our group, except that it is from the exterior, as mentioned above, that my teacher, Rabbi Moses Alshekh, may God protect and bless him, was the counterpart of my aspect. My teacher z"l wanted to include my teacher Rabbi Moses Alshekh, may God protect and bless him, Rabbi Moses Najara, Rabbi Jacob Mas'ud, and Rabbi Shabbetai Meyuḥas z"l in our group. He told me that they are from the two drops which are from the early morning. They are from the aspect prior to midnight, but since they are from the early morning, it is possible for them to join us.

I do not know the details of our group, which of us are those who are literally from the early morning of the union after midnight.

I am also uncertain if two of the above-mentioned four are literally in our group, since there were only ten in our group and there should be twelve. The other two are from the darkness before dawn, prior to midnight, in [the period] after midnight.

59. Two days before his death, my teacher z"l told me that even those colleagues who were in the first group with me needed to be clarified once more and a few of them may be replaced by others. The secret of the matter is according to what we have explained concerning the verse "If your enemy is hungry, give him bread to eat" [Prv 25:21]. Since these colleagues are not complete, that is, there are those among them who have a small amount of that aspect of the garment of the superior Soul, mentioned above, which is from the drop from after midnight, as mentioned above, they are not all equal. There are some who are majority good and a minority bad and there are those who are majority bad and a minority good and some who are in the middle. In this way there are several levels. He told me that those who are majority good will certainly remain that way. The others who are majority bad and minority good will take the bad from the above-mentioned and give them the good which is in them. Then, there will remain those who are completely good and those who are completely bad. My teacher told me that this was his intention in gathering them. By means of the fellowship and love that are between the colleagues, they will flow from one to another. The good will migrate to those who are majority good and they will be completed. The minority of bad will become associated with those who are majority bad. Then, those who are completely from the bad aspect will depart and the others who are completely from the good aspect will remain. My teacher z"l told me that for this reason it is important for a person to associate with those evil people who are majority bad and minority good, in order to return them in penance, since through this he

will take the good that is in them, particularly if he will encounter a person who has the portion of good that is missing from the source of his own Soul, so he can take it and be completed with it. Therefore, my teacher z"l cautioned me to love the above-mentioned colleagues very much and teach them, since through this I can clarify my good part that is mixed within them and I will take it and will complete myself. Indeed, for the person who is in between and average, it depends on his deeds. If he desires, he can become entirely good or the opposite. My teacher z"l told me on that day that R. Elia Falco z"l was average and this is the secret of what the sages said about the verse "All the host of heaven standing in attendance, etc." "Who will entice Ahab, etc." [1 Kgs 22:19-20]. The Talmudic sages said, "Ahab was indecisive."[174] Because of this he could not be punished until he turned to the evil side, since while he was indecisive he could not be punished. Similarly, from Ahab to R. Elia Falco, both of whom were from the same source, they always remained in between and indecisive. This is the reason that my teacher z"l wanted to dismiss him from our fraternity. He did not remove him because he was indecisive, until there occurred the great vexations with Rabbi Joseph Arzin, may God protect him, and then he began to turn to the evil side. However, despite this, the minority of good still remained and then he was dismissed from our fraternity. Concerning Rabbi Joseph Arzin, he told me that if his father would have come to Safed in that year, he too would be damaged. Aside from this, on the day that he expelled Rabbi Elia Falco, he certainly wanted to expel him also. Rabbi Jonathan Sagis z"l had a majority of good and there was no doubt that he might turn to the evil side. Rabbi Gedaliah Levi also had a majority of good and there was no doubt about him. Rabbi Isaac Cohen z"l had a majority of good, but there was a doubt about him, not out of lack of faith in my teacher z"l, but for another reason, which he did not want to explain. Rabbi Samuel Uceda had a majority of good, but there was a doubt if he would remain so. Rabbi Abraham Gabriel, Rabbi Shabbetai Menasseh, Rabbi Judah Mashan, and Rabbi Joseph Tabul Moghrabi were completely banished, but there is still some doubt about Rabbi Judah Mashan. He told me that in the future I will encounter a great trial, whether I will retain my love for my teacher z"l. Afterwards, my teacher z"l told me that his intention was to expel all of my colleagues and only leave three or four remaining.

My teacher z"l told me that I am required to favor sinners more than other people, since all the evil people of this generation are in the category of the mixed multitude.[175] The majority or almost all of them are from the source of Cain. His good sparks were mixed up with completely bad or mostly bad and therefore I am obligated to repair them, since they are from my source. Not only that, but I am able to repair through my deeds even the evil people of previous generations who are in *Gehenna*, to raise them from *Gehenna* and to put them into bodies which will return to this world to be repaired. The reason is that since my Animus is one of the primary ones from the Animus of Cain and also because I came now, in the final generation, as mentioned above. In addition, since I come from the aspect of the highest drops which are from the *Moaḥ* of *Da'at* itself and not from the six points which are disseminated through the body, therefore I have the above-mentioned divine power, if I will want to improve my deeds. He said that for this reason if I would favor the sinners of this generation, they would listen to my voice and my words would enter their ears. In the very week that he died, he taught me a Unification to raise seventy sparks which still remained in *Gehenna* among the *kelippot*, which were from Cain's source and from the source of my Animus. He also cautioned me about a few things as I will write, and taught me to raise them by means of their source with which they are united. This is the matter:

There are seven aspects and each has a few sparks and they correspond to the seven *sefirot*. This is their order: Korah in *Ḥesed* and he has thirteen sparks; Jethro in *Gevurah* and he has six sparks; Yuval in *Tiferet* and he has nine sparks; Dathan and Abiram in *Nezaḥ* and *Hod* and they have twelve sparks; Jabal in *Yesod* and he has eight sparks; Lamech in *Malkhut* and he has twenty-two sparks. He commanded me to raise them by means of their

237

sources and they are these: Korah with Elisha the prophet; Jethro with *Rabban* Johanan ben Zakkai; Yuval with Rabbi Judah Handoah; Dathan and Abiram with *Rabban* Gamaliel; Jabal with Bali, mentioned in the Talmud; Lamech with *Rav* Malchio. He commanded me to raise them by means of seven angels, and they are: the abbreviations of Argamon, Akatriel, and Metatron and all of them with vowels. Each and every letter of all of them with two vowels, and they are *Shewa, Kamez.* He commanded me to be careful about several things that are related to them, and they are: eye, ear, and mouth, contemplation of evil, the nose, and kabbalistic knowledge, to the extent possible. He commanded me to raise them by means of intentions with a few names. See and understand that each spark is one *Yud,* since each Soul is composed of ten *sefirot.* Therefore, thirteen sparks are related to the name of 130 *Alephs* and twelve sparks are related to the 120 combinations of *Elohim.* It is so with all of them until *Malkhut,* which is the twenty-two sparks related to the twenty-two letters, which when written out in full are the Tetragrammaton and Lord. In my humble opinion, the source of my Animus is united with *Rabban* Johanan ben Zakkai in [*Gevurah*]. Therefore, I will briefly arrange them in the order that my teacher z"l did, each by itself. They are:

Korah. Thirteen sparks. Elisha. *Yud Yud Heh Yud Heh Vav Yud Heh Vav Heh.* Eye beyond four ells. *Hesed.* Michael, Uriel.

Dathan and Abiram. Twelve sparks. *Rabban* Gamaliel. 120 combinations of *Elohim.* Contemplation of wisdom. *Nezah* and *Hod.* Raphael and Gabriel.

Jethro. Six sparks. *Rabban* Johanan ben Zakkai. *Y"H Yud Heh Vav Heh.* An ear which listens to slander and idle talk. *Gevurah.* Michael.

Jabal. Eight sparks. Bali. *Yah Adonai.* A nose which smells the odor of excrement and the odor of illicit sex. *Yesod.* Nuriel.

Yuval. Nine sparks. *Rav* Judah Handoah. *YHV"H ADN"Y.* A mouth that speaks idle things and gossip. *Tiferet.* Akatriel.

Lamech. Twenty-two sparks. *Rav* Malchio. *Yud Heh Vav Heh ALPh DLT NUN YUD.* Knowledge and much study of kabbalistic wisdom. *Malkhut.* Metatron.

He also commanded me to be careful about several other things, and they are: striding boldly; arrogance; eating little; intention in prayer; respecting our judges; blessings over enjoyments; salt should be on the table; not to drink water after the Grace after meals; to be careful with the honor of colleagues.

He commanded me further with regard to the following: To put my feet together and concentrate on the name *Abgitaz,* as mentioned above and as explained in its place.[176] To concentrate on the name Zohariel, while putting on the Sabbath garments, as is explained in its place. Not to stroke the beard and thereby pull out even one hair, even during activities, and to concentrate that two times "beard" [in *gematria*] equals "Shaddai," as is explained in its place. Not to join and interlace the ten fingers of the right and left hand and to concentrate on them with the name *AHV"H*, which is finger in *gematria,* as is explained in its place. To be careful that the straps of the phylacteries do not touch the ground and to concentrate that "strap" equals twice the name *El* fully spelled out, in *gematria,* as is mentioned in its place. To look at the cup of [wine] over which the blessing is made and to concentrate that the water which you are pouring into the wine equals, in *gematria,* the nine *Yuds* which are found in the four divine names of seventy-two letters, sixty-three letters, forty-five letters, and fifty-two letters.[177]

Until here is what he told me on the above-mentioned day, three days before my teacher z"l became ill.

60. My teacher z"l told me that I should be very careful to wake up at midnight for the following reason.[178] I am from the union of Jacob and Leah after midnight and if on some occasion I was not able to remain awake the whole second half of the night, I should get up and perform the ritual, which is known, and return to sleep. In any event, I should arise before dawn, which is the union of the darkness before dawn, mentioned above.

My teacher z"l told me that I have now already begun to repair the damage of Cain's sin. Therefore, when I think about the order that my teacher z"l arranged for me to concentrate on when the depths of the sea overwhelm me to sadden me and tempt me to sin, to concentrate on "Extending kindness to the thousandth generation" [Ex 34:7], as is known, in the word *Alafim* [thousands] I should concentrate on the names *Adonai* and *Elohim*, which are two thousands and equal that in *gematria*. He told me that this name of God will be thousands when fully spelled out and equals *Erez* [land] in *gematria*. I should concentrate on this every day and if I will concentrate on it and think about it, it will be very helpful. I need to be particularly careful about this on those days when I study Torah. The secret of the matter is that since Cain brought flax seed as his offering,[179] and we have already explained this matter at length, since it weakens the power of the land, and since *Malkhut* is called land, it returned to being barren. Therefore, it was decreed concerning Cain: "You shall become a ceaseless wanderer on the land" [Gn 4:12]. The name *Elohim* with the addition of *Alephs* equals *Malkhut*, as mentioned, during the time it is called *Erez*, which is another name for the [divine] name mentioned. I should concentrate on repairing this defect which made her barren because of the flax, and now return to repair her and to make her *Erez*, by means of this substitution. All the external ones cling to the evil *kelippot* which adhered to Cain and all of them want to cleave to and comprehend the letter *Aleph*, which is substituted for the letter *Heh* of *Elohim*, as mentioned, and they are not able to comprehend it.

61. My teacher z"l told me that my wife is now pregnant. If it will be a girl, there won't be anyone with as much sense as her. If it is a boy, there won't be anyone like him in the world and there won't be found anywhere such great love as there will be between him and me. In the future, he will teach me kabbalistic wisdom. He is not from my source. His level is three thousand levels higher than mine; he will never be separated from my source, even after the resurrection, as I have explained elsewhere. When there is a difference of 500 levels or more between father and son, they are made one source. Specifically, we relate in two aspects: first, the aspect of father and son; second, the aspect of teacher and student. He will be connected to me by being my teacher.

62. He commanded me to be very careful after reciting the *Olenu* prayer, to recite the verse "And the Lord shall be king over

all the earth, etc." [Zec 14:9]. I should concentrate on beginning with the letter *Vav* and concluding with the letter *Dalet*, which equal ten in *gematria*. I should concentrate on the verse "Am I not more devoted to you than ten sons?" [1 Sm 1:8]; I should concentrate on illuminating and drawing forth the ten children in Leah, as has been explained concerning that verse. See there.[180]

63. He commanded me about a Unification that I should perform on Friday night. It seems to me that it would also be beneficial on weekday nights. This is briefly what I should concentrate on. I should cleave to and connect my Animus with the Animus of Simeon ha-Pakuli and I should concentrate on connecting the aspect of my Soul with his Soul in the world of *Beriah*. This is by means of the name Akatriel, with each letter punctuated with the vowel *Kamez*. I should concentrate on connecting my Soul with his Soul in all ten *sefirot* of *Beriah*. Therefore, I need to concentrate on the above-mentioned name ten times in the ten *sefirot* of *Beriah* and I should always connect my Soul with his Soul, by means of this name. Afterwards, I should concentrate on connecting my Spirit with the Spirit of *Rabban* Johanan ben Zakkai in the world of *Yezirah* by means of the name Hafniel, completely punctuated with [the vowel] *Patah*. I should concentrate on this name ten times in the ten *sefirot* of *Yezirah*, in the above-mentioned manner. Afterwards, I should concentrate on connecting my Animus with the Animus of *Rav* Yeivi Saba in the world of *Asiyyah* by means of the name Yohakh, completely punctuated with [the vowel] *Zeire*. I should concentrate on this name ten times in the ten *sefirot* of *Asiyyah*, in the above-mentioned manner. As I concentrate on this name of *Yohakh*, I need to imagine him as a man with a child riding on his shoulders and the name *Yohakh* written on his heart.

The abbreviation of these three names is *AH"Y* and equals nineteen in *gematria*. They are the secret of the nineteen blessings that Simeon ha-Pakuli arranged for *Rabban* Gamaliel.[181] My teacher z"l told me that during that time I was able to connect my Soul with Simeon ha-Pakuli even in the world of *Beriah*, by means of some commandment or repair that I had, and I have the power to cleave to him even in the world of *Beriah*. However, I was only able to cleave to *Rabban* Johanan ben Zakkai in the world of *Yezirah*, and this was through the commandments I had, by means of which I was able to cleave to him. However, I do not yet have the power to cleave to *Rav* Yeivi Saba, except in the world of *Asiyyah*. I find that the matter does not depend on the level or attributes of the above mentioned *zaddiqim*, but on the specific commandments which I perform, by means of which I will be able to cleave to this one more than that one. There is one commandment that *Rav* Yeivi Saba performed and I do the same and thereby I am connected with him in the world of *Asiyyah*. There is another commandment that *Rabban* Johanan ben Zakkai performed and I also perform it with great zeal and by means of it I am able to cleave to him even in the world of *Yezirah*. Similarly, in the same manner with Simeon ha-Pakuli. Simeon ha-Pakuli is not literally from my source, but he is one of the group who entered and were connected with the palace of love, like Rabbi Akiva, as is mentioned in the *Zohar, parshat Pekudai*, in the palace mentioned.[182] Simeon ha-Pakuli is one of them and in this way they are connected to each other.

64. My teacher z"l told me that since the sparks of Cain's source were among the *kelippah* of Sisera, as is explained by us, the Soul of Rabbi Akiva was there and therefore he was born to the descendants of Sisera, as is known.[183] He told me that my Animus was also situated there.

He told me that when I lie down [I should recite] the verse "Into Your hand I entrust my spirit, etc." [Ps 31:6]. I should concentrate on the divine name in this verse with addition of *HYHY"N*, which is called the name of fifty-two, particularly for me, since I am a double transmigration, since there is in me part of my Animus and part of Rabbi Akiva. I should be careful to always revere this name with *HYHY"N* and never remove it from my heart. This name is called the cave of Machpelah because *Yud* is two *Yuds, Heh* is two *Hehs, Vav* is two *Vavs, Heh* is two *Hehs*.[184]

My teacher z"l cautioned me concerning the order of "A Prayer of David" [Ps 86] which is recited after the *Kedushah* of "And a redeemer shall come to Zion," that I should recite it with complete concentration, since the primary source of my illumination is from *Yezirah*. Since all the Psalms are in the world of *Yezirah* and that is the source of my Soul and comprehension, since all the Psalms are in the category of *Gevurot*, as is known, my Soul is also from the *Gevurot*, as is known.

In my book which I wrote on the *Kavvanot* for the morning prayers, in the prayer "Merciful Father, hear our voice," I explained the *Kavvanah* of the divine name which is there. See there, and you will know that it is required for me and it is to raise the person Heavenward through this *Kavvanah*.[185]

In the above-mentioned book, I explained what a person should concentrate on when he arises at midnight to mourn the destruction of the Temple. The primary reason is that the central point and source of Rachel begins to descend to the world of *Beriah* at midnight. The reason for her descent into exile is to collect the Soul sparks that are scattered among the *kelippot*. Therefore, we cry and are anguished about the exile of the *Shekhinah*, since we caused it by our sins and our grafting of evil on good and good on evil, as is known. My teacher z"l told me that in particular one who knows that he is from the source of Cain, in which the filth of the Serpent predominates, and the pure Souls are immersed in this filth, his hand is in this treachery more than other people. Therefore, my teacher z"l cautioned me very much concerning this crying and that I am required to do it more than other people.[186]

Part Five

— ADDITIONS AND MISCELLANIA —

1. Rabbi Isaac ha-Cohen z"l told me: When my teacher z"l was dying, as I left his side, he went over [to my teacher] and cried before him, saying: Is this the hope we all longed for in your lifetime, to see goodness, Torah, and great wisdom in the world? He answered him: If I had found that only one of you was completely righteous, I would not have been taken from this world. In the course of the conversation, he asked him about me, and he said: Where did he go? Has he left me in such an hour? He was very anguished. [R. Isaac] understood from his words that he had wanted to transmit something esoteric. Then [R. Isaac] said to him: What will we do from now on? He said: Tell the colleagues in my name, from this day forth they should not occupy themselves at all with this wisdom that I have taught them since they did not understand it properly. They will come to heresy and spiritual ruin, Heaven forbid. Indeed, only Rabbi Ḥayyim should engage in it, alone, silently and in secret. He responded: Have we no further hope, God forbid? He said to him: If you will be worthy, I will come and teach you. He said: How will you come to teach us, after you have departed from this world? He said to him: You have no concern with esoteric matters, about how I will come to you, whether in a dream, awake, or in a vision. Suddenly he said to him: Hurry, leave the house since you are a *cohen* and my time has come.[1] I have no leave to expand on anything. Before he could cross the threshold, he opened his mouth and his Soul left with a kiss.[2]

2. It is a basic principle that the Souls of *Abba* and *Imma* of *Beriah* are not incorporated in Adam, but only from *Zeir* and *Nukvah* and below. There are ten *Parzufim: Zeir* and *Nukvah* of *Beriah; Abba, Imma, Zeir,* and *Nukvah* of *Yezirah; Abba, Imma, Zeir,* and *Nukvah* of *Asiyyah.* Each of these ten *Parzufim* is composed of

244

ten *sefirot* (and all ten consist of ten *sefirot*), therefore the ten *Parzufim* are one thousand *sefirot*. Each *Parzuf* contains one hundred *sefirot* and one-tenth of them are in the category of *Keter*. We find that in the ten *Parzufim* there are one hundred *Keters*. These alone remained within Adam after the sin and are called the hundred conduits which were diminished. All nine hundred *sefirot* fell into the *kelippot*. These hundred *Keters* also had a defect, since the light of the nine first *sefirot*, which is called the "*Zihara Ila'ah*,"[3] disappeared from them. The ten *sefirot* within each *Keter* were left with the light of their Animus, which is the lower *Malkhut* which is in each *Keter*. These three aspects in the Souls were incorporated in Adam before he sinned in the ten *Parzufim* which are found from *Zeir* of *Beriah* until the end of *Nukvah* of *Asiyyah*. The first is the aspect of the lights called *Yehidah*, *Hayyah, Neshamah, Ruah*,[4] which are in the one hundred *Keters* which are in them. These left him when he sinned and ascended above and are called the Supernal splendor of Enoch. The second one is inferior to it and remained in Adam after he sinned. It did not leave him nor did it descend to the *kelippot*. This is the aspect of the light which is called Animus which is in the hundred *Keters* which is in each of the ten *sefirot* which is in each *Parzuf* of the ten *Parzufim* mentioned above. The third aspect is the most inferior of all and it is all the Souls which are all the lights of the nine lower aspects which are in each *sefirah* of the ten *sefirot* which is in each of the ten *Parzufim* mentioned. These descended to the depths of the *kelippot* and every day they rise and are slowly repaired. The Supernal splendor is divided into two types of splendor. The first is in the world of *Azilut* and they are the *Yehidah, Hayyah, Neshamah, Ruah*, which are in *Azilut*. The second is the splendor of the three worlds of *Beriah, Yezirah*, and *Asiyyah*. They are *Yehidah, Hayyah, Neshamah, Ruah*, which are in the hundred *Keters* which are found in the ten *Parzufim* from the *Zeir* of *Beriah* until the end of *Nukvah* of *Asiyyah*. These left Adam completely. There is a second inferior splendor and it too is divided into two. The first is the Animus which is in *Azilut* and the second is the Animus which is in the hundred *Keters* which are in the ten *Parzufim* of *Beriah, Yezirah,* and *Asiyyah,* as above. These remained with Adam. Part of them remained with him and part were bequeathed to Cain and Abel when they were born. There is a third level and these are the nine hundred *sefirot* which are contained in the above-mentioned ten *Parzufim,* minus their hundred *Keters.* These remained and were embodied in the *kelippot.*

3. One day, I asked my teacher z"l the reason why in my youth, when I asked several dream questions, not only was I not answered but I did not have dreams like ordinary people. He told me that the dream comes from lowly levels and my Soul ascends at night to a place higher than that of dreams. Therefore, my Animus did not tarry at the place of dreams when it ascended at night. As a result, [my Soul] does not see dreams as do other Souls, which are on a lower level than mine.

4. He also told me that as a result of Cain's sin his Animus, Spirit, and Soul were damaged and became mixed together with *kelippot.* This is the meaning of what I said that the majority of Cain was evil, but Abel was only damaged in his Animus and Spirit and this is the meaning of what I said that the majority of Abel was good. His Animus departed from the good contained in it and was given to Kenan and from him onward was repaired in him. The evil part was placed in an Egyptian and it too had a small admixture of good which had not yet been clarified. The evil portion of the Spirit which also had an admixture of a few good sparks was taken by Korah, who disputed with Moses a"h,[5] through the secret of impregnation. The Spirit of good was transmigrated into Samuel and repaired there. After the Egyptian was killed [by Moses],[6] Jethro took the [Egyptian's] evil Animus in him, which had already been repaired by his having been killed and in this way he was converted to Judaism. Afterwards, he took the part of Cain's Soul which was from the good aspect. The evil Soul which had a small admixture of good was given to Amalek the son of Eliphaz.[7] Samuel repaired the portion of Spirit more than Jethro repaired the portion of the Soul. I have already informed you of several other transmigrations which

were transmigrated on a number of occasions before and after this.

5. According to the previously mentioned page 4d,[8] it seems that the source of the aspect of Cain is literally in the left arm [of the cosmic Adam]. However, afterwards from the evidence of the hair that I have it seems that it is in the left shoulder. On page 9b it also begins in the arm and ends in the shoulder. On pages 3 and 6 and particularly page 7a it seems explicitly that it is at the shoulder where it joins the arm to the body. I have written in my book, part 1, gate 3, page 213b, that each arm is composed of three joints and the two upper joints of the two arms of *Arikh Anpin* which are the joints that are connected to the two shoulders from which is made *Da'at* of *Zeir Anpin* which is composed of *Hasadim* and *Gevurot*. It is known that in this *Da'at* were implanted Cain and Abel, the children of Adam. It needs study.

6. Know that Cain is from the three *Gevurot* of *Tiferet, Nezah*, and *Hod* minus the upper third of the *Gevurot* of *Tiferet*, since it is covered with the crown of the *Yesod* of *Imma*, as is known. Nadav and Avihu are from the two *Gevurot* of *Nezah* and *Hod*, from the *Keters* which are in them, but they are only from the aspect of their Animus and are only from the "encompassing light [or *makif*]" which is in them. Elijah z"l is from the "inner light [or *penimi*]" which is in them. The whole source of Rabbi Akiva's Animus is from the *Gevurot* of *Hod*, from the aspect of the *Keter*, which is in it, in the aspect of the Animus which is in it. We find that it is the Animus of the Spirit, since *Hod* is called Spirit and is one of the six directions. I do not know if the source of Rabbi Akiva is from the "inner light" or from the "encompassing light." Know also that his source is from the heel of this *Hod*, which is the *Malkhut* of the *Gevurot* which are in *Da'at*.

7. I once asked my teacher z"l how he could tell me that my Soul was so elevated, as mentioned above. Behold, the most insignificant one of the first generations was so righteous and pious that I do not even reach his heel. He said to me: Know that the greatness of the Soul does not depend on a person's deeds, but is according to the times and his generation, since a very insignificant deed in a generation like this is equivalent to several

great deeds in other generations, because in this generation the *kelippot* are incredibly powerful, which was not true in the first generations. If I had been in those first generations, my deeds and wisdom would have been more wonderful than many of the early *zaddiqim*. As Resh Lakish z"l says concerning Noah: "'He was blameless in his age' [Gn 6:9], and if he had been in the generations of the righteous, he would have been more righteous,"⁹ therefore, I am not at all disturbed by this, since my Soul undoubtedly is on a higher level than some of the early *zaddiqim* from the time of the Talmudic sages.

8. Another time I said to him: Am I not foolish to believe about myself, that you did not find anyone in this whole generation worthy to learn this wisdom except for myself? Am I not cognizant of myself and my deeds, that there are greater ones, *zaddiqim*, and more accomplished people than me in this generation? What do I care if you will praise me, for I know myself and it is not so. There is Rabbi Joseph Karo, Rabbi David ibn Zimra¹⁰ your teacher, Rabbi Moses Alshekh, Rabbi Abraham ha-Levi, Rabbi I"G,¹¹ the rabbi my grandfather, and so forth. Then he said to me: And what relationship did you ever have to me and what pleasure did I derive from you? On the contrary, you are the youngest and smallest of them all. I should not have brought you closer instead of them, since they are the great scholars of the generation and I would have acquired great honor with this. This demonstrates that I did not choose you for no reason, but for your attributes which are greater than all of theirs. Do not think in your heart that the attributes of people are as people think them to be. If you knew how many secret faults people have, you would be amazed. However, I do not wish to reveal people's secrets to you. You should know that I have already examined and weighed them all in the scales and I have not found a vessel as pure, as innocent, and as worthy as you. This should be enough for you. I do not have permission to speak explicitly about everything, and concerning this it is written: "Man sees only what is visible, but the Lord sees into the heart" [1 Sm 16:7]. Be strong and of good courage in your heart and rejoice in the portion of your Soul and its attributes. This is enough.

9. Rachel, the wife of R. J[udah][12] Aberlin, told me that when my teacher, Rabbi Moses Alshekh z"l, was teaching in the study house in her courtyard, she saw him sitting depressed. She asked him what he was depressed about. He said to her: Should I not be upset about Rabbi Hayyim who was my student and now does not want to take me on as a student to teach me the wisdom of the *Kabbalah?* She said to him: Is he greater than you in this discipline? He told her how during the lifetime of my teacher, the Ashkenazi z"l, he went to him one day and cried and pleaded that he should teach him this wisdom himself, and not through me. He responded that he came into this world only to teach me alone and it is impossible for him to reveal this wisdom except through me. Not only that, but were it not for what the Talmudic sages said, "Of everyone a man is jealous, except his son and disciple,"[13] I would be envious of the multitude of his Soul's attributes and what he will comprehend in the future—something that is immeasurable.

His son, Rabbi Hayyim Alshekh, told me the same thing, in the name of his father, my teacher, Rabbi Moses Alshekh z"l.

My teacher, the Ashkenazi z"l, told me similar things that transpired between him and Rabbi Solomon Sagis z"l, who envied me and did not want to learn this wisdom from me, but from him. My teacher z"l did not want to teach him and said to him: If you do not wish to study with Rabbi Hayyim, you will never learn this wisdom.

My teacher z"l said to me that I should live in Jerusalem, may it be speedily rebuilt, for there is my true dwelling place and there is the essence of my comprehension and all of my welfare.

10. Some brief principles concerning the source of my Soul. Cain is one organ of the 248 organs which are incorporated in Adam and this organ is an aspect of the five *Gevurot* of *Da'at,* and it is the innermost aspect of this organ. As a result of Adam's sin they descended into the left shoulder. Therefore, this whole shoulder is the external aspect of Cain's source. It is one large source of the 613 large sources which are incorporated in the whole body of Adam. This source of Cain is divided into 613 sparks of great Souls. Indeed, this great source is divided into

seventy small sources, each of which is no less than 613 small sparks of Souls. The totality of these seventy small sources is sixty myriads of small Soul sparks. Hence, everything incorporated into Cain is called one great source and it is one great *Parzuf* which is called Cain and is divided into seventy small sources and they are seventy small *Parzufim*. One of these seventy small *Parzufim* is the left back part of the great *Parzuf* called Cain. This small *Parzuf* which is the left back part of Cain is the one called the true source of my Soul, and we are all close to one another. This *Parzuf* has more than 613 small sparks and they are all scholars, except for other branches who are householders. So the [ultimate] source of my Soul is the left back part of the left shoulder of Adam. This is the external aspect of the source of my Soul, but the internal aspect of the source of my Soul is *Malkhut* in *Gevurah* which is called *Hod* which is in *Da'at*. This *Malkhut* is the aspect of Leah, whose place is behind *Da'at*; however, she is still in a Masculine aspect internally. The Soul of Rabbi Akiva is the left back part of the *Parzuf* of the totality of Cain in the lower back part of the *Hod* of the *Malkhut* of *Keter* of *Da'at* from the aspect of the *Gevurot* of the small Greatness which has been mentioned, in the manner in which it is *Malkhut* of Leah, as mentioned. However, my Soul, of me Hayyim, is the light which is emitted by this *Malkhut* of Leah and continues to illumine the external *Malkhut* of Leah which is behind *Da'at* and is completely Feminine. One still needs to know that all of this is from the aspect of the *Keter* of *Hod*, from the aspect of *Malkhut* of *Keter*, as mentioned, since all of Cain is only from the aspect of the *Keters*, which are called the bulwark of the world, as is known. If you will be more precise, you will find that the source of my Animus is in *Malkhut* of *Hod* of *Keter* of the totality of the crown of *Gevurah*, which is internal and which in its external garb is *Malkhut* of *Hod* of the *Keter* of every great *Parzuf*, which is called the left shoulder of Adam. The specific [place] of my Animus is the illumination which emanates from *Malkhut* of the *Malkhut* of *Hod* which is in *Keter* the crown of *Gevurot* and illumines the *Malkhut* of the *Malkhut* of *Hod* of the *Keter* of external Leah, the wife of Jacob, who is called *Zeir Anpin*.

11. During *Tammuz*, 5331 [1571], I said to my teacher that he should teach me one Unification, in order that I should achieve comprehension. He said to me: You will not yet be able [to do it]. I pleaded with him and he gave me a short Unification. I arose at midnight and I performed the Unification. I felt my body shaking and I had a headache. I was beginning to lose my mind, and my mouth was twisted to one side. I desisted from further Unifications. In the morning, my teacher z"l said to me: I told you that what happened to Ben Zoma, who was mentally spoiled,[14] would happen to you. Were you not Rabbi Akiva, there would be no cure for you. He then touched my lips with a mystical intention known to him, every morning for three days, and I was healed. On the eve of *Rosh Hodesh Ellul*, he said to me: Now you are ready, and he sent me to the caves of Abbaye, as mentioned above.

12. In the year 5332 [1572], we went out in the fields and we passed the grave of a gentile that was more than a thousand years old. His Animus was seen on his tombstone and he tried to harm me and kill me. There were many angels and innumerable souls of *zaddiqim* to my right and left and he was powerless to harm me. My teacher commanded me that when I return, I should not do so on that road. Afterwards, the soul of that gentile followed me at a distance. There in the field I became angry at Rabbi I"M,[15] and the Animus of the gentile began to attach itself to me and cause me to sin even more and I did not want to listen to my teacher's z"l teachings. He began to cry and said: All the Souls and angels have left him because of the anger and as a result that Animus rules over him. What shall I do? I wish that he would harm him and let him remain living; then I will be able to heal him. However, I fear that he will kill him and everything that I think will repair the world will be not accomplished by him, as is known to me. I could not tell, since I had not been given permission, whether I have struggled for nothing and the world would be destroyed. He did not eat the whole night out of anguish and worry. I returned on that road alone. When I reached his grave, a wind lifted me and I saw myself in the air, running twenty stories above the ground until I reached a land at nightfall and was left there. I slept soundly until morning. I wanted to get up, but

all of my limbs were very weak and painful, but I slowly reached the door of my teacher z"l. When I arrived, I was barely alive, like Jonah, and my teacher laid me on his bed, closed the door, and prayed. Afterwards, he entered the house alone, walked around the house, returned to the bed, and stretched himself over me.[16] He did this until noon, when I was almost dead, and at noon I saw myself that my Soul was slowly returning to me until I opened my eyes, got up, and recited the blessing "He who resurrects the dead." All this is absolutely and undoubtedly true.

13. In my humble opinion, undoubtedly, since it is known that *Azilut* continues until the end of *Asiyyah* and is clothed within *Beriah* since it expands until that point. We find that in *Asiyyah*, the four worlds of *Azilut, Beriah, Yezirah,* and *Asiyyah* are clothed one in the other, in *Yezirah* only three and they are *Azilut, Beriah,* and *Yezirah*, and in *Beriah* only two and they are *Azilut* and *Beriah*, and in *Azilut* only one. The categories of Cain and Abel incorporate all aspects of *Azilut* which exist from the beginning of the Animus of *Azilut* until the end of *Azilut* which is at the end of *Asiyyah*. This is what Adam their father bequeathed to them. However, they are themselves all the aspects of *Beriah, Yezirah,* and *Asiyyah*, which clothe all the parts of the Animus of *Azilut*, mentioned above, which continues until the end of *Asiyyah*. They are the Animus of the *Keters* which are in *Beriah, Yezirah,* and *Asiyyah*, that is, the *Malkhut* which is in the *Keters*. There are aspects which are higher than these. They are the nine higher *sefirot* which are in every *Keter* and they are called the Splendor of Unity *[Ziharah de-Yehidah]*, Life *[Hayyah]*, Soul, and Spirit. All the other aspects aside from the *Keters* are all the other Souls which lie below the aspect of the legacy of Adam to Cain and Abel, as mentioned.

This is the abbreviated set of rules that my teacher z"l commanded me concerning comprehension according to the needs of my Soul. First, I should always comport myself with the following practices: To be careful to the extreme to stay away from anger and pedantry, depression, arrogance, slander, mockery, gossip, idle chatter, nocturnal emissions, menstruating women, forbidden fats, embarrassing people, slaughtering, and the killing of any living thing, even insects. I should conduct myself with humility, joy, silence, and fear of sin. I should study Bible, *Mishnah*, Talmud, and *Kabbalah*, with their mystical intentions, every day. My primary study should be the *Zohar*. Every day, the awe of the divine name of fifty-two letters should be before my eyes always. I should always think about cleaving to the Soul of my teacher z"l. Before each of the daily prayers I should cleave to Rabbi Akiva z"l by mentioning his name ten times in a row. [To recite] "A prayer of David. Incline your ear, O Lord" [Ps 86], with great intention. To arise after midnight every night to cry over the exile of the *Shekhinah*, Heaven forbid, in the world of *Beriah*, and over the destruction of the Temple, the exile of Israel, and to cry over the sins [of the people]. Diligence in performing Unifications, particularly, on weekday nights after midnight. The fifteenth Unification of the *Yuds* and *Vavs* of the tenth Unification of the verse "They are renewed every morning–[Ample is your Grace]" [Lam 3:23]. On the nights of *Rosh Ḥodesh* after midnight, the sixteenth Unification of the [divine] name *Shaddai*. On Friday nights, after the meal and before midnight two Unifications, on weekday nights, and they are the tenth and the fifteenth and also the eleventh Unification of the ten divine names which are in *Da'at*.

14. A second practice is that I should fast for forty consecutive days with sackcloth and ashes in the place where the phylacteries for the head are normally placed and with crying over the sins, but not the nights. Nights, I should lie on the ground dressed in sackcloth, a stone beneath my head, and I should meditate on the divine name of fifty-two of *HYHY"N* with the addition of an *Aleph* between the two *Vavs*, which equals *even* [stone] in *gematria*. After the completion of the forty consecutive days mentioned, I should observe all these practices, fasting, sackcloth and ashes, and weeping during the day and sackcloth, sleeping on the ground with a stone under my head during the night, every Monday and Thursday of every week. Know that these forty days and the Monday and Thursday observances are only on days that it is appropriate to fast and not on any day when it is

forbidden to fast, such as Sabbaths, festivals, *Rosh Ḥodesh*, the fifteenth of *Shevat*, and so forth. I followed this practice every Monday and Thursday until the two and one-half years were completed.[17]

15. He also warned me about observing the Sabbath and honoring it in all its particulars, both in deeds and words even more than all the other commandments. Similarly, I should recite all the blessings over food with intention and don the phylacteries of *Rabbenu* Tam every day. I should strive to understand what I do not understand in each passage of the *Zohar* without giving up until I understand it. Great joy should be mine when I study Torah or when performing commandments or praying. The study of Torah should be in the following manner: Daily study of Bible, *Mishnah*, Talmud, *Kabbalah*, with their appropriate intentions and you should intend to connect your Soul with its Supernal source through the Torah and in this way the Supernal Adam will be repaired. [I should] rise after midnight and meditate on the Psalm "Hallelujah" and after completing it [meditate] on the name "*MNZPKh*."[18]

16. A brief excursus concerning the source of my Animus. Cain is the whole left shoulder and he is one source and one organ of the 613 sources of Adam and is divided into seventy small sources. The source of my Soul is one source of these seventy and I do not know if it is the greatest of them or the least of them, and so forth. It is obvious to me that my Animus itself is from the aspect of the heel which is called *Malkhut* and it is from the aspect of the Supernal Leah. However, I have two questions about this. The first is that the source of my Animus is the last of the seventy and it is the very end of the whole shoulder which is the lower *Malkhut*. Not only that, but the spark of my Animus is the very end of this end. The second one is that my source is the highest of the seventy sources and my particular Animus spark is the bottom of this source alone. But this is only externally. That is to say, on the outer garment of my Animus, excluding the light of the Animus which is in this garment, my Animus has an additional inner garment. It is in the *Gevurot* of *Hod* from *Malkhut*

which is in the *Moaḥ* of *Da'at*, except for the light of the Animus which is in this garment. Hence there are two vessels and two lights and all together they are called one Animus. The conclusion of the matter is that my Animus is from the aspect of greatness which is the Soul which is from the side of *Imma* of the *Gevurót* which contains the *sefirot* of *Da'at* of *Zeir* in *Hod* which is in *Da'at*, which is in *Malkhut*, which is in the *Keter* of *Da'at*. This is in each of the five *Parzufim* and it is in each world of the four worlds of *Azilut, Beriah, Yezirah,* and *Asiyyah.* Adam himself is from the aspect of Cain and above and he is of the three first *[sefirot], Keter, Hokhmah, Binah,* which is in all the *Malkhuts* which is in every *Keter* which is in the ten *sefirot* of *Zeir.* What Adam bequeathed to Cain are all the *Gevurot* of *Da'at* and the seven lower *[sefirot]* which are in *Malkhut* which is in *Keter* and Cain himself, all the lower nine *[sefirot]* in *Da'at.* His descendants are from the seven lower *[sefirot]* of every *sefirah* of the ten *sefirot* of *Zeir.*

17. I, Isaac ben Nun, the humblest of my clan, was dreaming on Friday night, the seventeenth of *Ab,* in the year 5368 [1608]. I saw in my dream that I was going to Jawbar, to the synagogue for an early-morning service on the eve of *Rosh Hodesh.* As I was walking, I met an extremely dignified person and he asked me if we had already made peace with the sage, our teacher, the divine rabbi, may God preserve him.[19] I answered him that we had agreed to make peace with him. He then said to me: If you knew who this sage is, you would go to his house daily to kiss his hands and feet, and be under his patronage. I responded to him: Do I not know that he is a great scholar? He said to me: Everyone knows that he is a great scholar, but you do not know who he is. Then I pleaded with him to tell me who he is. He then said that he is the Messiah. He said to me: I will bring you proof from the Torah, the Prophets, and the Writings.[20] From the Torah, he said: In Genesis [5:28–29], it is written: "And Lamech lived"—the letters of Lamech [can be transposed]—*melekh* [king]. It is further written: "He begot a son" and it does not say "he begot so and so" as above. Furthermore: "He named him Noah," and so forth. He said: This Noaḥ is the Messiah. Concerning that which it is written, "He begot a son"

and he did not say "He begot Noah," then he said: The letters of "*ben* [son]" are the same as the letters of Noah, in the following way: Both have the letter *Nun* and the *Bet* is the same as the *Het*— both have the same number of sides.[21] Thus it is as if he had said: He begot Noah. Why did he change it? Because he was not circumcised by man,[22] and when he was circumcised on the eighth day, he was called Noah and then the *Het* had the strength to stand.[23] He further said: The two musical accents on the word "*zeh* [this one]" [Gn 5:29] are a clue to the first and last redemption; furthermore: "from our work"—from the generation of the Flood, "and from the toil of our hands"—from this long exile. Furthermore: Why was his name doubled, Noah Noah? This is hinted at in the *haftorah* "Shout for joy" [Zec 2:14-4:7], which concludes "*hen hen*."[24] This is the secret of Noah. Had his name been *hen*, we would not be sitting in exile. However, because he was called Noah, the *Nun* overpowered the *Het*, since it is the power of *nahash* [the Serpent] and therefore the exile has been lengthened. In the future, the *Nun* will no longer be mentioned and the Messiah's name is Hayyim, which in *gematria* equals Noah. Furthermore: Noah Noah in *gematria* equals Hayyim in the following way: The word *Mem* equals eighty, and the two *yuds* add up to 100. The *Het* is not called *Het* [in the world to come] but *heh*, as you say *Mem, Nun, Heh, Vav* in the mundane world. I have alluded that the letters of "Hayyim" are Noah Noah in *gematria* which are the same as *hen hen*. If so, they equal Hayyim in *gematria* and the *Nun* is not mentioned above, as in Noah, where it is first, and not below, as in *hen*, where it is last. Therefore, Psalm 145 does not contain [a verse beginning with] the letter *Nun*.[25]

He further told me: I have given my words into your mouth. Listen to wisdom from the Writings. It is written: "While the sun lasts, may his name endure *[yinnon]*" [Ps 72:17]. *Yinnon* equals Noah Noah in *gematria* and also *hen, hen* and Hayyim as I told you.

I will bring you evidence from the Talmud: It says: "With the footsteps of the Messiah *[iqveh de-Meshihe]*, insolence will increase."[26] The meaning is: Footsteps *[iqveh]* is composed of the same letters as Jacob and "*Meshihe*" is Messiah as I told you. Further: Jacob [Yaaqov]—will hinder *[yeakev]*.

I asked him: How can you equate Yaaqov and *yeakev?* Yaaqov is with a *qaf* and *yeakev* is written with a *kaf!* He then said to me: Open your eyes to my words: The letter *kaf* spelled out equals 100. If so: Yaakov and *yeakev* are the same. This is what I said to you: "With the footsteps of the Messiah, insolence will increase." The person who told me all this gave me two myrtle branches to smell. I awoke and this is the dream.[27]

18. ...[28] the spirit of a certain person entered the body of the daughter of Raphael Anav here in Damascus and many wondrous things....He was in Paradise the whole time mentioned and now about three weeks ago he was sent from Heaven to suffer this trouble because of the primordial sin. He also said that the time of redemption had come and the coming of the Messiah is but a hair's breadth away, but the sins of the generation and particularly from Damascus cause iron chains to be placed on his neck to delay him. Indeed, he will not delay for more than twelve years. We find that he will come speedily in our days, in the year 5381 [1621], in any event. Indeed, in the course of these years many awesome troubles will occur...all the lands will be overthrown like Sodom seven times and Jerusalem will be burned seven times, but Safed will not be overthrown and will not be burned. First some insignificant people will come, like Gog and Magog. Afterwards, very important people of the Israelite nation will come together with the Messiah, among them the ancient worthies who have already died and who were brought to life. They will come with him and then will be the end.

They also told me that in Aleppo, literally during the same time, a spirit entered a young girl and preached to them concerning repentance, on the eve of *Rosh Hashanah*. They instituted fasts and repentance and after several months the girl died.

19. Here too in Damascus, in the month of *Shevat* 5370 [1610], a Muslim *sheikh* came from a distant land and people said about him that he could foretell the future. He said: So and so committed a sin with so and so on such and such a day, and so forth, and his words were found to be true. People began to gather around

him and he began to denigrate the Muslim religion and was incredibly crazy. They killed him immediately before his ideas could spread, on the ninth of *Shevat* of that year.

20. The physician Rabbi Abraham ibn Ya'ish told me that when he served the king of Spain, as he gave him water to wash his hands before the meal, a priest entered and said to the king: Know that fourteen years ago, I saw at night, while lying on my bed, a vision of two angels who said to me that I should tell your father, who was then alive, that he should be careful not to increase the burden on the Jewish Marranos. If he should increase the burden, he would die a terrible death. So it was when he was afflicted with lice, more numerous than the dust of the earth. As soon as they changed his bedding and sheets, the lice returned instantaneously in greater numbers. Everyone was amazed and they knew that it was "the finger of God" [Ex 8:15], and he died of this affliction. Afterwards, you reigned in his stead. Seven years ago today, I again saw the two above-mentioned angels in a vision in my bed and they said to me: Go to the king who is thinking evil thoughts about the Marranos to reassure them deceitfully so that they will all gather in his kingdom and afterwards he will kill them all. Great evil will befall him because of this. I did not want to come and tell you all this, not to you and not to your father, since I said: Perhaps it was a dream, and dreams are not truthful. Now, I was in Toledo and I again had a vision of the two above-mentioned angels and they had drawn swords in their hands and they wanted to cut off my head until I promised them that I would come to you.

They said to me: Go and tell the king that he too is a Marrano, the grandson of Palumba the Jewess—why does he hate and kill the Jews who are Marranos like him? He should know that the kingdom will be taken away from him. The king answered that henceforth his son would reign in his stead. He said to him: Know that in your lifetime a redeemer will arise from the tribe of Judah and will come from overseas, via the great ocean to the coast of Portugal, and he will destroy your kingdom and the kingdom of all the Christians.

The king then sent for the Grand Inquisitor to tell him the

punishment for that man. He said to the king: Throw him into prison. Then the priest said to the Inquisitor: Know that you will die tomorrow, and before you die a sign and wonder will be given in the sky that all will see, at midday a star like all the other stars, with its upper half red like blood and its lower half the color of pus and at its end two tails the length of ten spears, one shorter than the other. So it was. When the king saw this, he ordered that [the priest] be taken from the prison and imprisoned in his palace. All this was because of the nobles who were jealous of the Jews. Indeed, during all that time the king and priest secretly conversed about our Torah and he loved him like the apple of his eye. Then the priest said to him: Know that the above-mentioned angels told me that your father commanded you before his death that you should be careful not to make war on the king of France, since the existence and peace of all the Christian nations depends on his welfare. Now you will abrogate this testament. In order to begin the destruction of the kingdom of the Christians, you will do such and such cunningly until you will kill the king of France.

The king did so and after three years of cunning by a trusted agent, the king of Parnasia was killed and his son reigned in his stead.

He also advised him, through the angels, how to make peace with the nation of Flanders, which had been in a state of war for the past eighty years and had caused great damage and financial loss to the king of Spain. He could only do this by first making peace with the dukes of England and afterwards there would be peace. He did so and was successful.

The above-mentioned R. Abraham ibn Ya'ish was uncertain if the length of time was five years or if the time was only told to the king. This occurred in the year 1503 of the Christian calendar, on the fifteenth of March. The above-mentioned priest said that he was of Marrano descent.

21. The same Rabbi Abraham told me that he traveled with a ship of the king of Portugal on the great ocean to New Spain, Peru, and the New World.[29] From there the wind carried them to another island of immense size which was the kingdom of the

Indians, who were cannibals. They told them that on that island, far from them, was the kingdom of Daniel the Jew, a nation as numerous as the sands of the sea. Two of them could rout an army. Out of fear of him they hire desert people from the island who are very strong; one of them can rout a hundred people. They only have one eye in their forehead and they remain on the boundary of their land out of fear of King Daniel. Despite this, if two of Daniel's men would come they would devastate an army of the desert people. The king of Spain knows all this to be undoubtedly true.[30] He also heard from the above-named Indian that the name of this island is Ronfal,[31] and it is below the southern Pole.

22. On the fifteenth of *Ellul* 5368 [1608], a ship came from Venice to Sinim and on it was an old man, a Spanish noble whose name was Curiel, who had spent his life as captain of three galleons which plundered on the seas and he was an admiral in his land. His brother was a cardinal in Rome who was in line to become pope. This old man left his noble position and his fortune for the love of our holy Torah. He told that in his land, which is Portugal, someone close to the king came and said to him: Fourteen years ago he had a prophetic vision and he did not tell it then and now the angel has come a second time and said to him that if he does not tell these things, he will be killed. He said to himself: Woe is me if I tell; perhaps the king will throw me into prison, and if I don't tell—I will be killed. Therefore, it is better that he should throw me into prison until the time of the coming of the Redeemer, who will release me from there.

These are the words of his prophecy:

Between now and two years from now, the Redeemer will arise from the descendants of King David a"h and return all the kingdoms to his Torah and they will all serve God and all idolatry and its practices will be eliminated and he will be released from prison. This will be your first sign. The Grand Inquisitor will die between now and eight days from now. The second is that on this night a star with a long tail [a comet] will pass over the palace of the king and the king himself will die between now and two years from now. Until here.

The two signs mentioned occurred as he said. When the king

saw that the first two signs had occurred, he enthroned his young son during his lifetime, because he was afraid of the third sign, lest he die and someone who was not of his family would reign instead. He put the above-mentioned seer in prison, as he himself had said. The two years mentioned were completed on *Hanukkah* of the year 5370 [1610].

Many who came with the old man testified similarly, that it was as the above-mentioned seer said.

Rabbi Isaac Berakhah wrote this from Sinim to Damascus. In a letter from Venice to Aleppo it was added that there were two inquisitors and both of them died. He also added that three kingdoms would be destroyed during that time, and they are: Spain, Tangiers, and the Turks. Therefore, the king of Spain enthroned his six-month-old son, so that through a change of destiny, perhaps his kingdom would not be destroyed. Indeed, the death of the king was not mentioned in this letter. They also wrote that in most Christian countries, and particularly in Mantua, the people mitigated their behavior toward the Marranos in the extreme and treated them with respect, for the reasons stated by the above-mentioned Catholic priest.

23. Afterwards, a certain person came from Spain, who was...and told me that the essence of what was verified there (concerning the above-mentioned *Clerigo*[32] i.e., a priest who is not obligated to serve strange gods) was the matter of the first sign, that the Grand Inquisitor, who hated Jews, would die [at the end of] eight days. So it was and he saw his death. He also gave a sign that the king and queen would die within eighteen months—and he died by the end of *Ellul* 5369 [1599]—and afterwards would come a descendant of David and return the kingdom and the Jewish religion to their former place and he would be released from prison. Then, for this reason he enthroned his infant son in his place, as mentioned above. Indeed, the other aspects of the above-mentioned story in Spain were not verified, if he said them or not. Thus, it is uncertain if he said the above-mentioned things through astrology or a vision, since in Spain itself this was not sufficiently verified or clarified.

The above-mentioned man also told that a year and a half ago there was another scholar there, who was very learned in astrology. There were other lesser scholars who asked him to explain to them the judgment of the stars in the sixth year of that period. He looked at the astrological signs and became very alarmed and he said to them: In that year, I see that Jupiter and Saturn will come together and they will battle. Saturn will rule, vanquish, and subdue Jupiter. This is a sign that the Jews, who are under the influence of Saturn, will vanquish and rule over the Christians, who are under the influence of Jupiter, without doubt.[33] The king of Spain heard his words and killed him. The six-year period mentioned ended on the festival of Passover, which is January of the year 5373 [1613]. The man who told me this said that he received a letter from Flanders, that the above-mentioned man was not a priest but a great astrologer and for the past thirteen years he had been told at night many prophecies and insights for people. Now they were pleading with him at night that he should reveal things. He then began to speak prophetic things to people. The matter became known to the king and he imprisoned him. Then he said to them: I will tell you further that the Grand Inquisitor, the enemy of the Jews, will die on the eighth day and also that the king will die before the end of two years. Afterwards, many wars will arise in the world and the lowly Jewish religion and people will be established and it will be established forever. These two years were completed on *Rosh Hodesh Iyyar* 5370 [1610]. The above-mentioned Inquisitor died and the above-mentioned man was thrown into prison.

24. This is the actual text of the letter from Spain, and I saw it: A *Clerigo* came from Toledo to the royal city, Valladolid. He was dignified, charitable, of Christian descent, and a scholar. He said that for the past fourteen years a spirit has been talking to him during the nights. Now he has requested and strongly pleaded with him that he should come and make known the things in the annals, how in the month of *Adar* I of the year 5369 [1609][34] of creation until twelve months later, three great houses will fall, the kingdom of Spain, the kingdom of France, and the kingdom of Turkey. The king of the Jews will come and inherit these three kingdoms and his kingdom will be established for-

ever. When he was imprisoned...from speaking these words. The above-mentioned spirit will rescue him. He gave a sign that the Grand Inquisitor would die within eight days and that a star with the sign...would be seen in the sky on that night and so it was. He also said many other things and the hands of the king of Spain trembled and he enthroned (his baby son) in his place....

Book of Secrets

Translator's Introduction
to the Text

Rabbi Yizḥak Isaac Yeḥiel Safrin of Komarno[1] (1806–1874) was an important Hasidic leader of the nineteenth century and a prolific author. Among his writings is a small volume entitled *Book of Secrets* (*Megillat Setarim*) which is divided into two distinct parts. The first part, entitled "Book of Visions," is a fragmentary mystical autobiography closely modeled on R. Ḥayyim Vital's *Book of Visions*. The second part, called "The Deeds of the Lord," is a collection of stories about Israel Baal Shem Tov (1700–1760), the founder of Hasidism which Komarno heard from his father-in-law and others. He called his work *Megillat Setarim*,[2] perhaps believing that this was one of the titles Vital had given his autobiographical work.[3] Komarno believed not that he was a transmigration of Vital, but of Vital's teacher, R. Isaac Luria.[4] His apparent connection to Vital was that he believed himself to be the Messiah of Joseph of his generation as Vital had been in his.[5] This identification is suggested by Komarno's equation of the year of his birth, 5566 (1806), with the phrase "Messiah of Joseph" through the process of *gematria*. The very existence of this autobiography and its close resemblance to Vital's work further adds to the identification. Perhaps this work was a veiled attempt to buttress this claim. Unlike Vital's *Book of Visions*, Komarno's work does not present a coherent narrative framework that explains the motivation that drove him to produce this book. One can only speculate about his self-identification as the transmigration of R. Isaac Luria instead of Vital. Komarno, like

Vital, was a prolific author.[6] Unfortunately, his writings have not yet been subjected to significant scholarly study and analysis. The only study of Komarno and his writings is a hagiographic account by H. J. Berl that is of relatively little scholarly value.[7] A more definitive understanding of how Komarno saw himself, particularly in relation to Vital, must await an analysis of his large oeuvre, which is an important desideratum.

Komarno began writing his work shortly before his fortieth birthday, traditionally considered the age of esoteric understanding. It is also the time of the first dream that he records. He does not give any indication of what event motivated him to begin writing this work. Perhaps the first dreams that he records provided the impetus. Similarly, there is no indication why he stopped recording the dreams in 1857, though he lived another seventeen years, dying in 1874. The dreams he records begin and end mysteriously, without apparent cause or explanation.

The first part of Komarno's "Book of Visions" is a narrative of highlights of his life from his birth until the age of twenty. This narrative autobiographical section has as its common thread a number of incidents that illustrate his own greatness and the holiness of his father. He begins with the circumstances of his birth and the great sacrifice his father made so that he might be born. R. Jacob Isaac, better known as the Seer of Lublin (1745–1815), the leading Hasidic figure of the period, had predicted his greatness before his birth. His greatness was confirmed by a disciple of the Besht[8] who was visiting the city of his birth three days after his circumcision. His "recognition" by a disciple of the Besht is significant in light of his later claim to having a special spiritual relationship with the Besht. From the age of two to five he had prophetic visions, which were recognized by his uncle, R. Zevi Hirsch of Zhidachov (1763–1833), whose soul ancestry derived from R. Ḥayyim Vital, according to Komarno.[9] He does not tell us why these visions ceased after the age of five. When he was six, his father took him to visit the Seer of Lublin for Passover. During the Seder, the Seer took the shank bone from the Seder plate and held it out to him and pulled it back. The third time he did this he gave it to him. Komarno implies that this act was another sign of the greatness of his Soul. Elsewhere, he is more explicit and states that this was the Seer's way of "ordaining" his disciples and passing on the charisma that can be traced back directly to the Besht. He claimed to be the fourth in the direct line of spiritual succession to the Besht.[10] The prophet Elijah visited him at the age of seven disguised as a gentile peasant, but he was not spiritually worthy at that time to see Elijah in his true guise. He did not realize who this "peasant" was until his father informed him that it was Elijah. This is also an indirect way of praising his father, who was on a sufficient spiritual level to realize the true identity of the "peasant."

Komarno's father died when he was twelve, as had been foretold by the Seer of Lublin. After his father's death, he was raised and educated by his uncle, R. Zevi Hirsch of Zhidachov. He explains that in this way, R. Hayyim Vital's Soul was able to return the favor of the earlier transmigration when R. Isaac Luria was Vital's teacher. When he was fifteen he had an unexplained spiritual crisis, reminiscent of Vital's. He even uses the same phrase to describe his situation and the positive outcome of this trial. He married at the age of sixteen. His father-in-law, who had supported him financially after his marriage, died when he was twenty. He moved his family to Zhidachov to be near his uncle, at the latter's urging. Komarno ends his autobiographical narrative at this point and continues his text with a series of dreams he had, which began twenty years later, when he reached the age of forty. As with other aspects of this work, there is no overt explanation for why he ends his narrative at this point.

The second part of Komarno's "Book of Visions" consists of a series of dreams he describes, which begin in the spring of 1845, about the time he began to write his *Book of Secrets*. The last dream he records is in 1857. The majority of dreams are between 1845 and 1850, with only a handful between 1850 and 1857. There is no consistent theme or motif in his dreams as we find in Vital, although several dreams have themes that are reminiscent of Vital. On 19 *Adar* II 5605 (1845), he complains that he cannot cause the people to repent and is reassured that "God will answer him in the day of trouble."[11] In another dream he asks about the greatness of his Soul, his place in Paradise, and whether his teachings are accepted in Heaven. He is assured that his teachings are studied in all the Heavenly academies.[12] In a similar dream, his uncle, who is in Heaven, shows him a scroll containing his teachings.[13]

Though he identifies with Vital in many respects, there is one important area where his work differs from that of Vital: His writing does not have the obsessive egocentrism that one finds in Vital. Komarno finds place to discuss and praise others, while Vital is concerned only with himself. To the extent that others are mentioned in Vital's book, including his teacher, R. Isaac Luria, it is only when they have an impact on Vital and his mission.

Another noteworthy group of dreams are those in which he sees the Besht. On 19 *Adar* 5610 (1850), he was given a garment that once belonged to the Besht.[14] Three weeks later he meets the Besht in another dream.[15] He connects this dream with an exegetical comment on a Talmudic passage about the coming of the Messiah. It is unclear what the connection is between the comment and the dream. Implicitly, it can be assumed that this vision of the Besht was seen by him as further confirmation of his messianic mission. In a third dream, the Besht gives him a book to peruse.[16] This dream is also highly significant in that Komarno saw himself not only as a transmigration of the Besht, but also as directly continuing the teachings of the Besht. According to H. J. Berl, Komarno, in his own writings, comments on every passage in the writings of R. Jacob Joseph of Polonnoye (d. c. 1782), the Besht's closest disciple, which begins with the phrase "I heard from my teacher (the Besht)."[17] Perhaps his most explicit identification with the Besht is the remarkable statement at the end of the autobiographical section: "I was once standing near him [his uncle] and he said that our teacher, the Besht, was again in the world. He had grown greater in the light of Unification than his previous levels. He did not know where he was, and I was amazed."[18] Komarno was amazed, because in his eyes, the reference was clearly to himself. He had come to see himself not only as coming from the same soul-root, but as the Besht himself reborn in that generation.

Komarno's close identification with the Besht explains the significance of the second part of the *Book of Secrets*, entitled "The Deeds of the Lord." This section consists of a selection of stories about the Besht, most of which he heard from his father-in-law, R. Abraham Mordecai of Pinczow (d. 1824). The common thread that runs through these stories is the supernatural and magical abilities of the Besht, which are signs of his greatness. The majority of these stories are known from other sources.

The *Book of Secrets* was first published in its entirety by N. Ben Menachem in 1944 from two extant manuscripts.[19] This translation is based on the Ben Menachem edition. A brief sample of this work had previously been published by G. Scholem in his *Kitve Yad be-Kabbalah*.[20]

Notes to the
Translator's Introduction

1. Hasidic masters are traditionally known by the name of their city or town. I will use Komarno for Rabbi Yizhak Isaac Yehiel Safrin, following this convention.

2. This term has differing meanings. It can mean "Book of Secrets," "Intimate Diary," "Secret Book," or "Private Book."

3. D. Tamar, "Ollelot Sefer ha-Hezyonot," *Sinai* 91 (1982): 82. Vital's autobiography is referred to by this title in H. Y. D. Azulai's *Shem ha-Gedolim* (Vilna, 1853), pp. 104f., s.v. "Rabbenu ha-Ari." Komarno was probably influenced by this reference.

4. My translation, p. 278.

5. See above in the Introduction to the *Book of Visions*, where the concept of a Messiah of Joseph in every generation is discussed.

6. N. Ben Menachem, *Megillat Setarim* (Jerusalem, 1944), pp. 75–88, has a complete bibliography of his writings.

7. H. J. Berl, *R. Yizhak Isaac mi-Komarno* (Jerusalem, 1965).

8. The acronym by which R. Israel Baal Shem Tov, the founder of Hasidism, is usually known.

9. My translation, p. 276f.

10. Ben Menachem, *Megillat Setarim*, p. 52.

11. My translation, p. 282.

12. Ibid., p. 288.

13. Ibid., p. 288.

14. Ibid., p. 291.

15. Ibid., p. 292.

16. Ibid.

17. Berl, *Komarno*, p. 214.

18. Ibid., p. 183

19. Jerusalem, 1944.

20. Jerusalem, 1930, p. 174.

The Text of
Book of Secrets
by Rabbi Yiẓḥak Isaac Safrin
of Komarno

BOOK OF VISIONS

I will give my brethren a glimpse of God's ways: Who I am, what I am, and why I came into this lowly world. I was born on the twenty-fifth of *Shevat* 5566 [1806], under the sign of Jupiter, in the year "Messiah ben Joseph."[1] Today is the eleventh of *Adar* II 5605 [1845], and I have been in this world 14,281 days. I have celebrated 2,040 Sabbaths in this world. Until the end of the year *"halakhah le-Moshe mi-Sinai," "be-Tuv Yerushalayim," Hesed, Emet, Pahad,"*[2] I will have 14,476 days and 2,068 Sabbaths. On the twenty-fifth of *Shevat* 5606 [1846] I will attain the age of understanding.[3] When I complete my fortieth year, I will have 14,619 days and I will attain the crown of Torah.

Now I will tell about the greatness of my Soul: Who and what I am and why I came into the world. However, I have not yet received permission to discuss where I was and from which place I am derived in the body of Adam.[4]

I was my father's firstborn. Because of the evil decree which was caused by the face of the dog[5] of the Second Temple, a *kelippah* which has not yet been annulled caused a division in the whole world and the evil side of my Soul was included in it. My hatred of this side is great, for it caused me profound transmigrations. If my Soul had been repaired, I would not have needed to come into this world and the redemption would have come to all Israel. Because of the confusion and damage caused by the evil dog, the son of Tar..., I...[6] caused an exchange and substitution to my father and as a result I was not in this world more than a year since I needed more purification.[7] Afterwards, my sisters were born, righteous women. My father did not have a male child and I did not want to come into this world because the controversy over the face of the dog still existed. When my father, the *zaddiq*, was visiting our teacher and holy rabbi, the holy one of

275

the God of Israel, [Rabbi Jacob Isaac] of Lublin,[8] he pleaded with him that he should intercede in Heaven on his behalf, that he should have a son. He responded: If I decree that you should have a son, it will certainly be so. However, you will not live long, since you cannot both coexist in this world. My father accepted this upon himself and [the Seer of Lublin] transmitted to him an awesome [divine] name that would bring down my Soul. He said [to my father]: You will have a son who will be a great light. As soon as I came to my mother from the highest world, I said to her: Bring me back to you, for thus has it been decreed. I was born in the year "Messiah ben Joseph," on the twenty-fifth of *Shevat*, and to this day, the eleventh of *Adar* II, the fast of Haman,[9] the year "the memory of Mordecai is forever," the year "blessed be Mordecai the Jewish prophet,"[10] 14,281 days—I still have not repaired all the days I idled away and did not serve the King.

On the third day after my circumcision, one of the disciples of our divine teacher, the Besht,[11] was visiting the city of my birth, Sambor. Many townspeople and women with their children came to him. This is the accepted custom among the *zaddiqim* of our generation, to bless the holy people Israel, young and old, with the love of the Jewish Soul. My mother was among those who came, bringing me, so that the *zaddiq* should bless me. When he put his hand on my head, he cried out in a loud voice and said in Yiddish: This small one has a great and awesome mind and a wondrous Soul. My mother was very frightened by his great outcry and he said to her: Do not be afraid; this child will be a great light.

Between the ages of two to five years I attained wondrous visions and divine inspiration. I spoke prophetic words when a person would ask about divine matters, and literally gazed from one end of the world to the other.[12] My teacher and uncle, the awesome holy person, our teacher, Rabbi Zevi of Zhidachov,[13] gave me two Rhenish coins every week so that I would tell him and respond to everything that he would ask of me. I clearly and precisely answered all the questions that he asked me and donated the money to charity.

The Soul of my teacher and uncle was from the same source as

Rabbi Ḥayyim Vital, from the source close to the Soul of Rabbi Akiva, as is explained in Rabbi Ḥayyim Vital's *Book of Visions*, the passage beginning "My Teacher said to me."[14] Afterwards, through his wondrous deeds, it ascended several more levels. Similarly, the Soul of the holy rabbi, our teacher, Rabbi Levi Yizhak of Berdichev,[15] was also from there, from the source of the Soul of Rabbi Ḥayyim Vital. These sources and others like them were created by the Supernal King with great burning intensity, Unifications, and self-sacrifice that was rarely found even in the days of the *Tannaim*. The divine teacher, Rabbi Isaac Luria, praised the Soul of Rabbi Ḥayyim Vital with many praises. His source was very precious, encompassing the Souls of many righteous and saintly people. The redemption depends on this source. I have said enough about this. The Soul of the great sage, our teacher, Rabbi Ḥayyim ben Attar,[16] was also dependent on this source, which Rabbi Isaac Luria praised greatly, but was not from the source of Rabbi Akiva. Above all, our divine teacher the light of the seven days, the delight of Israel, our holy teacher Rabbi Israel Besht, whose Soul is in Paradise, was also from the above-mentioned source, but not from the side of Rabbi Akiva, but rather from other roots close to the above-mentioned source. He was, on his own, a great and awesome tree, the choicest of the Soul of Rabbi Ḥayyim Vital, and was included close to this source (see the *Book of Visions*: "To whom all the delight of Israel" [1 Sm 9:20]).[17]

My father, whose soul is in Paradise, was from the source of Maimonides z"l. He was righteous, pious, and holy, and was also close to the source of Rabbi Eleazar of Worms[18] and Rabbi Solomon ibn Adret.[19] Nonetheless, he did not completely attain the essence of kabbalistic wisdom. However, his heart was a fire burning for Torah and worship with self-sacrifice. He died with the Unification of self-sacrifice of Rabbi Akiva, one of the ten martyrs. A pillar of fire was seen over his grave on Friday afternoon that reached to the heart of heaven.[20] When he was lying on his bier, the *zaddiq* of Ohel said to him that he should pray that a certain evil decree should be annulled. [His body] moved twice as if alive, for such was his way, in fear and awe. He was a disciple of the divine master, the Rabbi of Lublin, the source of whose

Soul stretched from one end of the world to the other, and was of the source of Moses our Teacher and Rabbi Isaac Luria. He attained [a level of] divine inspiration the like of which was not seen in our times. From the divine master, the Besht, until his day there was no revelation like that which he received.

I was worthy to see him [the Seer of Lublin] during Passover. When I was six, I traveled with my father to celebrate Passover with him. I saw several wondrous examples of divine inspiration, on a very high level, and his wondrous worship with self-sacrifice, a burning torch. On the second day, during the second Seder after the recitation of the *Haggadah*, he took the bone from his Seder plate and extended it to me. Three times he pulled back his holy hand[21] and he did not want to give it to me until he saw, with divine inspiration, the source of my Soul and then gave it to me with awe and fear as was his holy manner. I understood his intent, in the secret of the source of my Soul, "Upon whom has the arm of the Lord been revealed" [Is 53:1]. Just as the letter *Lamed* ascends higher than all the other letters, so too you will ascend above all people, because you ascend to the [divine] name of *Yud, Yud, Yud*."[22] With these three *Yuds* there will be fulfilled in you, "Be exalted and raised to great heights" [Is 52:13]. They are: "bless you," "shine," "turn."[23] It is explained in our sermons that this is the spiritual mind from which emanates the Spirit of life to make the Feminine a vessel to arouse her to the conjugal union and from there comes the essential source of my Animus, Isaac Judah Yehiel, from the source of Rabbi Isaac Luria, very close to this holy person. "Your descendants will seize the gates of their foes" [Gn 22:17], "Show deference to the old; You shall fear your God" [Lv 19:32] [in *gematria*—Isaac, Judah, Yehiel], from the source of Beneyahu and Rabbi Hamnuna Saba and his son. My teacher and uncle was from the source of Rabbi Hayyim Vital. In this instance it was reversed, in that I learned from him. Therefore, the love between us was very great. If I had not been in this inferior generation and had not needed to restore a number of Animi with a broken and depressed heart, I would have attained some of the levels of our teacher, Rabbi

Isaac Luria. I was very depressed, since my only desire was to give pleasure to the Creator of the world with truth and a pure heart.

When I was seven, [a desire for] the wisdom of our divine teacher, Rabbi Isaac Luria, burned in me like a torch. I studied his writings with awe, fear, and great enthusiasm. I asked my father about the difficult passages. I studied in want and poverty and I was worthy of several wondrous things and holy levels. Once, I did not have food for more than a day. My father was walking back and forth in his *talit* and *tefillin*, his face burning like a flame as he studied a very profound doctrine. He called me over and taught me the doctrine of "Shila taught: A girl has three attributes"[24] in its plain and esoteric meanings. I was ravenously hungry. My father said to me: Go to the neighbor and get something to eat. I was very surprised, since I knew that this neighbor would not give me anything, not even for a good pledge. However, I believed him and I went there and stood at the door. A gentile was sitting there. He said to me: My son, would you like some bread and brandy? He gave me everything. As a result of my great hunger I did not have the leisure to comprehend this. Afterwards, my father said to me: My son, I see the greatness of your sins, that you were not worthy to see Elijah, except in this guise.[25]

When I was twelve years old, my father traveled to Hungary. I cried for seven days and nights and I was close to madness. I begged him not to go because I foresaw his death there. He answered me: So His blessed wisdom has decreed. He commanded me to observe certain practices. He traveled there and died on the twenty-first of *Ab* 5578 [1818], in the city of Ohel in the above-mentioned country. Afterwards, I was raised by my holy teacher and uncle, who was the brother of my father, his Soul is in Paradise. There I studied Torah in want and poverty and all my joy was from the great sweetness of the wondrous sermons that my teacher and uncle revealed. He also revealed wondrous things to me. In the course of this, I once saw our teacher, the *Bet Joseph*,[26] and my father together. My father asked him to bring me close to Torah, both exoteric and esoteric. Therefore, he brought me near to him, laid his hands on me, and transmitted to me all the paths of Torah that were within his understanding. A short time later, I was overcome by Satan, may his name be erased. I was not careful where I cast my gaze and two paths lay before me, *Gehenna* and Paradise. The good was awakened within me and one day I entered the synagogue alone and wept copious tears, like an overflowing spring, before the Creator of the world. I asked Him to forgive me, until I became excited and called to Him, "And I will mete out solace to them, etc." [Is 57:18]. From that day until today, twenty-five years, I have not looked at and have not seen any evidence of a [strange] woman's form. I am protected by Heaven that this should not occur, even by chance. I returned to the worship of the Creator of the world, to Torah and prayer.

At the age of sixteen I married my destined bride, who was from my aspect of the Spirit. There were several who opposed this match because the Spirit was not yet within me. However, as a result of my great penance and diligence in Torah study no stranger came between us. Afterwards, I [attained] several high and great levels of divine inspiration through diligence in Torah study and worship. In truth, I did not understand that this was not mine, since I was still far from the essence of worship. Afterwards, I contemplated this and separated myself from all things of this world. This was in the year 5583 [1823], at the beginning of winter. I had a private room which was very cold and was not heated even once during the whole winter. It was my custom to sleep only two hours every day and the rest was spent [in the study of] Torah, Talmud and commentaries, *Zohar*, the writings of our teacher, Rabbi Isaac Luria, and Rabbi Moses Cordovero. As a result of all this, I fell into a state of great *katnut*[27] for more than three months, and I was faced with many difficult and evil *kelippot* that attempted to entice me to leave my study of Torah. Worst of all was the depression that descended on me. During this period my heart was strong as a stone and I did not eat anything during that period except for a little bread and water each day, and I had no pleasure from Torah study and prayer. The extreme cold and the *kelippot* were very powerful, and I was literally caught between two paths with free will to choose. The bitterness from these enticements that passed over me were literally worse than a thousand deaths. Suddenly one day, after I overcame these enticements, while I sat studying tractate *Yevamot* for the sake of the Lord of the world and to adorn the *Shekhinah*[28] with all my strength, a great and wondrous light descended on me which filled the whole house with the indwelling of the *Shekhinah*.[29] This was the first time that I tasted a little of His light, may He be Blessed, without error or confusion and with wondrous pleasure. It is a light so pleasant that the mind cannot comprehend it. From then on, I entered into the worship of the Creator of the world with a wondrous infinite light and I was no longer overcome by enticements, as I had been previously. After this I again fell [spiritually] for a period of time and I understood that I needed to visit *zaddiqim* so that they would bring down His light, may He be Blessed, for me since I was already a clarified vessel. I traveled to Medzibozh to my rabbi and teacher, the holy rabbi, the man of God, Rabbi Abraham Joshua Heschel.[30] During this time, my daughter, the modest, pious, and holy Hinda Sarah, may she live, was born. I returned to my house and had good and luminous days because of the wondrous lights. In the midst of this, my teacher and father-in-law z"l died and I was left devastated. My teacher and father-in-law was a complete and holy *zaddiq*, my teacher in piety and fear [of the Lord]. I traveled to my teacher and uncle at the end of the year 5585 [1825] and stayed with him for three years. He ordered me to move my household from the holy community of Pinczow and live with him. I returned to my house and my holy uncle and teacher illuminated for me a wondrous and lucid light that the intellect cannot encompass. Therefore, I decided, come what may, I will live near this *zaddiq*. I was once standing near him and he said that our teacher, the Besht, was again in this world. He has grown greater in the light of Unification than his previous levels. He did not know where he was, and I was amazed.

5605 [1845], the ninth of *Adar* II. I washed my hands and recited a prayer of praise. I was not yet able to stand because of physical weakness. I unified myself with a Unification and connected myself to the Animus of the divine teacher, Rabbi Isaac

Luria. As a result of this communion, a deep sleep descended on me and I saw a number of Souls until a fright and trembling fell on me, according to my manner. It appeared from these events that I would attain great things. I ascended further and I saw R. Joshua Heschel, from here. I called loudly, R. Joshua Heschel, until the members of my household heard my voice. He said to me that he was well. I asked him why and for what reason was this apportioned to me. He told me that he once heard a sermon from a certain evil person and from this an evil spark entered him and turned his heart to oppose me. Afterwards, I was associated with him in love and affection. A great fear and trembling descended on me, and I awoke.

5605 [1845], the nineteenth of *Adar* II. On the eve of the holy Sabbath I had a long dream and in the course of it [received] an explanation of Psalm 20, "May the Lord answer you in time of trouble." When will He answer you, "The name of Jacob's God keep you safe?"[31] [He will answer you] when your strength and might will be in the name of Jacob's God, and he will connect the name of Heaven, the name of Jacob's God, with the anguish. The essence of the anguish is the aspect of the limbs of the *Shekhinah* which is clothed in this anguish. When you will be on this path, He will answer you immediately. The whole Psalm was explained to me in this manner. The secret of "The name of Jacob's God keep you safe" amounts to 903. In all degradations and deaths, until poverty which is the most difficult of all,[32] the name of Heaven will connect with him and then "He will send you help from the Sanctuary." The holiness will be assisted "from Zion"— the *zaddiq*, the foundation of the world, "will sustain you." It will be in this manner that "He will grant your desire." The scholar will understand how to interpret the whole [Psalm] in this manner. This occurred to me because I had been in great anguish the previous day over my great want, poverty, and degradation, as a result of which I had wasted much time from Torah study and worship. I was particularly anguished over my weakness. During the day I was very depressed about God's behavior toward me. I forgot the divine name, that my anguish over the lack of income and physical fatigue are insignificant, when today I am here and tomorrow in the grave giving an accounting before the Supernal King. (The essential anguish that I should have been anguished over was the decline and defect of the Supernal Holiness, the *Shekhinah*, for there is no greater anguish than this.) The most intense defects are those of the Supernal *Zaddiq [Yesod]*, the foundation of the world, and *Tiferet*. Woe to me that, Heaven forbid, my many sins caused me to sunder the unity and sever my Soul from unification with the *Shekhinah*. For I am in an infernal generation, and especially in the city of..., among inferior people, whose like is not to be found. I cannot cause even one of them to repent, since they are as full of mockery as the clouds. As the result of having caused a separation between "Blessed be He," it was hinted to me "God will answer you in the day of trouble," the abbreviation of which is *ZYB"Y*. The sages praised Zivi because of this Unity,[33] while I sundered it and because of this I have an intense defect. I woke up and said: "Blessed be He and blessed be His name which lives and exists forever, amen."

5605 [1845]. Sunday night, *[parshat] Shemini*, the twenty-second of *Adar* II. I dreamed that I was sitting at a gathering of *zaddiqim* and I gave a long sermon on the verse "And you shall serve the Lord your God" [Ex 23:25] on *Rosh Hashanah*, because *Rosh Hashanah* is an esoteric secret, as is explained in the *Raya Mehemna*.[34] It covers the light and is the secret of *Hesed*. The *Samekh* is joined to *Hayyim* [life] and *Din* [judgment] because *Het* is the abbreviation for *Hayyim* and *Dalet* is the abbreviation for *Din*. In addition, *Het, Samekh* in *gematria* is *Hayyim*, and *Samekh, Dalet* in *gematria* is *Din*. The secret of five times *Hesed* amounts to *seter* in this manner, and the secret of *Hayyim, Din* amounts to "The Lord, your God."[35] Through the sound of the *shofar, Hesed* is turned into *Din* in the secret of *kol* and *Hesed shalom* to *Hesed* and *Din* from the secret of *Emet* in the Unification of the face, the secret of truth. "He will bless your bread" on *Rosh Hashanah*, because all of a person's sustenance is gathered on *Rosh Hashanah*. The secret of "your bread" amounts to *Zevaot* [hosts].[36] Through this name his sustenance is provided with *Nezah* and *Hod*, with the sacrificial parts joined to the *Aleph* of *Zevaot*, as is explained in the words of our teacher, to the initiates. There the manna is ground for the righteous,[37] with the influences over sustenance. "Your bread" and the names of the Lord of Hosts encompass the upper and lower [worlds]. They all need blessing and the influence of sustenance, as is explained in the words of our master on the creation of the world with the letter *Bet*. "Blessed be He and the world came into existence," upper and lower are all called *Zevaot*, as in "the Lord of Hosts is with us," for His name will also be called "with us" as in the secret of the Unification of blessing the flow of sustenance. "The Lord of Jacob is our haven" [hints] at the Unification of procreation, face-to-face, [and] the letter *Aleph* which is superfluous in the lower compared to the upper [worlds]. "He will bless your bread" is the secret of the letter *Bet*, the blessing in the divine flow of sustenance which flows down on *Rosh Hashanah* through the divine name *Zevaot*, the secret of truth. "And your water"—this is *Yom Kippur* in the secret of the sealed spring. Afterwards, I immediately corrected myself and said: "And your water"—this is the festival of *Sukkot* and the drawing of living water for pouring [on the altar] and for joy, since *Yom Kippur* is included in the secret of "and your bread." One needs to eat physical bread on the eve of *Yom Kippur* in order to receive (the category of) spiritual bread on *Yom Kippur*, in the secret of judgment, life. "He is the Lord your God" encompasses sustenance and life. "When the Lord gives abundance on *Rosh Hashanah*, He gives it for life."[38] The seal of life and peace is sealed on *Yom Kippur* and everything depends on abundant sustenance. "And your water"—during the time when we are judged concerning water, during the festival of "your water"....[39]

"And I will remove sickness from your midst"—this is the evil beast which depends on the attribute that accuses Israel. It should not accuse, it should not accuse. Afterwards, I said, it should not accuse, it should not accuse many times. After this, I spoke more words of Torah and I repeated them many times so that I should not forget them and I concluded "it should not accuse, it should not accuse" many times. In the midst of these things I awoke and, because of my sins, I forgot everything immediately when I left to return to this world, except for the explanation of the above-mentioned verse.

5605 [1845]. The eve of *Shabbat Shemini*, the twenty-sixth of *Adar* II. I saw my teacher and uncle, the holy Rabbi Zevi, praying while walking back and forth in his *bet midrash*. He told me that he has permission to go to his *bet midrash* and pray as he did during his lifetime. I was amazed at how great and holy a *zaddiq* he was, that he has permission to behave as though he were still alive. I gazed at his holy face and I was filled with strength and joy that I should be worthy to see his holy splendor. It was fourteen years after his death, and he appeared as in life, as I had seen him thousands of times. Nothing good will occur to anyone who sits in his place. I saw what happened to my uncle R. Moses [of Sambor] a"h[40] and also to others, that it was unacceptable to the *zaddiq* that someone sits in his place. It is almost half a year since he honored me and said that I will sit in his place. Everything was loving and friendly, and still I found it unacceptable as I explained the matter at great length to my friend....Nonetheless, he said to me that he disagreed and I would be compelled.

5605 [1845]. On the seventh night of Passover I saw a *zaddiq* whose face shone light, the light of the sun. I asked him who he was and he answered that his name was Menachem. He greeted me with great and wondrous joy. I was too greatly overjoyed from seeing his face and I awoke.

5605 [1845]. On the twentieth day of the *Omer*, I was in the city of Dukla.[41] I arrived on a dark and gloomy night and there was nobody to take me home, until a tanner came and took me to his house. I wanted to recite the evening prayers and count the *Omer*, but I could not do it there. I went to the local *bet midrash* and prayed there. From this I understood the concept of the descent of the *Shekhinah* and her pain in standing in the tanner's market.[42] I wept many tears before the Lord of all, because of the *Shekhinah's* anguish. I fainted from my own great anguish and dozed a little. I had a vision of a great light in the image of an adorned young woman, a glowing light, but I was not worthy to see her face. More cannot be written down. Her light was brighter than the noonday sun.

5606 [1846]. On the first day of *Rosh Hashanah*, I did several spiritual exercises on behalf of the community of Israel in Russia. I overcame their guardian angel and because of the severity of the decree against them, there occurred to me what occurred. On the second day, I did what I had to do and at night I saw the above-mentioned guardian angel with a drawn sword. He wanted to kill me if I did not leave him alone....I promised him that I would leave him alone. Afterwards, I saw the guardian angel of Edom and he assured me that he would not do anything bad as a result of the decree and I blessed him with the blessing for a king, and then awoke. Thus it was that all the decrees against the Jews of Edom were annulled.

Regarding the *mitzvah* of sending the mother,[43] which I fulfilled, we find in the Midrash,[44] "and the children you shall take so that you will have children."

5607 [1846]. On the first night of *Rosh Hashanah*, I had a long dream. I saw that there were judgments against me. (Afterwards, I saw that I was walking with hair on my head. I said in my heart that these hairs certainly point to severe judgments, Heaven forbid.) During the day I prayed with great joy and self-sacrifice. When the Torah was lifted, I noticed the verse "When you have seen it, you too shall be gathered to your kin" [Nm 27:13]. I paid no attention to this and recited the *musaf* prayer in a pure light. On the second night, I dreamed that the Supernal Crown was revealed in His mercy and the judgments were sweetened.[45] The rabbi, the *Bet Joseph*, interceded on my behalf and only robbery remained. This too was sweetened and only a knife and silver spoon were stolen.

5607 [1846]. The Sabbath of Return.[46] On that day I dreamed that I was in the Holy Land and for many days I saw the disciples of my teacher, the *zaddiq*, Rabbi Joseph Zevi, the *zaddiq*, Rabbi Moshe Abele, Rabbi Israel Baer, and all of them kissed me with joy.

5607 [1846]. The twenty-eighth of *Tishrei*, after the conclusion of the Sabbath, I saw my uncle and teacher. He ordered me not to quote anything in his name when I give the sermon at a propitious time. In the year "there shall be a redeemer for Israel," on the night of the holy Sabbath, *parshat Noah*, the fourth of *Heshvan*, I had a long dream. However, it was not pure and clear, but confused. Afterwards, I ascended with great clarity and saw my uncle, the *zaddiq*, Rabbi Baerish, may his merit protect us, and I knew that I was dreaming. I saw his Soul and afterwards I went to another place where I saw this same uncle. I thought that I was awake and I was in a state of great translucence and clear thought. I said to myself: What great merit do I have that I see the souls of the *zaddiqim* while awake, without agitation? I was filled with light as a result of my great joy at having this privilege. I washed his hand, kissed it, and joyfully recited the blessing, *Shehehianu*. I enjoyed this vision very much. I said to him: Please forgive me for embracing and kissing you, for I am clothed in physical flesh and blood and his honor is clothed in pure light. It is therefore not appropriate to approach such pure light in foul garments. He laughed at me. Afterwards, I began to beg, implore, and beseech him and I asked him saying: May the master please tell me and reveal to me why I came to this world, what is my defect, what am I lacking, where is my place in Paradise? Reveal to me the greatness of my Soul, if I have not, Heaven forbid, been exiled from my greatness. I embraced and kissed him and continued to implore and plead with him a great deal, but he did not want to answer me, because he had not received permission to do so. When I saw that my pleas were of no avail, I asked him: At the very least sir, reveal the greatness of my teachings to me. Are they acceptable above, before the Lord of all, especially my book *Ozar ha-Hayyim* on the commandments and what I wrote there, in the 275th commandment concerning the mouth of *Attika Kadisha* and the renewal of creation?[47] He stood up with great agitation and fear and said: The Torah, the Torah (many times). He raised both hands in fear and said: Your teachings and novellae are studied in all the academies. I was filled with boundless joy and I awoke....

The year 5607 [1846]. The night of *Rosh Hodesh Heshvan* I recited the *piyyut* "*Hoshanah Sukkat Shalom*" with much weeping. I awoke, fell asleep again, and I saw in my dream that it was now *Rosh Hashanah* and the cantor began to say aloud, "Who shall be

at rest, who shall be humbled, who shall be exalted."[48] I understood that I still had to accept exile and afterwards my prestige
will be raised....

The year 5607 [1846]. The night of the holy Sabbath, the
twenty-fifth of *Heshvan*. I dreamed that I saw my friend, the pious
Joshua of Brody, and I forgot if he was still alive in this world or
already in the Supernal world. I asked him with great longing:
Tell me, dear brother, from where have you come? He answered
me: From the Supernal world. I asked him with great longing:
Tell me my brother, what am I in the Supernal world? He
answered: With goodness and great importance. Afterwards, I
questioned him further. The previous week I had been very
angry with my wife, for she had disturbed me greatly, and lights,
souls, and angels which had accompanied me for almost two days
disappeared from me. Was there great damage above, as a result
of this? He did not answer me at all concerning this. I said to him
with warmth and friendliness: Do not suspect me of asking you
these things because I want to be a rabbi or a *Rebbe*, but rather
because I desire that my portion be with the Lord of Israel and
the people of Israel. He answered me that all was well and I
awoke.

The year 5607 [1847]. In the month of *Shevat* I dreamed that I
saw a scroll of the Torah and between every verse it was full of
great and exalted secrets. I stood with my teacher and master, my
uncle Rabbi Zevi, may his merit protect us. He showed me this
scroll and told me that this was my scroll that I had written with
my teachings and the new interpretations which I had innovated.
I saw many times that I was donning *tefillin*, a sign of the magni-
tude of Israel's greatness....[49]

The year 5607 [1847], the twelfth of *Adar*. I saw that it was *Yom
Kippur* and I repented with great intention, out of the depths of
my heart. I recited the *musaf* prayers and recited the *avodah* service, prostrating myself with arms and legs outstretched. When I
said "And the Priests," I did a great penance and I awoke, a sign
that my sins were forgiven.

The year 5607 [1847]. The holy Sabbath, the eighteenth of

Adar. I saw several Souls who objected to my book *Ozar ha-Hayyim*,[50] on the 613 commandments, that I should not write more and reveal so many secrets. They showed me my book and complained about several things that were contained in it. I said to them: Praise God, I have already explained a number of commandments, up to *parshat Behar* [Lv 25] and it contains true and wondrous reasons. They admitted that this was true, but nonetheless, I should not write more. I said, if God will grant me life, I will certainly write, for we are commanded and required to know the reasons for the commandments. Afterwards, I was worthy to see a spark of Elijah z"l. I pleaded with him, my lord, please greet me. He greeted me and I was filled with great joy. I encountered several Souls and I said to them: I was worthy that Elijah should greet me, and I awoke. At the conclusion of the Sabbath I saw a beautiful but terrifying lion, a symbol of kingship. My prayers were accepted by the Supernal Lion.

5607 [1847]. At the end of the first day of *selihot*, I dreamed that at dawn I donned two pairs of *tefillin* as was my custom, with great joy. I did not attain such joy when awake, a sign that I will attain tranquillity and greatness. I got up and recited the *selihot* with the community. Before the prayers I took a brief nap and I dreamed again that I donned *tefillin*, a sign that I will quickly attain greatness, satisfaction, and joy....I saw Rabbi Mordecai of Drohobycz and I swore to him in my dream that I would not be in Drohobycz for ten years unless there is a compelling need to travel through there or to stay overnight. Even this was doubtful, for originally the oath was that I would not be there for ten years—however, afterwards I said, except for a compelling reason. Perhaps this conclusion falls into the category of idle words.[51] Therefore it is presently forbidden to me to travel to the above-named city for ten years. The whole matter is very strange to me....

I saw my teacher and he had complaints against Rabbi Ze'ev of this community, who is buried in Jerusalem, because of a certain matter. I argued much on his behalf. I also saw Rabbi Ze'ev that time and pleaded, as described above. I saw my teacher the whole week after *Simhat Torah*.

5608 [1847], Monday, the third of *Heshvan*. I saw that it was the eve of *Yom Kippur*, close to evening. I went and took out a Torah scroll from the holy Ark. I embraced and kissed it and recited "Light is sown for the righteous."[52] My intent was to repair the sparks, as is known. It appeared to me that this *Yom Kippur* occurred on the Sabbath. I began to recite *"Am ha-Sefer"* and it was a good sign that I had certainly repaired some sparks. It was further shown to me that my friend Rabbi Yehuda Zevi of Radziwill had died and with his death had repaired everything, including many sparks. Blessed is his portion that he directed his intention with the Unification of "Light is sown for the righteous" in the secret of the thirteen complete ones, as in the [divine] names of 72, 63, 45, 52, which as is known add up to 754, and with this his Soul expired with purity and in Unification....

The year 5609 [1848]. During the intermediate days of *Sukkot*, I saw a very bright moon and I saw a major eclipse of the moon. I said that this was a bad sign for the Turks....[53] On the fourteenth of *Tammuz*, during the day, I saw a palm tree and they said to me that I only have one heart for my Father in Heaven.[54] They also told me that my soul contains a spark from the *tanna Rav*. Thus, whoever tries to harm me will be punished. From this spark, my Animus burns to comprehend the secrets of the Torah. I was a disciple of Rabbi Simeon bar Yohai, a disciple of our teacher Rabbi Isaac Luria, and a disciple of the Besht, until now. I am in a dark, contemptible, and insignificant generation, Yizhak, Yehuda, Yehiel. I was told that the *tanna Rav* also donned his holy *tefillin* to the right side of the brain and all the disciples of Rabbi Simeon bar Yohai also followed this custom. My teacher and uncle told me in a dream at night that he saw in the Supernal world that several myriads of worlds depend on the holy *tefillin* that are on the right side of the brain and this is the appropriate practice. And in the city of Zhidichov....[55]

The year 5607 [1847]. On the eve of *Shabbat Va-Yehi*, I dreamt, during an afternoon nap, that I recited the *Neilah* service and, praise God, the harsh decrees were erased and the evil decree was annulled. I fasted until the night.

The year 5607 [1847]. Thursday night, the ninth of *Adar*. I saw the face of the Rabbi from Belz,[56] may he live, and afterwards the face of the Rabbi from Radziwill.[57] I saw that he was sitting on the ground and he was mourning the death of a relative. Afterwards, he gave me some coins and said that I should forgive everything....I do not know the meaning of this dream.

The year 5610 [1850]. Tuesday, [*parshat*] *Bo*, the second of *Shevat*. I dreamed that two of my teeth fell out together. The meaning is that I was told that two of my enemies will be uprooted together in one day.

5610 [1850]. The conclusion of *Shabbat*, the nineteenth of *Adar*. I saw that I was brought a garment belonging to our teacher the Besht, may his merit protect us, and I was told of a wondrous miracle that our teacher performed while wearing the garment, but I forgot what it was. I took the garment and rejoiced with it as with a treasure. The meaning of this dream is that when I gave my sermon during the third meal [of the Sabbath] a number of lights, Souls, and angels were present and among them was a Soul from the Soul sparks of the disciples of our teacher.

On Tuesday night, the twenty-first of *Adar*, I saw my teacher, Rabbi Naphtali of Ropshits,[58] may his merit protect us. I spoke to him about many matters and afterwards I asked him: Why was I worthy to see Souls when wide awake? He said: From the reward of the Sabbath and its light. We had a Sabbath illumined with a wondrous light.

5610 [1850]. The second of *Nisan*, Thursday night. It was the night of immersion in the *mikvah* and I studied Torah until midnight. I completed the study of the laws of Passover in the *Tur* and went to sleep. I had a dream and vision in the night. I saw our master Elimelech of Lyzhansk[59] and he was very affectionate toward me. I was told that the place of our divine master, the Besht, was not far from that of the above-mentioned master. I quickly went to his dwelling, with great desire, to see the face of the holy master. I stood outside his house and was told that he was inside, in the midst of his prayers. Afterwards, the door opened and I was worthy to see the face of our master, the Besht, may his merit protect us. As a result of my great joy and fear I was not able to move from my spot. He walked over to me and greeted me with a joyful face and I had great pleasure. His visage is engraved in my mind and is always before me. Perhaps I had been worthy to attain this because I had given charity that day, as is right and proper.

"The son of David will not come until a fish is sought for a sick person and will not be found."[60] There are two Messiahs: Messiah, the son of David, in the western lands, and Messiah, the son of Joseph—Messiah, the son of David, will redeem the *Shekhinah* along with all the clarified sparks of the primordial kings who were annihilated during the six days of creation.[61] The Messiah, son of Joseph, will redeem the transmigrated Souls that fell through sins, transgressions, and rebellions and were transmigrated into inanimate, vegetable, animal, and human. "Then the Lord your God will restore your fortunes and take you back in love" [Dt 30:3]. The Messiah, son of Joseph, will be sick, "Wounded because of our sins" [Is 53:5], to raise the Souls and return them, to accept exile upon himself for the Souls of the righteous which were transmigrated into fish,[62] their repair thus spoiled. As a result of this, fish are not found in their places, not in rivers and pools of fish; even those that are found are immediately spoiled and abandoned in exile. The tribulations atone for the transmigrations of the righteous, so that they should not need to transmigrate, and the righteous will be raised up.

The year 5613 [1852]. The eve of *Rosh Hashanah*. After I recited the *selihot* with great concentration, I lay down to sleep a little and I saw my teacher and uncle z"l. I spent about an hour with him, and during this hour he told me[63]—I do not know the meaning of the matter, for it was obscure. Nonetheless, I wrote it down.

The year 5615 [1855], 23 *Adar*. I saw the divine teacher, the Besht, and out of great awe I was not able to move from my spot. He came over, greeted me, and gave me a book that I should peruse. I asked of him that there should be peace in my city, that their hearts would be awakened to awe. Afterwards, I asked him many questions, that he should show me which path is good and proper. He was silent and did not answer at all.

The year 5618 [1857]. *Ḥeshvan.* I saw a sun that was eclipsed and I was told that this was the sun of the Feminine side. I saw another sun and it was also eclipsed and the world was dark for me... and I saw a bright moon....

5618 [1857]. The third night of *Ḥanukkah.* I saw a very bright star and the moon was eclipsed and the eclipse passed. They told me: "The children of Israel" are the *Neẓaḥ* and *Hod* of the Masculine and "you are children" are the *Neẓaḥ* and *Hod* of the Feminine.

THE DEEDS OF THE LORD

Now I will write about the deeds of the Lord, for the deeds done by the zaddiqim of our times are great.

My teacher and father-in-law, R. Abraham Mordecai of Pinczow, told me (I can testify that he would not change the story for everything in the world) that a righteous old man told him: My son, I once went to the mikvah at night with our teacher, the Besht. He tarried in the mikvah for a long time. I said to him: Master, the candle is almost extinguished! He responded in Yiddish: Thorn, take an icicle and light it. "He who told the oil to burn will tell the icicle to burn."[1] This means in Hebrew: Fool, take the icicle hanging from the roof during the winter and light it. The old man said that it burned until he accompanied the divine master to his house. When he arrived at the house, where there were lit candles, only a little water was left in his hand, which had melted from the heat of the flame. I heard this from my teacher and father-in-law. Believe me, my brothers, this and all the stories are true as the Lord your God is true.

My teacher and father-in-law told me, during his travels of more than two years to serve zaddiqim, he was also with the grandson of the divine teacher, the Besht, the author of *Degel Mahne Ephraim*.[2] Once he said to him: Come and I will tell you a wise thing that my grandfather did. In the city of Medzibozh there was a wealthy man who opposed my grandfather, the Besht, like the simpletons, sons of fools, who oppose the zaddiqim. Once, on the first night of Passover, an evil thing happened to him, Heaven forbid. The gentiles took a corpse and put it in the courtyard of the wealthy man, in order to falsely accuse him of having killed him for the Passover, as was the way of the evil gentiles in earlier times (and also in our time). It was the habit of these evildoers to leave guards after they left [the corpse], to ensure that nobody from the house left with a bundle on their shoulders. Afterwards, they would attack the inhabitants of the house and the other Jews, killing and robbing them, without fear of punishment (may God see the suffering of Israel and have mercy). When the wife of the wealthy man went out into the courtyard and found the corpse, she fainted from great fear and anguish. She was revived with great effort. Crying, screaming, and hitting her forehead, she told her husband about the nefarious evildoers and their leaving a corpse in their courtyard. They would certainly return soon to torment them mercilessly and kill them for no reason, as was their way. Out of great fear and anguish, she told her husband to go to the *zaddiq* and he would save them. He said to her: How can I go, I am his opponent? She responded: He is a *zaddiq* and will not bear a grudge. He went to our master, my grandfather, weeping greatly and told him the whole story, that he was in great danger. My grandfather said to me: Ephraim, my dear grandson, take the staff and go with this man to his house and say to the corpse, my grandfather sent me to you. You should immediately get up and come with me. I went with the man and spoke thus to the above-mentioned corpse. The corpse immediately got up and went with the bier in his hands to my grandfather, who lay him back on his bier. Afterwards, the plotters descended on the house of the wealthy man and they found nothing. Since our divine master was also famous among the gentiles as a wonder worker, they decided to also search my grandfather's house. My grandfather took the hat from my brother Baruch, may he live, who was then very young, and put it on the head of the corpse. He put the *Haggadah* in his hands and said to him: Mumble! He began to sway back and forth and read inarticulately, in a loud voice, from the *Haggadah*. When the plotters came, they searched the whole house but did not find the corpse. They did not recognize him, since he moved and made loud noises like the living. The gentiles went on their way. Afterwards, my grandfather sent for the rich man and told him: Take the corpse and bury it! He did so.

My teacher and father-in-law z"l heard all this from the above-mentioned *zaddiq*, the grandson of the Besht z"l, who was himself involved in the story. I heard the rest of the story from my teacher and father-in-law, who heard it from others. The follow-ing year, they gathered again to do a similar evil deed, to attack Israel with a blood libel. Among them was an anti-Semitic priest. When the *matzot* were being baked, the Besht went to the priest. Taking a walk with him, [the Besht] said to him: Why do you want to do this to a holy people, to shed blood like water for nothing, in a false and despicable accusation? Do you not know that I am in the world and I know all your secrets, those that you did and those that you want to do? You did not succeed last year when you left the corpse at the house of R. Lipa, the wealthy man. I resurrected him temporarily and you saw him sitting at my feet, at the edge of the bed, and did not recognize him. The priest then admitted to him that on his advice the corpse was thrown into the wealthy man's courtyard the previous year. In addition, he had already prepared a corpse to put into a Jewish house this coming Passover, in order to accuse them. The priest swore that he would never again do this to Israel. Afterwards, our divine teacher went to celebrate the festival of Passover with joy and gladness.

My teacher and father-in-law told me what he had been told by our teacher, the light of the seven days, Rabbi Jehiel Michel [of Zloczow],[3] the disciple of our master [the Baal Shem Tov]. Once he and two other disciples were walking in a field with our mas-ter. When the time came for the *minha* prayer, he said to them: We do not have water to wash our hands before the prayer. Our master took his staff and hit the ground and a spring broke forth and they washed their hands and prayed. To this day, the gentiles call it the Baal Shem's spring.

I was told by reliable persons that his holy disciple, the great *cohen*, Jacob Joseph [of Polnnoye],[4] said: I wish I would profit from all my good deeds in this world that which my teacher, the divine master, the Besht, profits when he smokes his pipe.[5] He unites awesome Unifications with every movement. He does not move the smallest limb without Unifications. Who can talk about, who can praise, and who can evaluate his holiness?

My uncle and teacher, Rabbi Zevi of Zhidachov, told me that once a woman came to our master [the Besht] to receive an amulet to cure a certain malady. Our master told her that if she would give him fifty ducats, he would give her the amulet. The woman went home, sold all of her belongings, but she only had thirty ducats. She traveled to our master and told him that she only had thirty ducats. He did not want to give her the amulet. The woman then traveled to the Council of the Four Lands[6] (its head then was the sage, Rabbi David of Ostrog), in order that they should collect another twenty ducats for her, to give to the zaddiq. When they heard the woman's request, they were filled with anger and rage and sent a message to him that he should immediately appear before the tribunal. The divine master traveled to them. When he arrived there, he stood in the doorway and smoked his pipe until the house was filled with smoke. None of them had the strength to open his mouth from fright of the *Shekhinah* that fell heavily upon them. Afterwards, the master went to the above-mentioned sage, Rabbi David, and said to him: David, David, come and I will show you a new Heaven and a new earth that I created in smoking this pipe, with the Unifications that I did during this time. He showed him and Rabbi David fainted. When he awoke, he said to his colleagues: One does not argue with God Himself. Believe me, this is no ordinary man. The woman, because of her great desire to give the *zaddiq* what he wanted, became extremely wealthy through a great and wondrous miracle. This too was his holy intent. May his merit protect us, amen.

Once, our divine master was traveling from Brody and the sage, Rabbi Ḥayyim Cohen of Lvov, was on his way to Brody and they met each other. The rabbi said to our master: Israel, they say about you that you have divine inspiration. He said this in a joking manner. Our master responded: Why do you jest, sir? After all, we find in books that whoever recites "*Ata Ḥonein*" on the Sabbath should be concerned the whole week,[7] and what are you joking about, sir? No creature in the world knew that this happened to the rabbi the previous Sabbath. He stood and kissed him on the head.

My teacher and father-in-law, the *zaddiq*, told me that once our master was sitting with his well-known colleague, and both of them were studying with the prophet Ahijah the Shilonite. (The [Soul] source of our divine master, the Besht, and our master, Rabbi Isaac Luria, were both from the source of Rabbi Simeon bar Yohai, who was of the source of Ahijah the Shilonite.) They all came [into the world] to repair the sin of the evil dog, the evil Jereboam ben Nebat, who after his sin contained the evil of the Soul of Messiah, the son of Joseph. The evil dog, the face of the dog of the Second Temple, opposes and troubles these holy ones in every generation, as does the face of the dog in our generation. It has ruined the whole world and increased heresy in Israel. Certainly the redemption was near in those holy days, especially through the source of our divine master, the Besht. The whole redemption depended on him and the holy Rabbi Hayyim ben Attar, but this evil ruined everything through the controversy and causeless hatred which it brought.

Once, our master was studying with his teacher, Ahijah the Shilonite, and they needed to ask a secret of the prince of the Torah. They made a mistake and brought down the prince of fire. As a result, a fire broke out in his house and burned the whole city.[8] Our divine master was afraid of accusations by the gentiles. He ran away and needed to cross the river Dniester. He put a piece of his belt on the river and crossed on it, not by means of a divine name, but through great faith. He believed and trusted in God that he would not drown, Heaven forbid.[9]

My teacher and father-in-law, the *zaddiq*, told me that when our divine master, the Holy of Holies, was secluded in the high mountains in communion with the Lord his God and studying with his well-known teacher, a group of thieves decided to kill him. They sat at a distance to observe his actions. They saw that when he quickly walked from mountain to mountain, the mountains quickly stuck to each other, as he went from mountain to mountain, so that he would not fall into the valleys between them, which were very abundant. A great fear fell upon them and they came before him and said: Man of God, if you wish, come with us to the Holy Land through a shortcut. The desire of our master for the Holy Land was very great (as has been told before) and he went with them. They came to a small and very dangerous crossing. He did not want to rely on a miracle and returned to his home, to connect his Soul with God.[10]

Once a singer came with musicians to sing for him. Our master understood through this all the sins that he had committed from the day of his birth until now. As a result, he thanked [the singer]. For even though our master saw from one end of the world to the other and [knew] all the thoughts of a person from the day of his birth, nonetheless, "When he sees iniquity, does he not discern it?" [Jb 11:11], until he sang before him and the Holy of Holies entered his ears....

My teacher and father-in-law, our master, Rabbi Abraham Mordecai of Pinczow z"l, told me that once in a certain village there was a priest, a great sorcerer, who would kill Jewish children before their circumcision with his magic. Once a Jew who lived in the above-mentioned village had a son to be circumcised. Our divine master saw that the priest was preparing to kill the child. Our master traveled there miraculously quickly with his disciples, arriving the evening before the circumcision was to take place. The Jew honored him greatly. Our master told the Jew to close the door and every opening, leaving not even a keyhole unsealed. He also prepared large thick staves, and when he will say to him "strike!," he should strike with all his strength. That night someone knocked at the door asking to be admitted, but the Jew did not want to [let him in], as he had been instructed by the man of God. The priest went and magically changed his form into a cat and unclean animals. He began to dig under the house and when he stuck his head into the house, our master commanded him to strike and the Jew struck terrible blows until [the priest's] hand and leg were broken. The priest went to his house. In the morning there was a great and joyous circumcision celebration. When it became known to the priest that our master had done all this to him, he complained about him before the nobility, that they should compel our master to dispute with him. The nobles finally agreed and set a time that both should appear, when each one would perform a wonder until one would be able to overcome the other and be victorious in front of a large assembly. On the appointed day, a large crowd gathered along with all the nobility and priests. Our master said to him: First, you do what you can. The priest conjured up all sorts of spirits, demons, wild animals, snakes, and scorpions. Our master quickly took his staff and drew a circle around himself. He stood in the middle and they could not enter the circle, until [the priest] conjured up a wild boar. When he saw it, our master said: This one is very insolent. He quickly drew another circle inside the first circle. The boar, in its insolence, put its front feet inside the first circle but could not penetrate [the second circle], and it turned and retreated. When the sorcerer saw that all of his magic was of no avail and could not penetrate the circle to harm him, he said to our master: You do something! He responded: I will not do anything except to call the children you murdered and they will take vengeance. Immediately, there gathered a great many small children who fell upon him, and not even a small bone of his was left intact. So may all your enemies be destroyed Lord, amen.[11]

My teacher and father-in-law told me: A disciple once asked him: What will be my fate and occupation? He told him that he will be a cantor. He responded: I cannot sing. Our master told him: I will connect you to the world of song and you will be able to sing. My teacher and father-in-law told me that he was himself familiar with the above-mentioned cantor and there was no more wonderful a singer in the whole world. Once, the above-mentioned cantor came to our teacher, the light of the seven days, Rabbi Elimelech of Lyzhansk, may his merit protect us. [He brought] two choristers, one called a bass and the other simply called a singer. There was confusion between the above-named master and his son, R. Eleazar, whether they would honor the cantor [with leading the prayers] welcoming the Sabbath. Our master was afraid that the cantor's holiness would perturb him, out of great awe of the great holiness of our divine master, since he was called the Besht's cantor. They immediately decided to honor him, come what may. When the cantor began to pray, the above-mentioned master sent word that he should cease and not lead the prayers any further, because he would expire from the great light, holiness, and divine illuminations that were opened for our master through the songs of this righteous one. Afterwards, our master honored him the whole Sabbath, but he did not lead the prayers. At the conclusion of the Sabbath, he asked the cantor to tell him of the levels and holiness of our divine master, the light of Israel. He told him wondrous things that ears had not heard. Primarily, he told him about his awe and love of God and how his Soul ascended while awake, every movement in all the worlds to see all the chambers of the *Merkavah*. When he recited the "great *Hallel*" [Ps 136], he did not recite each chapter until he saw the angel of that chapter and heard the sweetness of his song, and they recited it together. From the day he was born, his holiness and asceticism were awesome. He spoke with the Souls of the righteous, with Elijah z"l, and in particular with the divine teacher, Rabbi Isaac Luria z"l, who was with him all the time.

Our master, Rabbi Israel Besht, once asked our master, Rabbi Isaac Luria z"l: Why did he speak of the secrets so openly and not in the path of worship? He answered him that if he had lived two more years everything would have been repaired.[12] He also told him how he spoke with the Messiah and with R"M[13] and their responses to him. He was an expert in the secrets of creation and of the Chariot, in the whole Torah, in the speech of all living things and the heavenly angels. He was full of love and fear of God, good attributes, piety, humility, and love of Israel. The above-mentioned master said that all of the attributes that were written about Rabbi Isaac Luria z"l, our master, the Besht, had them all and even more. In addition, that which was written about Rabbi Isaac Luria z"l was like a drop in the ocean compared to what he truly had. He also told him how every Sabbath eve, at the time of *minha*, myriads of Souls gathered around him. He repaired them all and raised them to their source.

He told him that once our master chuckled a little, as was the manner of the *zaddiqim*. They asked him the reason for this laughter. He said that in a distant land a nobleman built a very beautiful palace, over a period of years. When a certain *zaddiq* was going to the synagogue for *minha*, it began to rain and hail very heavily. The *zaddiq* took refuge in the palace because of the hail. When the *zaddiq* left it and continued to the synagogue, the whole building immediately fell down. How can I not laugh at the great guidance of this world? The primary reason for the building of this great house was only as a refuge for the Soul of one *zaddiq* for a short time. All the sparks that were in the stones were repaired and there was no reason for them to stand for nothing. Therefore, they fell to the ground. Afterwards, the story of this building and its falling down without reason was in the newspapers. It occurred at the hour [that our master chuckled].

He further told the above-named master that when our master saw a bench or other artifact, he knew all the thoughts that the artisan had when he made the artifact. The above-named master was very astonished by this. Afterwards, the righteous cantor stood up and testified that once they were studying Torah with our divine master and a burning flame surrounded them until they were so purified that they received Torah from our master in the same way that Israel received it on Mount Sinai, with thunder and lightning and the loud sound of the *shofar*. The sounds did not diminish, since they were divine (in my opinion, this is the meaning of the verse "A loud voice and no more" [Dt 5:19]), but they needed holiness and purification. The above-mentioned master responded: I never attained this. It is no wonder, since the worship and holiness of Israel, our divine master, were extremely great, especially when his holiness and worship came through Ahijah the Shilonite and was at the river Dniester, a place of purity. Happy is the one born of woman who is worthy of this. The pious ones who heard this understood that everything mentioned above also applied to our master Elimelech, may his merit protect us. In time, that cantor died, and during the month after his death, on the eve of the Sabbath, when his bass chorister came from the bath and ritual immersion, he said to his wife: Quickly, call the burial society and "prepare my shrouds."[14] My cantor has been honored with bringing in the Sabbath in Paradise and he does not want to [do it] without me. He lay down on his bed and gave up the ghost.

My teacher and father-in-law z"l told me that our master had a disciple, that whoever entered within his four ells when he prayed, immediately died and passed from the world, because of the great holiness of the *Shekhinah* which rested on him.

I was told by reliable witnesses, truly righteous people, that in a certain place there was a rabbi. Once, a question was brought to him concerning a duck, on the eve of the Sabbath. He would have been able to declare it kosher because of poverty, in honor of the Sabbath, or excessive financial loss. He did not permit it because he was a strict decisor. Afterwards, when he died, the rabbi came before the Heavenly Tribunal and was acquitted, because he was completely righteous. In the midst of this, a certain duck came and complained that there was within it a Soul that had wandered for many years until the time for its repair had come in this duck. It is still wandering because he had declared it not kosher, for no reason. They decided that the righteous rabbi will have to wander. He went on in this way for several years until he was advised that he should go to our master, for he repairs all the (wandering) Souls. If he repairs the Soul, then there will no longer be any judgment against him. He did so and in a short time he ascended to his place.

There once occurred an incident in which our master came to a certain place and a householder made a great banquet in his honor. Before the banquet our master said that under no circumstances would he eat with him. The householder pleaded mightily with him, but to no avail. He left there and the householder was forced to eat the banquet with the members of his family. In the course of the meal, his son ate a piece of meat and a bone got stuck in his throat and he choked, Heaven forbid. The householder traveled to our master and said to him: If our master foresaw all of this, why did he not save a Jewish Soul? Our master responded that the reason was that the child in his previous transmigration was a rabbi who erred and declared a certain fowl not kosher, without proper consideration. It was decreed that he should transmigrate into this world again and the spark of the fowl should kill him. He saw all this and was unable to annul the Heavenly decree and therefore he left....

A man once came to our master and asked if he should learn the laws of slaughtering, in order to become a ritual slaughterer.

He said to him: My son, come and I will show you something! They went outside and he said to him: Look up on the roof! The man lifted his eyes and he saw a man standing next to the chimney, sharpening a knife. The man was very frightened, and [our master] said to him: My son, this was a ritual slaughterer several hundred years ago and he thoughtlessly slaughtered with a defective knife, and he still has not been repaired. Afterwards, it was decreed that he should come to me and show me a correctly prepared knife. He has been standing on my roof for three years and he cannot present a properly prepared knife. And you want to be a slaughterer? He responded that he no longer wanted it. This is the last story I heard from my teacher and father-in-law z"l. He heard all of these stories from his teacher, our master Jeḥiel of Zloczow, a disciple of our divine master. All of their words are true as the words of God.

Our master, Rabbi Isaac Luria z"l, hinted at our master, the Besht, when he responded to Rabbi Ḥayyim Vital z"l, concerning his achievement: To whom are all the delights of Israel. The achievement of R. Israel Baal Shem Tov is surely yours. See in the *Book of Visions*.[15]

Once, our master prayed with his disciples on *Rosh Hashanah* as was their holy manner. A box of snuff [belonging to] one of the disciples fell down and he bent down to pick it up in the midst of the prayers. A second one saw this and complained greatly that he had interrupted his prayers in order to take some snuff. These complaints brought a death decree upon that *zaddiq*, Heaven forbid. Our master, the Besht, saw all this and ascended through a Soul ascent[16] to the Heavenly Tribunal and argued vigorously on behalf of this *zaddiq*. Nothing helped until the night of *Hoshanah Rabah*, when he ascended through the power of his prayer to the upper heights and secured agreement that if the accuser himself found some merit, the judgment would be set aside. Our master entered his *bet midrash* and he found the disciple, who was occupied with the *tikkun* of the night. He could not concentrate and was unable to continue further. He walked back and forth to think about the greatness of God and about Unifications, when the thought occurred to him:

304

Why was the tobacco leaf revealed in the previous generation, to be smoked and [used] for snuff? He decided that this was because there are some worthy, precious Souls and sparks that it is impossible to raise them except through a pleasant odor. He decided to ask our master about this. On *Hoshanah Rabba* it was the custom of our master to be in a jovial mood and he answered questions about anything in the world, both plainly, with insight, with divine inspiration, with secrets, and in plain language. In the morning, the disciple asked our master about this and our master said to him: I will tell you. And he answered him as above. In the meantime he understood an explanation for his friend's [behavior] that he had interrupted his prayers because of the tobacco. Perhaps he had within him such a precious thing. Tell me what else is on your mind! He told him everything, how he was angry with his friend previously, but now he was satisfied. Our master told him all of the above and our master warned him that he should not suspect his friend again, but "judge every person positively."[17]

He once said to his disciples on *Hoshanah Rabba:* Prepare yourselves a teacher and rabbi, because I will die this year. His disciples said to him: Our master, the light of Israel, we have heard that there is one *zaddiq* in this land. Will we be able to affiliate with him? He answered them. When you travel to him, come to him when he is praying a certain prayer. Afterwards, examine him and ask him to give you some advice about how to remove haughtiness and arrogance. If he will tell you that he literally has no advice and will respond to you: God will help, for there is no advice for this—you will know that it is truthful, and he is a complete *zaddiq*. They traveled there and it happened as above. They asked him as above and he responded: Gentlemen, my dear and beloved ones, what can I tell you? There is no advice for this. There are those who can lower themselves to the ground, but their purest inner intent is arrogance and a wicked heart. There is also the opposite: One who behaves with haughtiness, but is brokenhearted. There is no counsel for this, but God's help, in His infinite mercy. They became attached to him in love, as our divine master had commanded, may his merit protect us, amen.

Once our master was on his way to the holy community of Brody and he was in [the city of] Radwill. In the city of Brody there was a woman who was having a difficult childbirth, the daughter of a wealthy man. She was already in labor for seven days and messengers were sent with offerings to all the *zaddiqim*, to the *zaddiq* R. Ḥayyim of Sanz, to R. Moses of Ostrog and others. Nothing helped and they sent word that our master should come there....[18]

Notes to the Texts

BOOK OF VISIONS

Many of the footnotes are based on the notes in the Hebrew edition edited by A. Z. Aescoli. These are indicated by [A].

Part One: Events in My Life

1. [A] This is a reference to the period when Vital neglected the study of Torah in favor of alchemy. See below Part 4, sect. 11. [M.M.F.— On Vital and Alchemy, see R. Patai, *The Jewish Alchemists* (Princeton, 1994), pp. 340–364. See also G. Bos, "Hayyim Vital's 'Practical Kabbalah and Alchemy': A 17th Century Book of Secrets," *Journal of Jewish Thought and Philosophy* 4 (1994): 55–112.]

2. (1488–1575) The most important *halakhic* authority in Safed and author of the standard code of Jewish law, the *Shulḥan Arukh*.

3. (d. after 1593) *Halakhic* scholar and biblical commentator in Safed and Vital's teacher in *halakhah*. He gave Vital rabbinic ordination in 1590.

4. Karo's angelic mentor, which was the personification of the *Mishnah*. On Karo and his *Maggid* see R. J. Z. Werblowsky, *Joseph Karo, Lawyer and Mystic* (Philadelphia, 1977); and M. Beneyahu, *Yosef Beḥiri* (Jerusalem, 1991), pp. 391–512.

5. The reference is to the biblical texts, written on parchment, which are contained within the *tefillin* boxes.

6. A kabbalist mentioned in a number of sources. M. Idel, "R. Yehuda Halliwa and his book, *Sefer Zofnat Paneaḥ*" (Hebrew), *Shalem* 4 (1984): 126f., 146–148. See also D. Ruderman, *A Valley of Vision–The Heavenly Journey of Abraham ben Hananiah Yagel* (Philadelphia, 1990),

NOTES TO VISIONS, PART I

pp. 200–202, where Yagel reports a story about R. Lapidot Ashkenazi that also alludes to his ability to predict the future.

7. A reference to his teacher, Rabbi Issac Luria, who was of *Ashkenazi* (i.e. Central European) descent, as opposed to *Sephardi* or Spanish and Portuguese descent.

8. On this form of divination, see S. Daiches, *Babylonian Oil Magic in the Talmud and in later Jewish Literature* (London, 1913); J. Trachtenberg, *Jewish Magic and Superstition* (New York, 1939), pp. 219–222; and J. Dan, "Archons of the Cup and Archons of the Toenail," in *Studies in Ashkenazi-Hasidic Literature* (Hebrew) (Ramat Gan, 1975), pp. 34–43.

9. Soniadora means female dreamer in Spanish.

10. [A] This passage is related to *Song of Songs Rabbah* 1.8. However, it is a different version. See L. Zunz, *Derashot be-Yisrael* (Jerusalem, 1974), p. 129.

11. [A] See below, Part 4.

12. Unifications are among the most important Lurianic meditative exercises. For a description and analysis of these practices, see L. Fine, "The Contemplative Practice of *Yihudim* in Lurianic Kabbalah," in *Jewish Spirituality*, ed. A. Green (New York, 1987), vol. 2, pp. 64–98; and A. Kaplan, *Meditation and Kabbalah* (York Beach, 1982), pp. 218–260.

13. G. Scholem, "Shtar Hitkasherut shel Talmidei ha-Ari," *Zion* 5 (1940): 138 n. 11, identifies R. Mas'ud Cohen with R. Mas'ud Cohen Azulai who was the teacher of R. Shlomiel Dresnitz in *Kabbalah*. D. Tamar, *Mehkarim be-Toldot ha-Yehudim be-Erez Yisrael U-be-Italia* (Jerusalem, 1970), p. 174 n. 25, disagrees with this opinion.

14. [A] A region in the south of Morocco.

15. [A] B. *Sukkah*, 52a, where the Messiah of David will plead for the life of the Messiah of Joseph.

16. In this method of divination, the person asks a divinatory question as soon as he or she awakens and receives an answer while still drowsy. This practice is based on Psalms 17:15, "Awake, I am filled with the vision of you." My thanks to Prof. Elliot Wolfson for this reference.

17. This is the name given in rabbinic sources to Tinneius Rufus, governor of Judea at the outbreak of the Bar Kochba revolt. According to Talmudic legend (B. *Avodah Zarah*, 20a: B. *Nedarim*, 50b), his wife became a proselyte and married Rabbi Akiva, bringing with her a considerable fortune.

18. [A] In other words, he could not see beyond this period in his vision.

19. A colleague of R. Hayyim Vital and student of R. Isaac Luria.

20. There is a tradition that R. Moses Cordovero said before he died that whoever would see the pillar of fire that would precede his coffin would be his successor. The only one who saw it was R. Isaac Luria. See D. Tamar, "The Greatness and Wisdom of Rabbi Ḥayyim Vital" (Hebrew), in *Rabbi Joseph B. Soloveichik Jubilee Volume* (Jerusalem/New York, 1984), vol. 2, p. 1300. The pillar of fire seen over Vital undoubtedly was meant to validate that he was Luria's successor.

21. Most likely what is meant is that he was a servant of Dome of the Rock mosque, which is on the Temple mount.

22. I.e., modern-day Iraq.

23. [A] B. *Sanhedrin*, 105b.

24. (d. between 1587 and 1589) Disciple of R. Isaac Luria and according to one source, his son-in-law.

25. Is 29:4.

26. B. *Sanhedrin*, 65b.

27. The term used in the *Sephardi* tradition for the commemorative meal partaken of on the anniversary of the death of a deceased relative.

28. [A] Joseph Sambari, in his chronicle, calls her a wise woman who had a *Maggid* and could foretell the future; *Sefer Divrei Yosef* (Jerusalem, 1994), ed. S. Shtober, pp. 364f.

29. (1505–1584) Important kabbalist, teacher of R. Moses Cordovero and author of "*Lekha Dodi*" hymn for *Kabbalat Shabbat*.

30. *Sifra, Leviticus*, 2.

31. [A] A city to the north of Damascus.

32. The term in Hebrew is *palil*, which normally means judge, perhaps the equivalent of a *Qadi* or religious dignitary.

33. The four basic elements of medieval science were air, fire, earth, and water. Everything was believed to composed of one of these elements or some combination of them.

34. [A] This may be a version of the Spanish word *careta*, which means mask. [M.M.F.–It could also be the Arabic term *Qarina*, female demon. My thanks to Prof. Paul Fenton for this suggestion.]

35. [A] This is probably a reference to the Turkish conquest of Malta in 1530. See H. Y. D. Azulai, *Shem ha-Gedolim*, s.v. R. Abraham ha-Levi; M. Steinschneider, "Ma'amar al R. Abraham ha-Levi" *Oẓar Neḥmad*, 2 (1857): 147–157; G. Scholem, "Ha-Mekubal R. Abraham ben Eliezer ha-Levi," *Kiryat Sefer* 2 (1925): 101f.

36. This is an allusion to the statement by R. Simeon bar Yoḥai in *Genesis Rabbah* 35.2 (Theodor-Albeck ed., pp. 329f.). My thanks to Prof. Ze'ev Gries for this reference.

37. [A] It would appear that this is not a reference to his son, R. Samuel Vital, who edited his writings. [M.M.F.—Perhaps this is a reference to one of his two sons who died young—Joseph, mentioned in Part 2, sect. 6, or Nehemiah, mentioned in Part 2, sect. 20.]

38. [A] A reference to the concept of "impregnation." See below, Part 4, sect. 3. See also *Sha'ar ha-Gilgulim* (Jerusalem, 1912), pp. 3, 6.

39. [A] A reference to Rav Yeivi Saba, a mythic figure mentioned in the *Zohar*. See below, Part 4, sect. 9, 31, 32, and others.

40. "The concepts of the various 'airs [ethers]' between the earth and the divine world reflect the influence of terms from the Book of Creation *(Sefer Yezirah)* and the commentaries on that book." J. Dan, "Samael, Lilith and the Concept of Evil in Early Kabbalah," *AJS Review* 5 (1980): 26f.

41. This story is one of the original prototypes for the story of the *Dybbuk*. It was repeated in a wide variety of sources. See M. Beneyahu, *Toldot ha-Ari* (Jerusalem, 1967), p. 292 n. 1. On the historical development of the *dybbuk* motif see G. Nigal, *Sippurei Dybbuk be-Sifrut Yisrael* (Jerusalem, 1983).

42. The term *Anav* means "humble." It is probably a reference to the well-known Italian family Anau. My thanks to Prof. Paul Fenton for this suggestion.

43. Joshua al-Boom was a kabbalist in Damascus who was an expert in the magical aspects of *Kabbalah*. He owned an ancient manuscript that taught him how to expel demons and spirits from persons who were possessed. He taught these practices to Vital. See Beneyahu, *Toldot ha-Ari*, pp. 291–295.

44. A kabbalistic custom. Wine represents *din* (judgment) and water represents *Hesed* (mercy), therefore the "judgments" are "sweetened" with "mercy."

45. Rabbi in Damascus. Cf. Sambari, *Sefer*, p. 375.

46. Rabbi in Damascus. Cf. ibid.

47. (1555?–1625?) Important Hebrew poet. Author of many hymns still sung.

48. (1550?–1622?) Rabbi of the Spanish congregation in Damascus. He was Vital's nemesis in Damascus and is mentioned often in this work.

49. A war with Gog and Magog is one of the precursors of the messianic age. See Ez 38.

50. An angel often mentioned in kabbalistic literature. R. Margulies, *Malakhei Elyon* (Jerusalem, 1964), pp. 169f.

51. [A] I.e., he had a prophetic mission. See Ez 3 and 33, and the end of this section.

52. [A] See below, Part 3, "The Dreams of Others."

53. [A] See above, sect. 17.

54. [A] A reference to *Rabban* Johanan ben Zakkai and Rabbi Akiva. See below, Part 4, sect. 5.

55. The most important angelic figure in the Jewish mystical tradition. *Encyclopedia Judaica* (Jerusalem, 1971), index, s.v. Metatron.

56. [A] See below, Part 4, sect. 58.

57. This is a paraphrase of Ps 84:5, which is cited in the Talmud (B. *Sanhedrin,* 91b) as a prooftext for the doctrine of the resurrection of the dead.

58. See below, Part 5, sect. 12.

59. The name in Hebrew sources for Tripoli, a port in northern Lebanon.

60. [A] The wife of R. Judah Aberlin, one of R. Isaac Luria's disciples, or perhaps she is the Rachel Ashkenazi mentioned above in sect. 16.

61. Rabbi in Damascus. Sambari, *Sefer,* p. 375.

62. [A] This issue, whether it is permitted and appropriate to force people to take an oath that they are reporting their income honestly for purposes of taxation, was a subject of much discussion in the rabbinic responsa literature of that generation and previous generations.

63. [A] A town near Damascus. There was an ancient synagogue there and the residents of Damascus would go there to pray on Sabbaths and holidays.

64. Not an oven in the modern sense. More like a closed brick fireplace built into the wall, which had a large area on top of it where one could sleep.

65. Rabbi in Damascus. Sambari, *Sefer,* p. 376.

66. (d. after 1612) Important rabbi in Safed.

67. (?1555–?1625). Important Hebrew poet. He was also criticized by other rabbis for his unconventional behavior.

68. The three weeks between the seventeenth of *Tammuz* and the ninth of *Ab,* two fast days relating to the destruction of the Temple. It is customary not to eat meat and to abstain from joyous activities during this period, as a sign of mourning for the Temple.

69. All are activities prohibited during this period.

70. Fasting is normally prohibited on the Sabbath.

71. He was a scribe and is mentioned in the responsa of R. M. A. Fano. Sambari, *Sefer*, p. 414.

72. An anonymous medieval compendium of *halakhic* rulings and explanations.

73. [A] The text of this Unification is in *Sha'ar Ruah ha-Kodesh* (Jerusalem, 1963), pp. 88f.

74. El, a name of God.

75. The year 1622 C.E. corresponds to the year 1000 A.H. in the Muslim calendar.

76. [A] The Muslim name for Jesus.

77. The word for lives, *hai*, is an allusion to Hayyim Vital, whose first name "Hayyim" means "life."

78. This dream may have been influenced by the approach of the year 1000 in the Muslim calendar, which Vital and the dreamer of the dream may have seen as the end of the dominion of Islam and Christianity. See Dan, "Archons of the Cup," p. 36, n. 19.

Part Two: My Dreams

1. G. Scholem, in his personal copy of the *Book of Visions*, which is in the Scholem Library of the Jewish National and University Library in Jerusalem, suggested a number of emendations to Aescoli's text. The emendations by Scholem are from this copy. He emends this name to Verga.

2. Scholem emends this to 422.

3. See M. Beneyahu, *Toldot ha-Ari* (Jerusalem, 1967), p. 103 n. 1, for many parallels to this story in other sources.

4. In a different version of this story, the person is punished in this manner because he committed adultery or slept with a gentile woman. See ibid., p. 200 n. 1.

5. [A] See below, Part 4, sect. 49, concerning the levites who will be priests in the messianic age, after the repair of Cain. This is the secret of the incident of Korah.

6. B. *Sanhedrin*, 92b, "In that day what will the righteous do, God will give them wings of eagles and they will fly over the face of the waters." See also *Zohar*, I:12b. My thanks to Prof. Ze'ev Gries for this reference. See also G. Scholem, "A Homily on the Redemption by R. Solomon of the House of Turiel" (Hebrew), *Sefunot* 1 (1957): 75, where

the kabbalists will be transformed into semi-physical and semi-spiritual beings and they will be given wings like those of eagles.

7. "Tying is a well-known device connected to causing sexual impotence in the bridegroom..."; see M. Idel, *Kabbalah–New Perspectives* (New Haven, 1988), p. 81 n. 43

8. [A] See below, Part 4, sect. 6, where this reference is discussed in greater detail.

9. [A] See above, Part 1, sect. 2. See also below, Part 4, in several places.

10. See Idel's analysis of the relationship of crying and revelation, as it relates to this dream in *Kabbalah–New Perspectives*, pp. 81–88.

11. This refers to the practice started by the kabbalists of Safed to go out into the fields to welcome the "Sabbath Queen" at the beginning of the Sabbath. On this ritual see G. Scholem, "Tradition and New Creation in the Ritual of the Kabbalists," in *On the Kabbalah and Its Symbolism* (New York, 1965), pp. 139–144.

12. [A] This vision is found in *Sefer ha-Peliah (Sefer ha-Qanah u-Sefer ha-Peliah)*, (Koretz, 1784), p. 48. The source of this vision seems to be Rabbi Abraham Abulafia. Solomon Molcho had a similar vision. See A. Z. Aescoli, *Hayyat Kanah* (Paris, 1938); and idem, "Hearot Ahadot le-Toldot ha-Tenuah ha-Meshihit," *Sinai*, 12 (1943): 84–89.

13. The prophet Elijah.

14. A paraphrase of Gn 28:12.

15. A paraphrase of Ez 1:14.

16. The concept of wool extinguishing Heavenly fire is found in *Midrash Tanhuma, va-Yishlah*, 2.

17. This is a technical term found in earlier kabbalistic literature referring to exoteric scholars who are not kabbalists. P. Giller, *The Enlightened Will Shine* (Albany, 1993), index, s.v. Masters of the Mishnah.

18. This term can be understood in two ways. Normally, it means "men of sublime spirituality" or spiritual elite. However, it can also be translated literally as "sons of the attic or upper story." In both cases it refers to kabbalists.

19. [A] B. *Berakhot*, 57a.

20. B. *Sanhedrin*, 92b; See also *Zohar*, I, 12b.

21. *Tikkunei Zohar*, Introduction, 1b (Margulies ed.).

22. A paraphrase of the prayer of R. Alexanderai in B. *Berakhot*, 17a.

23. The person who holds the child during the circumcision. The godfather, a position of great honor.

24. [A] Abraham ben Eliezer ha-Levi Berukhim (1515–1593), Safed kabbalist. [M.M.F.–See L. Fine, *Safed Spirituality* (New York, 1984), pp. 47–53.]

25. Intertwined snakes as a symbol of evil can be traced back to antiquity and occurs in earlier Jewish mystical sources. See M. Idel, "Studies in the Doctrine of *Sefer ha-Meshiv*" (Hebrew), *Sefunot* N.S. 3 [18] (1985): 247 n. 13.

26. This is a mythic motif that occurs in earlier sources. J. Dan, "The Story of Joseph Della Reina" (Hebrew), *Sefunot* 6 (1962): 321f.

27. (1522–1570) The most important kabbalist in Safed before R. Isaac Luria. He died shortly after Luria came to Safed.

28. This incident has many strange aspects. He is asked to lead a festival service and instead he recites the weekday version of this prayer. He stops about two-thirds of the way through the repetition at a messianic passage and then concludes the *amidah* with the final verse, leaving out the whole last third of the *amidah*.

29. There were also earlier groups of kabbalists who adopted this practice. D. Tamar, "On the *Havurot* of Safed" (Hebrew), in *Studies in the History of the Jews in Israel and Italy* (Hebrew) (Jerusalem, 1970), pp. 95–100; idem, "The Beginnings of the Ari in Egypt" (Hebrew), in *Studies in the History of the Jews in Israel and the Near East* (Hebrew) (Jerusalem, 1981), pp. 74–77.

30. Safed rabbi.

31. (d. between 1587 and 1589) Son of R. Moses Sagis. According to one tradition, he was the son-in-law of R. Isaac Luria.

32. [A] Perhaps this is a reference to a Jewish hermit or a Muslim dervish, according to the description?

33. I.e., the synagogue of those whose forebears had come from Aragon, in Spain.

34. [A] This verse is discussed in *Zohar Hadash* to Ruth (Margulies ed.), p. 88a, and in *Zohar*, III:281 (*Raya Mehemna*). The theme of the discussions is the nearness of redemption by the Messiah.

35. On this technique, see L. Fine, "Recitation of Mishnah as a Vehicle for Mystical Inspiration: A Contemplative Technique Taught by Hayyim Vital," *Revue des Etudes Juives* 141 (1982): 183–199. On the concept of meditation (*hitbodedut*) in Jewish mysticism, see M. Idel, "*Hitbodedut* as Concentration in Ecstatic Kabbalah," in *Studies in Ecstatic Kabbalah* (Albany, 1988), pp. 103–169; P. B. Fenton, "La *hitbodedut* chez la premiers qabbalistes en orient et chez les soufis," in *Priere, mystique et judaisme*, ed. R. Goetschel (Paris, 1987), pp. 133–157; idem, "Solitary

Meditation in Jewish and Islamic Mysticism in Light of a Recent Archeological Discovery," *Medieval Encounters* 1, 2 (1995): 271–296.

36. Three important *Tannaim.*

37. Both are names of God.

38. On the additional soul, see B. *Beẓah,* 16a and B. *Ta'anit* 24b. For a more extensive discussion of this theme, see E. Ginsburg, *The Sabbath in Classical Kabbalah* (Albany, 1989), pp. 121–136.

39. The redactor of the *Mishnah.*

40. In Hebrew.

41. [A] *Zohar,* II:104a *(Sabah de–Mishpatim).*

42. An important *Tanna.*

43. [A] M. *Avot,* 2:19.

44. A contemporary of Vital's, not the son of R. Simeon bar Yohai. See above, sect. 9.

45. I have translated this verse somewhat differently from the NJPS translation, in accord with its context.

46. [A] See below, Part 4, sect. 55.

47. The verse [Is 17:6] continues—"as when one beats an olive tree. Two berries or three on the topmost branch, four or five on the bough of the crown—declares the God of Israel." The discussion that follows seeks to explicate this part of the verse.

48. [A] See below, Part 4, sect. 57–58.

49. (c. 1545–beginning of 17th cent.) One of Luria's foremost students. He became a rival of Vital's after Luria's death and published his own version of Luria's teachings.

50. According to Vital, R. Isaac Luria divided his disciples according to their spiritual worthiness. The first group were his closest disciples.

51. [A] For the mystical reasons concerning Luria's death, see N. Bacharach, *Emek ha-Melekh* (Amsterdam, 1648), Introduction 3, ch. 6 (pp. 12a–13a) and *Shivhei ha-Ari* (p. 15). [M.M.F.—See also B.V. 4.44 and Beneyahu, *Toldot ha-Ari,* pp. 200–205.]

52. [A] *Emek ha-Melekh,* Introduction 2, ch. 2.

53. [A] For a discussion of the concept of *Parẓufim,* see below, Part 4, sect. 54, and in the Supplement, sect. 2.

54. A name of God.

55. [A] *Lamentations Rabbati, Petikhta* 24.

56. See H. Vital, *Etz Hayyim* (Koretz, 1784), pp. 17f.

57. [A] This is the abbreviation derived from a group of verses from the prayer of Rabbi Nehuniah ha-Kanah [from the liturgy for blowing the *shofar* on *Rosh Hashanah*]. See H. Vital, *Sha'ar Ruah ha-Kodesh*

(Jerusalem, 1912), p. 6. It is mentioned there by R. Solomon Sagis, in the name of R. Isaac Luria, that this is the second version of the divine name of 42 letters.

58. This interpretation is found in R. Moses Cordovero, *Pardes Rimmonim*, Part II, 29:2 (p. 67c). E. Wolfson, "Biblical Accentuation in a Mystical Key: Kabbalistic Interpretation of the *Te'amim*," *Journal of Music and Liturgy* 12 (1989–1990): 11, n. 84. My thanks to Prof. Elliot Wolfson for this reference.

59. A village in the Galilee.

60. A Talmudic sage.

61. 2 Chr 24:20.

62. Ne 8:9. G. Scholem suggests that this is also an allusion to Nehemiah ben Hushiel, who is a Messiah ben Joseph figure—"*Shtar Hitkashrut shel Talmidei ha-Ari*," *Zion* 5 (1940): 141. Nehemiah ben Hushiel is mentioned in *Sefer Zerubbabel*, in Y. Even Shmuel, *Midrashei Geulah* (Jerusalem, 1954), p. 78.

63. [A] *Zohar*, II:13a–b.

64. One of the prayers in the *amidah*.

65. The pulse point is a conduit to the Soul. Vital reports that his teacher, R. Isaac Luria, was able to diagnose spiritual ailments by touching the pulse point. See Vital, *Sha'ar Ruah ha-Kodesh* (Jerusalem, 1963), p. 14.

66. [A] Vital was the last transmigration of Cain. See below, Part 4. ["Father (*avikha*)" also has the meaning of ancestor.]

67. Samael is one of the primary names of Satan. See *Encyclopedia Judaica* 14: 719–722; R. Margulies, *Malakhei Elyon* (Jerusalem, 1964), pp. 248–270.

68. This is based on a combination of several statements. In the Talmud (B. *Shabbat*, 152b) it says that the souls of the righteous are hidden under the Throne of Glory. The *Zohar* expands on this theme. See *Zohar*, I:113a (*Midrash ha-Ne'lam*) and the parallels cited in R. Margulies, *Nizozei Zohar*, op.cit., n. 11. Also, *Zohar Hadash*, 24a (*Midrash ha-Ne'lam*); *Tikkunei Zohar*, tikkun 57 (p. 91b), and *Zohar*, I:125b (*Midrash ha-Ne'lam*). All references are to the respective R. Margulies editions. My thanks to Prof. Ze'ev Gries for these observations.

69. *Rashi* on Gn 17:22. Rashi's comment is a paraphrase of *Genesis Rabbah* 47.6 (ed. Theodor-Albeck, p. 475); see also *Genesis Rabbah* 82.6 (ed. Theodor-Albeck, p. 983). My thanks to Prof. Ze'ev Gries for this reference.

70. "Elijah is the face of the Eagle in the Chariot." Cf. *Hupat Eliyahu*

Rabah, 4:4, in *Reshit Hokhmah ha-Shalem*, ed. H. Waldman (Jerusalem, 1984), vol. 3, p. 230. My thanks to Prof. Ze'ev Gries for this reference.

71. Possibly a reference to the Copper Serpent of Nm 21:9.

72. This is the Arabic name for Eim Zeitim, a village north of Safed.

73. I.e., the completion of the study of a Talmudic tractate, which is considered a religious celebration.

74. A similar story occurs in R. Judah Halliwah's *Zofnat Paneah*—M. Idel, "R. Judah Halliwah and His Work—*Sefer Zofnat Paneah*" (Hebrew), *Shalem* 4 (1984): 126f. See also Beneyahu, *Toldot ha-Ari*, pp. 111f., for other parallels to this story.

75. A reference to Gn 32:25–30. The identification of the angel Jacob wrestled with as Samael is found in *Zohar*, I:146a.

76. Gn 36:43.

77. [A] See *Pirke de Rabbi Eliezer*, ch. 38; *Targum Jonathan ben Uziel*, Gn 36:43; *Genesis Rabah* 83.43 (ed. Theodor-Albeck, p. 1000).

78. Ob 1:1–21. See also *Midrash Tanhuma* (ed. S. Buber), *Va-Yishlah* 8 (p. 84), on the relation of Obadiah to Esau.

79. [A] *Sefer Zerubbabel* is found in J. Even-Shmuel, ed., *Midrashei Geulah* (Jerusalem, 1954). The identification of Nineveh and Rome is found on pp. 79 and 379, in this edition.

80. An allusion to B. *Sanhedrin*, 98a, which states that the Messiah is to be found among the beggars of Rome. On this motif, see A. Berger, "Captive at the Gate of Rome: The Story of a Messianic Motif," *Proceedings of the American Academy for Jewish Research* 44 (1977): 1–17.

81. An allusion to Gn 45:1.

82. An allusion to Gn 41:39.

83. M. Idel suggests that this dream may be a reflection of Solomon Molcho's attempts to meet the pope. M. Idel, "Solomon Molcho as Magician" (Hebrew), *Sefunot* N.S. 3 [18] (1985): 216f.

84. One of the prayers of the *amidah*.

85. Which is not found in the standard text of the prayerbook.

86. Two mythic sages from the *Zohar*.

87. R"B (*Resh "Bet*) is an abbreviation whose meaning in this context is unclear. Perhaps it is an allusion to "*Rabbenu*," as in Moses Our Teacher (*Rabbenu*).

88. Normally the *shofar* is blown by the rabbi or other distinguished member of the congregation.

89. M. *Sotah*, 9:15.

90. The meaning of this word is unclear.

91. See above sect. 3.

92. (1598–c. 1678) Vital's youngest son and editor of his writings.

93. M. Idel suggests that this should be emended to the Arabic term *"talmas"* [talisman]—"Introduction to the Second Edition," in A. Z. Aescoli, *Sippur David ha-Reuveni* (Jerusalem, 1993), p. XXXVIII. This whole dream draws on a tradition from the *Sippur David ha-Reuveni—* ibid., pp. XXXVI–XXXIX.

94. The term clarification (*berur*) is a synonym for repair (*tikkun*).

95. *Segol* is a Hebrew vowel consisting of three dots in a triangular pattern with the point downward.

96. [A] See below, Part 4, sect. 48, and Part 5, sect. 16.

97. On the soul garment (*Malbush*), see E. Wolfson, "The Secret of the Garment in Nahmanides," *Daat* 24 (1990): xxv–xlix; D. Cohen-Alloro, *The Secret of the Garment in the Zohar* [Hebrew] (Jerusalem, 1987), pp. 50–67.

98. *Midrash Alfa Beta de-Rabbi Akiva,* version A, in A. Jellinek, *Bet ha-Midrash* (Jerusalem, 1938), vol. 3, pp. 27f.; *Midrash Otiyyot de Rabbi Akiva,* version A, in A. Wertheimer, *Batei Midrashot* (Jerusalem, 1968), vol. 2, p. 368.

99. *Het* has the numerical value of eight.

100. [A] Ex 6:21. Koraḥ was also from the source of Cain's Soul and his repair was effected by Vital. See below, Part 4.

101. [A] B. *Sukkah*, 53a. The passage continues, "They lead him to the place where he is wanted."

102. Ex 1:1–6:1.

103. [A] Both activities were traditionally in Jewish hands in the countries of the Near East at this time.

104. Dt 34:6 says that no one knows Moses' burial place. However, the death of Moses is part of the *Sephardi* liturgy for *Simhat Torah* and may be the source for this evocation in his dream. My thanks to Prof. Paul Fenton for this observation.

105. This phrase is the beginning of the fourth prayer of Sabbath morning *shaharit amidah*. The "portion" Moses rejoices with in this prayer is the Sabbath.

106. Moses was ten cubits tall. B. *Berakhot*, 54b.

107. Dt 33:1–34:12.

108. [A] I could not find such a reference in this tractate in the versions known today.

109. Aescoli has Asumado. Scholem emends this to Apumado. He is mentioned in Israel Najara's *Zemirot Israel* (Venice, 1600), p. 143b. He was a physician. See Beneyahu, *Toldot ha-Ari,* pp. 210f.

110. *Tekiah, Shevarim, Teruah.*

111. (1502?–after 1571) Important Safed rabbi. Brother-in-law of R. Israel Najara.

112. [A] *Midrash Kohelet,* 9.8.

113. [A] B. *Berakhot,* 56a. The interpretations of this story and the previous one, in their original texts, are somewhat different from the way Vital presents them. He interprets them more positively than the original context warrants.

114. [A] In earlier versions this paragraph is placed at the beginning of this part and it belongs there.

115. [A] J. *Kelayim,* 9.3.

116. The term *"hagurah"* can mean belt. It can also mean loincloth and this is how modern scholars understand the term in its biblical context.

117. The circumcision takes place on the eighth day after birth.

118. An encomium for the dead.

119. The last letter of the word *"Erez."*

120. I.e., the last two letters of Cain in Hebrew.

121. The first letter of the word *kelippah.*

122. [A] See *Sha'ar ha-Gilgulim,* ch. 1, and below Part 4, in several places. [M.M.F.—*Haya"h* is one of the parts of the Soul, lit. "life force."]

123. This might be the Moshe Mizrahi who is the author of a manuscript on "popular science" studied by G. Bos, in "Moses Mizrachi on Popular Science in 17th Century Syria-Palestine." See note 79 of the Introduction.

Part Three: The Dreams of Others

1. [A] Near the grave of the prophet Samuel was a synagogue that was taken over by the Christians and turned into a church. Later Muslims turned it into a mosque.

2. A reference to Ps 119:169–175.

3. A reference to Ps 119:41–48.

4. (c. 1474–1547) *Halakhic* authority and leader of the Jewish communities of Israel, Egypt, and Syria.

5. Kabbalist and rabbi in Damascus.

6. [A] It seems that this is not a reference to his son Samuel Vital. See below, Part 4.

7. Scholem emends this to Sajjah. See n. 1, Part 2.

8. (1533–1600) Safed kabbalist, author of *Sefer Ḥaredim* and the mystical diary *Milei de Shemaya*.

9. (d. after 1612) Disciple of R. Joseph Karo and R. Moses Cordovero. Served as rabbi (*Av Bet Din*) in Safed after 1580.

10. [A] See below, Part 4, sect. 37, and elsewhere. [M.M.F.–*Zohar*, III:143a. My thanks to Prof. Ze'ev Gries for this reference.]

11. A paraphrase of Gn 41:7; 1 Kgs 3:15.

12. There is a tradition, based on Gn 5:29, that Noah was called Menachem (consoler) by Lamech and others. See L. Ginzberg, *Legends of the Jews* (Philadelphia, 1937), I:146, for the sources. Menachem is one of the names of the Messiah. See *Midrash Mishle*, 19.2.

13. Ginzberg, *Legends of the Jews*, vol. 1, p. 147.

14. A symbolic drop of blood must be drawn even if someone has been born circumcised.

15. The letter *ḥet* has the numerical value of eight.

16. On the relation of the foreskin to the forces of evil symbolized by the serpent, see E. Wolfson, *Circle in the Square* (Albany, 1995), p. 148 n. 49, and the sources cited there.

17. The Torah is chanted according to a system of cantilation that is indicated by a musical note or notes over the word.

18. [A] See R. Solomon Molcho, *Sefer ha-Mefoar* (Warsaw, 1884), p. 13. "The *nun* alludes to defeat." This is also alluded to in Ps 145 where the verse that should begin with the letter *nun* is missing.

19. [A] M. *Sotah*, 9:15.

20. This is a word play on the two words that are spelled the same way except for one letter, which he has equated via *gematria* and therefore feels entitled to substitute one word for the other.

21. [A] See also the source of this dream in Part 5, sect. 17.

22. [A] This seems to have been a form of predicting the future that is not known from other sources.

23. [A] The Jumblatt were a Kurdish clan who were appointed the governors of Syria already by Selim, the Ottoman ruler who conquered Syria.

24. [A] In this form of *gematria*, zeroes are deleted, i.e., 40 becomes 4. Using this method Ḥayyim equals 14, which is the same numerical value as David.

25. [A] *Genesis Rabbah*, 20.12 (ed. Theodor-Albeck, pp. 196f.); *Tanḥuma* (ed. S. Buber), Genesis, p. 18; *Zohar*, II:208b.

26. [A] *Leviticus Rabbah*, 29.1; *Pesikta* (ed. S. Buber), p. 150a.

27. An allusion to 1 Kgs 19:12.

28. The color green is significant. In Muslim lands, it is the color of sovereignty and non-Muslims are not allowed to wear this color.

29. In Lebanon.

30. B. *Sanhedrin*, 68a.

31. [A] M. *Sanhedrin*, 10:2.

32. *Deuteronomy Rabbah*, 1.24.

33. Og is identified with Eliezer, Abraham's servant in Tractate *Soferim*, chap. 21. Abraham circumcised all the male members of his household, which included Eliezer; see Gn 17:23.

34. This is an allusion to B. *Baba Bathra*, 121b, which states that seven figures overlapped, forming a chain that extends from creation to the end of time. These figures are Adam, Methuselah, Shem, Jacob, Amram, Ahijah, and Elijah, who continues to live. Vital added King David, probably because of his association with the Messiah.

35. A prayer recited before three people whose purpose is to negate a bad omen or portent that one had in a dream the previous night.

36. [A] The regional governor.

37. (1506–1589) Important *halakhic* authority and communal leader of Salonika.

38. Riding a horse was forbidden to non-Muslims in Islamic society.

39. Rabbi in Damascus. Sambari, *Sefer,* p. 375.

40. [A] The intention is clear. Luria would repair Vital alone and Vital would repair the others.

41. The scribe and assistant of the prophet Jeremiah. See Jer 36.

42. B. *Gittin*, 46b.

43. [A] See below, Part 4, sect. 58. R. Joseph ibn Tabul [another of Luria's disciples] who was at odds with R. Ḥayyim Vital was a transmigration of Baruch ben Neriah's soul.

44. [A] See below, Part 4, sect. 37, 41, and others; *Sha'ar ha-Gilgulim,* p. 12b and 32.

45. B. *Avodah Zara,* 11a. My thanks to Prof. Paul Fenton for this reference.

46. [A] *Genesis Rabbah*, 78.10 (ed. Theodor-Albeck, p. 928).

47. Which requires a quorum of ten to be recited.

48. A posture for taking an oath.

49. (second half of 16th cent.) Talmudic scholar and kabbalist in Safed.

50. See above, sect. 45.

51. (1479–1573) Important Tamudic scholar, *halakhic* authority, and kabbalist in Egypt and in Safed.

52. [A] See above, Part 1, sect. 23.

53. Purple, in Spanish.

54. For the foundations of the Temple. See B. *Sukkah,* 53a.

55. The *kollel,* the inclusion, means adding the number of letters in the word to the final number. E.g., for a three-letter word, you add three to the final *gematria,* calculation.

56. [A] Lv 26:42; Jer 30:18, 33:26, 46:27, 51:19.

57. A paraphrase of M. *Avot,* 2.21.

58. *Yemot ha-Mashiah,* in Y. Even Shmuel *Midrashei Geulah* (Jerusalem, 1954), p. 97; A. Jellinek *Bet ha-Midrash* (Jerusalem, 1938) vol. 3, p. 75.

59. A prayer from the *Yom Kippur* liturgy asking for God's mercy.

60. See above, Part 1, sect. 22.

61. [A] B. *Sanhedrin,* 102a. In the Talmud, this refers to Jereboam.

62. A negative paraphrase of Ex 24:7.

63. A parphrase of Zec 7:2, 8:21–22.

64. A Tel is a mound formed over the remains of a city that has been destroyed.

65. A paraphrase of Gn 19:13.

66. [A] Perhaps because the tribe of Dan went north to conquer lands beyond the area of conquest of the other tribes and therefore needed to be gathered.

67. 1 Sm 9:2.

68. 1 Sm 28:8–20.

69. [A] B. *Berakhot,* 55b. "Three dreams are fulfilled: A morning dream, a dream that his friend also dreams, and a dream that is interpreted within a dream."

70. See above, Part 1, sect. 22.

71. [A] 1 Sm 6:19. They were struck down.

72. [A] J. *Shekalim,* 6.1; R. Menahem Azariah Fano, *Asarah Ma'amarot* (Venice, 1597), Part 2, ch. 2.

Part Four: Things My Teacher Told Me About My Soul

1. *Aravot* is the seventh heaven.

2. [A] Vital is the Italian and Vidal the Spanish translation of the name "Hayyim," meaning life. The *Maggid Mishneh* is one of the important commentaries on Maimonides' *halakhic* compendium, *Mishneh Torah.*

3. Animus, Spirit, and Soul are the three parts of the Soul. I have consistently used these terms for their Hebrew equivalents. This tripartite division of the Soul is already found in the *Zohar*. See I. Tishby, *The Wisdom of the Zohar* (Oxford, 1991), vol. 2, pp. 684–698.

4. Impregnation (*ibbur*) differs from transmigration (*gilgul*) in that impregnation is the temporary entry of an additional soul. Normally, this is for a specific purpose, usually to perform a commandment or other act that the incoming Soul is deficient in or needs to complete a task left unfinished in the previous life.

5. A reference to the ten rabbis martyred during the Bar Kochba revolt.

6. [A] By R. Gershom ben Asher, Mantua, 1561.

7. [A] *Sifre*, ed. M. Ish Shalom (Vienna, 1864), p. 150a.

8. [A] B. *Sukkah*, 28a.

9. [A] B. *Yevamot*, 24a.

10. Zerahiah ben Isac ha-Levi Gerondi (12th cent.) was author of *Ha-Maor*, an important *halakhic* work.

11. Maimonides' work is also called *Mishneh Torah*.

12. An eighth-century aggadic work attributed to R. Eliezer ben Hyrcanus, because it opens with the words "It is related of Eliezer ben Hyrcanus," a sage of the second century.

13. [A] B. *Pesahim*, 49b.

14. [A] B. *Sotah*, 36b; *Bereshit Rabbah*, 39.1 (ed. Theodor-Albeck, p. 1072) and others.

15. According to L. Ginzberg, "Akiba ben Joseph," in *Jewish Encyclopedia* (New York, 1912), I:304, the idea that R. Akiva was descended from proselytes is "a misunderstanding of the expression '*Zekut Abot*' (B. *Berakhot*, 27b), joined to a tradition concerning Sisera, captain of the army of Hazor (B. *Gittin*, 57b, B. *Sanhedrin*, 96b), is the source of another tradition (Nissim Gaon to B. *Berakhot*, 27b), which makes Akiba a descendant of Sisera."

16. [A] More details about this incident can be found in Vital's *Sha'ar ha-Gilgulim, hakdamah*, 36.

17. M. *Avot*, 4:2.

18. *Genesis Rabbah*, 98.4 (98.3, p. 1253, in the Theodor-Albeck edition).

19. See M. Beneyahu, *Toldot ha-Ari* (Jerusalem, 1967), pp. 235f.

20. M. *Avot*, 4:2.

21. [A] See *Sha'ar Ruah ha-Kodesh*, (Jerusalem, 1972), p. 7a and sect. 20 below.

22. See below, sect. 46.

23. The second Passover was a day to celebrate Passover for those who could not bring the Paschal lamb to the Temple, for reasons of ritual impurity or distance—Nm 9:6–12.

24. *Zohar,* I:28b; I:36b.

25. [A] See below, sect. 39, 40, and 42 where Vital explains that the source of Jacob's Soul is from the heel of the *Parzuf* of Esau. Vital's soul is also from this source.

26. *Zohar Hadash* (ed. Margulies), p. 89c–d.

27. [A] *Pirke de Rabbi Eliezer,* chap. 44 and others.

28. *Rav* Yeivi Saba is the central character in the section called *Saba de-Mishpatim,* in *Zohar,* II:94b–114a.

29. [A] B. *Yevamot,* 24a.

30. A section of the *Zohar.*

31. *Zohar,* III: 187a; 188a–b.

32. [A] B. *Shabbat,* 99b; J. *Shabbat,* 1.1.

33. In this case Rav is a name rather than a title.

34. [A] B. *Shabbat,* 23b.

35. [A] Ibid., 56b.

36. [A] B. *Menahot,* 29b; B. *Hullin,* 110a.

37. [A] B. *Ta'anit,* 7b.

38. [A] Should be R. Hanina. See B. *Baba Kama,* 91b; B. *Baba Bathra,* 26a and below sect. 34.

39. [A] B. *Sanhedrin,* 26a.

40. [A] B. *Erubin,* 36b and others.

41. [A] B. *Berakhot,* 25b and others.

42. [A] B. *Kedushin,* 22b; B. *Baba Bathra,* 74b.

43. [A] B. *Bezah,* 28b and others.

44. [A] *Sha'ar ha-Gilgulim* (Jerusalem, 1912), p. 41.

45. [A] B. *Yoma,* 82b.

46. In Hebrew, the term for stone (*even*) and the particular spelling of the Tetragrammaton that Vital uses both have the same numerical value.

47. These are the Hebrew letters whose form changes when they are at the end of a word.

48. This is a custom adopted only by pietists. On this custom and its history, see Y. Gartner, "The Influence of the Ari (R. Isaac Luria) on the Custom of Donning Two Pairs of Phylacteries" (Hebrew), *Daat* 28 (1992): 51–64.

49. [A] *Sha'ar Ruah ha-Kodesh,* p. 9 b–c.

50. [A] Ibid., pp. 9c, 10a, and 34b.

51. [A] Ibid., p. 4d.

52. [A] J. *Berakhot,* 9; *Zohar,* III:36a.

53. An aspect of *Arikh Anpin.*

54. A *Sefirotic* reference. Vital, *Likutei Torah ve-Ta'amei ha-Mitzvot, Beshallah* (ed. Ashlag), (Jerusalem, 1970), p. 144.

55. [A] See above, sect. 8.

56. [A] J. *Nazir,* 7.1.

57. [A] *Sha'ar Ruah ha-Kodesh,* p. 37b.

58. The first letters of the words in this phrase spell out the name Yuval.

59. The *Idra Rabba* is a section of the *Zohar.* The term means "great assembly" and is supposed to be the record of a gathering of Rabbi Simeon bar Yohai and his disciples.

60. [A] B. *Shabbat,* 146a.

61. On this tradition, called *"Tikkun leyl Shavuot,"* see Y. D. Wilhelm, *"Sidrei Tikkunim," Alei Ayin* (Jerusalem, 1948–1952), pp. 125–130.

62. See above, sect. 7.

63. The sixth of the seven lower *sefirot.* In the anatomy of the cosmic Adam it also corresponds to the phallus.

64. See above, sect 7.

65. [A] B. *Pesahim,* 112a.

66. Dt 22:6–7.

67. A reference to the Paschal lamb and how it is roasted.

68. 365 is the number of negative commandments and 248 is the number of positive commandments.

69. B. *Baba Mezia,* 58b.

70. This is similar to the highest form of charity espoused by Maimonides in his *Mishnah Torah, Hilkhot Mattenot Aniyyim,* 10:7.

71. The letters are the same, only the vowel changes.

72. On this concept see, M. Hallamish, "Hanhagah min ha-Kabbalah be-Sifrut ha-Halakhah," *Niv ha-Midrashia* 13 (1978): 161–165; idem, "Gilgulo shel Minhag Kabbali," *Kiryat Sefer* 53 (1978): 534–556; Z. Gries, *Sifrut ha-Hanhagot: Toldoteha u-Mekomah be-Hayyei Hasidav shel ha-Besht* (Jerusalem, 1990), pp. 128f. n. 94; idem, "Mi-Mythos le-Ethos— Kavim le-Demuto shel R. Abraham mi-Kalisk," in *Uma ve-Toldoteha* ed. S. Ettinger (Jerusalem, 1984), vol. 2, pp. 120–126. See also the discussion below, Part 4, para. 59. My thanks to Prof. Ze'ev Gries for these references.

NOTES TO VISIONS, PART IV

73. Abel and breath are the same word in Hebrew, *hevel*.

74. [A] M. *Avot*, 2:15.

75. *Pirke Hekhalot Rabbati*, para. 3–5, in A. Wertheimer, *Batei Midrashot* (Jerusalem, 1968), vol. 1, pp. 71–75.

76. This abbreviation is the first letters of the first verse of the prayer "*Ana be-Koah.*" This prayer consists of seven verses of six words each. The initial letters of each word form the forty-two letter name of God. See *Encyclopedia Judaica*, 3:25.

77. *Zohar*, III:27b.

78. [A] *Yalkut Shimoni*, Numbers, para. 771; *Pirke de Rabbi Eliezer*, ch. 44; *Zohar Hadash* (Warsaw, 1902), p. 168.

79. On the additional Soul, see B. *Bezah*, 16a, and B. *Ta'anit*, 24b. For a more extensive discussion of this theme, see E. Ginsburg, *The Sabbath in the Classical Kabbalah* (Albany, 1989), pp. 121–136.

80. The *sefirah* of *Hokhmah*.

81. Both names are composed of the same letters, rearranged.

82. See above, sect. 6.

83. *Tikkun*, 69 (p. 118b, Margulies edition).

84. See above, sect. 9.

85. B. *Menahot*, 29b.

86. [A] *Bereshit Rabbah*, 96.1 (ed. Theodor-Albeck, p. 1192); *Tanhuma*, *Vayehi*, 8; *Tanhuma* (ed. S. Buber), *Vayehi*, 9; B. *Pesahim*, 56a.

87. J. *Ta'anit*, 4:7.

88. [A] B. *Yevamot*, 47b.

89. [A] See above, sect. 5

90. *Ottiyot de Rabbi Akiva* in A. Wertheimer, *Batei Midrashot* (Jerusalem, 1968), vol. 2, p. 388 n. 148.

91. B. *Berakhot*, 54b.

92. Ibid. 28a. For the significance of Luria's ability to read letters on people's foreheads, see L. Fine, "The Art of Metoposcopy: A Study in Isaac Luria's Charismatic Knowledge," *AJS Review* 9, 1 (Spring 1986): 79–101.

93. [A] B. *Ketubot*, 63a.

94. Akiva is spelled with an *aleph* in the Babylonian Talmud and with a *heh* in the Jerusalem Talmud.

95. On this concept, see M. Elon, *Jewish Law* (Philadelphia, 1994), index s.v., deserted corpse.

96. [A] B. *Yevamot*, 50a.

97. Which has the same spelling as Dimi.

98. [A] B. *Baba Bathra*, 22a.

99. The first two letters of the Tetragrammaton.

100. The word *Mishoresh* and *Y"H*, when combined, create the name "Mushrashia."

101. [A] *Zohar*, II:92a.

102. [A] *Bereshit Rabbah*, 22.12 (ed. Theodor Albeck, p. 219).

103. [A] B. *Ketubot*, 63a.

104. [A] Commentary of Rashi on Nm 25:10 (B. *Sanhedrin*, 82b).

105. The first letter of the alphabet is substituted for the last and so on down the alphabet.

106. [A] A. Hyman, *Toldot Tannaim ve-Amoraim* (London, 1910), vol. 1, p. 80, where all the occurrences of this phrase are collected.

107. [A] B. *Nedarim*, 50b.

108. B. *Nedarim*, 50a; B. *Ketubot*, 62b–63a.

109. [A] M. *Eduyot*, 5:6.

110. This section is also numbered 32 in the Hebrew text. Therefore, I have numbered it 32a.

111. The Tetragrammaton with the letters fully spelled out equals 52 [*Bet"Nun*] in *gematria*.

112. [A] B. *Baba Bathra*, 12b.

113. [A] Ibid.

114. [A] *Sha'ar ha-Gilgulim*, p. 41.

115. [A] B. *Yevamot*, 16a; J. *Yevamot*, 1:6.

116. The number 613 refers to the number of biblical commandments. According to R. Simlai in the Talmud, "613 commandments were revealed to Moses on Sinai, 365 prohibitions equal in number to the solar year and 248 positive commandments equal to the limbs of the human body" (B. *Makkot*, 23a). Later the meaning of the number 365 was changed to refer to the number of sinews and blood vessels in the human body.

117. [A] M. *Ohelot*, 1:8.

118. 600,000 is the traditional rabbinic number for the Israelites present at Sinai.

119. P. 112a (Margulies edition) There are differing approaches to the concept of transmigration in the Zoharic corpus. Cf. G. Scholem, "Gilgul: The Transmigration of Souls," in *On the Mystical Shape of the Godhead* (New York, 1991), pp. 209–211. Cf. also Y. Liebes, *Sections of the Zohar Lexicon* (Hebrew), Ph.D. Thesis, The Hebrew University, 1976, p. 303 n. 32; pp. 321f. n. 109. My Thanks to Prof. Ze'ev Gries for these references.

120. According to medieval biology, semen is produced in the brain and descends via the spinal column.

121. [A] The beginning of sect. 37.

122. All three names are permutations of the same letters in Hebrew.

123. A term for the highest *sefirah, Ein Sof.* Can also apply to the second and third *sefirot, Hokhmah* and *Binah.*

124. Liebes, *Lexicon,* pp. 50f. n. 123.

125. The number of people who went to Egypt with Jacob—see Ex 1:5. The term *nefesh* used in this verse can mean Soul or person.

126. *TaRYaG* equals 613. *T*—400, *R*—200, *Y*—10, *G*—3.

127. [A] See below, sect. 45.

128. [A] *Zohar,* III:288a.

129. For an analysis of the contents of these secret teachings that led to the death of R. Isaac Luria, see Y. Liebes, "Two Young Roes of a Doe: The Secret Sermon of Isaac Luria before His Death" [Hebrew], *Jerusalem Studies in Jewish Thought* 10 (1992): 113–169.

130. [A] B. *Berakhot,* 28b.

131. See above, sect. 16.

132. [A] *Sha'ar ha-Gilgulim, Hakdamah,* 7.

133. The age at which one becomes an adult in the Jewish tradition.

134. *Zohar,* II:94b.

135. [A] See above, n. 132.

136. In Jos 2:4, the word for "and she hid them" is in the singular form.

137. [A] *Numbers Rabbah,* 16.1.

138. R. Margulies, *Malakhei Elyon* (Jerusalem, 1964), p. 16.

139. I.e., in the land of Israel.

140. [A] B. *Baba Bathra,* 75a.

141. [A] B. *Shabbat,* 25b.

142. Enoch is identified with the angel Metatron. For the sources of this identification, see Ginzberg, *Legends of the Jews,* vol. 5, pp. 162ff.

143. Abel in Hebrew is *HeBeL. H* = 5, *B* = 2, *L* = 30.

144. See, above, n. 90.

145. Vital cites tractate *Shabbat,* which is incorrect. I have inserted the correct citation.

146. [A] *Sha'ar ha-Gilgulim, Hakdamah,* 35.

147. [A] B. *Pesahim,* 50a; B. *Baba Bathra,* 10b.

148. For a fuller discussion see *Sha'ar ha-Pesukim,* Ezekiel (ed. Ashlag), p. 240.

149. [A] *Sha'ar ha-Gilgulim, Hakdamah,* 20.

150. For Vital's understanding of this concept, see G. Scholem, "Tse-lem: The Concept of the Astral Body," in *On the Mystical Shape of the Godhead* (New York, 1991), p. 272 n. 45.

151. (c. 1270–1340) Poet and philosopher.

152. [A] Part 1, sect. 418. [M.M.F.–(c. 1235-c. 1310) One of the foremost *halakhic* authorities of the medieval period.]

153. *Zohar,* II:95b.

154. [A] *Sha'ar ha-Gilgulim, Hakdamah,* 27.

155. [A] See above, sect. 16.

156. [A] *Sha'ar ha-Gilgulim, Hakdamah,* 7, 12.

157. [A] B. *Sanhedrin,* 38b.

158. *Sha'ar ha-Mitzvot* (Jerusalem, 1905), *Tezei,* p. 55.

159. [A] *Tikkun,* 69 (Livorno, 1802), pp. 112f.

160. [A] B. *Yevamot,* 80b.

161. *Zohar,* I:59b–60a.

162. It is not clear to what this is a reference.

163. [A] See above, sect. 6, 25.

164. The ten rabbinic martyrs of the Bar Kochba revolt, in 132–135 C.E.

165. *Zohar,* III:144a.

166. Jacob ben Meir (c. 1100–1171) Leading French scholar of the 12th century and grandson of Rashi. His arrangement of the texts in the phylacteries differed from that of his grandfather, which is the most commonly used type.

167. *Zohar,* I:39a; II:254a.

168. *Zohar,* II:10a.

169. Two martyrs mentioned in Talmudic literature. *Encyclopedia Judaica,* 13:69.

170. Bethar was the last Jewish stronghold to fall in the Bar Kochba revolt in 135 C.E.

171. J. *Ta'anit* (Venice, 1520–1524), 4.8, p. 68d.

172. Both *Leyl* and *Laylah* are forms of the word for night.

173. This is not R. Moses Alshekh, his teacher, but someone else. D. Tamar, "Ollelot Sefer Hezyonot," *Sinai* 91 (1982): 85.

174. [A] B. *Sanhedrin,* 102a.

175. Those who accompanied the Israelites when they left Egypt during the Exodus—Ex 12:38.

176. See above, n. 76.

177. [A] These practices are described in greater detail in Vital's *Sha'ar Ruah ha-Kodesh.*

178. This ritual is called "*Tikkun Hazot.*" For a description and discussion, see G. Scholem, "Tradition and New Creation in the Ritual of the Kabbalists," in *On the Kabbalah and Its Symbolism* (New York, 1965), pp. 146–150; S. Magid, "Conjugal Union, Mourning and *Talmud Torah* in R. Isaac Luria's *Tikkun Hazot,*" *Daat* 36 (Winter 1996): XVII–XLV.

179. *Pirke de-Rabbi Eliezer,* ch. 21.

180. [A] This is explained in *Shaar ha-Likkutim,* on 1 Samuel (ed. Ashlag), p. 291.

181. [A] B. *Berakhot,* 28b.

182. The palace of love is the fifth of the seven palaces—*Zohar,* II:253 a–b.

183. See above, n. 15.

184. The root of "Machpelah" is *kafal,* double.

185. [A] *Sha'ar ha-Kavvanot, kavvanot ha-Amidah,* sermon 6 [(Jerusalem, 1963), p. 236].

186. [A] *Sha'ar ha-Kavvanot, kavvanot keriat Shema,* sermon 4. [M.M.F.–Crying has theurgic significance in Lurianic *Kabbalah*; see M. Idel, *Kabbalah–New Perspectives* (New Haven, 1988), pp. 75–82, 197–199. See also, E. R. Wolfson, "Weeping, Death, and Spiritual Ascent in Sixteenth Century Jewish Mysticism" in J. J. Collins and M. Fishbane ed., *Death, Ecstacy, and Other Worldly Journeys* (Albany, 1995), pp. 209–247.]

Part Five: Additions and Miscellania

1. A *cohen* (priestly descendant of Aaron) is not allowed to become ritually impure by being in the same house with a corpse.

2. On this motif in Judaism see M. Fishbane, *The Kiss of God: Spiritual and Mystical Death in Judaism* (Seattle, 1994).

3. Lit. "Supernal Splendor." This is a central concept that is widely discussed in the *Zohar.* For recent discussions, see E. Wolfson, *Through a Speculum That Shines: Vision and Imagination in Medieval Jewish Mysticism* (Princeton, 1994), pp. 355–357, and Y. Liebes, "Zohar ve-Eros," *Alpai'im* 9 (1994): 67–119. My thanks to Prof. Ze'ev Gries for this note.

4. All four are terms for aspects of the Soul.

5. Nm 16:1–20.

6. Ex 2:11–12.

7. Gn 36:12.

8. It is unclear to what book the page references in this section refer.

9. B. *Sanhedrin,* 108a.

10. (1479–1573) Important *halakhic* authority and kabbalist.

11. It is not clear to whom this refers.

12. As emended by G. Scholem.

13. [A] B. *Sanhedrin,* 105b.

14. B. *Hagigah,* 14b.

15. It is not clear to whom this refers.

16. An allusion to 2 Kgs 4:32–35.

17. A reference to the period in which he neglected the study of Torah for the study of alchemy. See Part 1, sect. 2, n. 1.

18. The five letters of the Hebrew alphabet that change their form when they are at the end of a word.

19. I.e., Vital.

20. The three parts of the Hebrew Bible.

21. The letters *Bet* and *Het* both have three sides. When one of them is rotated 90 degrees, it looks like the other one.

22. [A] *Avot de Rabbi Nathan,* ed. S. Schechter (New York, 1967), p. 12.

23. I.e., the *Bet,* which can be seen as a *Het* on its side, rotated and became a *Het.*

24. *Hen* is composed of the same letters as Noah.

25. [A] R. Solomon Molcho in his *Sefer ha-Mefoar* (Warsaw, 1884), p. 13, suggests that *Nun* refers to failure (*nefilah*) and therefore is missing from Psalm 145, which is an alphabetic acrostic.

26. [A] M. *Sotah,* 9:15.

27. [A] This story is the source, in the first person, of the dream that is related in the third person, above, Part 3, sect. 13.

28. This section is an abbreviated version of Part 1, sect. 21. The text is fragmentary.

29. I.e., the Americas.

30. [A] The source of the story of Daniel's kingdom is *Sippur Eldad ha-Dani* (The Story of Eldad the Danite), which contains many stories of the ten lost tribes. *Kitve A. Epstein,* ed. A. M. Haberman (Jerusalem, 1950), vol. 1.

31. [A] It is uncertain to which island this refers.

32. As emended by G. Scholem.

33. [A] See Abraham bar Hiyya, *Meggilat ha-Megaleh* (Berlin, 1924): section on "signs of the end in the conjunction of the constellations and planets."

34. Vital says "69," but it should be 5369.

BOOK OF SECRETS

[B] Indicates notes by N. Ben Menahem in the Hebrew edition of the *Megillat Setarim*.

Book of Visions

1. [B] The numerical value of this phrase equals 566, which refers to the year 5566 [1806].

2. [B] The numerical value of each of these three phases equals 605, referring to the year 5605 [1845].

3. [B] M. *Avot,* 5:21. Forty is the age of understanding.

4. [B] R. Hayyim Vital, *Sha'ar ha-Gilgulim* (Jerusalem, 1912), *hakdamah* 31, p. 31b.

5. An allusion to the statement in B. *Yoma,* 21b. See also the discussion of this motif in *Zohar,* I:6b, and the additional sources cited by R. Margulies in *Nizozei Zohar, ad. loc.,* n. 4. Additional sources are *Zohar Hadash,* 2nd ed., ed. R. Margulies (Jerusalem, 1978), *Terumah,* p. 43b; *Tikkunei Zohar,* 2nd ed., ed. R. Margulies (Jerusalem, 1978), *tikkun* 18, p. 33b; ibid., *tikkun* 21, pp. 45a and 62b. My Thanks to Prof. Ze'ev Gries for this reference.

6. [B] Later in the text the "evil dog" is a reference to Jerboam ben Nebat, the king of Israel who is considered responsible for splitting Israel into two kingdoms after Solomon's death. In rabbinic literature, he is an archetype of evil.

7. This would appear to be an allusion to a male child that was born and died at the age of one year, before R. Yizhak Isaac was born. He assumes that he had the same Soul, which had to be returned to Heaven for further purification.

8. R. Jacob Isaac (1745–1815), known as the Seer of Lublin. One of the most important Hasidic masters of the early 19th century. The majority of Hasidic figures in Poland were his disciples.

9. [B] There is no such fast day.

10. [B] Both passages have the numerical value of 605, a reference to the year 5605 [1845].

11. An acronym for Rabbi Israel Baal Shem Tov, the founder of Hasidism.

12. [B] B. *Hagigah,* 12a: "On the first day, God created a light by

means of which a person can see from one end of the world to the other....He hid it....For whom did he hide it? For future *zaddiqim*."

13. R. Zevi (d. 1831) was a disciple of the Seer of Lublin. A prolific author and kabbalist.

14. Part 4, sect. 6.

15. R. Levi Yizhak (c. 1740–1810), disciple of Maggid of Mezhirech, author of *Kedushat Levi* and one of the most legendary figures in Hasidism.

16. Seventeenth-century Morrocan rabbi and author of Torah commentary *Or ha-Hayyim*. It was much quoted by Hasidic masters.

17. Part 4, sect. 23.

18. R. Eleazar (c. 1165–c. 1230). Last major figure in the medieval *Hasidei Ashkenaz* movement, which is not related to Beshtian Hasidism.

19. R. Solomon ibn Adret (c. 1235–c. 1310). Spanish rabbi. One of the most influential medieval *halakhic* authorities.

20. This is based on the Talmudic tradition about R. Abahu, cf. B. *Ketubot*, 17a. There are also accounts of a pillar of fire over the grave of the prophet Ezekiel. See L. Ginzberg, *Legends of the Jews* (Philadelphia, 1928), vol. 4, p. 326, and vol. 6, p. 413 n. 75. My thanks to Prof. Ze'ev Gries for this reference.

21. Hand in Hebrew is *yad*, which has the same spelling as the letter *yud*. Thus the fact that he extended his hand three times is related to the secret of the three *Yuds*, which follows. My thanks to Prof. Paul Fenton for this observation.

22. *Zohar*, III:246b (*Raya Mehemna*). My thanks to Prof. Elliot Wolfson for indicating this source to me.

23. The first words of each sentence of the Priestly Blessing in Nm 6:24–26. Each word begins with the letter *yud* in Hebrew.

24. [B] B. *Ketubot*, 44b.

25. Elijah appears in a number of guises in the rabbinic tradition, including as a gentile—e.g., as an Arab (B. *Berakhot*, 6b), as a Roman (B. *Sanhedrin*, 109a), and many others. See the discussion by M. Ish Shalom in his Introduction to *Seder Eliyahu Rabah ve-Seder Eliyahu Zutah* (*Tanna Debey Eliyahu*) third edition (Jerusalem, 1969), pp. 28–32. My thanks to Prof. Ze'ev Gries for this reference.

26. The title of a major work by Rabbi Joseph Karo. Famous rabbis are often referred to by the titles of their works.

27. The term *katnut* has a variety of meanings in ethical and kabbalistic literature. In the ethical literature it means humility, in contrast to *gadlut* or arrogance. In Lurianic *Kabbalah* it acquired the meaning of

distance from God. In Hasidic literature, it is used in both senses at different times. On the evolution of this term, see G. Scholem, "Devekut or Communion with God," in *The Messianic Idea in Judaism* (New York, 1971), pp. 218–222. On the Hasidic uses of this term, see Z. Gries, "Mi-Mythos le-Ethos—Kavim le-Demuto shel R. Abraham mi-Kalisk," in *Uma ve-Toldoteha*, ed. S. Ettinger (Jerusalem, 1984), vol. 2, pp. 143f. My thanks to Prof. Ze'ev Gries for this reference.

28. Adorning the *Shekhinah* through the study of Torah is a motif found in rabbinic and mystical sources. See Y. Liebes, "Ha-Mashiah shel ha-Zohar—Le-Demuto shel ha-Meshihit shel R. Simeon bar Yohai," in *Ha-Ra'ayon ha-Meshihi be-Yisrael* (Jerusalem, 1982), p. 208 n. 4. In addition to the above, R. Isaac Luria interpreted *ha-Kalah* (the bride) as *halakhah*. See *Shulhan Arukh ha-Ari* (Jerusalem, 1961), pp. 71f.; *Nagid u-Metzaveh* (Jerusalem, 1965), p. 73. R. Eleazar Azikri, *Milei de-Shemaya*, ed. M. Pachter (Jerusalem, 1991), p. 144, calls *halakhah*, "the inner essence of the *Shekhinah*." The Lurianic concept migrated to the writings of early Hasidism; cf. *Toldot Ya'akov Yosef* (Jerusalem, 1963), *Behukotai*, p. 435a. My thanks to Prof. Ze'ev Gries for this information.

29. This is an exact parallel to the description of what happened when the Baal Shem Tov studied. Cf. *In Praise of the Baal Shem Tov*, ed. and trans. J. Mintz and D. Ben Amos (Bloomington, 1970), pp. 45f.

30. Abraham Joshua Heschel of Apta (Opatow) (d. 1825) was one of the senior Hasidic masters of the early 19th century. Author of *Ohev Yisrael*.

31. This whole paragraph is an interpretation of this Psalm.

32. *Ecclesiastes Rabah*, 7.26.

33. [B] B. *Gittin*, 56a.

34. *Zohar*, III:98b.

35. [B] The numerical value of both phrases equals 132.

36. [B] The numerical value of both equals 499.

37. [B] B. *Hagigah*, 12b.

38. [B] B. *Ta'anit*, 8b.

39. The text is incomplete here. However, it refers to *Sukkot*.

40. R. Moses (d. 1840) Minor Hasidic master.

41. Town in central Poland.

42. *Zohar*, III:115b.

43. Dt 22:6–7.

44. [B] *Deuteronomy Rabah*, 6.5.

45. I.e., they were annulled. The sweetening of harsh judgments is an important concept in Hasidic theology.

46. The Sabbath between *Rosh Hashanah* and *Yom Kippur.*

47. My thanks to Prof. Elliot Wolfson for clarifying aspects of this sentence. This part of Komarno's *Ozar ha-Hayyim* was not published as a separate book but was incorporated into his commentary on the Torah, *Heikhal ha-Berakhah.*

48. A passage from *Unetane Tokef,* a central prayer of the High Holiday *musaf* service.

49. [B] B. *Berakhot,* 57a: "He who dreams that he is donning his *tefillin* may look forward to greatness."

50. Lemberg, 1858. Published together with his book *Netiv Mitzvotekha.*

51. [B] B. *Berakhot,* 55a: "No dream is without idle words."

52. Ps 97:11. The opening words of the *Kol Nidre* service.

53. The Hebrew word used is "Ishmaelites," which also means Muslim.

54. [B] B. *Megillah,* 14a.

55. [B] The text breaks off at this point.

56. [B] Rabbi Shalom Rokeah of Belz.

57. [B] Rabbi Yehudah Zevi, the son of Rabbi Moses of Sambor.

58. R. Naphtali (1760–1827), disciple of R. Elimelech of Lyzhansk and major Hasidic leader in Galicia.

59. R. Elimelech (1717–1787), disciple of the *Maggid* of Mezhirech and one of the founders of Hasidism in Galicia.

60. [B] B. *Sanhedrin,* 97a.

61. *Zohar,* III:135a–b.

62. [B] R. Moses Teitelbaum, *Yismah Moshe* (Lemberg, 1849), p. 39b: "We find in the writings of R. Isaac Luria that the majority of *zaddikim* are transmigrated into fish."

63. [B] The text is missing in the manuscripts.

The Deeds of the Lord

1. [B] A paraphrase of B. *Ta'anit,* 25a.

2. Rabbi Moses Hayyim Ephraim of Sudylkow (c. 1740–1800?).

3. R. Jehiel Michel (c. 1731–1786).

4. R. Jacob Joseph (d. c. 1782) Leading disciple of the Besht and our most important source for the Besht's teachings.

5. Rabbi Gershon of Kuty, the Besht's brother-in-law, is reported as saying "I wish I would have a portion of the next world that the Besht

gains from smoking one pipeful of tobacco"—*In Praise of the Baal Shem Tov*, ed. D. Ben Amos and J. Mintz (Bloomington, 1970), p. 105.

6. The central institution of Jewish self-government in Poland and Lithuania from the middle of the 16th century until 1764 when it was dissolved by decree of the Polish *Sejm* (parliament).

7. [B] *Be'er Hetev on Shulḥan Arukh Oreḥ Hayyim, Hilkhot Shabbat*, sect. 268. Cited in the name of R. Isaiah Horowitz, *Shnei Luḥot ha-Berit*.

8. A similar story is found in *In Praise of the Baal Shem Tov*, p. 18.

9. [B] This story is found in *Degel Mahne Ephraim, parshat Vayishlaḥ* (p. 48 in the Jerusalem, 1963 edition).

10. See *In Praise of the Baal Shem Tov*, pp. 23f., for another version of this story.

11. [B] See *Adat Zaddiqim* (Lublin, 1900), p. 11, for a similar story.

12. An allusion to the belief that the Messiah was expected in 1575. D. Tamar, "The Expectations in Italy for the Year of Redemption—1575," in *Studies in the History of the Jews in Israel and Italy* (Hebrew) (Jerusalem, 1970), pp. 11–38.

13. It is not clear to whom this is a reference.

14. [B] B. *Avodah Zarah*, 17a; *B. Rosh Hashannah*, 17a.

15. [B] Part 4, sect. 6.

16. The Besht describes a Soul ascent in his letter to his brother-in-law, R. Gershon of Kuty. N. Lamm, "The Letter of the Besht to R. Gershom of Kuty," *Tradition* 14 (1974): 110–125; L. Jacobs, *Jewish Mystical Testimonies* (New York, 1977), pp. 148–155.

17. M. *Avot*, 1:6.

18. [B] Both manuscripts break off at this point.

Glossary

Abba—*Parzuf* composed of *Ḥokhmah*.

A"H—Peace be upon him. A standard encomium for the dead.

Amidah—Central prayer of the liturgy. The core prayer of every worship service.

Amora (pl. *Amoraim*)—Scholars in Israel and Babylon in the third to sixth centuries who compiled the part of the Talmud called the *Gemara*.

Arikh (*Arikh Anpin*)—(lit. long face) *Parzuf* relating to *Keter*.

Arvit—The evening prayer, also called *ma'ariv*.

Ashkenazi (pl. *Ashkenazim*)—Person whose ancestry is from Central or Eastern Europe.

Asiyyah—(lit. action) Lowest of the four kabbalistic worlds.

Attika Kadisha—(lit. The Ancient Holy One) Another term for *Arikh Anpin*.

Attik Yomin—(lit. Ancient of Days) The upper *Parzuf* relating to *Keter*.

Azilut—(lit. emanation) Highest of the four kabbalistic worlds.

Beriah—(lit. creation) Third of the four kabbalistic worlds.

Bet Midrash—House of study.

Binah—(lit. Understanding) The third of the ten *sefirot*. Often described in maternal images.

337

GLOSSARY

Cohen—Priest, descendant of Aaron.

Da'at—(lit. knowledge) The third *sefirah* in some kabbalistic systems where *Keter* is not counted among the ten *sefirot*. It is a synthesis of *Hokhmah* and *Binah*.

Elohim—Name of God.

El Shaddai—Name of God.

Gaon (pl. *Geonim*)—Head of the academy in post-Talmudic Babylonia.

Gehenna—Hell.

Gematria—Numerology. A method of tallying the numerical value of the Hebrew letters of words and making associations based on the numbers derived.

Gevurah (pl. *Gevurot*)—(lit. power) The fifth *sefirah*. Also called *din*, stern judgment.

Haftorah—A section of Prophets related to the Torah reading on Sabbaths and festivals.

Haggadah—Book containing service for Passover *Seder*.

Hakham—Sage; the *Sephardi* title for a scholar who is rabbi of the community.

Halakhah—Jewish Law, Jewish legal traditions.

Hanukkah—Festival of Lights.

Havdalah—Ceremony marking the conclusion of the Sabbath.

Hayyah—An aspect of the soul.

Hesed (pl. *Hasadim*)—(lit. love, grace) The fourth *sefirah;* the right hand or love of God.

Hod—(lit. Majesty) The eighth *sefirah.*

Hokhmah—(lit. wisdom) The second *sefirah.*

338

GLOSSARY

Holam—Vowel, pronounced "oh."

Hoshana Rabba—Minor festival, seventh day of *Sukkot*.

Imma—(lit. Mother) *Parzuf* composed of *Binah*.

Kaddish—Liturgical doxology.

Kamez—Vowel pronounced "ah."

Kedushah—Prayer added to reader's repetition of the *Amidah*.

Kelippah (pl. *Kelippot*)—(lit. husks) Mystical term for the forces of evil.

Keter—(lit. crown) The first *sefirah*.

Khan—An inn for travelers.

Kiddush—Blessing over wine that sanctifies the Sabbath or a festival.

Kol Nidre—Opening prayer for the eve of *Yom Kippur*.

Ma'ariv—The daily evening prayer service.

Malkhut—The tenth *sefirah*. Represents the Feminine element within the Godhead. Another name for *Shekhinah*.

Matzot—Unleavened bread.

Merkavah—The divine chariot or throne.

Mikvah—Place for ritual immersion.

Minha—The daily afternoon prayer service.

Mishnah—Oral teachings redacted by Rabbi Judah the Prince at the beginning of the third century.

Mitzvah—Commandment or good deed.

Moghrabi—Someone of North African origin (e.g., Morroco, Algeria).

Mohel (pl. *mohelim*)—One who performs circumcisions.

GLOSSARY

Mohin—(sing. *Moah*) The inner aspect of *Neshamah,* which is found only in the first three *sefirot.*

Musaf—Additional prayer service on Sabbaths and festivals.

Mustarab—A term referring to Jews who were Arabic-speaking natives to Syria and Israel, as distinct from *Sephardim* or *Ashkenazim.*

Nefesh—Aspect of the Soul.

Neilah—Concluding service of *Yom Kippur.*

Neshamah—Aspect of the Soul.

Nezah—(lit. Endurance) The seventh *sefirah.*

Notarikon—Method of abbreviating Hebrew words or phrases by writing single letters.

Nukvah (Nukvah de Zeir)—(lit. Feminine) Fifth *Parzuf;* Name for *Malkhut.*

Omer—The forty-nine days between Passover and *Shavuot;* ritual of counting the days during this period.

Parshat—Weekly Torah portion, followed by name of section of Torah.

Parzuf (pl. *Parzufim*)—(lit. Face) Reconfiguration of the *sefirot* in parts of the *Zohar* and in Lurianic *Kabbalah.* There are five *Parzufim: Arikh Anpin, Abba, Imma, Zeir Anpin,* and *Nukvah de Zeir.*

Piyyut—liturgical poem.

Posek (pl. *Posekim*)—*Halakhic* decisor; rabbinic authority in medieval and modern period.

Qadi—A Muslim judge or official.

R.—Rabbi.

Rav—Rabbi.

Rebbe—Hasidic Master.

Rosh Hashanah—Jewish New Year.

GLOSSARY

Rosh Ḥodesh—The first day of the month, a semi-holiday.

Ruaḥ—Aspect of the soul.

Saboraim—Babylonian scholars in the immediate post-Talmudic period (fifth–eighth centuries).

Sandek—Person who holds the child during circumcision; considered a great honor.

Sefirah (Sefirot)—The ten emanations of *Ein Sof,* the Infinite, through which the world is created and sustained.

Seliḥot—Penitential prayers recited the week before *Rosh Hashanah.*

Sephardi (pl. *Sephardim*)—Person whose family origins are in the Iberian Peninsula.

Shaḥarit—The morning prayer service.

Shavuot—Feast of weeks; Pentecost.

Shekhinah—The tenth *sefirah, malkhut;* the divine presence.

Shema—Deuteronomy 6:4, "Hear O Israel"; Judaism's confession of faith.

Shewa—Vowel, silent.

Shofar—Ram's horn, blown on *Rosh Hashanah.*

Simḥat Torah—Festival of rejoicing with the Torah; last day of *Sukkot.*

Sukkah—Booth or tabernacle in which one dwells during *Sukkot.*

Sukkot—Feast of Tabernacles.

Talit—Prayer shawl with fringes (*zizit*) at four corners.

Talit katan—Garment with *zizit* worn under outer garments during the day by observant Jewish males.

Tanna (pl. *Tannaim*)—Rabbinic teacher of the Mishnaic period.

GLOSSARY

Tefillin—Phylacteries, worn during the weekday prayers; some scholars and mystics wear them all day.

Tiferet—(lit. glory) The sixth *sefirah;* center of the lower sefirotic world; the male principle of God that unites with *Malkhut*.

Tikkun—Repair or restoration of the cosmos; kabbalist prayers and meditations.

Tikkunei Zohar—A work that is part of the *Zoharic* corpus by a later author.

Yeḥidah—Aspect of the soul.

Yesod—(lit. foundation) The ninth *sefirah;* often symbolized by the male membrum.

Yezirah—One of the four kabbalistic worlds.

Yom Kippur—Day of Atonement; holiest day of the Jewish year.

Yozer—Liturgical hymn inserted in the first benediction of the morning *Shema* prayer.

Zaddiq (pl. *Zaddiqim*)—Person of outstanding faith and piety; in Hasidism, refers to a Hasidic Master.

Zeir (*Zeir Anpin*)—(lit. short face) *Parzuf* composed of the six *sefirot* from *Tiferet* to *Yesod*.

Zeire—Vowel pronounced "ey."

Zizit—Fringes attached to *talit*.

Z"L—May his memory be for a blessing. A standard encomium for the dead.

Months of the Hebrew Year

The Hebrew year begins with the month of *Tishrei*, which usually occurs in September.

Tishrei

Heshvan

Kislev

Tevet

Shevat

Adar I and II (In leap years there is a second month of *Adar*.)

Nisan

Iyyar

Sivan

Tammuz

Ab

Ellul

Bibliography

PRIMARY SOURCES

Biblical texts are quoted from *The TANAKH: The New JPS Translation According to the Traditional Hebrew Text* (Jewish Publication Society, 1985) with occasional variances required by the text. Rabbinic (i.e., Talmudic and Midrashic) texts are quoted from the standard editions. When scholarly editions have been cited, they are indicated in the notes. All citations from the *Zoharic* corpus (*Zohar, Tikkunei Zohar*, etc.) are from the respective editions of R. Margulies (Mossad Ha-Rav Kook, Jerusalem).

SECONDARY SOURCES

Aescoli, A. Z. "Hearot Aḥadot le-Toldot ha-Tenuah ha-Meshiḥit." *Sinai* 12 (1943): 84–89.

———. *Messianic Movements in Israel* [Hebrew]. Jerusalem, 1956.

———. *Sippur David-ha-Reubeni*. 2nd ed. Jerusalem, 1993.

Avitsur, S. "Safed—Center for the Manufacture of Woven Woolens in the Fifteenth Century" [Hebrew]. *Sefunot* 6 (1962): 43–69.

Avivi, Joseph. *Binyan Ariel*. Jerusalem, 1987.

Azikri, E. *Milei De-Shemaya*, ed. M. Pachter. Tel Aviv, 1991.

Azulai, H. Y. D. *Shem ha-Gedolim*. Vilna, 1853.

Bacharach, N. *Emek ha-Melekh*. Amsterdam, 1648.

BIBLIOGRAPHY

Beneyahu, M. "Rabbi Hayyim Vital in Jerusalem" [Hebrew]. *Sinai* 30 (1951): 65–75.

———. "The Revival of Ordination in Safed" [Hebrew]. In *Yizhak F. Baer Jubilee Volume.* Jerusalem, 1960, pp. 248–269.

———. *Toldot ha-Ari.* Jerusalem, 1967.

———. *Yosef Behiri.* Jerusalem, 1991.

Berger, A. "Captive at the Gate of Rome: The Story of a Messianic Motif." *Proceedings of the American Academy for Jewish Research* 44 (1977): 1–17.

Bloch, C. *Lebenserinnerungen des Kabbalisten Vital.* Vienna, 1927.

Bos, G. "Hayyim Vital's Practical Kabbalah and Alchemy: A 17th Century Book of Secrets." *Journal of Jewish Thought and Philosophy* 4 (1994): 55–112.

———. "Moshe Mizrachi on Popular Science in 17th Century Syria-Palestine." *Jewish Studies Quarterly* 3, 3 (1996): 250–279.

Cohen-Alloro, D. *The Secret of the Garment in the Zohar* [Hebrew]. Jerusalem, 1987.

Daiches, S. *Babylonian Oil Magic in the Talmud and in Later Jewish Literature.* London, 1913.

Dan, J. "Archons of the Cup and Archons of the Toenail." In *Studies in Ashkenai-Hasidic Literature* [Hebrew]. Ramat Gan, 1975, pp. 34–43.

———. "Samael, Lilith and the Concept of Evil in Early Kabbalah." *AJS Review* 5 (1980): 17–40.

———. "The Story of Joseph Della Reina" [Hebrew]. *Sefunot* 6 (1962): 313–326.

Davis, N. Z. "Fame and Secrecy: Leon Modena's *Life* as an Early Modern Autobiography." In *The Autobiography of a Seventeenth-Century Rabbi–Leon Modena's Life of Judah,* ed. and trans. M. R. Cohen. Princeton, 1988, pp. 50–70.

BIBLIOGRAPHY

De Vidas, E. *Reshit Hokhmah ha-Shalem*, ed. H. Waldman. Jerusalem, 1984. 3 vols.

Dimitrovsky, H. Z. "New Documents Regarding the Semicha Controversy in Safed" [Hebrew]. *Sefunot* 10 (1966): 113–192.

Elior, R. "The Doctrine of *Gilgul* in *Galya Raza*" [Hebrew]. *Jerusalem Studies in Jewish Thought* 3, 1–2 (1983–1984): 207–239.

————. "Messianic Expectations and Spiritualization of Religious Life in the Sixteenth Century." *Revue des Etudes Juives* 145 (1986): 35–49.

Elon, M. *Jewish Law*. Philadelphia, 1994. 4 vols.

Emden, J. *Megillat Sefer*, ed. D. Kahana. Warsaw, 1897.

Epstein, A. "Sippur Eldad ha-Dani." In *Kitve A. Epstein*. Jerusalem, 1950, Vol. 1.

Even Shmuel, Y. *Midrashei Geulah* [Hebrew]. Jerusalem, 1954.

Fano, M. A. *Asarah Ma'amarot*. Venice, 1597.

Fenton, P. B. "La 'hitbodedut' chez les premiers qabbalistes en orient et chez les soufis." In *Priere, mystique et judaisme*, ed. R. Goetschel. Paris, 1987, pp. 133–157.

————. "Solitary Meditation in Jewish and Islamic Mysticism in the Light of a Recent Archeological Discovery." *Medieval Encounters* 1, 2 (1995): 271–296.

Fine, L. "The Art of Metoposcopy: A Study in Isaac Luria's Charismatic Knowledge." *AJS Review* 9 (1986): 79–101.

————. "The Contemplative Practice of *Yihudim* in Lurianic Kabbalah." In *Jewish Spirituality*, ed. A. Green. New York, 1987. Vol. 2, pp. 64–98.

————. "Recitation of Mishnah as a Vehicle for Mystical Inspiration: A Contemplative Technique Taught by Hayyim Vital." *Revue des Etudes Juives* 141 (1982): 183–199.

————. *Safed Spirituality*. Ramsey, 1984.

BIBLIOGRAPHY

Fishbane, M. *The Kiss of God: Spiritual and Mystical Death in Judaism.* Seattle, 1994.

Friedberg, C. B. *Bet Eked Sefarim.* Tel Aviv, 1954. 4 vols.

Gartner, Y. "The Influence of the Ari (R. Isaac Luria) on the Custom of Donning Two Pairs of Phylacteries" [Hebrew]. *Da'at* 28 (1992): 51–64.

Giller, P. *The Enlightened Will Shine.* Albany, 1993.

Ginsburg, E. *The Sabbath in the Classical Kabbalah.* Albany, 1989.

Ginzberg, L. *Legends of the Jews.* Philadelphia, 1937. 7 vols.

Gries, Z. "Mi-Mytos le-Ethos–Kavim le-Demuto shel R. Abraham mi-Kalisk." In *Uma ve-Toldoteha,* ed. S. Ettinger. Jerusalem, 1984, vol. 2, pp. 117–146.

————. *Sifrut ha-Hanhagot: Toldoteha u-Mekomah be-Hayyei Hasidiav shel ha-Besht.* Jerusalem, 1990.

Haberman, A. M., ed. *Kitve A. Epstein.* Jerusalem, 1950. 2 vols.

Hallamish, M. "Gilgulo shel Minhag Kabbali." *Kiryat Sefer* 53 (1978): 534–556.

————. "Hanhagah min ha-Kabbalah be-Sifrut ha-Halakhah." *Niv ha-Midrashia* 13 (1978): 161–165.

Helner, M. "The Doctrine of *Gilgul* in the Kabbalistic Writings of R. David Ibn Zimra" [Hebrew]. *Pa'amim* 43 (1990): 16–50.

Heschel, A. J. "Prophetic Inspiration in the Middle Ages." In *Prophetic Inspiration after the Prophets: Maimonides and Other Medieval Authorities,* ed. M. M. Faierstein. Hoboken, 1996.

Hyman, A. *Toldot Tannaim ve-Amoraim.* London, 1910.

Idel, M. "*Hitbodedut* as Concentration in Ecstatic Kabbalah." In *Studies in Ecstatic Kabbalah.* Albany, 1988, pp. 103–169.

————. *Kabbalah–New Perspectives.* New Haven, 1988.

————. "One from a Town, Two from a Clan–The Diffusion of Lurianic

BIBLIOGRAPHY

Kabbalah Sabbataeanism: A Re-Examination." *Jewish History* 7, 2 (1993): 79–104.

―――. "R. Yehuda Halliwah and His Work–*Sefer Zofnat Paneah*" [Hebrew]. *Shalem* 4 (1984): 118–148.

―――. "Solomon Molcho as Magician" [Hebrew]. *Sefunot* N.S. 3 [18] (1985): 193–219.

―――. "Studies in the Doctrine of *Sefer ha-Meshiv*" [Hebrew]. *Sefunot* N.S. 2 [17] (1983): 226–232, 244–250.

Jacobs, L. *Jewish Mystical Testimonies*. New York, 1977.

Jellinek, A. *Bet ha-Midrash*. Jerusalem, 1938. 6 vols.

Kaplan, A. *Meditation and Kabbalah*. York Beach, 1982.

Kupfer, E. "The Visions of R. Asher ben R. Meir Called Lemlein Reutlingen" [Hebrew]. *Kovez al-Yad* N.S. 8 [18] (1976): 385–423.

Lamm, N. "The Letter of the Besht to R. Gershon of Kuty." *Tradition* 14 (1974): 110–125.

Liebes, Y. "*De Natura Dei:* On the Development of the Jewish Myth." In *Studies in Jewish Myth and Jewish Messianism*. Albany, 1993, pp. 1–64.

―――. "Early Lurianic Compositions?" [Hebrew]. In *Mashuot: Studies in Kabbalah and Jewish Thought in Memory of E. Gottlieb,* ed. M. Oron and A. Goldreich. Jerusalem, 1994, pp. 339–342.

―――. "Ha-Mashiah shel ha-Zohar–Le-Demuto ha-Meshihit shel R. Simeon bar Yohai." In *Ha-Ra'ayon ha-Meshihi be-Yisrael.* Jerusalem, 1982, pp. 87–236.

―――. *Sections of the Zohar Lexicon* [Hebrew]. Ph.D. Thesis, Hebrew University, Jerusalem, 1976.

―――. "Two Young Roes of a Deer: The Secret Sermon of Isaac Luria Before His Death" [Hebrew]. *Jerusalem Studies in Jewish Thought* 10 (1992): 113–169.

―――. "Zohar ve-Eros." *Alpai'im* 9 (1994): 67–119.

BIBLIOGRAPHY

Magid, S. "Conjugal Union, Mourning and *Talmud Torah* in R. Isaac Luria's *Tikkun Hazot.*" *Daat* 36 (Winter 1996): XVII–XLV.

Margulies, R. *Malakhei Elyon.* Jerusalem, 1964.

————. *Responsa from Heaven* [Hebrew]. Jerusalem, n.d.

Meroz, R. "Early Lurianic Compositions" [Hebrew]. In *Mashuot: Studies in Kabbalah and Jewish Thought in Memory of E. Gottlieb,* ed. M. Oron and A. Goldreich. Jerusalem, 1994, pp. 311–338.

————. "Faithful Transmission Versus Innovation: Luria and His Disciples." In *Gershom Scholem's Major Trends in Jewish Mysticism 50 Years After,* ed. P. Schaefer and J. Dan. Tübingen, 1993, pp. 257–274.

Molcho, S. *Sefer ha-Mefoar.* Warsaw, 1884.

Najara, I. *Zemirot Yisrael.* Venice, 1600.

Netanyahu, B. *Don Isaac Abravanel.* Philadelphia, 1972.

Nigal, G. *Sippurei Dybbuk be-Sifrut Yisrael.* Jerusalem, 1983.

Oron, M. "Dream, Vision and Reality in Hayyim Vital's *Book of Visions*" [Hebrew]. *Jerusalem Studies in Jewish Thought* 10 (1992): 299–309.

————. "Waiting for Salvation—History and Literature in the Metamorphosis of the Legend of R. Joseph Della Reina" [Hebrew]. In *Between History and Literature.* Tel Aviv, 1983, pp. 79–90.

Patai, R. *The Jewish Alchemists.* Princeton, 1994.

————. *The Messiah Texts.* Detroit, 1979.

Rosenthal, F. "Die arabische Autobiographie." In *Studia Arabica I* (*=Analecta Orientalia*). Rome, 1937, pp. 3–40. Reprinted in F. Rosenthal, *Muslim Intellectual and Social History: A Collection of Essays.* Aldershot, 1990.

Ruderman, D. *A Valley of Vision–The Heavenly Journey of Abraham ben Hananiah Yagel.* Philadelphia, 1990.

Sambari, Joseph. *Sefer Divrei Yosef,* ed. S. Shtober. Jerusalem, 1994.

BIBLIOGRAPHY

Schechter, S. *Avot de Rabbi Nathan*. New York, 1967.

————. "Safed in the Sixteenth Century." In *Studies in Judaism*, Second Series. Philadelphia, 1908, pp. 202–306.

Scholem, G. "The Authentic Kabbalistic Writings of R. Isaac Luria" [Hebrew]. *Kiryat Sefer* 19 (1942): 184–199.

————. "Gilgul: The Transmigration of Souls." In *On the Mystical Shape of the Godhead*. New York, 1991, pp. 197–250.

————. "Ha-Mekubal R. Abraham ben Eliezer ha-Levi." *Kiryat Sefer* 2 (1925): 101–141, 269–273.

————. "A Homily on the Redemption by R. Solomon of the House of Turiel" [Hebrew]. *Sefunot* 1 (1957): 62–79.

————. *Kabbalah*. New York, 1974.

————. *Major Trends in Jewish Mysticism*. New York, 1961.

————. "On the Legend of R. Joseph Della Reina" [Hebrew]. In *Studies in Jewish Religious and Intellectual History*, ed. R. Leowe and S. Stein. University of Alabama, 1979, pp. 101–108.

————. *Sabbatai Sevi*. Princeton, 1973.

————. "Shtar Hitkasherut shel Talmidei ha-Ari." *Zion* 5 (1941): 131–160.

————. "Tradition and New Creation in the Ritual of the Kabbalists." In *On the Kabbalah and Its Symbolism*. New York, 1965, pp. 118–157.

————. "Tselem: The Concept of the Astral Body." In *On the Mystical Shape of the Godhead*. New York, 1991, pp. 251–273.

Silver, A. H. *A History of Messianic Speculation in Israel*. Boston, 1959.

Tamar, D. "The Greatness and Wisdom of Rabbi Hayyim Vital" [Hebrew]. *Rabbi Joseph B. Soloveichik Jubilee Volume*. Jerusalem/New York, 1984, Vol. 2, pp. 1297–1311.

————. *Mehkarim be-Toldot ha-Yehudim be-Erez Yisrael u-be-Italia*. Jerusalem, 1970.

BIBLIOGRAPHY

—————. "Ollelot Sefer Hezyonot." *Sinai* 91 (1982): 82–86.

—————. *Studies in the History of the Jews in Israel and the Near East* [Hebrew]. Jerusalem, 1981.

Teitelbaum, M. *Yismaḥ Moshe.* Lemberg, 1849.

Tishby, I. *The Doctrine of Evil and the Qelippah in Lurianic Kabbalah* [Hebrew]. Jerusalem, 1942.

—————. *Messianism in the Time of the Expulsion from Spain and Portugal* [Hebrew]. Jerusalem, 1985.

—————. *The Wisdom of the Zohar.* Oxford, 1991. 3 vols.

Trachtenberg, J. *Jewish Magic and Superstition.* New York, 1939.

Weintraub, K. J. *The Value of the Individual: Self and Circumstance in Autobiography.* Chicago, 1978.

Werblowsky, R. J. Z. *Joseph Karo–Lawyer and Mystic.* Philadelphia, 1977.

Werthheimer, A. *Batei Midrashot.* Jerusalem, 1968. 2 vols.

Wilhelm, Y. D. "Sidrei Tikkunim." In *Alei Ayin.* Jerusalem, 1948–1952, pp. 125–146.

Wolfson, E. "Biblical Accentuation in a Mystical Key: Kabbalistic Interpretation of the *Te'amim.*" *Journal of Music and Liturgy* 12 (1989–1990): 1–13.

—————. *Circle in the Square.* Albany, 1995.

—————. "The Secret of the Garment in Nachmanides." *Daat* 24 (1990): xxv–xliv.

—————. *Through a Speculum That Shines: Vision and Imagination in Medieval Jewish Mysticism.* Princeton, 1994.

—————. "Weeping, Death, and Spiritual Ascent in Sixteenth Century Jewish Mysticism." In J. J. Collins and M. Fishbane ed., *Death Ecstacy, and Other Worldly Journeys* (Albany, 1995), pp. 209–247.

BIBLIOGRAPHY

Yuval, I. J. "A German Jewish Autobiography from the Fourteenth Century" [Hebrew]. *Tarbiz* 55 (1986): 541–566.

Zunz, L. *Ha-Derashot be-Yisrael.* Jerusalem, 1974.

Index

(References in **boldface** are to material in Introductions)

INDEX

Assiyah, 104
Attik Yomin, 202-03
Attika Kaddisha, 188, 191, 287
Augustine, St., **3**
Avshalom, Abraham, 46, 47
Azikri, Eleazar, 10
Azilut, 210, 211, 212, 213, 224,
    245, 252, 255

Baal Shem Tov, Israel, **267, 268,
    269, 270-71;** in Komarno's
    Book of Secrets, 276, 277, 281,
    290, 291-92, 293, 294, 296,
    297, 298, 300-01, 304
Beneyahu, M., **8**
Berab, Jacob, 115
Beriah, 223, 224, 231, 241, 244,
    245, 246, 252, 253, 255
Berl, H. J., **268, 269**
Besht, Israel. *See* Baal Shem Tov,
    Israel
Binah, **29**, 76, 203, 204, 255
Book of the Responding Angel, The,
    4, 277
Book of Secrets (Komarno), 11,
    267-71; text, 275-306; Vital's
    Book of Visions distin-
    guished, **267, 269, 270**
Book of Visions (Vital), **4, 8, 9,
    10-31;** Komarno's *Book of
    Secrets* distinguished, **267,
    269, 270;** text, 43-263
Boom, Joshua al-, **22**, 58, 62-63,
    65, 68, 72, 73-74

Cain, **30-31**, 171-72, 176-77,
    181,186, 197, 198, 200-01,
    202, 203, 206, 210-16, 218,
    219-20, 227, 237, 240, 242,
    247, 249, 252, 254, 255; sin

of, 111, 163, 175, 182, 183,
    196, 239, 246
Calabrese, Hayyim Vital. *See*
    Vital, Hayyim
Calabrese, Joseph Vital, **6**
Caro, Joseph. *See* Karo, Joseph
Cohen, Isaac ha-. *See* Ha Cohen,
    Isaac
Cohen, Mas'ud, **8**, 45-46
Cordovero, Moses, **6, 7, 10, 17,
    18**, 85, 86, 87, 90, 137, 280;
    pillar of fire, 17; in Vital's
    dreams, **18**, 85, 86, 87, 90,
    137
Creation, **27-28**
Curiel, Israel, 109

Da'at, 193, 194, 195, 203, 204,
    225, 231, 233, 234, 247,
    249, 250, 255
Demons, 56-57, 138
Din, **28, 29.** *See also Gevurot*
Dresnitz, Shlomel, **9, 16-17**

Eleazar ben Arakh, **26**, 88-89,
    157, 158
Eleazar ben Shammua, **26**
Eleazar ben Yohai, 89
Eleazar of Worms, 277
Elijah, 47, 79, 80, 84, 92, 112,
    153, 164, 191, 211, 212, 247
    269, 289, 301
Elimelech of Lyzhansk, 291, 302
Elior, Rachel, **5**
Esau, **163**
Ethers, 57
Eyn-Sof, **27, 28**

Feminine, 230-31, 293
Fine, Lawrence, **27**

354

INDEX

INDEX

Other Volumes in This Series

Other Volumes in This Series

Other Volumes in This Series